BREAKING FINANCIAL BOUNDARIES

BREAKING FINANCIAL BOUNDARIES

Global Capital, National Deregulation, and Financial Services Firms

DAVID M. MEERSCHWAM

Harvard Business School

HARVARD BUSINESS SCHOOL PRESS

Boston, Massachusetts

Library of Congress Cataloging-in-Publication Data

Meerschwam, David M.
   Breaking financial boundaries : global capital, national
deregulation, and financial services firms / David M.
Meerschwam.
     p. cm.
   Includes bibliographical references (p.) and index.
   ISBN 0-87584-253-4 (acid-free) :
   1. Financial institutions—United States. 2. Financial
institutions—Great Britain. 3. Financial institutions—Japan.
4. International finance. I. Title.
HG181.M44 1991   90-15472
332.1—dc20   CIP

95 94 93 92 91   5 4 3 2 1

The paper used in this publication meets the requirements of the American National Standard for Permanence of
Paper for Printed Library Materials Z39.49-1984.

CONTENTS

PREFACE

I decided to write this book in 1987 after finishing a consulting project with several prominent investment bankers. My assignment had been to prepare discussion materials for a series of breakfast meetings about the major issues affecting the U.S. and international economy. The assignment itself was unusual. Why would a group of highly sophisticated, senior managers turn to a young, academically trained economist to lead them through these issues? Why were the issues of interest to them and what were the links between their world and the macro- and international economy?

The answer to the first question was relatively simple: trained as an international macroeconomist, I worked at the Harvard Business School, which so often provides a link between academe and the corporate world. Thus my training and work environment had made me sensitive to the general interests of my clients. The questions of which issues to discuss and how to establish the links between the macroenvironment and the business world were much harder to answer. Still, over the course of many breakfast meetings three things became clear to me: (1) macroeconomic events—especially international capital flows—had changed so much that many noneconomists found them increasingly difficult to place in context; (2) the changes in the international capital markets, especially in New York, Tokyo, and London were profound, related to the macroevents, and of great relevance to managers; (3) the firms that these managers were running were undergoing major change.

As I prepared for each meeting and then took part in the discussion, I realized how wide the gulf was between the work of academic economists and the experience of this sophisticated group of leaders whose industry is as close to the world of economics as any. Many valuable ideas were unfamiliar to these managers, not because of their inherent complexity, but simply because they are rarely presented other than in academic journals. On the other hand, scholars frequently omit important real-life institutional considerations from their economic models, either because they are "intractable," because they would lead to a loss of generality, or because the academic theorist is simply unaware of them. And yet, as I shuttled between Wall Street and Cambridge, I noticed that my investment banking group was genuinely interested in the fundamental economic ideas being developed by academics, provided these ideas were "translated." By the same token, many of my academic colleagues found the institutional issues interesting and relevant, once they were brought to their attention.

For my part, I began to see more and more links between these two perspectives. I decided to integrate them by studying global macroeconomic forces, changes in the national financial systems of the United States, Japan, and the United Kingdom, and how financial services firms have responded to them. Each of the subjects carried with it a vast literature. I worked my way through much of that, but also did extensive fieldwork, visiting U.S., Japanese, and British companies. The results of that research are contained in this book. Its focus is the breaking of financial boundaries, and it is itself an attempt to break an important boundary—the one that separates the academic economist and the financial practitioner. For this reason my study spans several academic and professional disciplines, is cross-national and comparative, and moves through time. The best way to judge its success is whether or not those who read it will say that they learned something useful.

ACKNOWLEDGMENTS

Many people have contributed to the writing of this book, including the economists with whom I have worked and the practitioners with whom I discussed the issues presented here. My colleagues at the Harvard Business School deserve special mention; they highlighted the importance of cross-disciplinary and cross-national research and helped me understand the importance of institutional research. Of the many who have made valuable suggestions, I am especially grateful to Professors Baldwin, Caves, Crane, Cuff, Fruhan, Goldberg, Light, Mason, McCraw, Perold, Reiling, Stevenson, and Vietor. Colleagues at other institutions who offered help and advice are Professors Blinder (Princeton), Eichengreen (University of California at Berkeley), Hannah (London School of Economics), Krugman (MIT), Parker (Stanford Business School), Stein (MIT), and Walter (NYU).

I am particularly indebted to my colleagues M. Colyer Crum and Samuel L. Hayes. Crum introduced me to many of the issues that I have researched over the past few years, and provided invaluable help in my transition from the world of theoretical economics to that of applied research. Hayes's help, insights, and suggestions went well beyond the call of professional duty; the many hours he labored over my manuscript greatly improved it. Of course, none of those mentioned bear responsibility for its shortcomings.

I am grateful to Dean McArthur of the Harvard Business School, who supported this project in many ways, including generous financial support from the Division of Research. Richard Luecke and Natalie Greenberg of the Harvard Business School Press were a valuable resource. Also, Barbara Feinberg and John Simon edited parts of the book, and Earl Harbert edited the whole. Over time, several research assistants helped with various chapters: Nilgün Gökgür, Mike Baldwin, and Donna Hill. My secretaries Erin McCormack and Brenda Fucillo uncomplainingly prepared successive versions of the manuscript.

Boston, Massachusetts   David M. Meerschwam
October 1990

BREAKING FINANCIAL BOUNDARIES

INTRODUCTION

The only constant was change. Commonplace as this expression may be, few popular maxims so well reflected the complex reality of financial transactions, institutions, and systems during the 1980s. Changes were pervasive in all three areas, and they affected many different players. The following examples show the diversity of these changes. In 1986, Sumitomo Bank, a leading Japanese commercial bank, which had been forbidden to engage in investment banking activities in Japan for more than thirty-five years, announced a capital investment of $500 million in a leading U.S. investment bank, Goldman Sachs. In 1989, after several years of building its equity capability in London, Citicorp reversed direction, reducing its activities in the London equity markets. Finally, in 1990, another major player, Drexel Burnham Lambert, filed under Chapter 11 of the bankruptcy code. After a decade of rapid growth, during which the firm climbed from relative obscurity to prominence, achieving both remarkable profitability and extraordinary visibility, Drexel suddenly ceased to be a factor in the U.S. financial industry. Overall, dramatic change—bringing with it innovative strategies—qualified as one of the few constants that could be fairly applied to financial services firms in a turbulent decade.

The national financial systems in which these firms operated experienced no less drastic upheaval. In 1986, the London Stock Exchange faced the "Big Bang." After a long history of operating by informal traditions, formal rules were introduced that altered the nature of the exchange. In 1988, Japanese regulators approved new freedoms in the domestic CD market. This was but one of an avalanche of changes that reshaped a national system whose foundations had been laid a century earlier. In 1989, the United States allowed commercial banks to underwrite certain types of corporate debt securities for the first time since the 1930s. This action furthered the reversal of the policy that had created segmentation of the securities and commercial banking industry, originally instituted in response to the financial dislocations of the 1920s. And these are only a few of the many momentous changes and constant adjustments in financial regulation and organization that altered the national systems of the United States, Japan, and the United Kingdom during the 1980s.

1

During this period, global economic relationships were being redefined, and hence they became increasingly difficult to predict. This made it even harder for financial services vendors to set their strategic courses. In the early 1980s, the United States stood as the world's largest international creditor; by 1985, the country had turned into a net debtor nation, and by 1990, it was the largest debtor in the world. Similarly, within a period of five years, the American dollar first doubled and then lost half its value against other major currencies. And after having faced, in the early 1980s, the most severe recession of the postwar era, by 1990 the United States was continuing to experience an economic recovery that had lasted longer than any before it. So, enormous changes also characterized international and macroeconomic conditions.

Individually, each of these incidents provides some limited insight into the multitude of extraordinary events in worldwide financial affairs that occurred in the 1980s. Although interesting in themselves, these incidents of change can be pieced together to form a larger, more complex, and much more important story. In this book, I tell that story.

To do this, I tie together various changes in the financial industry of the 1980s and show how they were the consequences of long-term evolutions. This demonstration requires several levels of analysis—the firm, the national financial system, and the global economy—and their interactions. My discussion contrasts with other narratives, which focus narrowly on the sort of incidents I have mentioned and analyze them by concentrating on only one of what I believe are three significant and *interrelated* levels of change.

These levels are:

1. Changes in business strategies of financial services firms.
2. Changes in organization of the three major centers of finance.
3. Changes in international and macroeconomic relationships.

By treating one or more of these levels in isolation, one misses important insights. The changes that have taken place on these three levels actually represent complementary parts of a single story, which spans decades and crosses national borders. It is a story of the breakdown of financial boundaries both internationally and domestically, and of an attendant increase in choices. As barriers broke down in international financing, countries gained new choices and increased flexibility in making domestic macroeconomic policy. As barriers broke down in the tightly controlled national financial systems of the three major centers of finance (the United States, the United Kingdom, and Japan), both issuers and investors discovered new choices. And as financial product market segmentation eroded, price competition increased among close substitutes, which diminished the value of traditional relationships that had long served to tie issuers, investors, and intermediaries together.[1] For financial services firms, the emerging environment offered tremendous opportunity, great potential rewards—and new risks. The strategic choices rapidly multiplied.

In making strategic choices, a player must understand the changed environment and the forces that have created it. Observers have described the financial environment as reflecting deregulation, internationalization, securitization, and disintermediation. This book goes beyond such characterizations to identify more fundamental levels of cause and effect. In fact, deregulation, internationalization, securitization, and the

---

1. In discussing changes in the U.S. financial system, I identify a transition from *relationship banking* to *price-driven banking*. Because these concepts are central to all three systems, they warrant a brief explanation here. By a relationship system I mean a financial system in which price signals are neither sufficient nor fully necessary to determine the allocation of funds in the economy. Under a price-regulated system (which sets interest rate controls) alternatives to the price mechanism have to be found. This circumstance does not imply, however, that, for the financial systems that operated in the postwar years, prices played no role; what mattered was that suppliers and demanders of funds did not have the full freedom to competitively place or seek their funds.

Economics literature, especially in finance, has developed many models to explain why perfectly free competitive markets may not offer the first best solution from the perspective of social welfare maximization. Notions such as imperfect (or asymmetric) information or agency problems are particularly powerful in finance. Financial transactions, by their very nature secretive and tentative, since part of the contract always depends on an unproven ability to pay back at some future date, are affected by these problems. Thus, an institutional attempt to deal with these information problems may well be expected. To put it differently, a relationship between a lender and borrower may be economically efficient even if the transaction does not take place at "fully competitive" market prices. Instead, the transaction price reflects the value of the relationship and should be seen as the outcome of an intertemporal maximization problem under information asymmetries.

There may be a second, institutional reason for the suppression of the price mechanism in finance. Regulation that does not reduce information problems may have been instituted for different, perhaps outdated, reasons, related to (perceived) social welfare maximization. Here, we can expect that firms and their financial intermediaries will try to break the restrictions imposed on them, especially if other pressures, such as increased asset price fluctuations, enhance the possible rewards for escape from regulation.

How policymakers should determine such regulation is not a topic I address; this is not a book about regulation. In fact, the following pages offer little normative judgment when the subject of regulation does crop up. Regulation may affect the boundaries within which strategy formulation of the financial intermediaries takes place (the focus of Part III), but I consider the subject to lie outside the direct influence of the financial services firm, and thus beyond the scope of this book.

like did not arise in a vacuum. Instead of accepting them at face value, I propose further questions: What brought about greater price freedoms in the financial markets of the United States, Japan, and the United Kingdom? Why did they occur in all three markets at approximately the same time? Why did the regulators allow traditional product market segmentation to be eroded? Why did the large international capital account imbalances appear in the 1980s? The answers to these questions are complex, but they are also essential in order to provide an adequate evalution of the current environment in which financial services firms have to operate. Satisfactory answers require, moreover, an understanding of longer-term evolution in international, macroeconomic, and institutional events.

In essence, this book explores the principal consequences of 40 years of evolution in financial transactions in the three most important national capital markets and in the international capital markets. It chronicles a dramatic change—the breaking of local boundaries and the replacement of relatively simple arrangements (based on lack of choice) with more complex ones, as financial transactions were increasingly influenced by competitive market forces.

Thus a central theme of this book is the acceptance of flexible prices (for currencies and financial products) and the sanctioning of new financial freedoms (as international capital controls receded and domestic product market segmentation was reduced). These changes had, in turn, a strong impact on the strategies of financial services firms. By dealing with the three levels of change I have outlined, I am able to highlight a remarkable, and long-term, difference in the attitude of policymakers toward the desirability of free, competitive markets in "real" transactions versus "financial" transactions. First, I discuss how the international economic organization set up after World War II was predicated on the principle of unimpeded international goods transactions. At the same time, international agreements made it clear that capital flows would *not* be accorded equal favor, while the prices of currencies were fixed. In domestic systems, meanwhile, a similar acceptance of price regulation and market restrictions for financial products and transactions prevailed. With regard to these conditions, I show: (1) that this regulated financial world entered a transition to increased reliance on prices; (2) that, because of underlying global forces, the three national systems were affected in similar ways; and (3) that, as a result, financial services vendors were under greater pressure to create value by defining strategies that exploited their competitive strengths and fit the needs of their clients—needs that could increasingly be fulfilled in many different ways.

For example, individual corporate issuers were faced with a multiplying number of financing alternatives. Traditionally, most U.S. firms enjoyed only limited access to the public debt market and only infrequent access to the equity market; for them, bank financing often proved the most practical choice. Today, a spectrum of price-sensitive close substitutes exists to offer these firms a seemingly limitless variety of financing strategies in both domestic and international capital markets. It is the present environment of choice, which contrasts with earlier environments in the major financial systems, that I intend to sketch.

In these traditional regulated environments, the lack of choice reduced the role of *financial* strategy for most corporations. This meant that for the financial services vendors, the role of *corporate* strategy was limited. For example, U.S. commercial banks offered few financing alternatives to their clients, and they were themselves faced with restrictions on product development and interest rates. In Japan, the funding and lending opportunities for city banks were likewise restricted. In both countries, investment bankers operated with a fixed commission structure and well-understood syndication rules. Insurance companies faced a similarly simple environment.

But after the collapse of the Bretton Woods system of fixed exchange rates in 1971, all this would dramatically change. As more volatile and generally higher interest rates appeared, investors and issuers became more interest rate (price) sensitive. This change promised rewards to the financial entrepreneur and innovator that could devise financial products that took advantage of new attitudes, especially as capital began to flow ever more swiftly across international markets. In this environment, product innovation and deregulation forced new strategies on financial intermediaries. To understand these novel business strategies, one must consider general international and macroeconomic conditions, which exercised a direct influence on the activities of the financial firms.

It has always been hard to do justice to the intricacies of macroeconomic relationships, but during the 1980s the subject seemed more clouded than ever. The confidence that economists and policymakers showed in the outcome of macroeconomic management during the 1960s was replaced, in the 1980s, by doubt and uncertainty. One illustration of this emerged in the rumors concerning the abolition of the Council of Economic Advisors during the Reagan presidency—a time of sharp public disagreements between Treasury Secretary Regan and Chairman of the Council Feldstein over the causes and effects of macroeconomic policy. With international accounts deeply out of balance and the United States and many other Western economies seemingly impervious to the business cycle, the always complex topic of macroeconomics appeared even more abstruse; it made it more difficult for financial services firms to set their strategic courses in the rapidly changing national financial systems.

In order to clarify the environment in which these courses have to be charted, this book explores the changing picture of financial transactions as reflected in: (1) massive capital flows between developed nations (Part I); (2) fundamental reorganization of the financial systems in the three world centers of finance, New York, Tokyo, and London (Part II); and (3) new strategies employed by financial intermediaries in response to changed conditions (Part III). Combined, these themes become parts of a single puzzle, which can only be understood when all the pieces are considered together.

As an example, consider the United States during the 1970s, when a very tightly regulated financial market relaxed to provide increased freedoms as regulators lost control. This loss of control came about as international markets outside the jurisdiction of national regulators began to offer serious competition to the national marketplace (the growing Eurodollar deposit market, for instance, presented an attractive alternative to the price-regulated CD market). One reason for wanting to circumvent the regulators' control was a higher level of interest rates, accompanied by their increased volatility; this situation provided investors with a new incentive to shop for the best financial product prices. Interest rates themselves had risen more readily because the revised system of exchange rates gave policymakers the freedom to concentrate on *domestic* policy objectives, neglecting international accounts on the grounds that the flexible exchange rate would take care of them. When stiff commodity (energy) price shocks threatened to produce domestic recession, the domestic policy focus would lead to expansionary monetary policy, inflation, and higher nominal interest rates. And while the macro- and international economic changes helped break the regulated system, the new product and price freedoms offered financial firms new rewards and risks. It led some to embark on rapid growth strategies that must now be regarded as ill-advised. In fact, spectacular failures resulted, as present problems in the U.S. savings and loan industry testify. Interactions among the three levels I have outlined are not merely short-term; it often takes a long time for changes in one to have visible effects on the others, and thus it is all the more important to understand the mechanics of that interaction.

A second example of interaction across the three levels may be identified in the massive U.S. capital account imbalances observed in the 1980s. Here, the widely perceived failure of Keynesian demand management during the late 1970s and the companion ascendancy of supply side economics coincided with a benign neglect of the foreign accounts; the resulting U.S. international borrowing placed large quantities of U.S. assets in foreign hands, changed the relative importance of various capital markets, and caused many U.S. and foreign financial institutions to enter each other's national marketplaces—exerting greater pressure on national regulators. Generally, as regulators provided new freedom, financial innovations popular in one market invaded the others. Then, following their clients and products, several financial institutions embarked on international expansion. Many leading U.S. investment banks, for example, now have more employees stationed abroad than constituted their entire workforce a decade and a half ago.

These interrelated examples show why this book must treat many different subjects. This is a study in which breadth is indispensable, and important details may occasionally be ignored, or dealt with only briefly, or relegated to footnotes, in the interest of reserving space for what is essential to the development of the text. The risks of this approach are evident. Specialists in international finance may find Part I to be oversimplified; experts on the financial system of Japan may have a similar reaction to Chapter 4. And financial services firm strategists may already be familiar with at least some of the material in Part III. The advantage of my method will be found, however, in the broader perspective on all these matters that the book as a whole presents. My overriding purpose is to show that all three levels belong to a single story.

Here, the analogy with a puzzle may be helpful. The puzzle-solver can stare at one individual piece and absorb its nuances, but the full meaning of that piece can only be appreciated as a part of the whole.

PART I

INTERNATIONAL CAPITAL IMBALANCES
IN THE 1980s

1

THE THEORY OF TRADE AND THE BRETTON WOODS SYSTEM

In February 1989, when the U.S. Department of Commerce announced the nation's trade figures for 1988, financial markets around the world reacted with satisfaction. With the U.S. trade deficit at "only" $154 billion, many commentators speculated that it might be the start of a long awaited reversal in the seemingly ever-increasing U.S. current account deficits. The news, at least for the moment, was good; yet only a decade earlier the announcement of an equal deficit (even when adjusted for inflation) would surely have been met with shock and disbelief. Compared to pre-1980s levels of current account and capital account imbalance (see Charts 1.1 and 1.2), the world in the 1980s had changed.

In order to explain the causes of these imbalances, this chapter and the next will emphasize the interaction of institutional events and macroeconomic forces. The chief result of this interaction was the breakdown of national boundaries in capital flows, which in turn affected the transitions of the U.S., Japanese, and U.K. financial systems discussed in Part II.[1] These changes in the national financial systems in turn led to new business opportunities and strategies for financial services firms, which are the subject of Part III. Thus, to understand this single story of change on three levels, one must begin by looking at the operation of fundamental forces.

Chapters 1 and 2 show how these forces manifested themselves in a reconstituted international financial system in the early 1970s, giving policymakers the hope that, by adopting flexible exchange rates, they could have more freedom in monetary and fiscal policymaking. These institutional reforms had unexpected consequences, however. Not only did they facilitate imbalances, they failed to relieve ultimate policy pres-

1. For an excellent treatment of the history of the international monetary system, see K. Dam, *The Rules of the Game: Reform and Evolution in the International Monetary System* (Chicago: University of Chicago Press, 1982).

CHART 1.1
Current Account as % of GNP
1960–1989

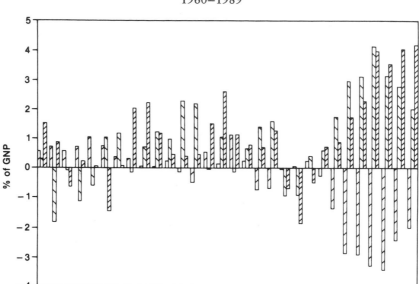

Source: *International Financial Statistics*, various editions.

sures. They simply delayed such pressures. In other words, policymakers won the freedom to procrastinate over unpopular choices, not to escape them. Also, the new institutional freedoms encouraged inflation and subsequent asset price (interest rate) volatility. Such volatility became one incentive to alter the national financial systems of the United States, Japan, and the United Kingdom, as well as the behavior of the financial intermediaries operating in these countries. To trace this development, I begin by briefly reviewing the history of thought about international trade transactions. Once established, the pure theory of international trade would influence the mindset of academics and policymakers for a long time.

THE PURE THEORY OF INTERNATIONAL TRADE

Chart 1.3 shows one of the many indicators that demonstrate the growth of international trade. It is certainly no surprise that, with improvements in transportation and communication, international trade

CHART 1.2
U.S. Net Asset Position
1970–1988

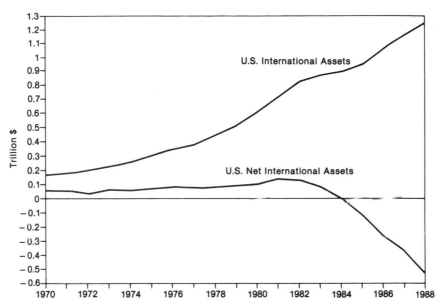

Source: *Economic Report of the President* (1990).

has greatly increased. Under most conditions, free trade should benefit both trading partners and should grow as technological improvements make more goods tradable. Few other paradigms in economics are so well accepted by both theorists and policymakers as the one presenting gains (under most circumstances) from free international trade.[2]

In international economics, there are two types of transactions: the exports and imports of goods and services, which make up the *current account*; and the exports and imports of assets, which make up the *capital account*. Early investigations into international transactions focused on the goods side. In the pure theory of trade, the exchange of goods between nations is the result of production and consumption patterns; the financing of the trade is not much considered. Given a "correct" set of international prices, world output can be distributed through balanced trade in order to maximize the consumption of the various players. Countries produce according to what they do most effectively *before* they exchange goods. Through trade they are able to

2. Exceptions to this result obtain, for example, when one country has world-market power and benefits from an "optimal tariff."

CHART 1.3
Dollar Value of World Exports
1960–1989

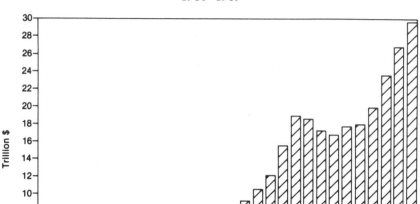

Source: *International Financial Statistics,* various editions.

acquire and then consume whatever goods they lack. In short, traditional models of international trade seek optimal global production patterns, which can be used to maximize world output.

In such a theoretical world, gains from trade have little to do with
the way in which trade is financed. One can imagine perfectly balanced
trade, whereby the value of the imported goods will equal the value of
the exported goods, so that no net financing is needed. The gains from
trade are measured by comparing consumption after free trade to consumption without trade. The theoretical development of this field of
economics focused initially on the causes of trade and on a robust formulation of potential gains to be realized from it. In the early stages, it
was particularly important to show that trade could benefit *all* participants. Early in the nineteenth century, David Ricardo argued that the
weakest as well as the strongest (technological) nations could benefit
from trade. He showed that mutually beneficial international goods
exchanges did not require one country to be better at producing goods
than another country, but only that the two countries be different in
their abilities to do so. By concentrating in production on what a country did relatively well, and subsequently trading these goods in the inter-

national markets for goods produced by others that specialized in what they did best, gains from trade could arise for even the weakest country. *Comparative* rather than *absolute* advantage mattered. So the trade game was open to any nation, however weak its perceived technological capabilities, and widely accepted theory predicted real welfare improvements for all nations from perfectly balanced trade.[3]

Over the next two centuries, continuing research into the causes and effects of trade refined the notion of comparative advantage. Older models, which categorized countries by technological capabilities, were supplanted by models that segmented nations by the relative amounts of the factors of production available to them. Thus, one country could be relatively well endowed with labor, another with land. The former would specialize in the production of goods that made heavy use of labor, the latter in those that relied heavily on land. Because of such specialization, trade would subsequently allow both countries to consume both kinds of goods.[4] Later, during the 1970s, industrial organiza-

---

3. Ricardo's insights seemed even more surprising in his own time, when the notions of an "invisible hand" and the exchange economy were not generally accepted. On the relationships among Ricardo, Smith, and Quesnay's ideas about models of production and exchange, see E. Wolff, "Models of Production and Exchange in the Thought of Adam Smith and David Ricardo," unpublished Ph.D. diss., Yale 1974. The earliest statement of theory of comparative disadvantage, as presented in Chap. 7 of D. Ricardo, *On the Principles of Political Economy and Taxation* (London: J. Murray, 1821) has also been attributed to Robert Torrens, another early nineteenth-century economist. (R. Torrens, *An Essay on the External Corn Trade* [London: Hatchard, 1815].) Ricardo's model relied on technology (or labor productivity) differentials, since it assumed the use of only one factor of production. The model was extended to include many goods (see, for example, R. Dornbusch, S. Fischer, and P. Samuelson, "Comparative Advantage, Trade and Payments in a Ricardian Model with a Continuum of Goods," *American Economic Review* 67 [1977]:823–839), and it was shown that the model is simplified when the number of goods becomes a smooth continuum.

4. Two Swedish economists, Hecksher and Ohlin, are most closely associated with the factor-endowment model of trade. Although it looked at relative factor abundance rather than relying on technology differentials for comparative advantage, their model was not a radical departure from the traditional Ricardian model, since it still showed that comparative rather than absolute advantages mattered. The Hecksher-Ohlin model of trade became the focus of the international trade literature; it was extended by several theorists to yield strong results. They showed that under certain conditions free trade in goods would be a substitute for trade in factors of production. Thus, factor price equalization was obtained, even though it was shown that in some situations it would fail. For example, with complete specialization of production, factor price differences would obtain. Another implication of the factor-endowment models was that international trade would yield income distribution effects inside the country. See W. Stolper and P. Samuelson, "Protection and Real Wages," *Review of Economic Studies* 9 (1941):58–73. Similar extensions, making more or less restrictive assumptions, constituted much of the

tion models provided yet another rationale for trade. They assumed that the nature of production technology was such that economies of scale in production would lead countries to specialize in certain products, and that these could be advantageously exchanged for products produced more efficiently elsewhere, due to similar economies of scale.[5]

Today, it is easy to understand how—given these successive models—the notion that free trade is beneficial gained wide currency. In practice, however, such conditions were only infrequently observed.[6] Over the history of international transactions, free trade has more often been an exception than the norm. But although tariffs, controls, and other impediments to free trade were commonly used, and the academic literature showed special cases in which optimal tariffs and other forms of protection would actually be better for a country than free trade, the basic idea that free trade was beneficial continued to be widely accepted in academic and policymaking circles. The formation of the General Agreement on Tariffs and Trade (GATT) in 1947, by establishing a general policy framework for multilateral tariff reductions, demonstrated this wide acceptance.

---

development of the trade literature. Considerable attention was given to the implications of the Hecksher-Ohlin model but little to its basic premises, until the next generation of models appeared.

5. One major advantage of this line of research was its ability to explain trade between countries with similar technologies and similar relative factor endowments. These trades have been much observed between developed nations. For an excellent treatment of industrial organization models of trade, see E. Helpman and P. Krugman, *Market Structure and Foreign Trade, Increasing Returns, Imperfect Competition and the International Economy* (Cambridge, MA: MIT Press, 1985). Also, see A. Dixit and J. Stiglitz, "Monopolistic Competition and Optimum Product Diversity," *American Economic Review* 67 (1977):297–308; P. Krugman, "Scale Economics, Product Differentiation and the Pattern of Trade," *American Economic Review* 70 (1980):950–959; and K. Lancaster, "A Theory of Intra-Industry Trade under Perfect Monopolistic Competition," *Journal of International Economics* 10 (1980):151–175.

6. Exceptions to the optimality of free trade were to be found, for example, in the optimum tariff literature. In the traditional trade literature, it was posited that a large enough country might have world-market power that could be exploited through an optimum tariff. In the more modern industrial organization literature of international trade, notions of strategic trade policy have emerged; see J. Brander and B. Spencer, "Export Subsidies and International Market Share Rivalry," *Journal of International Economics* 18 (1985):83–100. For a general evaluation, see G. Grossman, "Strategic Export Promotion: A Critique," in P. Krugman, ed., *Strategic Trade Policy and the New International Economics* (Cambridge, MA: MIT Press, 1986):47–68. Also see A. Dixit, "Trade Policy: An Agenda for Research," in Krugman, ed., *Strategic Trade Policy and the New International Economics*:283–304.

Gains from trade derived from more efficient world production through specialization, but the actual process of international trading involved the exchange of monies to settle the accounts. Such exchanges did not, however, figure prominently in the development of most models of international trade. In them, production was allocated geographically according to comparative advantage, and highly flexible relative prices sent clear signals as to what each country should produce and buy in international markets. That is, these models concentrated on current account transactions that left the account in balance—the monetary value of exports simply equalled that of imports.[7]

INTERNATIONAL TRADE AND THE MACROECONOMY

While trade theorists developed models of international trade that provided a rationale for free, balanced trade, other academics analyzed the role of international transactions in macroeconomics, focusing especially on unbalanced trade. They saw imbalances primarily as temporary deviations, and as a result they concentrated on the adjustment mechanism that would restore balanced trade. Again, the history of economic thought on this issue is long. The classical view, most frequently associated with the eighteenth-century writings of David Hume, took international trade as given and focused on the relative price changes that would guarantee overall balance.[8] For example, assuming a fixed (gold) exchange rate system, a country running a trade deficit would lose bullion as it sold gold to finance the excess of imports over exports. Since under the gold standard the money supply was directly tied to the amount of gold in the country, any gold loss would reduce the money supply and would lead to price deflation. Then, with cheaper prices for goods produced at home, the trade balance would return to equilibrium, as imports became comparatively more expensive and exports became

7. Models of international goods transactions, where prices were perfectly flexible and where production and consumption reacted smoothly to price signals, in effect ignored the monetary side of the economy; they considered only "real" transactions. Note that since the notion of price flexibility was well accepted by the classical economists, comparative advantage and reciprocal demand lay at the foundation of the models developed at that time. J.S. Mill's 1844 contribution had already identified the relationship between the terms of trade and reciprocal demand. See J. Viner, *Studies in the Theory of International Trade* (New York: Harper and Brothers, 1937):535–536.

8. Hume's work relied on monetary adjustment in the wake of a trade imbalance. A "miraculous" disturbance would set forces in motion to return equilibrium. Quoted ibid.:292.

more attractive to foreigners.[9] Thus, if deviations from balanced trade occurred, price signals induced by monetary contraction or expansion would allow for a return to balanced trade.[10]

The mechanism of the gold standard can easily be understood in the context of balance of payments, which countries use to record all their international transactions. The balance of payments consists of various subaccounts, but, as the term indicates, all those accounts in *combination* do balance. Just what subaccounts are looked at really matters, since individually each one can be out of balance, even though the sum of the subaccounts will always equal zero. Typically, three accounts are considered: the current account, which records goods and services transactions; the capital account, which records asset transactions by the private sector; and the official account, which records the international transactions of the authorities (mostly intervention in the foreign exchange market to buy or sell currencies in order to keep the exchange rate constant). With one account in deficit, at least one other has to be in surplus by a comparable amount. For example, with a current account deficit (i.e., imports of goods and services exceed exports), either the capital account or the official account has to be in surplus (i.e., more assets are sold than bought in order to finance the country's excess of imports of goods and services over exports).

The balance of payments also helps to illuminate the differences between fixed and flexible exchange rates. With fixed exchange rates, authorities will, if necessary, intervene in the foreign exchange market to keep the rate at the chosen level. Suppose that, at this rate, the sum of the current and capital accounts is not zero. Because the balance of payments in sum balances, the third account, the official account, will have to offset exactly the net effect of the two other accounts and thus guarantee overall balance. So the official account will be in surplus or deficit, reflecting the consequences of the authorities' intervention to keep the exchange rate fixed. In this way official reserves will be depleted or augmented, depending on whether these officials are net buyers or sellers in the currency markets.

With flexible rates, on the other hand, the authorities do not intervene in the foreign exchange market; thus the official account is always zero, and the level of foreign reserves remains unchanged. Because the three

9. Even within the context of the classical writers, other factors could influence the adjustment mechanism. See F. Taussig, "International Trade under Depreciated Paper," *Quarterly Journal of Economics* 31 (1917):380–403.

10. Another mechanism, accepted by classical economists but never put forth with much emphasis, was an income-expenditure channel.

subaccounts that make up the balance of payments also add up to zero under flexible rates—here with the zero official account—the current and capital accounts have to offset each other exactly. They will do so because the variation of the exchange rate affects both current and capital accounts, allowing the free market rate to achieve a balance-of-payments equilibrium.[11]

Thus, under fixed rates the exchange rate remains stable. To achieve stability, however, the authorities have to intervene in the markets, and this causes the levels of official reserves either to rise or fall. Under flexible rates, the exchange rate is set by the market, and it rises or falls according to supply and demand pressures. But the country's official

11. The work of Joan Robinson was fundamental in analyzing the effects of an exchange rate change on the international balances. Her contributions are now viewed in light of the effects of an exchange rate change on the balance of trade, but the description of exchange rate determination in the first paragraph of her 1937 essay remains instructive: "The exchange rate is determined from day to day by supply and demand of home currency in terms of foreign currency. Each transaction is two-sided, and sales are equal to purchases. Any change in the conditions of demand and supply reflects itself in a change in the exchange rate, and at the ruling rate, the balance of payments balances from day to day or from moment to moment." See J. Robinson, *Essays on the Theory of Employment* (New York: Macmillan, 1937):183. The capital account (or balance of lending, in Robinson's terminology) was not accorded much importance: "The volume of imports and exports is determined by tastes, techniques, and resources the world over, and by cost and incomes at home and abroad, which in turn are determined by the level of money wages and effective demand. The balance of lending is determined (given wealth and income) by relative rates of interest at home and abroad, and by all those considerations which may be lumped together under the heading of 'the state of confidence.'...The theory of exchanges may be regarded as the manner in which movements of the balance of trade and the balance of lending are equated to each other." Ibid.:187–188. One outcome of this line of research appeared in the so-called elasticities approach. It posited that, given conditions on the responsiveness of imports and exports to exchange rate changes as seen through their elasticities, the desired change in the balance of trade could be observed. The importance of the elasticities was originally presented by A. Marshall, "The Pure Theory of Foreign Trade," *Scarce Tracts in Economics and Political Science*, no. 1 (London: The London School of Economics and Political Science, 1879). Later, C. Bickerdike, "The Instability of Foreign Exchange," *Economic Journal* 30 (1920):118–122, outlined the conditions discussed by Robinson. A. Lerner provided a full statement of these conditions in his *Economics of Control: Principles of Welfare Economics* (New York: Macmillan, 1944). In the late 1950s, Alexander developed the "absorption" approach, which argued that a devaluation undertaken at full employment could only affect the balance of trade if a reduction in domestic absorption took place. Alexander granted the basic correctness of the elasticities approach, but noted that a more fruitful line of thought could be based on the relationship between real expenditure and real income and on the relationship of both of these to the price levels. See S. Alexander, "Effects of a Devaluation on a Trade Balance," *International Monetary Fund Staff Papers* 2 (1952):263–278.

reserves remain stable, since no intervention by the national authorities in the currency markets ever takes place.

In many ways, the gold standard simply represented a fixed exchange rate system. When two countries each fix the price of gold in terms of their currencies, the exchange rate between their currencies becomes fixed as well. At the fixed rates a particular current account might or might not be in balance. If it were out of balance, then the official account would have to offset it in order to keep the overall balance of payments in balance, assuming for the moment that capital controls ruled capital flows out (so that the capital account was zero). Thus, authorities would have to sell or buy gold abroad. Furthermore, the gold flows would affect the money supplies in both countries. As prices rose or fell, depending on whether the money supply increased or contracted, trade transactions would return to balance.[12]

This elegant model of the world became a casualty of the Keynesian revolution.[13] In Keynes's new world prices could be "stuck" with the economy in a chronic state of underemployment. In such a situation, the classical adjustment mechanism, which relied on price changes to restore balance in the current account after the exchanges of gold between the trading nations, could become ineffectual. Without the requisite domestic price adjustments, an alternate response had to be considered—a change in the exchange rate. Thus attention shifted from the changing domestic prices (under a fixed exchange rate) to the rigid domestic prices that would nonetheless look cheaper or more expensive to foreigners after a change in the exchange rate.[14]

12. Another approach to trade balance was also suggested; it relied on income and expenditure effects, induced by the monetary effects of the gold flows.

13. Keynes had expressed misgivings about the adjustment mechanism within the context of German reparations following the First World War. He analyzed the effect of a unilateral transfer on the adjustment mechanism. See J. Keynes, "The German Transfer Problem," *Economic Journal* 39 (1929):1–7. However, the real impact of Keynesian economics was seen through the channels presented in his *General Theory of Employment, Interest and Money* (London: Macmillan, 1936).

14. Within the context of Keynesian thinking an income channel could help restore balance, since a surplus country with rising income would increase its imports. Most Keynesian theorists focused, however, on policy-induced exchange rate changes in the quest to restore trade balance. In 1948, Metzler, one of the major scholars of international economics, reviewed the "revolution in economic theory which occurred in the nineteen-thirties." He summarized the changes implied by the Keynesian revolution in these words: "The essence of the new theory is that an external event which increases a country's exports will also increase imports, even without price changes, since the change in exports affects the level of output and hence the demand for all goods." See L. Metzler, "The Theory of International

Over time modifications and syntheses of various models appeared, and the policy implications of each came under study, especially the interactions between a country's external balances and its fiscal and monetary policymaking.[15] In a theoretical world without an external sector, macroeconomic policymaking could concentrate on inflation, unemployment, and growth; adding the external sector now had the effect of adding an extra target for the policymaker. According to one important line of thinking, the government could use internal (i.e., fiscal and monetary) policies to achieve internal equilibrium—typically meant to be high growth and low inflation—and external (i.e., exchange rate) policies to achieve external equilibrium, typically meant to be current account balance. Later theoretical contributions completed the devel-

---

Trade," in H. Ellis, ed., *A Survey of Contemporary Economics*, vol. 1 (Philadelphia: The Blakiston Company, 1948):213. Contrary to Metzler's assertion, equilibration can occur within the Humean adjustment process when increased real money balances are reflected by increased imports at constant prices. Still, what matters is the shift in emphasis in the channel of adjustment away from price adjustment to income effects. By circumventing the domestic price adjustment as a means of equilibration, Metzler incorporated Keynesian thinking, but he was also forced to explore alternative channels of adjustment. Metzler noted that full adjustment through the income channel would be precluded either by an increase in savings because of higher income or by internal adjustment policies. He concluded that: "If induced changes in employment are prevented or greatly reduced, virtually the only method of balancing international accounts without resort to direct controls will be through changes in the terms of trade, i.e., through the price system....Even without general cost and price changes, the essential means of adjustment contemplated by the classical theory—a change in the terms of trade—can be accomplished through changes in the exchange rates." Ibid.:221.

15. J.E. Meade provided a synthesis between Robinson and Alexander's work, but not everyone was ready to view Meade's contribution as a synthesis, and the search for a middle ground continued. Machlup's criticisms of the absorption approach, for example, specifically called for a synthesis: "Neither of the two 'alternative' sets of tools can be spared; both are needed." F. Machlup, "The Terms of Trade Effect of Devaluation Upon Real Income and the Balance of Trade," *Kyklos* 9 (1956):417–452. Alexander provided such a synthesis and treated the income effect as the "reversal factor" induced by the elasticities effects on the balance of trade. See S. Alexander, "Effects of a Devaluation: A Simplified Synthesis of Elasticities and Absorption Approaches," *American Economic Review* 49 (1959):22–42. He derived a condition for a devaluation to improve the balance of trade, taking the reversal factor into account. Noting that Alexander's synthesis was similar to Harberger's (A. Harberger, "Currency Depreciation, Income and the Balance of Trade," *Journal of Political Economy* 58 [1950]:47–60), S. Tsiang, in "The Role of Money in Trade Balance Stability: Synthesis of the Elasticity and Absorption Approaches," *American Economic Review* 51 (1961):912–936, suggested instead a model that differed from Meade's only in that it allowed for interest rate variations (which had been ruled out by Meade's "Neutral Economy Assumption").

opment of these new models.[16] Theorists considered how a trade flow imbalance would interact with the domestic economy and how imbalances in trade could be ended.[17] Their models did not forsake the notion that trade was beneficial, but they did suggest that deviations from balanced trade could occur at full employment and that the system lacked automatic forces for driving a return to balance, as persistent imbalances showed. Faced with this unattractive and untenable conclusion, scholars began to shift away from models that looked at equilibration in trade flows (so-called flow equilibrium models). Instead, they directed their attention toward the asset (or financial) side of the world.[18] The implications of this thinking will be presented in the next chapter; first it is necessary to review the institutional developments that accompanied the changes in economic thinking already outlined.

FIXED VERSUS FLEXIBLE EXCHANGE RATES—THE BRETTON WOODS SYSTEM

The overwhelming evidence from the theoretical models, with their increasingly sophisticated assumptions, documented the benefits from trade. This view emerged so clearly that, while institutional barriers against free trade were repeatedly erected, the basic desirability of trade remained beyond serious question. What did resist consensus was the exact nature of a framework for the international payments system. Should exchange rates be fixed or flexible? Here, both theorists and policymakers failed to make unambiguous choices.

16. See R. Mundell, "The Appropriate Use of Monetary and Fiscal Policy for External and Internal Stability," *International Monetary Fund Staff Papers* 9 (1962):70–79; N. Fleming, "Domestic Financial Policies Under Fixed and Floating Exchange Rates," *International Monetary Fund Staff Papers* 9 (1962):369–380. Also see note 22.

17. Harry Johnson, by taking these models to their logical conclusions, considered their most troubling feature to be that "[b]y choosing a proper mix of demand-management policies and the exchange rate the authorities [could] obtain full employment consistent...with any current account surplus or deficit." H. Johnson, "The Monetary Approach to Balance of Payments Theory," *Further Essays in Monetary Theory* (New York: George Allen, 1972):234. Note the damaging implications of Johnson's conclusions: no automatic adjustment would be forthcoming.

18. First, the monetary approach was developed. Johnson noted that: "[T]he new approach to balance of payments theory, while basically Humean in spirit, places the emphasis not on relative price changes but on the direct influence of excess demand for or supply of money on the balance between income and expenditure." Ibid.:230. Later, the more general asset market approach was developed. "The unifying theme," wrote Frenkel and Mussa in their summary of the significance of this line of research, "was the 'asset market approach to exchange rates' which

I have noted that the historical gold standard represented one example of a fixed exchange rate system.[19] Several policymakers associated the operation of the gold standard between 1870 and 1914 with a smooth functioning of the payment system and satisfactory growth in the developed countries, but others questioned their comfortable assumptions about cause and effect.[20] Even so, after World War I, an attempt was made to restore the old system. Its failure can be traced to many difficulties, not the least of which was the dilemma of finding the "right" fixed rates. Because of this and other problems no major reorganization of the international financial system succeeded until the end of World War II.[21] At that time, defining the structure of a new system meant choosing between fixed and flexible rates; or, to put it differently, between intervention by the officials to support the fixed rate or reliance on the market mechanism to set prices (exchange rates) in the foreign currency markets. Academic debate over this choice concentrated on how the adjustment mechanism would operate; in particular, the effectiveness of policies to achieve external and internal equilibrium under different regimes was carefully analyzed.[22]

---

emphasizes conditions for equilibrium in the market for stocks of assets, especially national monies, as the proximate determinant of the behavior of exchange rates." See J. Frenkel and M. Mussa, "Asset Markets, Exchange Rates and the Balance of Payments," Chap. 14 in R. Jones and P. Kenen, eds., *Handbook of International Economics*, vol. 2 (New York: North Holland, 1985):680.

19. As early as 1819, Robert Torrens had advocated making exchange rates more flexible by widening the gold points. For a review of the gold standard, see A. Bloomfield, *Monetary Policy Under the International Gold Standard, 1880–1914* (New York: Federal Reserve Bank of New York, 1959). Also, see R. Cooper, "The Gold Standard: Historical Facts and Future Prospects," *Brookings Papers on Economic Activity* 1 (1982):1–56.

20. For an argument against the effectiveness of the gold standard, see R. Triffin, "The Evolution of the International Monetary System: Historical Reappraisal and Future Perspective," *Princeton Studies in International Finance*, No. 12 (Princeton, NJ: International Finance Section, 1964).

21. For an empirical evaluation of the interwar period, see S. Tsiang, "Fluctuating Exchange Rates in Countries with Relatively Stable Economies: Some European Experiences after World War I," *International Monetary Fund Staff Papers* 7 (1959):244–273.

22. Under flexible rates, for example, would monetary policy be more or less effective as a means to "cool off" the economy in a time of payments deficit? The results of the debate over exchange rate systems differed according to the assumptions of the models (which, since the 1930s, all displayed Keynesian features to a greater or lesser extent). By the middle 1960s, Mundell's work represented perhaps the most complete statement of the issues. Mundell concluded that internal equilibrium (i.e., full employment) was best achieved through fiscal policy and external equilibrium through monetary policy. Short-run capital flows played a major role, and capital mobility was essential, in the context of this "assignment rule." Mun-

But policymakers could not afford the luxury of long-term debate; after World War II, institutional arrangements had to be made, and these relied primarily on fixed rates.[23] At the Bretton Woods conference of 1944, an international monetary system in which currencies were pegged against the U.S. dollar came into existence. U.S. authorities took it upon themselves to exchange dollars for gold in official transactions at a fixed price of $35 per ounce. With the dollar's price set in terms of gold, and the other currencies pegged against the dollar, a "modified" gold standard reappeared. This outcome seems to have been less the result of economic analysis than of policymakers' memories of the relative prosperity enjoyed under the old gold standard and of the abysmal economic situation in the prewar years, when the international monetary system was not fully anchored in gold.[24] Still, when a fixed exchange rate regime was chosen in the wake of the war, the devastation of most the European countries combined with the relative good health of the U.S. economy to assure that the dollar would hold a special position.

There is little evidence to show that flexible exchange rates were

---

dell's model relied on fairly restrictive assumptions to explain exchange rate system interactions with fiscal and monetary policy choices. It assumed very simple linkages between monetary policy and interest rate effects, associating expansionary monetary policy with falling interest rates. Thus it ignored all kinds of expectation effects of future inflation changes on the nominal interest rate. Yet even with all their restrictive assumptions, the models could establish no clear dominance of fixed or flexible exchange rate systems. At best they could tie the choice of the system to the types of shocks observed in the international and domestic economy. Note how difficult this makes policy prescription. It is hard to base one's choice of a policy regime on the unanticipated shocks, precisely because they are unanticipated.

Another debate analyzed the stabilizing nature of speculation in a flexible exchange rate regime; see M. Friedman, "The Case for Flexible Exchange Rates," in *Essays in Positive Economics* (Chicago: University of Chicago Press, 1953):157–204.

23. Officially, according to Article IV, the rates were "fixed," even though adjustments were foreseen. IMF, *Articles of Agreement* (Washington, DC: International Monetary Fund, 1978):6–9.

24. The positions of the two major economic powers, the United States and the United Kingdom, were prepared by Harry Dexter White (U.S. Treasury) and John Maynard Keynes (Honorary Advisor to the British Treasury). The state of affairs at the onset of the war was characterized by Keith Horsefield as "[a]n international economics community where 'beggar-thy-neighbor' policies were the rule, and where the best international attempts to restore order to the financial system were endangered by the desperate attempts of weaker countries to hold their own in the face of cut-throat competition." See K. Horsefield, *The International Monetary Fund 1945–1965*, vol. 1 (Washington, DC: International Monetary Fund, 1969):5.

seriously considered at the time. Instead, trade constraints and international liquidity concerns dominated discussions at Bretton Woods, where the two plans presented—Keynes's British and White's American—differed mainly on the question of how international imbalances would be settled and how international liquidity would be created.[25] These preoccupations reflected the development of economic theory at a time when it focused primarily on trade flows and on the adjustment mechanisms to be used if and when a deviation from balanced trade occurred. At the conference the system adopted relied on fixed (but adjustable) rates, on liquidity creation through dollar balances, and on a strong recommendation to avoid trade restrictions.[26]

This emphasis on free trade, along with the notable absence of any corresponding pressure for free capital movements, deserves attention. It will play a central role in the story that unfolds in later chapters of the changes in the national financial systems of the United States, Japan, and the United Kingdom. These countries showed a similar dichotomy on the domestic level, where free trade in goods existed alongside severe restrictions in financial transactions. The widespread restrictions that governed the financial markets in these three countries severely reduced the choices of the financial services firms operating within them.

International capital restrictions can easily be understood if one keeps in mind the economic models reviewed earlier.[27] Recall that the various *trade* models demonstrated the superiority of free trade, which would allow optimal international production. International *capital* flows, on the other hand, were viewed differently: long-term investment flows, though they could be beneficial, played only a minor role in policymakers' thinking.[28] More attention was given to short-term capital flows, which were viewed as the parasitic outcome of speculation and thought capable of destabilizing the entire system. This attitude toward short-term flows was apparent in the consensus expressed by the IMF's first annual report on exchange restrictions:

25. Ibid.:3–78.

26. Most currencies remained nonconvertible for an interim period, but they were expected finally to become convertible.

27. Article I, *The Purpose of the Fund*, placed exclusive emphasis on the current account. IMF, *Articles of Agreement*:2–3.

28. See ibid.:26. Article VI, Section 3, *Controls of Capital Transfers*: "Members may exercise such controls as are necessary to regulate international capital movements, but no member may exercise these controls in a manner which will restrict payments for current transactions or which will unduly delay transfers of funds in settlement of commitments except as provided in Article VII, Section 3(b) and in Article XIV, Section 2."

Departures from the principle of unrestricted *current* international payments under conditions of convertibility of member countries would be exceptional....On the other hand, every member country may protect itself against the serious disturbing effects which erratic international capital movements have had in the past on the accounts of debtor and creditor nations alike (emphasis added).[29]

The role of long-term capital flows, although viewed more favorably, still did not attract much attention.[30] One basic principle of international economics may account for this: capital accumulations have to be reversed because, otherwise, the nation accumulating capital would eventually end up "owning the rest of the world"—an unlikely as well as undesirable outcome.[31] A 1970 report by the directors of the IMF explained this by looking back at the experiences of the 1960s:

Members of the Fund are specifically authorized to exercise such controls as are necessary to regulate international capital movements, provided these do not unduly delay or otherwise restrict payments for current transactions; in addition, the Articles limit the ability of members to use the Fund's resources to meet a large or sustained outflow of capital, and the Fund may request a member to exercise controls on capital movements to prevent such use of the Fund's resources.[32]

These very different attitudes toward controls on trade versus capital were nonetheless consistent; with long-term capital flows downplayed and short-term capital controls utilized, the capital account could be

29. See the *First Annual Report on Exchange Restrictions* (Washington, DC: International Monetary Fund, 1950):122.

30. The IMF and national authorities did recognize the need for international investment flows. These did not stand at the center of attention but were seen in relation to developing or rebuilding countries. See, for example, the exchange between Paul Brown (member of the House Committee on Banking and Currency) and Harry White, U.S. Congress, House Committee on Banking and Currency, *Bretton Woods Agreements Acts: Hearings on H.R. 2211*, 79th Cong., 1st sess., 1945, vol. I:90.

31. It is, of course, theoretically possible for a deficit on the long-term capital account to be offset by a surplus on the short-term capital account, so that no net accumulation of capital takes place. In such a situation only a maturity transformation of the obligations and assets of the countries would be involved. Also, the statement in the text is oversimplified. Suppose a country's asset stock grows faster than the accumulation rate of the foreign creditor. A continuous current account deficit and an offsetting capital account surplus could then be sustained, without the foreign creditor ending up "owning" the home country.

32. Quoted in B. Tew, *The Evolution of the International Monetary System, 1945–1977* (London: Hutchinson, 1977):87.

balanced. In the absence of official intervention, this meant that balanced free trade should occur at the "correct" set of exchange rates. Remember that the balance of payments consists of three accounts, the sum of which always equals zero—the current, capital, and official accounts. With a balanced capital account and no official transactions, the current account has to balance as well. Thus, if in the fixed exchange rate world with capital controls, the exchange rate is correctly set (here to mean that no continuous intervention has to occur), then all three accounts remain in balance. It was therefore agreed that fixed exchange rates would be set, even though they would be adjustable in the sense that a country facing fundamental "disequilibrium" (never carefully defined but apparently meaning a structural current account deficit) would be allowed to alter the pegged rate.[33] The only remaining question seemed to be how to set the rates so that they would yield current account equilibrium.

At Bretton Woods the IMF founders also attempted to ensure that sufficient international liquidity would be available to allow the system to operate smoothly.[34] This concern for liquidity derived from two factors: one was the expectation that at the agreed-upon exchange rates most countries would run net deficits vis-à-vis the United States, especially in the years immediately after the war; the other was the expectation that the need for dollar liquidity would be substantial, because many nations would use dollars in international transactions as long as their own currencies were not readily exchanged. This lack of convertibility among most currencies was expected to prevail for some time, even though the IMF called for the earliest possible return to convertibility. Since its own resources were relatively small, early liquidity had to be provided through U.S. grants (e.g., the Marshall Plan) and loans (e.g., the Export-Import Bank).[35] Only in 1958, when convertibility among

---

33. The members of the fund took it upon themselves to maintain exchange rate stability according to Sec. 4 of Article IV. This allowed the pegged rates to be adjusted only in the case of "fundamental disequilibrium," leading to the designation of the "adjustable peg" system. See M. de Vries, *The International Monetary Fund, 1945–1965*, vol. 2 (Washington, DC: International Monetary Fund, 1969):39–50.

34. The original Keynes plan proposed an international clearing union. The White plan envisaged a contributory system with the international agency providing liquidity if necessary. In the actual arrangement that led to the IMF's formation, a contributory scheme was adopted.

35. Concerns about international liquidity abated as the U.S. current account surplus fell from $4.7 billion to a deficit of $1.4 billion between 1957 and 1959. During the 1960s, the concerns about a dollar shortage were replaced with concerns about a dollar surplus or "overhang." It was at this time that Robert Triffin framed

most currencies was restored, did the Bretton Woods system begin to operate fully—it lasted only slightly more than a decade. During this decade, the international monetary system functioned according to rules set in the mid-1940s; the Bretton Woods system of pegged but adjustable exchange rates prevailed, while capital account restrictions were frequently observed in the system.[36] Still, weaknesses were soon to appear.

BREAKING THE SYSTEM
THE MOVE TO FLEXIBLE EXCHANGE RATES

Under the Bretton Woods system, two methods of adjustment could occur. Suppose a country ran a current account deficit (and again I abstract from the capital account): to support the exchange rate, the authorities could enter the currency markets and buy their own currency, thus losing foreign reserves. An alteration in the reserve levels was only temporarily possible, since countries losing reserves had to take measures to avoid running out of them. This need would force the authorities to take monetary and/or fiscal policy actions, changing demand and supply for imports and exports in their country in order to restore external balance.

If, however, the exchange rate had been pegged at a "fundamentally" wrong level, then, rather than forcing domestic policy actions or official intervention, the Bretton Woods system allowed for parity changes—as it turned out, for every nation *except* the United States. No parity change would be possible if the United States were to find itself in a position of fundamental disequilibrium on the current account, because

---

his famous "dollar dilemma": with dollars convertible into gold and required for international liquidity, growing use of the dollar would diminish the relative backing of gold to the dollar, which in turn would make the currency less desirable as a reserve currency. See R. Triffin, *Gold and the Dollar Crisis: The Future of Convertibility* (New Haven: Yale University Press, 1960).

36. In 1963, for example, the United States responded to sustained capital outflows with the Interest Equalization Tax, the Voluntary Foreign Credit Restraint Program, and the Foreign Direct Investment Program. The adoption of the Interest Equalization Tax (IET) in 1963 created the Eurosecurities market. Although a Euro-deposit market had functioned since the late 1950s, and several bonds had been issued outside the home country of the issuer (in particular, so-called Yankee bonds, issued by sovereign European borrowers in the United States), it was the IET of 1963 that gave the impetus for an Italian offering, managed by a London investment bank denominated in dollars; the Eurosecurities market was born, and it grew from issue volume of less than $150 million in 1963 to over $175 billion in 1986.

under the modified gold standard, all other countries pegged against the dollar.[37] Thus, another country like Britain could change the par value of its currency (as it did in 1967) by devaluing against the dollar (and therefore against all other currencies), but the United States, in contrast, could take no similar action. It could only ask all other countries to change their currency values against the dollar. This basic asymmetry was a serious drawback to the fixed dollar-linked rates system, which became increasingly apparent during the 1960s, as the international accounts of the United States worsened.[38]

During the late 1960s, fundamental pressures threatened the Bretton Woods system. Balance-of-payments surpluses in Germany and Japan, driven by their current accounts, were a persistent source of trouble (see Chart 1.4, page 31).

Between 1967 and 1969, the overall U.S. current account deteriorated sharply, and although Germany did revalue its currency upward against the dollar between September and October 1969, the U.S. current account showed only a short-term improvement during 1970 and then moved into deficit in 1971. The special position of the dollar combined with a lack of pressure on surplus nations to cause the entire system to break down. Reflecting on this phenomenon, the 1973 *Economic Report of the President* noted that the Articles of Agreement of the IMF

37. This issue has been analyzed by Robert Mundell as the redundancy problem and the world price level. Even though Mundell presents the analysis in terms of balance-of-payments equilibrium and general instruments to control the balance, a special case is a simple fixed-exchange rate world, with exchange rate adjustment as the balance-of-payments instrument. Here, with n-countries, only n-1 rates can be set independently. R. Mundell, *International Economics* (New York: Macmillan, 1968):195–198.

38. At the same time, the perceived need for international liquidity remained a second major concern. For example, on the probable future needs for liquidity, see the 1965 Ossola Report (Group of Ten, *Report of the Study Group on the Creation of Reserve Assets* [Washington, DC: G-10, 1965]). In early 1966, at a meeting of the IMF deputy directors, liquidity creation again took center stage. Various proposals were debated, among them plans presented by Otmar Emminger (for the Federal Republic of Germany, Italy, and the Netherlands), and by representatives of the United States, the United Kingdom, and Canada. The concern about liquidity also grew because the world monetary gold stock was rising only slowly. Gold reserves increased from $33.6 billion in 1952 to $38.9 billion in 1969; total world reserves (gold plus foreign exchange) rose during the same period, from $49.4 billion to $78.7 billion, *International Financial Statistics* (Washington, DC: International Monetary Fund, 1982). An implicit recognition that the United States might need to borrow from the fund can be found in President Kennedy, "Message to the Congress," February 16, 1961. The IMF's General Agreement to Borrow reflected this.

were not very explicit about circumstances under which countries should take action to remove balance of payments deficits or surpluses. The assumption was that deficit countries would sooner or later run out of reserves or borrowing facilities and therefore would have to adjust. However, surplus countries could postpone adjustment as long as they were willing to accumulate reserves. Since the major deficit country, the United States, could not adjust its exchange rate without endangering the operation of the system, and since most of the surplus countries were persistently reluctant to change their own rates, the disequilibrium in world payments increased through the latter half of the 1960s until it reached a breaking point in mid-1971.[39]

Up to this point, not much attention had been paid to the capital account; short-term capital movements remained heavily controlled and long-term flows were not a focus of policy debate. Yet the capital account was far more important than anyone had estimated, and it was soon to play a key role in the actual breakdown of the Bretton Woods system. Note that the deterioration in the U.S. current account during the latter half of 1960 left the country with a surplus that dwindled each year (see Chart 1.4, page 31). The immediate pressure, however, stemmed from large capital outflows, both recorded and nonrecorded (often a euphemism for legal and illegal). In 1970, the U.S. capital account registered a deficit of $12.9 billion; in 1971, $19.3 billion. This meant that private citizens were selling their dollars and buying foreign assets, a process made easier by the appearance of new markets such as the Euromarkets, which were outside the control of regulators.[40] Thus, with the current account barely in surplus and the capital account in large deficit, any offset had to come from the official account. So the official reserve account came under increasing pressure. It financed private transactions with almost $10 billion in 1970 and with $30 billion in 1971. Later chapters will explain how these pressures not only affected the current account but also set in motion a process that would ultimately lead to a radical reorganization of the U.S. financial system and to changes in the operations of financial intermediaries.

Such pressures manifested themselves through the capital account, but current account problems (i.e., increased imports compared to exports) continued to represent the underlying problem. With the U.S. current account moving toward deficit, market participants became convinced that some exchange rate adjustment was inevitable. This made

39. *Economic Report of the President* (Washington, DC: U.S. Government Printing Office, 1973):122.
40. See the passage from the 1971 *Economic Report of the President* quoted below.

CHART 1.4
Current Account
1965–1970

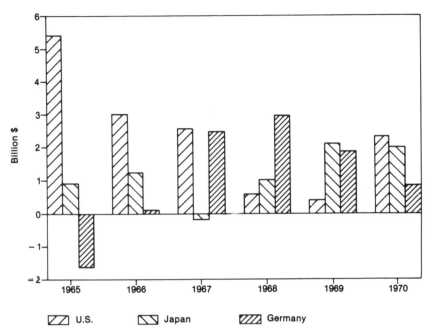

Source: International Financial Statistics, various editions.

the purchase of foreign assets attractive. Bought at the present exchange rate, these foreign assets would become much more valuable if and when monetary officials devalued the dollar. The sale of dollars used to purchase these assets put further strain on the capital account, just as the IMF had warned. The 1970 *Economic Report of the President* declared:

> While the gradual narrowing of our trade balance has dominated the general trend of the U.S. balance of payments, short-term fluctuations have become increasingly dominated by capital movements.[41]

The 1971 *Report* noted that:

> The large capital movements occurring...in response to changes in relative interest rates and monetary conditions are the outgrowth of the increasing internationalization of capital markets, especially the development of the

41. *Economic Report of the President* (Washington, DC: U.S. Government Printing Office, 1971):126.

Eurodollar-market. The increasing mobility of capital is a reflection of the growing flexibility and responsiveness of capital markets, which contribute to the efficient international allocation of investment and production. This mobility nevertheless involves some problems. The responsiveness of short-term capital flows to variations in timing and degree in the use of monetary policy can both undermine the effectiveness of monetary policy as a domestic stabilization tool and produce significant balance-of-payments disturbances. It is possible to argue that such short-term capital flows are largely temporary and usually self-reversing, and that therefore one need not be concerned about their balance-of-payments consequences. Traditionally, however, several courses of action have been suggested to alleviate the problems arising from interest-sensitive funds. One is to offset these capital flows through flexible official financing; another is to reduce reliance on monetary policy as an internal stabilization tool; and the third is to insulate domestic money markets by *direct control of capital movements* (emphasis added).[42]

Here again a difference in attitude is seen in the treatment of capital flows and trade flows.

With regard to the payments imbalance, the earlier 1970 *Report* described three "basic measures" that would ensure the needed adjustment. One measure depended on direct barriers, implicitly considered acceptable for capital flows but not for trade flows. The second looked only at trade flows and prescribed domestic demand-management techniques to stimulate (or reduce) imports and reduce (or stimulate) exports. The third relied on exchange rate changes, again mentioned only in relation to trade flows; it noted that this approach was irrelevant for the U.S. dollar because of the currency's special position as a key to the value of other national currencies. More generally, the 1970 *Report* observed: "[E]xchange rates can be altered (although, as a practical matter, the United States cannot adjust its exchange rate)."[43]

These quotations are important because they reflect the prevailing attitudes toward international flows of goods and capital. These attitudes provided policymakers with their frame of reference when, between 1971 and 1973, they reconsidered the postwar international financial system. First, the U.S. government closed the gold window in August 1971 and forced the replacement of bilateral exchange rate adjustments—whereby the position of the dollar represented the outcome of policy actions by America's international partners—with multilateral adjustments. In December 1971, in a conference at the Smithsonian Institute in Washington, DC, the major trading nations agreed that the

---

42. Ibid.:143–144.
43. *Economic Report of the President* (Washington, DC: U.S. Government Printing Office, 1970):134.

dollar's exchange rate could be changed through mutual consultation.[44] Still later, in 1973, a system of flexible exchange rates was adopted. As Chapters 2 and 3 will show, the effects of these actions were enormous. They facilitated the onset of inflation in the 1970s, the massive capital flows of the 1980s, and finally a vast reorganization of the U.S. financial system. Here one must examine motives rather than results: What was expected by the proponents of this new system of flexible rates? What problem was it designed to solve?

The Smithsonian conference dealt with the special position of the

44. Although the summer of 1971 marked the end of the United States' willingness to convert gold to central banks at $35/ounce, the second, and perhaps more significant, change in the system was the multilateral Smithsonian agreement to reset the fixed rates. (For an anecdotal account of the U.S. administration's view, see William Safire, *Before the Fall: An Inside View of the Pre-Watergate White House* [Garden City: Doubleday, 1975]:509–528.) Bilateral adjustments were superseded by multilateral adjustments that floated the Canadian dollar and revalued, relative to the U.S. dollar, the currencies of Belgium by 11.6%, the French franc by 8.6%, the deutsche mark by 13.6%, the Italian lira by 7.5%, the Japanese yen by 16.9%, the Dutch guilder by 11.6%, the Swedish kroner by 7.5%, and the pound sterling by 8.6%. In effect, the agreement depreciated the dollar against most other currencies and took the first step toward more flexible exchange rates, even though the official policy was to "repair" rather than "replace" Bretton Woods. These revaluations meant that the U.S. dollar was effectively devalued by actions of the other nations, but the price of the dollar in terms of gold was also officially revalued to $38/ounce, indicating that the responsibility to change parities was shared by the United States. The United States at first strenuously objected to a revaluation, but later relented. At the Smithsonian conference, Treasury Secretary Connally agreed to the devaluation of the dollar in terms of gold. The 1971 negotiations, in contrast to the preparations for the Bretton Woods Conference in 1944, took place in well-established forums. The IMF, the G-10, and the G-5 all played roles.

Multilateral currency realignments appear to have had two objectives. First, they addressed a weakness in the original Bretton Woods system. No longer dependent on the bilateral actions of individual trading partners, the United States could now change the value of its currency through multilateral consultation. Second, the realignment was expected to return the currency values to levels consistent with fundamental equilibrium as foreseen by the Articles of Agreement of the fund. As noted before, a move to floating exchange rates was not widely advocated (even though a widening of the parity bands found some support). The economic counsellor to the Executive Board of the IMF, speaking on behalf of "The Staff," stressed that a "satisfactory new pattern of exchange rates could not be found by letting all currencies float for a certain period." M. de Vries, *The International Monetary Fund, 1966–1971* Vol. I (Washington, DC: International Monetary Fund, 1976):537.

Here it seems that "equilibrium" was given a special interpretation. Balance-of-payments equilibrium could obtain under any level of the current account, provided the capital account would offset it, but "fundamental equilibrium" seemed to be related in the policymakers' minds to the current account (or even trade account) balance. See the analysis of the economic counsellor offered by Margaret Gerritsen de Vries: "[The Counsellor] emphasized that to create a sufficiently large current dollar in 1971. In order to understand the larger significance of events during the early 1970s, however, one must realize that the speculative flight from the dollar in 1970 was merely a symptom—not the disease itself. Deterioration of the *current account* revealed significant weaknesses in the U.S. economy, and the lack of any adequate adjustment mechanism within the existing institutional context set conditions right for the capital flows that brought on a crisis.[45] Such a diagnosis must have again strengthened policymakers' belief in the fundamental importance of the current account as a driving force in the economy. They saw financial transactions not as a cause but as an *outcome*.

In this environment, a flexible exchange rate system was enormously attractive.[46] Flexible rates would offset the current account against the capital account, since *no* official account transactions were needed to support a particular exchange rate. They would also do away with

---

account surplus in the U.S. balance of payments would require an adequate depreciation of the U.S. dollar against other currencies." Ibid.:538. Confusion between balance-of-payments equilibrium and current account equilibrium is seen in the following two examples. On August 15, 1971, President Nixon announced the closing of the gold window, which would lead to the Smithsonian agreement, and declared: "I am taking one further step to protect the dollar, to improve our *balance of payments* and to increase jobs for Americans. As a temporary measure I am today imposing an additional tax of 10% on goods imported into the United States. This is a better solution for *international trade* than the direct controls on the amount of imports (emphasis added)." Similarly, Treasury Secretary Connally explained: "We obviously had an unacceptable situation with respect to our *balance of trade* where it looked for the first time since 1893 that we might have a deficit in the balance of trade (emphasis added)." *New York Times*, August 17, 1971:16. Both statements are factually correct, but the emphasis in the adjustment process is strongly geared toward trade balance; the correct exchange rate is expected to bring about the desired balance.

The Smithsonian agreement was shorter-lived than the parties involved in it had hoped. Flexible exchange rates, instead of multilateral exchange rate adjustments, became the dominant form of international monetary arrangement after 1973.

45. For a U.S. interpretation of the Bretton Woods system, see the *Economic Report of the President* (1973):121, which noted that "the [Bretton Woods] rules permitted changes in a country's parity when its balance of payments was in fundamental disequilibrium. In practice the parities were changed only infrequently, generally after a prolonged period of disequilibrium in external payments. There was a widespread belief that, because of the importance of the United States in world trade and the central role of the dollar in the international monetary system, the United States could not change its exchange rate."

46. This did not mean that flexible rates were seriously considered in 1971. While the policymakers looked to find new par-values, fresh developments were adding weight to the argument in favor of flexible rates. Even inside the IMF, research progressed on the effects of an exchange rate change (e.g., the Multilateral Exchange Rate Model, or MERM). Although these models were consistent with adjustable pegs, they also affected thinking about flexible rates. For MERM, see P.

short-term speculative capital flows, because the movements of the exchange rate cannot be predicted. If policymakers were correct in their implicit assumption that long-term capital flows between developed nations were of only minor importance, then the capital account would be balanced. In a world with no official account transactions *and* balance on the capital account, *flexible rates would balance the current account*. And with current account equilibrium, policy coordination would be less important. Each country's monetary and fiscal policies could be designed simply to fulfill its own domestic objectives; external equilibrium would be guaranteed by the flexible exchange rate. I suggest that external (or current account) balance and policy independence were the true "problems" that flexible rates were intended to solve. The following chapters show that the reality was very different from this attractive, and seemingly elegant, solution.

Looking back at the events of 1971 through 1973, it is possible to identify both the interactions between institutional change and macroeconomic flows and the very different but important perceptions of monetary authorities. Short-term capital flows had always been viewed with suspicion by U.S. policymakers, and had indeed helped set the stage for key decisions about the exchange rate system in 1971 and again in 1973.[47] Such capital flows were facilitated by developments in the international capital markets, including the creation of the Euromarkets, to which U.S. capital could flee.[48] But short-term capital flows were

---

Armington, "A Theory of Demand for Products Distinguished by Place of Production," *International Monetary Fund Staff Papers* 16 (1969):159–178; and J. Artus and R. Rhomberg, "A Multi-Lateral Exchange Rate Model," *International Monetary Fund Staff Papers* 20 (1973):591–611. Still, the development of the MERM really indicated a belief that adjustable pegs could be set. See M. de Vries, *The International Monetary Fund 1972–1978*, vol. 1 (Washington, DC: International Monetary Fund, 1985):124–126.

47. The conditions necessary for the creation of a more successful adjustable peg for a smaller set of national players were later seen in the European Monetary System. There, the ECU would serve as numeraire, liquidity would be created through the ECFM, and a divergence indicator would call for adjustments of pegs when imbalances occurred. For an early discussion of the EMS, see B. Cohen, "The European Monetary System: An Outsider's View," *Essays in International Finance*, no. 142 (Princeton, NJ: International Finance Section, 1981).

48. The IMF noted that "the rapid growth in the size of international markets in short-term funds in the late 1960s, mainly in the form of 'Euro' markets in bank deposits denominated in foreign currency, induced a number of major countries to impose or extend regulatory measures....[However] comprehensive and effective restrictive controls on international capital movements were widely considered neither feasible nor, at least in their entirety, desirable....At the same time, partly in association with the increasing integration of the world economy, the actual movements have become very large—far larger than expected in 1958 on the eve of the

also symptoms of deeper underlying concerns about the sustainability of the U.S. current account position. As a result of the pressures exerted by these capital flows and of the basic forces they represented, the popular rationale for acceptable methods of realigning the exchange rates fully focused on current account transactions alone; policymakers implicitly assumed that the operation of flexible exchange rates would balance both the current and capital accounts.

In this thinking an important point seemed forgotten: international trade can be used, as a means for a nation to *save*, rather than simply help bring about an optimal allocation of world production (the basic notion that runs through this chapter). When trade functions in this other role, unbalanced trade and an offsetting capital account are seen; a nation is accumulating or selling assets. A current account deficit financed by a capital account surplus simply means that assets are being sold—that the country is "dissaving." This means that even under flexible exchange rates the free market rate can be consistent with both current account *and* capital account imbalance.

Such equilibrium exchange rates did not figure largely in the thinking of policymakers during the early 1970s (nor, it seems fair to suggest, in that of the academic scholars of international trade and finance). Policymakers apparently hoped that once institutional rigidities were removed, current account equilibrium would prevail. But flexible exchange rates promised more than mere current account equilibrium. Flexible rates gave policymakers the hope that they would have new freedom in dealing with domestic macroeconomic management—freedom from all worries about external accounts. They could then concentrate on the domestic economy. As the next chapter reveals, this expectation was a great miscalculation, and one with far-reaching consequences. The perceived new freedom in monetary and fiscal policies actually led to new problems, beginning with massive inflation and higher and more volatile interest rates. These problems provided a powerful incentive to fundamentally reshape the financial systems of every major center of finance (the subject of Chapters 3–6). This reshaping, in turn, effectively reformed the operating behavior of the financial services firms (the subject of Chapters 7 and 8). Finally, these changes became the seedbed for the massive trade imbalances and capital flows of the 1980s. In short, the 1970s and 1980s saw the breakdown of local boundaries in finance, which is the subject of the next chapter.

---

general move by European countries to external convertibility." IMF, *The Role of the Exchange Rate in the Adjustment of International Payments* (Washington, DC: International Monetary Fund, 1970):25. Also quoted in Tew, *The Evolution of the International Monetary System*:90–91.

2

MODELS OF EXCHANGE RATE DETERMINATION AND THE FLOATING RATE WORLD

The breakdown of the Bretton Woods system was only one of a series of worldwide financial changes. Widespread adoption of flexible exchange rates in 1973 coincided with major alterations in global patterns of trade and finance. After the rapid increase in oil prices in 1974, these new patterns showed clearly that nations such as those in the Middle East could engage in world trade without the slightest presumption of achieving balance on the current account in the near future.[1] In this case, trade did not exist to facilitate the exchange of goods but simply to transform one type of wealth (oil) into another (financial claims on the rest of the world). Such trade imbalances and the capital flows necessary to offset them were not restricted to a few oil producers and their consumers: many countries were affected by imbalances and by a variety of macroeconomic complications that followed. The net result was worldwide recession and inflation.

Even today it remains difficult to measure the impact of the new flexible exchange rate regime on these developments. Reconsideration of them leads to a whole series of important questions: Would fixed rates have resulted in different domestic fiscal and monetary policy responses to the oil shocks? In less consequent inflation? If so, at what costs?[2] From our perspective, there is one more pressing question: with

1. For example, between 1970 and 1972, Saudi Arabia's current account surplus doubled to $2 billion, then jumped from $2.5 billion to $23 billion between 1973 and 1974. Not until 1983 (excepting 1978) did the country begin to run significant current account deficits. Its cumulative current account stood at $170 billion between 1971 and 1983. See IMF, *International Financial Statistics* (Washington, DC: International Monetary Fund, 1986). Of course, the inflow of wealth into the country led to increased imports of goods and services. Still, it became clear that the notion of balanced trade would have to rely on long-term equilibration.

2. After the experience of the 1970s, many scholars questioned the theory that a flexible exchange rate regime would allow economic management to target domestic variables. For the view that monetary policy should target exchange rates, see

less inflation and less interest rate volatility, would there have been fewer incentives for financial entrepreneurs to find ways to restructure the national financial systems?

Because inflation has been related to growth in the money supply, speculation about what would have happened under fixed exchange rates could probably be based on one of the oft-cited advantages of a fixed exchange rate regime—the implicit discipline it imposes on policymakers' choices of domestic economic policies.[3] I noted earlier that when intervention appeared necessary to support the exchange rate in a fixed exchange rate regime, officials were often beset by fears of losing foreign reserves. Such fears forced them to consider macroeconomic adjustments as a means of dealing with external accounts. Under flexible rates, intervention was unnecessary, and governments were left free to pursue their own internal fiscal and monetary policy mix without much regard to the external sector.[4] Thus, expansionary monetary or fiscal policy could be pursued with the objective of sheltering an economy from the *domestic* impact of the oil shock. A flexible exchange rate was expected to deal with the external account; as I have suggested, many policymakers even considered flexible rates adequate to the task of balancing the current account.

The realities were quite different. Fundamental forces—oil price shocks, changes in savings behavior, and new types of macroeconomic management such as supply side economics—combined with the new

---

R. McKinnon, *An International Standard for Monetary Stabilization* (Washington, DC: Institute for International Economics, 1987), and J. Williamson and M. Miller, *Targets and Indicators* (Washington, DC: Institute for International Economics, 1987). For an empirical evaluation, see D. Papell, "Monetary Policy in the United States Under Flexible Exchange Rates," *American Economic Review* 79 (1989):1106–1116.

3. A simple example would show a rapidly inflating country increasing imports and consuming foreign exchange reserves in order to finance those imports. Here it is assumed that some sterilization of reserve loss occurs (if not, more automatic monetary contraction would be seen).

4. See R. Cooper, *The Economics of Interdependence: Economic Policy in the Atlantic Community* (New York: McGraw-Hill, 1968). A related advantage of floating exchange rates was that a domestic economy would be (to some extent, and depending on the shocks) isolated from the effects of foreign domestic policy actions. See, for example, G. Haberler, "The International Monetary System Again under Stress," in J. Dreyer, G. Haberler, and T. Willett, eds., *The International Monetary System: A Time of Turbulence* (Washington, DC: American Enterprise Institute, 1982):3–19. He concludes that "some incontrovertible facts refute the view that floating does virtually nothing to insulate a country from imported inflation or deflation. But this does not mean that floating shields a country from *all* foreign disturbances." Ibid.:12.

flexible rate system to produce higher levels of inflation during the 1970s, as well as large and sustained current and capital account imbalances between *developed* countries such as Japan and the United States during the 1980s.[5] In the early 1970s, such inflation and international financial pressures started the United States (and indirectly, Japan and the United Kingdom) on the road to national financial reform. The capital flows of the 1980s completed this job. They demonstrated capital market integration and international savings imbalances. The explanation of how all this happened begins with a brief review of the development of the economic models.

THE ASSET MARKET APPROACH TO EXCHANGE RATE DETERMINATION

The adoption of flexible exchange rates led both policymakers and academics to study exchange rate determination with special interest. Under the fixed exchange regime, the effects on the current account of changes in the pegged rates (such as those sanctioned by the IMF to deal with fundamental disequilibrium) had been well explored. The study of flexible rates, however, redirected attention to the *determination* of the rate in the international currency markets. The basic standard for determination seemed embarrassingly simple—demand and supply in these markets. But what drove demand and supply for currencies? In theory, at least, the answer was once again simple—overall demand and supply for a currency was determined by demands for imported goods, services, and assets. In practice, however, these demands were affected by the exchange rate itself, and thus it was not easy to state the relationships among them. The various effects of the exchange rate on current and capital accounts had to be considered if the fluctuations of demand and supply were to be understood. Chart 2.1 illustrates the U.S. dollar exchange rate against three major currencies.

In the previous chapter I argued that although the engineers of the flexible exchange rate system had hoped to achieve current account balance through market changes in the exchange rates, observers found it increasingly difficult to ignore exchange rate determination as it influ-

---

5. In Chapter 1 I noted repeatedly that policymakers did not focus on long-term capital flows. Net long-term flows were considered in the relations between countries in different stages of development, but they were not much looked at between developed nations. The notion that one country would accumulate the assets of another seemed relatively unimportant, especially in comparison to current account imbalances financed through reserves under the fixed exchange rate system.

CHART 2.1
Dollar Exchange Rates
1971(Q1)–1989(Q4)

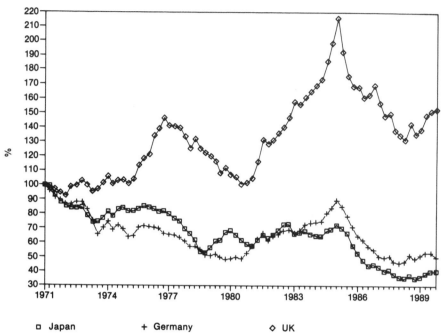

□ Japan   + Germany   ◇ UK

Note: The data are normalized so that 1971 (Q1) = 100%.
Source: International Financial Statistics, various editions.

enced capital account transactions.[6] This should not be surprising, since under flexible exchange rates the absence of official intervention in the exchange market made it necessary to match current account imbalances one-for-one on the capital account. Thus, current account deficit could immediately be seen as capital account surplus, and vice versa.

Under the fixed rate regime, this had not been the case. During the Bretton Woods era, the official account had broken the symmetry between the current and capital accounts. But by the mid- and late 1970s, in an era of flexible rates (and thus an era without changes in the official account), capital and current accounts had to be equal, though opposite in sign. Instead of studying the current account to determine the effect of flexible rates, an observer could just as usefully concentrate on the

6. This does not mean that no models of exchange rate determination were presented before 1973; it merely signalled a renewed interest, which surfaced in the 1970s. See J. Frenkel, Preface of *The Economics of Exchange Rates,* J. Frenkel and H. Johnson, eds. (Reading, MA: Addison-Wesley, 1978):vii.

capital account; one account simply represented the mirror image of the other.

This shift in attention to the capital market (or asset market) set the stage for the development of the asset market approach to exchange rate determination. Now, financial transactions began to play a larger role in the development of the theoretical models.[7] As I will explain below, this shift in theoretical emphasis accurately reflected events in the real world. There, the ascendancy of international asset transactions in the 1970s set the stage for the later appearance of massive international imbalances and helped explain the crucial developments that took place in national financial systems, where asset transactions attained equal prominence.

So models of exchange rate determination constructed in the mid- and late 1970s looked increasingly at financial, or asset, market phenomena.[8] The basic idea was that the foreign asset holdings of countries were central in determining the exchange rate, and that the exchange rate in turn would affect the current account. But the current account itself would also affect the foreign asset holdings of countries: since countries needed foreign currencies to buy foreign assets, they could do so only when they "earned" those currencies through current account surplus.

Of course, this process of accumulating foreign assets required time. But what would happen if U.S. citizens suddenly wanted to hold a greater portion of their wealth in foreign-denominated assets? Here, both the flexible exchange rate system and the currency markets would play a role. Suppose one day U.S. citizens decided to increase their

---

7. At first, only one asset was considered: money. See J. Frenkel, "A Monetary Approach to the Exchange Rate: Doctrinal Aspects and Empirical Evidence," *Scandinavian Journal of Economics* 78 (1976):200–224. "The approach that is taken," Frenkel notes, "reflects the current revival of a monetary view, or more generally, an asset view of the roles of the exchange rate." Later models included additional assets.

8. See R. Dornbusch, "The Theory of Flexible Exchange Rate Regimes and Macro-Economic Policy," *Scandinavian Journal of Economics* 78 (1976):255–275. "In the short-run," Dornbusch notes, "the scope for goods arbitrage may be limited, and accordingly, purchasing power parity may only obtain for a limited set of commodities. Under these conditions, it is useful to abstract altogether from the detail of goods markets and rather view the exchange rate as being determined entirely in the asset market." Examples of under- and overshooting of the exchange rate derived from such models. On impact, the exchange rate, driven by the asset market, could be different from the long-term equilibrium rate. For an elegant statement, see P. Kouri, "The Exchange Rate and the Balance of Payments in the Short Run and in the Long Run: A Monetary Approach," *Scandinavian Journal of Economics* 78 (1976):280–304.

foreign asset holdings by $10 billion, and they tried to buy $10 billion of foreign currency to pay for the intended asset purchases. In the currency markets, this action would *immediately* bid up the price of foreign currency, because the U.S. current account could not move to $10 billion surplus quickly enough to produce the required foreign earnings; a current account surplus or deficit occurs *over time*. The dollar would, therefore, depreciate, as those trying to buy more foreign currencies to finance their intended asset purchases failed to find new sellers. In the very short term, then, the exchange rate would be fully determined by asset market considerations.

But the influence of the asset market would carry over to the goods market. At first, the depreciated dollar would satisfy the initial desire of U.S. citizens to hold a greater portion of their wealth in foreign-denominated assets; so far, no actual purchases of foreign assets had taken place (the *amount* of foreign assets would not have changed) but at the new, depreciated, dollar rate, the *value* of the existing amount of foreign assets in dollar terms would be higher.

The process would not end there, however. Depreciation of the dollar would begin to affect the current account. With a depreciated dollar, imports would seem dearer and exports more attractive—so the current account would move to surplus.[9] As this occurred, the new current account earnings could be used to purchase foreign assets (making the capital account show capital inflows). The original desire of U.S. citizens to increase the amount of foreign assets could now be satisfied. Thus, the exchange rate would in the very short run be determined in the financial markets. Given this rate, over time a current account surplus would emerge, and its earnings could be used to buy the foreign assets (the capital account would turn negative). The whole model placed a novel emphasis on the role of the international asset position.

Although such models reflected changes in the real world, where asset markets had begun to play a more prominent role (which will be described in Chapters 3–6), many theoretical ideas were borrowed from developments in the literature of domestic finance.[10] Also, these new

9. It can easily be shown how stable and unstable equilibria obtain depending on the choice of assumption about the impact of the exchange rate mechanism on the current account.

10. See Robert Merton's seminal contribution, "Optimum Consumption and Portfolio Rules in a Continuous Time Model," *Journal of Economic Theory* 3 (1971):373–413. For the international models, see J. de Macedo, "Optimal Currency Diversification for a Class of Risk Averse International Investors," *Journal of Economic Dynamics and Control* 5 (1983):173–185. For a general review of this literature, see M. Adler and B. Dumas, "International Portfolio Choice and Corporation Finance: A Synthesis," *The Journal of Finance* 38 (1983):925–984.

models, by concentrating on financial assets, focused greater attention on expectations about the future.[11] Like domestic financial assets, foreign assets represented claims against *future* output. By buying a U.S. Treasury bond, the foreign holder gained an opportunity to sell that bond in the future and then to use the proceeds to purchase U.S. goods. *This meant that trade in goods had come to play a dual role.* On the one hand, goods were traded in order to establish an optimal world production pattern, fully consistent with the traditional models of *balanced trade* discussed in Chapter 1. On the other hand, *imbalanced trade* in goods (with the required offsetting capital account) could be seen as a vehicle for expressing the savings decisions of various nations.[12] A current account surplus and capital account deficit meant that the country gained foreign assets as it was building up claims on the rest of the world—claims expected to be used in the future. Likewise, a current account deficit and capital account surplus meant the loss of foreign assets and the accrual of debts to the rest of the world.

Capital flows thus assumed a meaning very different from that ascribed to them during the Bretton Woods years. Short-run capital flows in that era were viewed as a kind of casino built on top of the trading house, and long-term capital flows between developed nations were largely ignored. After Bretton Woods, capital flows attracted attention as the measure of national savings and investment desires.[13]

INTERNATIONAL CAPITAL AND THE FREEDOM TO PROCRASTINATE

At this point, the influence of institutional arrangements and their political effects on the predictions of the theoretical models must be considered. To begin, recall the earlier discussion of the discipline exerted by

11. The expectation-forming mechanism was assumed to be "rational." See R. Lucas, "Expectations and the Neutrality of Money," *Journal of Economic Theory* 4 (1972):103–124. For an earlier statement, see J. Muth, "Rational Expectations and the Theory of Price Movements," *Econometrica* 29 (1962):315–335. This implied that, rather than modelling expected future actions as a lagged response to present activity, actors in the economy would take full advantage of all available information, so that their expected actions would be consistent with the structure outlined in the model expected for each period of time in the future.

12. See J. Sachs, "The Current Account and Macro Economic Adjustment in the 1970s," *Brookings Papers in Economic Activity* 1 (1981):201–268.

13. A significant literature had earlier discussed trade in capital goods. See A. Smith, "Capital Theory and Trade Theory," in P. Jones and P. Kenen, eds., *Handbook of International Economics*, vol. 2 (New York: North Holland, 1985):289–324.

a fixed exchange rate on macroeconomic management.[14] There it was seen that the impact of official transactions on reserve levels would *force* policy adjustment. This rationale accounted for the early optimism that greeted flexible rates. The monetary and fiscal policy authorities had faith that policy independence would prevail once new international institutional arrangements freed them from foreign reserve constraints in setting optimal domestic policies.

But this optimistic assumption proved to be wrong. Even in a flexible exchange rate world, the external sector plays a role in domestic policy-making—a role that may at first be overlooked but that eventually becomes impossible to ignore. Suppose the authorities in one country decide to embark on a politically popular program of domestic expansion financed through heavy international borrowing. Through this program of borrowing, the authorities cause large and sustained deficits on the current account, which are mirrored in large and sustained capital account surpluses. Unlike a situation in which a country is anxious about depleting its foreign reserves in defense of a fixed exchange rate, in this case a nation is not *forced* to change its macroeconomic policies—at least not in the short run. Although the current account deficit means that liabilities are incurred that will have to be paid off in the future, politically undesirable adjustments of domestic policies (such as a monetary or fiscally induced recession) can be postponed as long as international markets finance domestic policies. In fact, only one thing happens immediately: the asset position of the expansive nation changes.

In such a case, policymakers only manage to procrastinate over unpopular adjustment decisions; they cannot avoid them permanently. Their initial desire for long-term policy independence produces an oversimplified view: When policymakers focus on domestic outcomes and ignore external accounts, their indifference lasts only until a new source of discipline appears. Eventually, the accumulation of external debt or credit provides the new constraint on policy.

What emerges from focusing on accumulations of assets and liabilities is a straightforward interpretation of the problems facing many third

14. The whole notion of discipline and the advantages of rules versus discretion in macroeconomic management relates, again, to developments in other fields of economics. See F. Kydland and E. Prescott, "Rules Rather than Discretion: The Inconsistency of Optimal Plans," *Journal of Political Economy* 85 (1977):473–493, which discusses issues of time inconsistency of optimal policies. For the difficulties in applying econometric methods to the rational expectations model, see J. Taylor, "Estimation and Control of a Macroeconomic Model with Rational Expectations," *Econometrica* 47 (1979):1267–1286.

world debtors. These debtors provide good examples of countries that have given priority to capital account rather than current account transactions. Consider the case of Brazil. From $5.3 billion in 1970, Brazil's debt grew over the next six years to $26 billion.[15] Only with large and sustained current account surpluses in the future could such an accumulation of debt be repaid. Brazil would have to generate future flows of income sufficient to reverse the flows of capital, and the eagerness with which foreigners financed Brazilian policies suggests that they expected this orderly reversal to take place.

Of course, one could argue that the third world debt crisis announced by the press in 1982 (and precipitated by balance-of-payments problems in Mexico) indicated that all was *not* well. This situation could not be considered novel; Latin American countries had a history of debt crises going back well into the nineteenth century. Still, the crisis in 1982 was significant because it signalled that new institutional constraints—such as renegotiating with commercial banks—had begun to play a major role in the adjustment mechanism.[16] In other words, financing current account deficits could allow for a debt buildup inconsistent with any realistic path of future surpluses. This inconsistency could relate to institutional considerations such as a desire by commercial banks to increase their reported earnings, or an expectation that other governments may bail banks out at difficult times. But whatever the reason for the debt accumulation, it may require institutional change for Latin American debtors to achieve equilibrium again.

These problems are not limited to the third world. During the 1980s, first world countries experienced some equally remarkable disillusionments. The United States' accumulation of international debt, and the rapidity with which this largest creditor nation turned into the largest debtor nation, provided an unprecedented example for both policymakers and scholars. Even when it is assumed that the country's deficits reflect an anticipated series of large future current-account surpluses, questions remain as to the future impact of such anticipated surpluses on the domestic U.S. economy. Will its adjustment be smooth or erratic, and will the international financial markets be able to handle, possibly

15. See Central Bank of Brazil, annual reports.

16. As a result, national policy adjustment is no longer sufficient; institutional responses must be developed to mitigate the problem. The emergence of debt-equity swaps and other financial instruments should be seen in this light. In particular, secondary market trades of third world debt at significant discount from face value reflect different evaluations of the potential future surpluses that could be generated to finance the obligations. See D. Meerschwam, "J.P. Morgan's Mexican Bank Debt-Bond Swap," 289-013. Boston: Harvard Business School, 1988.

in short periods of time, significant assets flows? Here a parallel with the decline on the stock exchanges in October 1987 can be drawn. Then, the issue was not so much that a large price drop occurred; the real concern had to do with the ability of markets to continue to function in an effective way under unprecedented order flows. In 1987, the chief danger lay in a breakdown of the system, not in the depression of stock prices. A similar concern lies at the heart of current discussions about "hard" versus "soft" landing scenarios for the U.S. economy, including the implications of such scenarios for the financial services firms that operate in the international markets as discussed in Chapters 7 and 8.

By the late 1980s, international capital flows had become so large that anxiety over a hard landing was widespread. This unease deflated the optimistic hopes of the engineers of the flexible exchange rate system about policy independence, as repeated attempts were made to coordinate domestic economic policies and stem imbalances. As the 1990s began, few experts were willing to argue that the observed imbalances on current and capital accounts could reach equilibrium over time without policy initiatives. New demands for policy coordination were heard, but as had so often happened in the past, policymakers loudly recommended that action be taken not by themselves but by their trading partners. To understand how the uncertainties of the 1980s came about, I first return briefly to the turbulent 1970s.

THE EVOLUTION OF ECONOMIC POLICY IN THE 1970s

Serious attempts to "fix" the Bretton Woods system at the Smithsonian conference in Washington in 1971 ultimately proved unsuccessful. Within three years of the agreed-upon multilateral parity adjustments, a generalized move to floating exchange rates took place (see Table 2.1). In the years that followed, however, it became clear that few countries were willing to let markets fully determine the values of their currencies; some market intervention occurred, mostly at undisclosed levels.[17] The major trading nations never fully realized their hopes of current account equilibrium under flexible rates, although the imbalances of the 1970s were not of unusual magnitude (see Table 2.2).

17. Although the remainder of this section focuses on floating exchange rates, the importance of market intervention and reserve asset management, as seen in the use of IMF "facilities," "credit trances," and "stand-by agreements," cannot be ignored. Central authorities also continued to use swaps for the purposes of intervention.

TABLE 2.1
IMF Classification of Exchange Rate Regimes

Classification Status	1960	1982	1983	1984	1985	1986	1987	1988	1989
Currency pegged									
to U.S. dollar	69*	38	33	34	31	32	38	36	31
French franc	—	13	13	13	14	14	14	14	14
SDR	—	15	12	11	12	10	8	8	7
Composite	—	23	27	31	32	30	27	31	34
Other	—	5	5	5	5	5	5	5	5
Flexibility limited vis-à-vis a single currency	—	10	9	7	5	5	4	4	4
Cooperative arrangements	—	8	8	8	8	8	8	8	9
Adjusted according to a set of indicators	—	5	5	5	5	6	5	5	5
Managed floating	—	20	25	20	21	21	23	22	22
Independently floating	—	8	8	12	15	19	18	17	20
Total	69	145	145	146	148	150	150	150	151

*At the beginning of 1960, there were 69 member countries in the IMF. Two withdrew at the end of the year.
Source: International Financial Statistics, various editions.

TABLE 2.2
Current Account as % of GNP* 1960–1989

	U.S.	Japan	U.K.	Germany
1960–1969	0.52	0.82	0.66	1.02
1970–1979	0.43	1.12	1.22	1.00
1980–1989	1.82	2.11	1.16	1.98

*Yearly average of absolute value of current account as % of GNP.
Source: International Financial Statistics, May 1990.

CHART 2.2
Inflation Rates
1961–1989

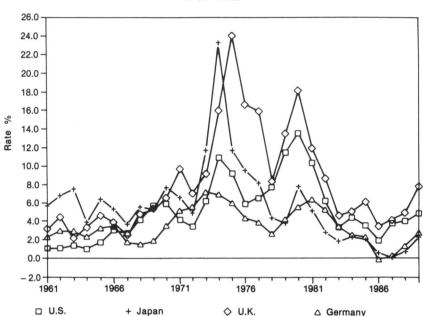

□ U.S.   + Japan   ◇ U.K.   △ Germany

* Annual Changes in Consumer Price Index

Source: International Financial Statistics, various editions.

The flexible rate system functioned during—and some critics would say, facilitated the emergence of—a period of a rising inflation and increasing levels of unemployment throughout the United States and several Western European countries. These developments were obviously related to the oil shocks of 1974 and 1979 (see Charts 2.2 and 2.3).[18]

In a burgeoning literature that sought to identify the basic causes of inflation, money supply growth was seen as an essential prerequisite. Hence economists studied the costs of policies aimed at reducing price increases. Most models predicted negative employment effects, although there was lively debate over the duration of the period of high unemployment. The "Volcker recession" of the early 1980s did indeed show

18. Some institutional change did occur in response to the oil shocks; the International Monetary Fund, for example, introduced a special "oil facility," partly to answer "recycling" concerns. Much has been written about the turbulent mid-1970s. An enlightening analysis with respect to the United States is R. Solow, "What To Do (Macro-economically) When OPEC Comes," in S. Fischer, ed., *Rational Expectations and Economic Policy* (Chicago: University of Chicago Press, 1980):249–267.

CHART 2.3
Unemployment Rates
1961–1989

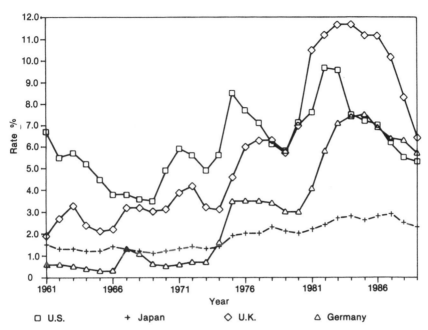

Source: United Nations Statistical Yearbook, various editions.

the short-term adverse impact of a contractionary monetary policy designed to wring inflation out of the system. Here the impact of the new international monetary arrangements should be considered: given the oil shock, would a different inflationary effect have occurred under fixed exchange rates? And if at the time of the energy price shock, fixed exchange rates had still been in operation, would they have survived the ensuing pressures? Models suggestive of various outcomes can be constructed, but the *perceived* (monetary) policy independence anticipated under the flexible exchange rate system actually amplified the inflationary shock.[19] In this light the many calls during the late 1970s

19. This does not suggest that the observed outcomes were *therefore* suboptimal; one can argue that even if under a fixed exchange rate regime the foreign reserve constraint had forced less accommodative policies, employment effects in response to the oil shock would have been severe. Thus, a model is needed that deals explicitly with the alternative impacts on the social welfare function of the two exchange rate regimes. Indeed, many sophisticated contributions along these lines have been made. For my purposes, however, it is only necessary to note that the new institutional arrangements facilitated inflation, which was later to have its effect on financial services firms.

for a return to the gold standard—which would have meant a return to fixed exchange rates—become more understandable, even though no such policy is advocated here. The possible advantages of such a system would rely at best on the policymakers' acceptance of discipline. Proponents of the gold standard typically take this discipline for granted, but there is no structural constraint to prevent authorities from frequent alteration of gold parities.[20]

In theory, almost all results that obtain under fixed exchange rates will eventually be observed under flexible rates as well; in practice, however, institutional arrangements actually *facilitated* the emergence of inflation. Without short-term international pressures to defend an exchange rate, expansionary monetary policy became a tool of domestic purposes and was liberally used. It created inflation and fueled increases and greater volatility in interest rates. Higher and more volatile rates, together with the increased international capital flows, provide a crucial link to the later chapters in this study; they were a major reason for the changes in the national financial systems of the United States, Japan, and the United Kingdom, and in the strategies of the financial firms that operate within those countries. In the new interest rate climate, profits could increasingly be made by active management of the liabilities side of the balance sheet, and the attractiveness of new interest-rate-sensitive financial products soared. Thus inflation became the stimulus for financial product innovation, causing a breakdown of existing boundaries between vendors and products within national financial systems.

Here interaction appears among the three levels of change that I identified in the Introduction. The policy focus on current account transactions, combined with the hope of monetary policy independence, led to the transformation of the international financial system. As a result, fundamental economic pressures (such as the diminishing U.S. trade account surplus and the oil shock) could be fought with new policies; these policies led to inflation in the 1970s. Inflation, in turn, changed the stable financial systems, which were no longer to be defined by regulatory functions, and forced financial services firms to develop new strategies.

But there is a second part to the story: international capital flows

20. Most advocates of the gold standard suggest that it would force monetary authorities to limit their inflationary policies. This depends, however, on the discipline exercised in keeping parities fixed. Thus, in theory, if one assumes such discipline, the same results could be achieved under strict monetary growth targets in the absence of a gold standard. As with the discussion of the impact of international institutional arrangements, the implicit assumption seems to rest on the institutional power to exert discipline.

allowed escape routes from the national systems to develop. In the early 1970s, for example, these flows helped break the tightly regulated national systems. In the 1980s, they added to other pressures on the systems to increase the pace of their transformation. In this sense, overall neglect of the external sector, made so much easier by the flexible exchange rate system, helped set the stage for the restructuring of the national financial systems.

This is not to say that the external sector managed without *any* attention from the authorities. It was, for example, continual monetary and fiscal policy adjustment in the late 1970s that eventually brought an end to the precipitous decline in the value of U.S. currency.[21] Similarly, the United Kingdom experienced financial difficulties between 1975 and 1977 that led it to rely on agreements with the IMF. Still, in the international financial system that emerged, monetary and fiscal policy could be geared more closely to the domestic sector.

During the 1970s, the foreign exchange markets operated largely in accordance with the expectations of the advocates of flexible exchange rates, but macroeconomic events in the major developed nations provided abundant surprises. Keynesian prescriptions for macroeconomic demand management had been widely accepted during the 1960s. A basic tenet of Keynesian thinking declared that authorities could, and should, use demand management in the economy in the pursuit of full employment. The so-called Phillips curve, discovered in 1958, identified an empirical relation between inflation and unemployment, showing an apparent trade-off between the two. This, it was believed, made possible the selection of some optimal combination of inflation and unemployment.[22] But the 1970s experience of high unemployment *coexisting with* rising inflation violated any expected trade-off between them and cast doubt on the effectiveness of Keynesian demand management.

Economic theory began to reflect these doubts. Just as the emphasis on the asset markets brought expectations about the future to the fore (since assets represented claims on *future* output), so expectations about the future played an increasingly important role in domestic macroeconomic theory. In particular, rational expectations models implied that

21. In 1978, for example, the U.S. government obtained swap agreements, and pressure on the dollar in the international markets led to discount rate increases.

22. See A. Phillips, "The Relation between Unemployment and the Rate of Change of Money Wages in the United Kingdom, 1861–1957," *Economica* 25 (1958):283–299. Although Phillips did not provide a theory for the phenomena he observed, he noted that empirically high wage inflation and unemployment were negatively correlated. Later, theoretical foundations were presented for the observed phenomena.

the real impact of demand management might well be much smaller than Keynesian models had presumed, because people in the economy would factor expected future policy actions into their present behavior. For example, it was suggested that expansionary monetary policy would simply create inflation, rather than cause unemployment to fall—especially if it didn't come as a surprise. Thus, the rational expectations school questioned the effectiveness of monetary and fiscal policy actions. It fitted the observed phenomena of the 1970s well: an environment where inflation and unemployment happily coexisted in apparent violation of both the Phillips curve and the predictions of Keynesian economics.[23]

During the late 1970s, the gradual decline in the stature of Keynesian economics and the effectiveness of demand management, especially in the United States, cast doubt on the role of monetary and fiscal authorities as active interventionists in the economy. Observers suggested that, in a world of rational expectations, the role of government policy should be limited to allowing for the maximum and unencumbered supply of goods without trying to manage demand: supply side economics became the popular term for this idea. Thus, authorities should attempt only to create the best environment for maximizing supply at each price level. This idea in itself was not controversial. What was controversial was the shift in policy *focus* to the supply side, as well as the conclusion that demand management was, at best, an exercise in futility.

With inflation running at 10.7% between 1977 and 1981, and unemployment reaching 7.5% in 1981, the United States entered the 1980s boasting its faith in supply side management, inflation reduction through tight monetary policy, and continued benign neglect of international accounts.[24] Serious internal imbalances and a relatively benign external sector constituted the legacy of the Carter presidency.[25] And

23. For the classic reference, see Lucas, "Expectations and the Neutrality of Money": 102–124. Several empirical studies have attempted to test the neutrality proposition. For example, in a number of articles Robert Barro claimed that only unanticipated changes in monetary policy matter. For an early statement, see R. Barro, "Unanticipated Money Growth and Unemployment in the United States," *American Economic Review* 67 (1977):101–115.

24. Inflation measured as an average annual change in the CPI. Unemployment reached a high of 9.5% in 1982. The emphasis on supply side economics was most clearly seen in the policy recommendations during and after Ronald Reagan's successful bid for the presidency in 1980.

25. Note the remarkable contrast with the economic situation at the close of the Reagan presidency. Then, internal balance (unemployment at approximately 5.4% and inflation at 4.7%) coexisted with external imbalance (current account deficit of $154 billion).

even though U.S. international accounts had shown a steady deterioration on the trade account between 1975 (a surplus of $8.91 billion) and 1980 (a deficit of $25.50 billion), the current account, while significantly reduced, again showed a surplus (of $1.86 billion) in 1980, as the United States accumulated foreign assets. As a percentage of GNP, even the trade account deficit did not appear exceptionally large.

It seemed as if the hopes and expectations of the architects of the post-Bretton Woods system had almost materialized. A caveat is in order, however. Even during these years, monetary policy intervention—in particular, interest rate changes—was sometimes used to affect the external sector. For example, contractionary monetary policy was used to raise interest rates (thus affecting the capital flows) and cool down the economy (thus reducing imports). But, overall, the choices in macroeconomic management multiplied, because the authorities no longer had to defend a fixed exchange rate. Thus, the Reagan administration came into office with approximate external balance and economic policies targeted to domestic problems.

Eight years later, at the close of the Reagan presidency, a dramatic reversal had occurred: internal balance with respect to inflation and unemployment coexisted and contrasted with the stagnation of the 1970s, but now serious external imbalance replaced the relatively innocuous capital flows of the late 1970s. The United States had gone from being the world's largest creditor to being the largest debtor nation. This remarkable transformation of the Carter legacy of domestic economic problems but relative international stability depended on: (1) a perception of policy independence made possible by the international financial system, which allowed authorities to avoid unpopular policy changes; (2) disenchantment with demand management, which allowed for a steady deterioration of government finances; and (3) a new belief in supply side stimuli. Just how the United States embarked on a policy of massive dissaving while financing itself in the international capital markets will become clear later. For the moment, it is more useful to put the story of United States in a comparative perspective.

THE REDISTRIBUTION OF INTERNATIONAL ASSETS, 1978–1988

The difficulties that faced the United States in the wake of the oil shocks also affected other major industrial nations. In 1978, inflation in the United Kingdom "fell" to 8.2%, and unemployment stood at 6.3%. West Germany, since World War II a consistent example of fiscal and monetary conservatism, also experienced inflation and unemployment increases.[26] In both the United Kingdom and Germany, real GNP growth declined—from an annual compound growth rate of 2.3% and 3.1%, respectively, between 1965 and 1975, to less than 1.8% and 2.1% between 1975 and 1985.[27] Even a star performer like Japan was not spared the impact of the oil shock and its aftermath: Japanese real GNP growth, which had been almost 10% in 1973, turned negative in 1974 and remained well below 5% throughout the 1980s. Overall, there was little doubt that the period of sustained worldwide growth experienced during the 1960s had ended, and that the world economy had entered a new phase in the 1970s.

Many countries had experienced satisfactory growth records during the 1960s, but it was the rise of the Japanese and, to a lesser extent, the German economies, following the devastation of World War II, that was especially striking.[28] By the close of the 1960s, the United States felt threatened by these reemerging economic powers.[29] But the threat was mitigated by the revision of the international financial system at that time, together with the impact of the oil shock and, later, the sustained depreciation of the dollar (which lasted well into 1978). These factors all helped to produce current account surpluses for the United States, first between 1973 and 1976 and again in 1980 and 1981. Measured by the current account performance of the United States, the overall balance in the world economy had not demonstrably shifted by the end of the 1970s, despite the growth of the trading partners' economic muscle (i.e., productivity, quality of exports, and technology).[30]

26. Especially during the final stage of the Bretton Woods system, and again in the mid-1970s, the United States voiced repeated requests for Germany to embrace expansionary economic policies. German annual average inflation was 2.5% between 1950 and 1971; 4.4% between 1975 and 1980; and 6.3% in 1981. Unemployment in 1981 was 4.1%.

27. *International Financial Statistics* (Washington, DC: International Monetary Fund, 1987).

28. Between 1960 and 1970, Japan's average annual growth rate exceeded 10%.

29. Germany revalued its currency in 1969, but persistent current account surpluses were seen. Japan, too, exhibited persistent surpluses during that period.

30. Note that several observers had much earlier warned the United States about the loss of its ability to compete with countries like Japan and Germany. In 1971, Peter Peterson, special assistant to President Nixon, presented an analysis to the administration pointing to this effect. See P. Peterson, *The United States in the Changing World Economy* (Washington, DC: U.S. Government Printing Office, 1971). Later, others sounded similar warnings. See, for example, B. Scott, "National Strategy for Stronger U.S. Competitiveness," *Harvard Business Review* 62 (1984):77–91; S. Wheelwright, "Restoring the Competitive Edge in U.S. Manufacturing," *California Management Review* 27 (1985):26–42; and R. Hayes and W. Abernathy, "Managing Our Way to Economic Decline," *Harvard Business Review* 58 (1980):67–77.

Even in terms of GNP growth rates, the performance of the United States during the late 1970s was not significantly worse than in previous decades. Actually, some convergence between countries such as Japan and Germany, on the one hand, and the United States on the other can be identified (see Table 2.3). The Japanese economy's exceptional growth performance had been interrupted, and the German economy also faced slower growth. (The performance of the U.K. economy dropped well below par on almost all counts.) This is not to say that no concerns were raised about U.S. performance. Analysts used the nebulous concept of international competitiveness to question the United States' ability to perform in an open international economy—a concern related to the worsening U.S. performance on the trade account.

Still, the truly important redistribution of international assets did not take place until the 1980s. Here it is sufficient to note that the performance of leading industrial nations, in terms of unemployment and inflation, was returning to more traditional levels by the mid-1980s, after the difficulties in the mid- and late 1970s and early 1980s. By the late 1980s, internal equilibrium, though perhaps not fully attained, did not seem as far off as it had appeared to be a decade earlier. What *had* changed dramatically were external balances. International capital flows had not increased in a balanced fashion; they had become a vehicle for a massive reallocation of international wealth.

As the U.S. capital account surpluses (i.e., the country's borrowing abroad to finance its current account deficits) grew during the 1980s, fewer and fewer observers were willing to believe that the U.S. accumulation of international debt could be considered as merely an innocuous step toward long-term equilibration. Various explanations appeared for the underlying problems. Popular accounts stressed twin deficits, linking the budget deficit to the international deficit.[31] Other explanations focused on a sustained rise in the value of the dollar (until 1985); they attributed the continued increase in the deficit after a significant depreciation of the U.S. dollar to the time interval required for imports and exports to respond to the currency depreciation.[32]

31. The direct link between the budget deficit and the current account was particularly appealing since the sizes of the two deficits had started to resemble each other. For example, in 1987 both the U.S. budget deficit and the current account deficit stood at approximately $150 billion. What curiously few commentators noted was that in other countries—for example, Japan—current account *surplus* and budget *deficit* had often been observed. In 1987, by coincidence, the Japanese budget and current account both stood at approximately $85 billion. However, the budget showed a deficit, the current account a surplus!

32. This phenomenon is the so-called J-Curve. It describes the lag time between a depreciation of the home currency and the improvement of the current account,

TABLE 2.3
U.S., U.K., Japanese, and German Performance
1961–1989

U.S.	CGR of Nominal GNP	Inflation Rate	CGR of Real GNP	Average Unempl. Rate	Cumulat. Current Account
1961–1970	7.0%	3.1%	3.8%	4.7%	$32.8b
1971–1975	9.5%	7.1%	2.2%	6.1%	$19.9b
1976–1980	11.3%	7.6%	3.4%	6.8%	− $25.9b
1981–1989	7.5%	4.4%	3.0%	7.3%	− $772.5b

U.K.	CGR of Nominal GDP	Inflation Rate	CGR of Real GDP	Average Unempl. Rate	Cumulat. Current Account
1961–1970	7.2%	4.2%	2.9%	2.7%	$0.3b
1971–1975	15.6%	13.2%	2.2%	3.8%	− $10.7b
1976–1980	16.8%	14.8%	1.8%	6.3%	$6.4b
1981–1989	9.1%	6.2%	2.7%	10.3%	− $18.1b

Japan	CGR of Nominal GNP	Inflation Rate	CGR of Real GNP	Average Unempl. Rate	Cumulat. Current Account
1961–1970	17.8%	5.5%	10.5%	1.3%	$4.9b
1971–1975	15.2%	10.4%	4.3%	1.5%	$16.4b
1976–1980	10.1%	4.9%	5.0%	2.1%	$11.7b
1981–1989	5.6%	1.3%	4.2%	2.6%	$346.2b

Germany	CGR of Nominal GNP	Inflation Rate	CGR of Real GNP	Average Unempl. Rate	Cumulat. Current Account
1961–1970	8.4%	3.7%	4.5%	0.6%	$7.2b
1971–1975	8.8%	6.5%	2.1%	1.4%	$22.2b
1976–1980	7.6%	4.1%	3.4%	3.2%	− $2.8b
1981–1989	4.8%	2.8%	2.0%	6.4%	$167.2b

Note: Sum of inflation rate and real growth rates may not add up to nominal growth rates because of rounding errors.

Source: Economic Report of the President, various editions.

Instead of looking at either the budget deficit or the exchange rate, it is more useful, in the quest to understand U.S. debt accumulation, to focus on basic relationships that generate imbalanced international transactions. Remember that financial assets should be seen as claims on future output, and that international trade can function as a means for allowing one country currently to consume more than it produces (and thus to run a current account deficit). In different terms, because national income can be consumed by either the private sector, the government, or foreigners, the sum of private plus government savings (borrowing) equals net national savings (borrowing) as reflected in the current or capital account under flexible rates. Given an amount of national production, the combined savings (borrowing) of the government and private sector are the excess (shortfall) of goods produced at home—and exported to (imported from) foreign countries. National savings (the sum of government and private sector savings) are exactly reflected in the current account.[33] For example, when a country incurs a current account deficit, claims on domestic future output have to be sold to foreigners in order to finance net imports. Thus, the country loses assets in an international redistribution of wealth, as Table 2.4 shows.

In the 1980s, domestic policies led U.S. production to trail domestic consumption.[34] A significant expansion of government borrowing, caused by new tax policies and continuing expenditures on government programs, financed the increasingly large budget deficits.[35] (See Chart

---

which is caused by differences in the speed of adjustments of prices and volumes of imports and exports. Although the J-Curve was exhaustively investigated, many empirical researchers found it difficult to fully explain the apparent duration of the adjustment mechanism in the 1980s. Subsequently, other hypotheses were presented that attempted to explain the sluggish response of the current account to the changing value of the dollar. Some of the models tried to incorporate strategic price behavior of international competitors, noting that such competitors may, for market share reasons, be willing to accept margin cuts in response to a depreciation of the importing country's currency.

33. For an account of U.S. savings behavior, see C. Caroll and L. Summers, "Why Is U.S. National Savings So Low?" *Brookings Papers on Economic Activities* 1 (1987):607–635.

34. In reality, "consumption" is not the correct term here. A better term to use would be "absorption," since it describes total national demands on production, including consumption and investment demand.

35. During the period 1980–1987, federal receipts (taxes) rose by 7.4%, national defense spending by 11.2%, and other government outlays by 6.8%, all in compound growth rates. As a result, the deficit rose from 2.7% of GNP to 3.8% of GNP. *Economic Report of the President* (Washington, DC: U.S. Government Printing Office, 1988):250, 338.

TABLE 2.4
U.S. and Japanese Savings
1960–1988

	U.S.				Japan			
	Net Savings as % of Net Invest.	% of GDP			Net Savings as % of Net Invest.	% of GDP		
		Net Savings	Net Invest.	Current Account		Net Savings	Net Invest.	Current Account
1960	114.64	9.18	8.00	0.62	101.42	22.12	21.81	0.60
1965	110.22	11.34	10.29	1.07	97.42	18.17	18.65	1.11
1970	106.85	7.84	7.33	0.39	104.42	26.89	25.75	1.01
1975	125.35	5.96	4.75	1.36	97.49	19.45	19.95	−0.10
1980	105.53	5.93	5.67	0.44	99.21	18.32	19.45	−1.03
1981	102.84	6.43	6.26	0.31	99.43	17.88	17.98	0.49
1982	98.94	2.68	2.71	−0.03	102.09	17.03	16.68	0.70
1983	65.79	2.22	3.37	−1.00	109.73	16.07	14.64	1.81
1984	62.86	4.38	6.97	−2.44	116.49	17.05	14.63	2.84
1985	53.09	3.15	5.94	−2.93	120.73	17.96	14.88	3.69
1986	42.70	2.47	5.79	−3.44	126.44	18.46	14.60	4.33
1987	39.22	2.11	5.38	−3.01	122.80	18.31	14.91	3.05
1988	56.76	2.94	5.18	−3.17	114.87	19.00	16.54	2.71

Note: Net Savings = Gross savings minus consumption of fixed capital. Net Investment = Gross capital formation minus consumption of fixed capital. Because of "statistical discrepancies," Net Savings − Net Investment may deviate from Current Account.

Source: OECD National Accounts (1989), pp. 32–35.

2.4.) In terms of output and consumption, greater government demand for the real resources produced in the economy was *not* offset by a smaller private sector claim. In financial terms, the budget deficits were *not* offset by greater savings in the private sector. Instead, to satisfy excess demand for goods required an increase in imports from abroad. Again, in financial terms, combined private and government financing needs made foreign borrowing unavoidable. The demand for net imports and the financing they required meant that the United States had to find partners in the world economy who were willing to buy its obligations. For the United States to be a net borrower in the world economy, others had to be net savers.

Given the importance of national savings in a country's international transactions, the actions of authorities in shaping the national savings are of great consequence. During the 1980s, U.S. government policies made national dissavings inevitable—only a sharp increase in the domestic savings rate could have maintained external equilibrium and pre-

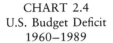

CHART 2.4
U.S. Budget Deficit
1960–1989

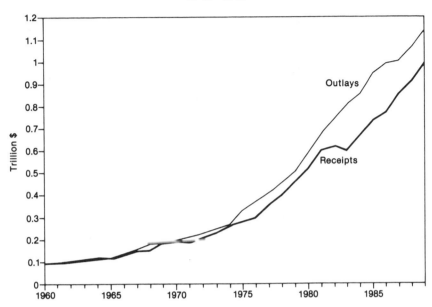

Source: Economic Report of the President, various editions.

served domestic investment. In contrast, policies pursued in Japan during this time led to massive current account surpluses.[36]

These shifts contrast sharply with the policymakers' expectations about the behavior of the current account under flexible exchange rates. As suggested earlier, the international financial system of flexible rates was expected to force major adjustments in import and export patterns and a return to balanced current (and therefore capital) account. Such hopes were a natural outgrowth of more than two centuries of emphasis on trade as the vehicle for optimal world production under balanced current accounts. In this imagined world, the U.S. policy described

36. Much has been written about the economic policies pursued in Japan, especially the interaction of business and government relations in that country. For an exhaustive account of the Japanese economy, see H. Patrick and H. Rosovsky, eds., *Asia's New Giant: How the Japanese Economy Works* (Washington, DC: The Brookings Institution, 1976). For a comparative business-government relations study, see T. McCraw, ed., *America versus Japan* (Boston: Harvard Business School Press, 1986).

above would not have led to large accumulations of international debt. A broad fiscal expansion, in the context of balanced international accounts, would lead to interest rate increases, an upward adjustment in savings, and/or a reduction in import demand.[37] In the real world, however, this did not happen. Instead, in a massive deficit-induced Keynesian expansion, the United States borrowed heavily in the international market at a time when other countries (e.g., Japan) with a different set of domestic policy preferences were willing and able to supply necessary financing. Thus, although little savings were generated *inside* the United States to finance growing budget deficits, foreigners stepped forward with savings to fill the gap.

Now, the other part of the earlier story falls into place: disenchantment with Keynesian policies led to emphasis on supply side effects and encouraged new macroeconomic policies. In retrospect these new policies actually seem to have caused a large Keynesian expansion. But they were neither perceived nor presented that way, as policymakers confidently declared that demand management had been superseded by supply side economics. Therefore, the standard risks associated with such a program caused little concern in policymaking circles; large budget deficits were officially abhorred but, in reality, allowed to build up. In a changed environment that emphasized supply side measures such as tax reductions and deregulation, government finances were benignly neglected; domestic economic policies were pursued while the external sector was virtually ignored. The Reagan administration's faith in deregulation, free markets, and flexible exchange rates allowed them all to flourish.

Thus, post-Keynesian ideas and new arrangements facilitated the financing of budget deficits in the international markets, and unpopular domestic measures such as spending cuts or tax increases were simply postponed. Needless to say, as national policymakers procrastinated

---

37. The implications of a Keynesian expansion in the context of a closed economy has been widely studied. Early on, concepts such as crowding out and the interest elasticity of investment played a major role. Later debate revolved around the role of expectations and the wealth effects of government obligations. Ricardian equivalence resurfaced as a popular notion, and the overall effectiveness of fiscal stimuli was questioned. In the context of an open economy with balanced trade, the relative importance of the interest rate channel or the income channel would depend on income and substitution effects. However, expansionary fiscal policy, financed in the international capital market and thus coupled with unbalanced trade, accorded policymakers a degree of apparent freedom.

over unattractive choices, the net asset position of the United States steadily deteriorated.

The use of foreign funds and associated international debt accumulations to finance domestic (private and government) absorption is of course doubly troublesome if the foreign proceeds are used to finance current consumption rather than investment. If the need for net foreign financing reflects an investment boom and if the returns on these investments exceed the foreign borrowing costs, long-term equilibration is attained once the investment returns are used to amortize the debt. If, however, the foreign borrowing is applied to current consumption, future debt amortization will be possible only if future consumption is curtailed (see Table 2.4).

Although nothing so far described is inconsistent with *long-term* equilibration, the magnitude of imbalances does raise questions about the nature and size of future adjustments. That such adjustments will occur remains inevitable, however, since no country can forever continue to build up debt (or to accumulate assets, in the case of Japan). So the chief question becomes: will these inevitable adjustments be smooth or disruptive? To find the answer, both practitioners and scholars of international trade began to consider the *costs* of exit and reentry in industries where international market share had already been lost (in accordance with the industrial organization literature).[38] The *risks* of protectionism and other trade barriers came to the fore, as the growth of imbalances was fueled by the inability of policymakers to take unpopular domestic policy action. Finally, the ability of an entire institutional framework to deal with possible large adjustments attracted special attention, as scenarios for a hard landing became less improbable. In short, there was a rising sense of uncertainty in the financial community.

Not surprisingly, during the mid-1980s, as imbalances grew rapidly, policy coordination resurfaced (for example, the Plaza meeting of September 1985) as a viable option, first, to affect the exchange rate, and later, to deal with domestic policies that influenced the net saving behavior of various countries.[39] What had become clear was that a system of flexible exchange rates could not guarantee policy independence, the hopes of its advocates notwithstanding.

---

38. See notes 5 and 6, Chapter 1.
39. For an account of the Plaza meeting and other coordination meetings, see Y. Funabashi, *Managing the Dollar: From the Plaza to the Louvre* (Washington, DC: Institute for International Economics, 1988).

AN OFFICIAL STORY: THE ECONOMIC REPORTS OF THE PRESIDENT

The *Economic Report of the President* in 1982 provides a thought-provoking view of the evolution of these issues as seen by senior U.S. administrators. The document is especially interesting when compared with the earlier *Reports* discussed in Chapter 1 and later *Reports* presented below (admittedly submitted by different authors). The 1982 version, after stating a preference for free, unregulated markets in most domestic sectors, as well as a free international currency market, addresses the worsening U.S. trade balance in these words:

> In most circumstances, a trade deficit by itself should not cause concern. A trade deficit is a narrow concept. Goods are only part of what the world trades; another major part is composed of services. Hence, the current account, which includes both, better indicates the country's international payments position. But the current account is not a complete measure of international competitiveness either. What also matters is how the current account deficits are financed.
>
> Concern with the country's international payments position is appropriate when the basis for that concern is that the country is simultaneously experiencing a sustained deficit in its current account and a persistent depreciation of its currency in the exchange markets. The joint occurrence of these two events should alert economic policymakers to the possibility that the country may be losing competitiveness.[40]

Although the second paragraph may, in retrospect, seem prophetic in its accurate description of events during the mid- and late 1980s, the international position of the United States in 1981 had only begun to conform to this picture. Current account equilibrium still prevailed, and the U.S. dollar had appreciated. External concerns were considered at most secondary to the domestic macroeconomic problems that the United States faced. "It is particularly important," the *Report* noted,

> not to become unduly preoccupied with the trade or current account balances with a single foreign country. Any policy to reduce a bilateral imbalance by restricting imports is likely to reduce the absolute volume of trade and, in consequence, the economic well-being of both countries, and could have wider repercussions. A far more constructive approach would be for the nations with restrictive trade practices and institutional barriers to imports to reduce systematically those obstacles to the freer flow of trade and invest-

---

40. *Economic Report of the President* (Washington, DC: U.S. Government Printing Office, 1982):179.

ment. Actions, like those recently taken by Japan, for example, should prove far more beneficial than measures by the United States to restrict imports.[41]

This focus on trade is fully consistent with the Ricardian trade notions discussed in Chapter 1. Furthermore, the appeal of leaving policy adjustment to the trade partner comes through loud and clear.

But the 1982 *Report* did not focus exclusively on the current account; instead, it considered the role of the capital account as well, albeit in a curious way:

> Nor should a current account deficit that is *comfortably* financed by net inflows of capital evoke concern. The relationship is straightforward: goods and services comprise one aspect of international commerce, financial and real assets another. If foreigners purchase more U.S. real and financial assets in the United States—land, buildings, equities, and bonds—then the United States can *afford* to import more goods and services from abroad. To look at one aspect without considering the others is misleading (emphasis added).[42]

This statement is conceptually sound, yet the peculiar use of the words "comfortably" and "afford" is striking, especially because it never becomes clear what the antonyms would be. In a flexible exchange-rate system, by definition, current and capital accounts will offset one another. If *unbalanced* goods transactions take place, offset by net capital movements, the asset position deteriorates. The "comfortable financing" thus may be of short duration, lasting only until the claims accumulated by foreigners are presented; "affordability" becomes difficult to measure!

Thinking about these issues shifted profoundly, as is evident when one compares the 1982 *Report* with that of 1988. By 1988, capital account surplus and current account deficit were looked upon less favorably. In the 1988 *Report,* the chapter dealing with the international position of the United States noted that "maintaining non-inflationary growth, *while reducing external imbalances,* is the primary objective of economic policy in the United States and other leading industrial nations (emphasis added)."[43] The increasingly large capital flows required to offset the current account deficits seem to have been comfortable no longer; instead, the external sector had begun to demand full attention. The same 1988 *Report* dealt with this matter more directly:

41. Ibid.:180.
42. Ibid.:181.
43. *Economic Report of the President* (1988):89.

While the current level of net foreign claims should not be cause for alarm, persistent growth of such claims at an annual rate equivalent to 3.5% of U.S. GNP (about $150 billion in 1987) would be a source of worry. At this rate, net foreign claims on the United States would reach 40% of U.S. GNP by the end of the century. Servicing these claims, assuming a 5% real rate of return, would consume about 2% of U.S. GNP—still not a large percentage, but a very substantial absolute sum. Relative to the size of the economy, U.S. net indebtedness would not be much larger than Canada's has been in recent years. However, the absolute figure would be very large—more than $2 trillion in 1987 dollars. This could present difficulties for the world financial system, especially if for some reason foreigners suddenly become less willing to hold claims on the United States.[44]

Here we see explicit concern for the institutional framework. Not surprisingly, the *Report* remarked that "it is especially important for countries with substantial external surpluses to increase their demand growth in order to maintain their own output and employment growth while their external surpluses contract."[45] In short, policy adjustments were still to be requested of international trade partners, and policy coordination among the major industrialized countries was once again an accepted goal, as was evidenced by the Louvre Accord in February 1987. Now, almost two decades after the forced revision of the Bretton Woods system, events appeared to have come full circle. In fact, external constraints, policy adjustment, and international coordination had not been made obsolete by the flexible exchange rate system. But by replacing one system with another, the institutional environment, both internationally and domestically, *had* been dramatically altered.

By the late 1980s, the ability of the international financial system to deal with the flows required to finance the United States had become a serious concern, and the role of institutional arrangements came under question.[46] Did such arrangements encourage policy procrastination? Or, using the terminology of the 1982 *Report,* would less "comfortable" capital flows have required more timely policy adjustment? And if the flexible system did indeed make large capital flows easier, would it also be able to deal with the large flows that could reverse the original shift?

44. Ibid.:99.
45. Ibid.:112.
46. The United States actually became a debtor nation in 1984; it went from a net foreign credit position of $141.1 billion in 1981 to a net liability position of $263.6 billion in 1986. The absolute international investment position of the United States should be viewed with some skepticism because of accounting treatment of international assets, but the change in the international asset position of the country was unambiguous. The U.S. cumulative current account deficit between 1982 and 1987 was approximately $600 billion.

Furthermore, did the dramatic changes in the financial systems at key financial centers make international transfers of capital easier?

Institutional changes were not the *cause* of the U.S. accumulation of international debt: differences in national savings can be acknowledged as the real underlying cause. Institutional changes did, however, facilitate rising debt levels, by enlarging the set of feasible financing instruments, heightening investors' sensitivity to complex, price-sensitive transactions, and increasing their financial sophistication.[47] Along with the domestic developments, new international financing opportunities appeared; together they encouraged procrastination over unpopular policy adjustments, allowing imbalances to grow.

These developments bring to mind the traditional notion of discipline as exercised by a fixed exchange rate regime. The lack of convertibility during the early years of the Bretton Woods system had made international capital transactions difficult, and many impediments to private international transactions remained in existence even after the restoration of official convertibility. Such restrictions were fully consistent with the highly regulated nature of domestic capital markets. With restrictions on international capital flows in force, and a fixed exchange rate system in place, an environment is created in which the comfortable financing of current account deficits (or the investment of a current account surplus) may not be possible. As a result, domestic policy adjustment can be expected.

Reviewing the experience of the 1980s, I have identified several factors that interacted to facilitate large international capital flows. The flexible exchange rate system brought with it a mistaken belief that benign neglect of the external sector was costless. Disenchantment with Keynesian policies allowed for an emphasis on supply side economics and a subsequent deterioration of the government's finances. Since the early 1970s, the economic outcomes in the United States were: first, highly inflationary policies, intended to accommodate the oil shock (using new freedoms created by an absence of any foreign reserves constraint); then, contractionary monetary policies designed to tame inflation; and finally, expansionary fiscal policy, put in place during the 1980s as U.S. budget deficits grew.

These ideas and policies led to huge imbalances. The resulting in-

47. The ease with which the new instruments can be acquired may be in itself due to learning and familiarization; it will also further the desire to invest in foreign assets. To put this more formally, using an international portfolio model, the desired shares of foreign assets as a percentage of total wealth may well be functionally dependent on the ease with which the various markets can offer price-sensitive financial instruments.

creased international capital flows provided escape routes from the tightly regulated national financial systems of the three major financial centers—New York, London, and Tokyo. A second channel of influence, which linked macroevents to national financial systems, relied on the effects of the inflation created by the new policies. Asset prices became more volatile than they had been in the 1950s and 1960s. This volatility, in turn, put additional pressure on market participants to create new freedoms from regulation. In sum, these new forces guaranteed that the financial centers of the world would be changed almost beyond recognition.

PART II

THE EVOLUTION OF THE FINANCIAL SYSTEMS OF THE UNITED STATES, JAPAN, AND THE UNITED KINGDOM

3

THE U.S. FINANCIAL SYSTEM

The previous chapters discussed changes in international financial transactions and the breakdown of national boundaries in finance. Changes
were no less remarkable during the 1970s and 1980s in the three major
national financial centers: the United States, Japan, and the United Kingdom. Observers at the time typically described these latter changes as
the outcome of deregulation, securitization, and disintermediation. But
the phenomena themselves were actually driven by the forces that I have
already outlined. In this chapter, I turn to the United States, where
financial changes have raised serious doubts, for the first time since the
1920s, about the stability of the financial system. During the 1980s a
series of factors caused U.S. financial stability to reemerge as an issue
of practical relevance, rather than theoretical interest only. These included the bailout of Continental Illinois Bank, the bankruptcy of
Drexel Burnham Lambert, the savings and loan associations fiasco, the
burgeoning of government debt, and the unsatisfactory asset quality of
some of the largest banks, along with the widespread use of high-yield
bonds and the dubious financial soundness of several firms that became
large holders of them. Concern about the national financial system
should be even greater now. For, at the beginning of the 1990s, the
U.S. economy has entered uncharted waters. Few observers expect the
buildup of international imbalances to continue forever, and momentous questions are arising: Will the adjustments process bring with it
serious recession? And if so, what impact will it have on financial institutions?

Deregulation and rapid product development were the short-term
causes of much of the instability, reorganization, and change that occurred in the 1980s. Together, they forced even the strongest institutions
to redefine their strategies, especially in light of the need to compete
with foreign firms at home and abroad. But what led U.S. financial firms
to make innovations in the first place? In this chapter, the roots of the
remarkable events that took place in the U.S. banking industry during

the late 1970s and 1980s are traced to earlier developments, which themselves relate to the changes discussed in the previous chapters.[1]

EARLY BANKING IN THE UNITED STATES

Just when banking began in the United States is difficult to determine. Financial intermediation services were available even in colonial times.[2] The Bank of Philadelphia, which opened in 1780, probably represents the earliest U.S. bank in the modern sense of the word.[3] Like later banks, it was chartered by the state in which it operated.[4] Such state chartered banks were, however, not the type advocated by the Federalists, who preferred national banks. Alexander Hamilton, in particular, favored a federally chartered bank that could both help the finances of government and create additional credit in the economy. But his views were not widely shared: the populist fear of powerful financial institutions, and especially of nationally chartered banks, became a consistent theme in the development of the U.S. financial system.[5] Congress sanctioned

1. Although much of this presentation concerns developments in the U.S. commercial banking industry, the phenomena described here have broader applicability throughout much of the financial industry.
2. For accounts of the development of the U.S. financial system, see A. Bolles, *The Financial History of the United States, 1774–1789, 1789–1860, 1861–1885,* vols. 1, 2, and 3 (New York: Appleton, 1884–1886); H. Krooss, ed., *Documentary History of Banking and Currency in the United States* (New York: Chelsea House, 1969); F. Redlich, *The Molding of American Banking: Men and Ideas* (New York: Hafner, 1947–1951); H. Krooss and M. Blyn, *A History of Financial Intermediaries* (New York: Random House, 1971); M. Myers, *A Financial History of the United States* (New York: Columbia University Press, 1970); W. Shultz and M. Caine, *Financial Development of the United States* (New York: Prentice-Hall, 1937); B. Klebaner, *Commercial Banking in the United States: A History* (Hinsdale, IL: Dryden Press, 1974); B. Hammond, *Banks and Politics in America from the Revolution to the Civil War* (Princeton, NJ: Princeton University Press, 1957).
3. In 1781, the Continental Congress rechartered this bank as the Bank of North America. See Shultz and Caine, *Financial Development of the United States:* 56–57. First to emerge in the United States were the so-called land banks, through which deeds to land holdings were transacted.
4. State banks were chartered in New York and Massachusetts in 1784 and in Maryland in 1790. See Hammond, *Banks and Politics in America:* 65–67.
5. Many doubted the constitutionality of a federally chartered bank; perhaps more importantly, they were fearful of large, powerful financial institutions, which they associated with federal control or with centralized power in general. This concern, which would shape the system for years to come, is crucial to understanding the development of banking in the United States. Although a proposal to allow the federal government to charter banks was rejected by the Constitutional Convention, Hamilton was able to convince the Congress of the desirability of such an institution, and in 1791 Washington signed a bill creating the first nationally char-

the existence of a national bank, only for a short period (1791–1811); when the charter of the National Bank of the United States expired in 1811, it was not renewed.

The same fate—the failure to be rechartered—destroyed the second Bank of the United States in 1836, providing fresh evidence of the nation's fear of centralized banking power. Again, opponents of a strong, federally chartered bank made use of the familiar arguments that such an institution was both unconstitutional and dangerous. Nicholas Biddle, the bank's president, overplayed his attempt to dispel these fears

---

tered U.S. bank. (See Shultz and Caine, *Financial Development of the United States*:90.) Its charter, granted for twenty years, gave rise to the dual banking system peculiar to the United States. On the duality of the U.S. banking system, see W. Brown, *The Dual Banking System in the United States* (New York: American Bankers Association, 1968); and T. Thompson, *Checks and Balances: A Study of the Dual Banking System in America* (Washington, DC: National Association of Supervisors of State Banks, 1962). In this dual structure, which allowed both state and nationally chartered banks to operate, we can see the fundamental trade-offs that had to be made: individually chartered state banks allowed for diversification of power, but their susceptibility to failure created potential instability. Larger and presumably much more stable national banks, on the other hand, held greater potential for abuse of power. Thompson, for example, presents the view that state banks safeguard the U.S. banking system from highly centralized federal government control: "The dual banking system is both product and result of our unique American plan of parallel State and national government. Its twofold premise is that the power to govern belongs to those who are governed, and that government must be by law—not by men. By its very nature, the dual banking system is a compromise between the unwelcome posturing of an omnipotent central bank and the vagaries of uncontrolled 'free banking.' In itself, this is a manifestation of the essential compromise that is the American character: individual freedom adjusting to a place within the national complex. Such adjustment has not always been perfect, seldom has it been easy; but the equilibrium between a *free* and a *controlled* society has ultimately been preserved." Thompson, *Checks and Balances*:71. Since state charters were granted on a case-by-case basis, the quality of individual banks varied widely, and the notes they issued sold at varying discounts. Despite these uncertainties, however, the system seemed to function. It grew from three banks in 1791 to more than 80 in 1811, when the national charter of the Bank of the United States lapsed. For the next five years only state chartered institutions opened. By 1816, the number of state chartered banks stood at almost 250. At that time a second Bank of the United States was chartered in part to finance the war debt and to restore stability to the currency. On the political problems concerning the rechartering of the bank, see Bolles, *The Financial History of the United States 1789–1860*:145–152. Branches of this bank, which opened in 1817 with another 20-year charter, were not welcomed in all states. The concept of a national bank was far from being broadly accepted. Some states were so much opposed to the national bank that they levied discriminatory taxes against it. See Shultz and Caine, *Financial Development in the United States*:177 and Hammond, *Bank and Politics in America*:251–404.

when he said: "There are very few banks that might not have been destroyed by an exertion of power of the [second Bank of the United States]."[6] Intended to show how responsible the bank had been, this statement suggested in a threatening way how powerful it might become. The controversy gave President Jackson, a professed opponent of the bank, the opportunity he had sought; he used Biddle's confession of the bank's potential for abuse to persuade Congress to let the bank die a natural death by not renewing its charter.

As a result, from 1836 onward only state banks operated in the United States.[7] This situation altered, however, with the National Banking Act of 1863. Now, public consciousness of the possible weaknesses of a fragmented system temporarily outweighed the fear of centralization.[8] Concern about the many state banks issuing notes (and the many state banks subsequently unable, or unwilling, to redeem them), together with the state banks' inability to be sufficiently active in wartime finance, spurred Congress to pass the reforming 1863 Banking Act, which created a class of nationally chartered banks to be supervised by the Comptroller of the Currency. When many state banks refused to obtain a national charter—electing instead to retain their state charters—the dual character of the U.S. banking system became firmly established.[9]

6. For further elaboration of this "most profound descent into indiscretion," see Hammond, *Banks and Politics in America*:297–298.

7. Although fragmentation was well established, there was a place for centralization in this system. New York City banks, for example, became increasingly important as the city became more prominent in domestic and international trade. The major New York banks cooperated to establish a clearinghouse, and banks located outside New York wanted their bank notes to trade at par there to enhance their credibility and improve stability. To achieve this, state banks started to hold balances with the New York banks. Thus, some of the features of today's system were in place even then. See Shultz and Caine, *Financial Development of the United States*:249.

8. For a discussion of the National Banking Act and its effects, see A. Davis, *The Origin of the National Banking System* (Washington, DC: U.S. Government Printing Office, 1911); and W. Swanson, *The Establishment of the National Banking System* (Kingston, NY: Jackson Press, 1910).

9. There were incentives for banks to retain a state charter, even when it meant foregoing the privileges associated with a national charter. Reserve requirements for national banks were typically higher than those set at the state level, and certain product areas were not open to national banks. The coexisting national and state banks offered similar products and services, though a tax law soon made it impossible for state banks to issue notes. The 1865 tax law, which levied a 10% surcharge on state issues, drove state notes out of existence. See Shultz and Caine, *Financial Development of the United States*:316–348.

Two important characteristics of the U.S. banking system could thus be distinguished at an early date: First, no dominant banks were permitted. Second, because banks could choose between state and national charters, competition was assured at the regulatory level. Still, neither the dual banking system nor the ingrained American antipathy toward financial power could prevent some financial institutions from growing stronger. But when they did, the old fear of centralized financial power resurfaced; once a certain threshold of power had been crossed, forces were set in motion to curtail an institution's growth and influence. A clear example of this process appeared in the rise and fall of financial trusts in the late nineteenth century. That chapter of national history served to dramatize the repeated fate of centralized banking in the United States.

FINANCIAL CENTRALIZATION

The Morgan Bank, for example, grew into a broad-based institution with major interests in widely diversified financial intermediaries; its financial products spanned insurance and commercial and trust banking. But as the power of Morgan and other select banks such as First National and National City grew, so did the nation's traditional suspicion of their power. In its 1912 congressional investigation, the Pujo Committee denounced centralization, describing the "Money Trusts" in the following terms:

> [A] community of interests between a few leaders of finance, created and held together through stock ownership, interlocking directorates, partnership and joint account transactions, and other forms of domination over banks, trust companies, railroads, and public service and industrial corporations, which has resulted in great and rapidly growing concentration of the control of money and credit in the hands of these few men.[10]

The Clayton Act of 1914 helped to break such trusts by strengthening the Sherman Act of 1890. Within a year of its passage, Morgan directors resigned their directorships of commercial banks, insurance companies, and trust companies.

10. Quoted in A. Chandler, Jr., and R. Tedlow, *The Coming of Managerial Capitalism: A Casebook on the History of American Economic Institutions* (Homewood, IL: Richard D. Irwin, 1985):286. It is interesting to contrast this with the development of the powerful banks at the center of zaibatsu in Japan (see Chapter 4). There the authorities fostered the kind of arrangements criticized by the Pujo Committee.

While the threat of dominant banks rose and then abated, the other side of the trade-off between stability and decentralization was not forgotten. For example, a 1908 act that authorized an extensive study of foreign financial systems led to a recommendation for a central government bank to enhance the stability of the U.S. financial system.[11] Made public at the height of the debate following the Pujo Committee deliberations, when popular sentiment weighed against centralized banking, this recommendation was turned down. But the need for a more powerful institution to guarantee stability remained. When finally the Federal Reserve Act of 1913 recognized the need for a more central institution, it established not one bank but twelve semicentral institutions with an overseeing board.[12] In this form, the U.S. central bank was much less like a truly central institution than most of its foreign counterparts. The American fear of concentrated bank power and the states' desire to preserve their rights would not permit anything stronger.

DEVELOPMENT OF THE MODERN SYSTEM: THE FEDERAL RESERVE SYSTEM

From its inception, the Federal Reserve System was a most unusual institution.[13] Its primary objectives were to keep the supply of currency elastic and to supervise the financial system. Because they were required to apply for membership, all nationally chartered banks came under the supervision of the Federal Reserve. State chartered banks also could elect to belong, provided they accepted several regulations, such as minimum reserve requirements.

In the dual banking system of the United States, many small banks

11. The Aldrich Freeland Act of 1908 allowed for special note issuance in times of financial distress. It also created a National Monetary Commission to study banking abroad. See Shultz and Caine, *Financial Development of the United States:*473–474.

12. Although the Democratic party had stated in its 1912 platform that it opposed the creation of a central bank, after its victory it decided to support the legislation of 1913, arguing that the Federal Reserve banks and board did not constitute a central bank.

13. For accounts of the creation and development of the Federal Reserve System, see R. Johnson, *Historical Beginnings: The Federal Reserve* (Boston: Federal Reserve Bank of Boston, 1977); Federal Reserve Bank of Philadelphia, *Fifty Years of the Federal Reserve Act* (Philadelphia: Federal Reserve Bank of Philadelphia, 1964); M. Friedman and A. Schwartz, *A Monetary History of the United States, 1867–1960* (Princeton, NJ: Princeton University Press, 1963); and Board of Governors of the Federal Reserve System, *The Federal Reserve System: Purposes and Functions* (Washington, DC: Federal Reserve Board, 1974).

found it difficult to establish the level of public confidence necessary to function effectively. Even the nationally chartered banks had trouble growing into powerful institutions that spread across state borders; federal legislation such as the McFadden Act of 1927 prevented national banks from becoming truly national institutions by mandating that they observe local regulations in the state in which each was headquartered.[14] This rendered interstate banking virtually impossible, since some states did not allow it. In this environment bank failures became common: between 1920 and 1929, 5,711 occurred. By the end of the 1920s, the instability of the U.S. financial system had once again become a major issue.[15] The fragmentation of banking had assured a diffusion of power, but it had also failed to check instability.

The Federal Reserve System, itself a curious blend of centralization and diffusion of powers, simply could not impose stability on this volatile arrangement. Internal disagreement about optimal policies surfaced between 1929 and 1932, when the full effects of widespread financial dislocation were painfully evident throughout the U.S. economy.[16] When Franklin D. Roosevelt became president, the banking crisis was at its height, and new banking legislation was a top priority.[17] The ensuing banking acts set the basic structure for the U.S. financial system for the next 35 years. The legislation of the 1930s, passed in response to the crises of that era, governed financial transactions even during the high-growth years of the postwar period. Not until the pressures of the late 1960s (described in earlier chapters) began to be felt did further significant changes occur in the banking system. Until that time, product market segmentation and price regulation were institutionalized.

THE GLASS-STEAGALL ACT

Known as the Glass-Steagall Act, the Banking Act of 1933 aimed at curbing the abuses of the 1920s and at guaranteeing both stability and

---

14. Still, loopholes remained, such as the possibility for bank holding companies to develop wider networks.

15. See Friedman and Schwartz, *A Monetary History of the United States, 1867–1960*:438–439.

16. On challenges to the banking system brought about by the Depression and subsequent reform measures, see P. Temin, *Did Monetary Forces Cause the Great Depression?* (New York: W.W. Norton, 1976); Friedman and Schwartz, *A Monetary History of the United States, 1867–1960*:299–492; and Shultz and Caine, *Financial Development of the United States*:628–720.

17. Not until 1935 was the power of the Federal Reserve Board significantly broadened. A reconstituted Board of Governors of the Federal Reserve System then provided more centralized authority.

diversity. To promote diversity and to avoid potential conflicts of interest between lending and underwriting securities, it segmented the financial industry, separating the banking and securities businesses. To achieve greater stability, the act strengthened the supervisory powers of the Federal Reserve and created the Federal Deposit Insurance Corporation (FDIC). In effect, the FDIC constituted the third federal regulator (together with the Comptroller of the Currency and the Federal Reserve) for commercial banks; it also offered deposit insurance.[18] But in spite of these multiple federal regulators, state banks could still elect to be supervised by the authorities of one state *only*. (State banks that wanted to operate without federal supervision had to forego membership in the Federal Reserve System and in the FDIC.) Thus, even in this new climate of intense regulation, diversity was still possible.

The statutory separation of the banking and securities businesses under the Glass-Steagall Act, along with the McFadden Act's insistence that even national banks adhere to state regulation, severely restricted both banks' branching policies and their product mix. With respect to branching policies, some states allowed only unit branch banking, which prohibited banks from even establishing networks of branches across a state to attract deposits from different geographical areas. With respect to product market segmentation, banks were excluded from the securities business, and they responded by retreating to their core businesses—lending and deposit gathering, typically in a well-defined geographical area.

Geographic and product market segmentation within the U.S. financial system greatly limited the alternatives available for carrying out financial transactions. But these were not the only factors that restricted the choices banks could offer in financial transactions. Price regulations drew another boundary. Regulation Q, in effect since 1933, set maximum rates for various types of deposit and savings accounts; it would later be extended to cover savings and loan institutions.[19]

18. The Comptroller of the Currency was concerned with chartering, supervising, and examining national banks only. The Federal Reserve System supervised all member banks. The FDIC regulated all banks that joined its program; Federal Reserve member banks were required to join, and other banks could elect to apply for membership.

19. For the effects of Regulation Q, see C. Haywood and C. Linke, *The Regulation of Deposit Interest Rates* (Chicago: Association of Reserve City Bankers, 1968); and C. Haywood, *Regulation Q and Monetary Policy* (Chicago: Association for Reserve City Bankers, 1971).

Note here the prevailing similarity in attitudes to financial transactions in both domestic and international capital markets. Although policymakers apparently believed that *real* transactions should be left free (at least they professed reliance on free trade and tried to enhance free domestic competitive markets through antitrust and antimonopoly legislation), *financial* transactions were viewed as fair game for regulation. Overall, policymakers believed that if financial transactions were left to free competitive markets, the result could only be instability. Chapters 1 and 2 noted the multiple barriers to *international* financial transactions; here similar impediments to free *domestic* capital markets are seen.

YEARS OF STABILITY

Between 1929 and 1933, more than 9,056 banks had failed in the United States, making total failures since 1921 more than 14,000. In the postwar years, however, such failures became rare.[20] Between 1945 and 1980 an average of only six FDIC member banks closed per year because of financial difficulty. Remarkably, the system that operated after World War II seems to have achieved the elusive goal of diversity coupled with stability.[21] Americans had earlier been unable to forge a financial system in which both qualities were consistently present, but had been forced to make periodic trade-offs in which one was obtained at the cost of sacrificing the other. In the postwar era, it seemed that they had at last formed a synthesis. Regulated diversity through sharp differentiation along product and geographical lines seemed to enhance financial stability.

But another factor also mattered. As I noted earlier, the 1950s and 1960s were characterized by a generally prosperous and stable economic environment.[22] In comparison to the 1970s and 1980s, interest rates were both low and stable. In this environment the rewards for financial innovation were minimal, and the value of switches between lenders and borrowers was similarly low.

---

20. See Friedman and Schwartz, *A Monetary History of the United States 1867–1960*:438–439.

21. Although stability came about after the Banking Act of 1933, I concentrate on the years after the war.

22. For a similar interpretation, see U.S. Department of the Treasury, *Report to the President: Geographic Restrictions on Commercial Banking in the U.S.* (Washington, DC: U.S. Department of the Treasury, 1981):1–2.

Long-standing relationships could flourish in this sort of environment. Borrowers who switched from one financial institution to another had to reestablish their credentials, as the information vested in the existing relationship was lost and the accumulated, mutual, noncontractual obligations were dissipated. At the same time, little interest rate advantage could be expected, since rates were generally regulated and low, because they were not primarily an outcome of competitive pressures among vendors. In funds-gathering, banks had to persuade depositors that the cost of turning to another bank was high: the depositor gained little through the switch, given product restrictions and regulated interest rates, but could lose a lot, because possible future access to funds was dependent on the relationship.[23]

The importance of increased switching costs can hardly be exaggerated, but there were other factors that kept borrowers faithful to old institutions. The authorities offered incentives such as FDIC insurance to maintain stable relationships. A good example of the operation of the system can be seen in the funds made available to commercial banks through demand deposit accounts—the purest form of relationship money. There was little incentive for depositors to switch banks, since the rates offered on time deposits were regulated (demand deposits could offer no interest at all), and since deposits (up to a maximum) were insured by the FDIC.[24] Banks could compete only through services and conveniences; they were also barred from accessing the growing accumulations of funds in several potentially important markets. In particular, two important sources—life insurance and pension funds—remained unavailable to them.

Furthermore, the existence of stable sources for low-cost funds, and the difficulties imposed by regulators both worked to reduce funding alternatives, so that any rapid growth of assets was unlikely. This mod-

23. Note that this was not unique to the United States. As I explain in Chapter 4, switching costs were equally high in the banking system that developed in Japan. There, however, centralization rather than decentralization was the operative philosophy.

24. It has been suggested that price regulation did not really matter, since the rates offered on the various accounts typically remained below the ceilings set by Regulation Q. If, according to this line of reasoning, banks had been willing to compete for funds on a price basis, they could have done so. But, given the geographical segmentation of the market, the general availability of credit (in contrast to the credit crunches of the late 1960s), and the limited profitability allowed by regulators, price competition for deposits seemed of only secondary importance to banks. Furthermore, for the most important source of funds, demand deposits, the ceiling was binding; it stood at 0%.

TABLE 3.1
Financial Assets of Selected Financial Institutions
(as a percentage of total)

Institution	1946	1950	1960	1970	1980	1988
Commercial banks	57.3	51.2	38.3	38.6	36.7	32.8
S&L associations	4.4	5.8	11.9	12.9	15.4	17.3
Mutual savings banks	8.0	7.6	6.9	5.9	4.2	3.6
Credit unions	0.2	0.3	1.0	1.3	1.7	2.2
Life insurance companies	20.3	21.3	19.3	15.0	11.5	13.2
Private pension funds	1.5	2.4	6.4	8.3	11.6	6.2
State & local pension funds	1.2	1.7	3.3	4.5	4.9	5.3
Other insurance companies	3.0	4.0	4.4	3.7	4.3	4.2
Finance companies	2.1	3.2	4.6	4.8	5.0	7.0
Real estate investment trusts	0.0	0.0	0.0	0.3	0.1	0.1
Mutual funds	0.6	1.1	2.8	3.5	1.5	4.2
Money market mutual funds	0.0	0.0	0.0	0.0	1.9	3.3
Securities brokers & dealers	1.5	1.4	1.1	1.2	1.1	0.7
Total	100.0	100.0	100.0	100.0	100.0	100.0
Total ($ billion)	234	294	600	1,342	4,040	6,817

Note: Columns may not add up to 100% because of rounding.
Source: Board of Governors of the Federal Reserve System, *Flow of Funds Accounts*, various editions.

erated return requirements on the asset side of a bank's balance sheet. With little to pay for deposits, spread banking—whereby profits arose from the difference between the cost of funds and the lending rate—became feasible. It provided a stable source of bank profits and reduced incentives to innovate. These circumstances also fostered conservative asset management and further stabilized the banking sector.

Another important contributor to banking relationships was regulated product differentiation, which encouraged the formation of many different types of institutions to service various market segments. Commercial banks, savings and loans, mutual savings banks, credit unions, life insurance companies, open-ended investment companies, securities dealers and brokers, real estate investment trusts, and money market funds—all competed in differentiated product areas, and each type maintained its own set of relationships. Table 3.1 gives an indication of their asset sizes.

In total assets, commercial banks comprised the largest single group.

Although they offered the most diversified product line, these banks nevertheless remained considerably restricted. Savings and loans were allowed to operate side by side with commercial banks, but the thrift institutions could not offer many standard banking services and were restricted in lending: legislation channeled the funds they collected into government securities and, through mortgage lending, into the housing markets.

Geographical segmentation and other regulation restricted the number of feasible banking partners for all but the largest corporations. And even for the largest borrowers, there were only a few possible bank fund suppliers. Smaller banks could not serve large corporations because of regulated limits on lending relative to bank capital. These corporations were therefore forced to establish relationships with only the largest banks, irrespective of location. The smaller corporations might have been able to do business with banks in other states, but the lack of convenient access effectively limited the practical alternatives and again stimulated local relationships.

Traditionally, the largest share of bank loans went to short- and medium-term commercial and industrial projects, at rates linked to the prime. In fact, there were only a few alternatives (e.g., private placements to insurance companies) to commercial bank loans in short- and medium-term finance. The commercial paper and bankers' acceptance markets had not yet attained their current importance, and they typically represented a funding source for only a few select, high-quality borrowers. Compared to bank credit, transactions in such markets remained unimportant (see Table 3.2). For example, total commercial paper outstanding in 1960 was only $4 billion. Another early alternative to the standard bank loan, bankers' acceptances, stood at $2 billion in 1960. In contrast, commercial and industrial loans outstanding totalled $42 billion.[25] Thus, for corporations, access to bank credit lines remained crucial. Such access was insured by having a stable relationship with a bank.

In long-term finance, both equity and debt issues were, at least in theory, available to all companies. Prices played a more direct role in placing debt or selling equity than in most other kinds of financial transactions. In the debt market, however, it was mostly a benchmark rate (government bond interest) that varied, and few companies habitually used the equity markets as an important source of external funds.

25. See Board of Governors of the Federal Reserve System, *Banking and Monetary Statistics, 1941–1970* (Washington, DC: U.S. Government Printing Office, 1976).

TABLE 3.2
Outstanding Credit Market Debt
($ billion)

Category	1946	1950	1960	1970	1980	1988
U.S. govt. securities	229	218	243	343	1,016	3,277
State & local obligations	15	24	71	144	350	760
Corporate & foreign bonds	28	39	90	202	495	1,392
Mortgages	42	73	209	471	1,452	3,261
Consumer credit	8	21	56	134	355	744
Bank loans n.e.c.*	18	28	63	152	457	758
Commercial paper	0	1	4	33	122	428
Bankers' acceptances	0	0	2	7	42	86
Misc. nonbank loans	13	21	39	110	376	796
Total	353	427	778	1,596	4,666	11,501

*Bank loans n.e.c. (not elsewhere classified) consist almost entirely of loans to businesses.

Note: Columns may not add up to totals because of rounding.

Source: Board of Governors of the Federal Reserve System, *Flow of Funds Accounts,* various editions.

Furthermore, relatively few companies had access to the public debt market, because rating agencies excluded the vast majority of American corporations, rating them below investment grade (see Table 3.3 for data on sources of funds).

Even companies with access to the public debt market were usually unable to take advantage of windows of opportunity in the capital markets (i.e., favorable price developments). A time-consuming and heavily regulated issue procedure hampered firms that wanted to match their funding requirements with favorable market developments. A complicated set of rules and complex negotiations between the issuer and the SEC led to a long delay in the publication of an acceptable prospectus.[26] And even for those firms that passed all the hurdles in gaining access to the public debt market, their ability to access funds depended not only on their credit rating, but also on their relationship with the securities firm that was expected to underwrite their new issue, since the underwriters made judgments about the timing and pricing of the issue.

26. It is remarkable that the prospectus, after careful evaluation and comment by the SEC, would always carry bold print stating, "These Securities Have Not Been Approved or Disapproved by the Securities and Exchange Commission Nor Has the Commission Passed upon the Accuracy or Adequacy of This Prospectus. Any Representation to the Contrary Is a Criminal Offense."

TABLE 3.3
Sources of Funds for Nonfinancial Corporate Businesses
(as a percentage of total)

Sources of Funds	1946–1950	1951–1955	1956–1960	1961–1965	1966–1970	1971–1975	1976–1980	1981–1985	1986–1988
Internal funds generated	56.6	66.0	68.8	66.5	57.7	52.2	58.8	67.7	61.6
Increase in liabilities & net new equity issues									
Net new equity issues	4.2	5.5	4.4	1.0	2.4	5.6	1.2	−5.9	−16.3
Tax-exempt bonds	0.0	0.0	0.0	0.0	0	0.8	2.5	3.8	3.5
Corporate bonds	9.3	10.2	9.6	6.6	13.2	11.1	7.4	8.2	30.5
Mortgages	4.6	3.6	5.1	6.0	5.2	9.1	0.9	0.0	0.7
Bank loans n.e.c.	6.1	4.3	5.3	6.7	7.9	8.1	8.6	8.7	4.2
Commercial paper	0.1	0.1	0.2	0.0	1.2	0.4	1.2	2.0	1.0
Acceptances	0.1	0.0	0.1	0.0	0.2	0.3	0.4	0.3	0.7
Nonbank finance loans	−0.1	0.8	1.3	0.6	1.2	2.0	3.1	3.4	4.6
U.S. govt. loans	0.0	−0.1	0.1	0.2	0.2	0.3	0.3	0.0	0.3
Profit taxes payable	4.8	1.6	−2.8	1.9	−1.6	0.3	0.7	−0.8	0.7
Trade debt	14.4	7.7	7.6	10.4	12.0	8.9	11.5	6.7	2.0
Misc. liabilities	0.1	0.4	0.4	0.1	0.5	1.0	3.1	5.8	6.5
Total external funds	43.4	34.0	31.2	33.5	42.3	47.8	41.2	32.3	38.4
Internal + external funds	100.0	100.0	100.0	100.0	100.0	100.0	100.0	100.0	100.0
Total funds ($ billion)	135	173	230	342	528	793	1,508	2,153	2,162

Notes: Columns may not add up to 100% because of rounding. Farms are excluded after 1975. Eurobond issues are included in corporate bonds after 1975. Miscellaneous liabilities include foreign direct investment in the U.S. and loans from foreigners.

Source: Board of Governors of the Federal Reserve System, *Flow of Funds Accounts*, various editions.

Though the 1950s and 1960s had their share of macroeconomic problems, overall growth was high. As I noted in the previous chapters,
inflation (and interest rates) remained low, at least in comparison with
the 1970s. Optimism about demand management and intervention prevailed in the minds of authorities; regulation was accepted in many fields
such as air and road transportation, and banking was no exception. The
U.S. financial system in the postwar years was marked by stability,
simplicity, and regulation. It was the culmination of almost two centuries of experimentation and evolution. Banking had become straightforward business; financial decisions were relatively simple, and comparatively few choices were available. One caricature suggested that bankers
adhered to a 3-6-3 rule: pay 3% for deposits, charge 6% for loans, and
tee off at the golf course at 3:00 p.m.! And if the simple set of financial
instruments available also made it possible for corporate CFOs to join
the bankers on the green, the third "3" made even more sense—it ce-
mented relationships.[27]

The U.S. financial system of the 1950s and 1960s engendered few
risks or failures. It was stable, but stability is not necessarily desirable.
In fact, there may be an optimal amount of exit and entry—or success
and failure—necessary for an industry to function at its best, and zero
exit may not be that optimum. Yet, given past experiences of widespread
financial instability and the dislocations associated with it, stability was
unquestionably a policy goal. The relationship system worked to achieve
this goal. But its success must also be attributed to the stable macroeconomic climate and to the strict national capital market segmentation

27. Financial sector stability has been achieved in other ways, too. In Germany,
for example, a few universal banks enforced stability through their size and ability
to compete in all product areas. See H. Francke and M. Hudson, *Banking and
Finance in West Germany* (New York: St. Martin's, 1984). In Japan, as in the
United States, relationship banking and stability were achieved by reducing financial
alternatives, but there financial restrictions were driven by a great desire to *centralize*
the system and to maximize the influence of the authorities over the distribution of
funds. See M. Crum and D. Meerschwam, "From Relationship to Price Banking:
The Loss of Regulatory Control," in McCraw, ed., *America versus Japan* (Boston:
Harvard Business School Press, 1986):261–297; Y. Suzuki, *Money and Banking in
Contemporary Japan: The Theoretical Setting and Its Application* (New Haven:
Yale University Press, 1980); H. Patrick, *Monetary Policy and Central Banking
in Contemporary Japan* (Bombay: University of Bombay, 1962); Bank of Japan,
Economic Research Department, *The Japanese Financial System* (Tokyo: Bank of
Japan, 1972); H. Wallich and M. Wallich, "Banking and Finance," in H. Patrick
and H. Rosovsky, eds., *Asia's New Giant: How the Japanese Economy Works*
(Washington, DC: The Brookings Institution, 1976):249–315; and W. Monroe,
Japan: Financial Markets and the World Economy (New York: Praeger, 1973). For
a presentation of events in the Japanese system, see Chapter 4.

created when international capital controls closed most escape routes. All this provided the fertile ground in which the relationship system could flourish.

Although the *transition* of this system has often been linked with internationalization, deregulation, and securitization, one should look deeper for the causal forces of change. By the 1970s, obvious signals of change had begun to register: international capital flows gained importance, and new financial markets like the Euromarkets began to appear outside of the control of U.S. regulators. Novel international institutional arrangements such as flexible exchange rates emerged, and energy price shocks occurred. Monetary policy was freed from external balance constraints, and inflation started to rise. A new attitude toward regulation eventually emerged: unencumbered free market mechanisms formed the ideological base of a new American administration. These were all parts of a process that first damaged and then permanently altered the relationship system of banking. The full set of implications would not become clear until late in the 1980s.

To explain these changes, I begin by returning to the late 1960s, when (as I explained in Chapters 1 and 2) the pressures for change began to make their presence felt. At first they were simple and few in number, and they affected only a small group of participants. But they ultimately created financial innovations that took full advantage of the changes in the underlying macroenvironment of international economic events.

INTEREST RATE VOLATILITY AND THE MOVE TOWARD PRICE BANKING

Before 1951, the Federal Reserve set interest rate policies in close consultation with the U.S. Treasury. These agencies shared the implicit understanding that rates should be kept low. Their close cooperation was a remnant of the war years, during which the Federal Reserve facilitated Treasury borrowing by buying the issues of government debt and paying for them with new money, thus allowing the money supply to rise. In 1951, the Federal Reserve decided to follow an independent policy. As a result, the 1950s were characterized by monetary policy that fluctuated between expansionary and contractionary, depending on the Fed's current views regarding the likelihood of inflation or recession. Monetary policy became a tool of demand management that employed interest rates to stimulate or cool down the economy. Though it continued to play this role during the 1960s, another goal became increasingly important—the management of interest rates to affect the external account of the United States.

During the 1960s, the United States continued to run a current account surplus, but in the same years the capital account deficit began to more than offset the current account, with the result that net foreign reserves were reduced. In 1970, the capital account deficit reached almost $13 billion; by 1971, it stood at $19 billion.[28] These rising capital account deficits meant that monetary policy, once used primarily as a domestic demand management tool, was now called upon increasingly to influence the external transactions of the United States, as required by the Bretton Woods system. Despite a host of regulations aimed at controlling international capital transactions, only a rise in U.S. interest rates could stem the persistent outflow of private capital and protect dwindling American foreign reserves. This effect of the external sector on monetary policy has already been identified as the foreign reserve constraint.[29]

* The dual role of monetary management—to affect *both* domestic and international events—was difficult to coordinate, and the Federal Reserve eventually made a brief attempt to separate the two effects. The Fed tried to employ long-term interest management for the home economy and short-term management for the international economy.[30] But international pressures on the system were not limited to the changing role of monetary policy alone: foreign financial markets, which had begun to offer nonregulated alternatives to the controlled domestic environment, played a role as well. The initiation of tight monetary policy toward the end of 1968, aimed at dealing with an unsatisfactory external financial position, made issuers more eager to flee the control of U.S. regulators.

The authorities continued to have serious problems. Hoping to save the Bretton Woods system, they fought capital outflows with higher short-term interest rates and monetary squeezes, which only made the offshore unregulated markets a more attractive alternative. As more U.S. banks began funding themselves in the Euromarkets, regulators

---

28. If net errors and omissions (which could be the result of nonreported capital transactions) are taken into account, another $11 billion and $20 billion, respectively, can be added for these years. See *International Financial Statistics* (Washington, DC: International Monetary Fund, 1987).

29. Policymakers hoped that by eliminating this constraint under the flexible exchange rate system, the United States could achieve monetary policy independence.

30. These policies, known as Operation Nudge or Operation Twist, suggested that long-term interest rates would influence domestic investment decisions, while short-term shifts in interest rates would be more effective in attracting short-term international capital. See L. Chandler, *The Economics of Money and Banking*, 6th ed. (New York: Harper & Row, 1973):566–567.

faced a choice between losing oversight of these banks and allowing more interest rate freedoms at home. A third alternative—building a Great Wall of regulatory protection around the domestic financial market—was impractical if not impossible. So authorities chose to allow *some* new domestic interest rate freedoms, in the hope that these would offer financial firms an incentive to remain in the domestic market.[31] In sum, this meant that (1) regulators had lost some control; (2) new funding opportunities had emerged; and (3) interest rates would determine the allocation of (large) deposits to banks in a less controlled domestic system. Banks could now *purchase* money, instead of having to rely on relationships to attract it.

This heightened emphasis on price factors (interest rates) came at a time when rates themselves were rising and becoming more volatile. It provides the second crucial link to the previous chapters. There I noted that as the exchange rate system moved to flexible exchange rates in 1973, hopes of policy independence rose. The oil shock led to expansionary monetary policy, aimed at fighting recession. But as supply side shocks invited monetary expansion, or at least accommodation, to smooth the contractionary impact of higher energy prices, a precipitous increase in both the level and volatility of interest rates became inevitable. Having already started to abolish some interest rate controls, regulators were establishing an environment suited to the development of more and more products that would escape their price control.[32]

Rising inflation and interest rate volatility provided the chief incentives for financial product innovation in the 1970s (Chart 3.1). New opportunities to realize profits from the liabilities side of the balance

31. During earlier years, when Regulation Q threatened to become a real constraint, the Fed had often responded by simply adjusting the ceilings it imposed. For example, in January 1962, when the maximum rates were becoming binding, Regulation Q was increased from 3% to 4% for time deposits. See Chandler, *The Economics of Money and Banking*:565. Interest rate ceilings on large CDs with short maturity (30–89 days) had been freed by the Fed in 1971. At the time, the incident that allowed for the new freedoms was the failure of Penn Central Transportation's CP and subsequent pressures in the credit markets. The underlying trend of avoidance of regulation through the Euromarkets may perhaps have mattered more than the particular incident itself. See Board of Governors of the Federal Reserve System, *57th Annual Report* (Washington, DC: Federal Reserve Board, 1970):42–43.

32. Later in the 1970s, in response to high inflation rates, the Fed changed policies. Monetary policy was no longer used to target interest rates, which in turn had to affect aggregate demand. Now the money supply itself became the target of the policymakers. This shift was consistent with the overall transition away from demand management described in previous chapters, and it left interest rates to fluctuate even more freely.

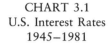

CHART 3.1
U.S. Interest Rates
1945–1981

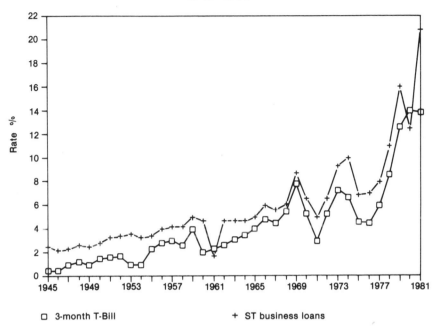

□ 3-month T-Bill   + ST business loans

Source: Federal Reserve Bulletin, various editions.

sheet—historically limited by low, stable interest rates—now emerged. Investors grew sensitive to the price performance of financial products; issuers felt concerned about their costs, and intermediaries became more innovative in response to changing demands and opportunities.[33]

THE EURODOLLAR MARKET

I have noted that, in the late 1960s, external and domestic pressures together created monetary squeezes. When interest rate ceilings on various products became binding in 1969, the ability of U.S. banks to obtain

33. The characterization of the 1950s and 1960s as a period of low interest rates and few innovations in finance should be understood in *comparison* to the 1970s and 1980s. During the mid-1960s, for example, terms such as "performance investing" arose, and the whole conglomerate movement of the late 1960s was largely based on financial engineering. Still, such innovations should be seen as exceptions to the rule. In contrast to the 1970s and 1980s, those who engaged in the new financing techniques were seen as outsiders rather than as part of the financial mainstream.

funds at negotiated prices was restricted, and the price-driven Eurodollar markets began to look attractive as an alternative means for getting additional funds.[34]

The term "Eurodollar" originally applied to the European markets in which dollar-denominated deposits and loans were made.[35] For a variety of reasons, these markets developed in London during the mid-1950s. East bloc countries, concerned about possible interference with their dollar accounts at U.S. banks, decided to transfer their accounts to European banks. Meanwhile, U.S. balance-of-payments deficits left dollar amounts in foreign hands, not all of which, owing to deposit rate restrictions, were eventually redeposited with U.S. banks.[36] Finally, the financing needs and deposit power of foreign subsidiaries of U.S.-based multinational corporations were a major force in fueling these Euromarkets. U.S. banks followed their customers abroad on the understanding that in these markets, success in obtaining funds did not rely on relationships. But more than that, these markets operated outside the control of U.S. regulators. In effect, the Euromarkets were unregulated; as long as international markets did not interfere with the domestic market, British authorities saw no reason to impose controls on them. (I will return to the British perspective in Chapter 5.)

Lack of regulation accounted for many of the differences between Eurocurrency markets and domestic financial markets. There are, for example, no minimum reserve requirements or interest rate restrictions in the Euromarkets. Equally important, it is not clear who bears responsibility for the transactions of the banks that operate in them, since no central bank has assumed a supervisory role, and there is no lender of last resort.[37] Thus, a market was created in which U.S. borrowers, lend-

34. On the development of the Eurocurrency markets, see M. Stigum, *The Money Market,* rev. ed. (Homewood, IL: Dow Jones-Irwin, 1983):129–192, 525–600; and D. Kane, *The Eurodollar Market and the Years of Crisis* (London: Croom Helm, 1983).

35. The name "Eurodollar" or any other Eurocurrency refers to a deposit or loan made in a currency other than the one of the country in which the bank that takes the deposit or makes the loan is located.

36. For example, the balance of payments, excluding official transactions, showed a deficit of $2.4 billion in 1958. This reversed a 1957 surplus of $1.6 billion. Also at this time, changes in convertibility rules facilitated the growth of the Euromarkets.

37. Central banks have obviously been aware of this. The failure of a German bank, Bankhaus I.D. Herstatt, was the kind of shock that reminded many of the inherent dangers. See Kane, *The Eurodollar Market*:118–119. Following a 1974 meeting in Basel, the governors of the central banks of the Group of Ten (United States, Canada, Japan, United Kingdom, France, West Germany, Italy, the Netherlands, Belgium, and Sweden, with Switzerland as the eleventh honorary member)

ers, and intermediaries found each other without having to consider price restraints. At first, only the largest players entered, but over time smaller firms gained access as well. In fact, the growth of the Eurocurrency markets has been remarkable: an estimated annual compound growth rate of 31% for the period 1964–1975.[38]

In the growing Euromarkets, some funds taken in by the branches of U.S. banks were booked "for head-office account"; they provided the U.S. operations of these banks with a competitive alternative to domestic relationship money.[39] But even so, the Eurodollar markets did not immediately become popular with U.S. bankers; only during and just after the period of tight money in 1968, when interest restrictions and credit crunches robbed the domestic market of its attractiveness, did domestic bankers begin to use the Euromarkets extensively. When U.S. officials tried to stem capital outflows with higher short-term rates, protecting their official reserves while keeping many price controls in the system, the new financial markets looked increasingly attractive for funding purposes.

Not surprisingly, the 1971 *Economic Report of the President,* which I quoted in Chapter 1, declared that the Euromarkets had furthered the country's problems in the late 1960s and early 1970s. This viewpoint is easily explained. A crisis was building in the international system, and many expected either a devaluation of the dollar or a further tightening of interest rates to contain the capital outflows. The impending crisis had two results: first, many investors tried to escape the dollar (legally or illegally), and, although good data is difficult to find, many must have turned to the unregulated markets; second, with interest

---

indicated in a carefully worded statement that they had reached an unspecified agreement about responsibilities. Skeptics argue that the statement generated just enough confidence to allow the markets to continue to ignore the issue. The Basel Concordat read: "While it is not practical to lay down in advance detailed rules and procedures for the provision of temporary support to banks experiencing liquidity difficulties, the means are available for that purpose and will be used if and when necessary." Quoted in Stigum, *The Money Market*:179. If a precise and well-defined plan that made specific central banks responsible for the behavior of specific commercial banks had been presented, regulation of the Euromarkets would have been inevitable and the major attraction of the market might have disappeared. Given the importance of the markets, for example, in recycling the dollar balances of the petroleum exporting countries after the oil shock of 1973, such an outcome would have been even less desirable than the precarious stability that existed as a result of the lack of regulatory power.

38. Derived from A. Crockett, *International Money: Issues and Analysis* (Sunbury-on-Thames, England: Nelson, 1977):168.

39. The number of U.S. banks with offices in London grew from 9 in 1960 to 48 in 1980.

rates rising at home—mostly for international balance reasons—the regulatory interest rate constraints on funding caused banks enough financial pain that they attempted to escape as well. When U.S. regulators faced this diminution of their sphere of influence, they decided to make some concessions at home, rather than tighten their grip on the system even further.

After the regulators gave in, the funding alternative provided by the Euromarkets worked to bring an end to U.S. interest rate restrictions on CDs. Restrictions on CDs were abolished between 1971 and 1973, first for large-denominated certificates, later for smaller ones. The purely price-driven money provided by the Euro- and (as will be seen below) the CD markets together would infect other financial markets over time and spell the end of the relationship system. Although interest rates provided the motivation for increased reliance on prices, financial products became the enabling factor in the creation of a new environment.

THE CD MARKET

The negotiable certificate of deposit is an excellent example of a product developed early in this period of change, and one that grew rapidly in the new environment (see Chart 3.2). Invented by Citibank in 1961, it was a CD with a new feature: it could be sold in secondary markets. And though Regulation Q was extended in 1961 to cover CD rates, the secondary trading feature offered novel opportunities. Because the CD could be traded, it decoupled the depositor from the banks. Furthermore, in secondary transactions, market conditions could be reflected in CD prices. Thus, the rates offered on the CD were determined by the quality of the issuing institution and the overall availability of money—as long as the ceilings remained above rates in the market.

The CD market enabled banks to circumvent the strict geographical restrictions that had traditionally determined their supply of stable relationship money through deposit accounts. Instead of merely matching loan commitments to the supply of funds available (through the relationship system), banks could now grow their lending, knowing that CDs could be used to gather funds from more diverse areas.

The CD revolution not only changed the dynamics of funding, it altered the *kind* of money that banks had at their disposal. Unlike deposit money, large CDs moved quickly in response to price stimuli or credit quality. They did not have stability, and because the minimum size of large CDs exceeded the FDIC's insurance maximum, they carried no protection. When the product was developed, few seemed troubled about the new risks; but in the 1980s these dangers would jolt the entire

CHART 3.2
Growth of CD Market
1965–1981

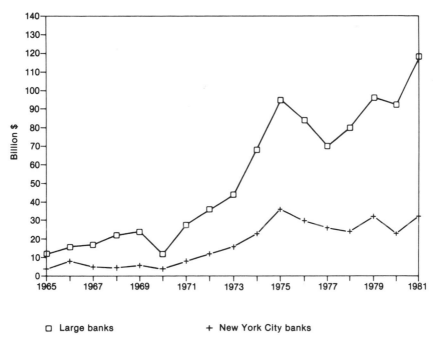

□ Large banks   + New York City banks

Source: Federal Reserve Bulletin, various editions.

financial system. In finance, the full effects of change often take time to become visible.

At first, the new instruments enjoyed only modest popularity. About $10 billion in domestic CDs were outstanding in 1965, and only moderate growth occurred before the early 1970s (see Chart 3.2). More rapid growth occurred after the removal of rate restrictions. By 1975, the CD market had grown tenfold, for an annual compound growth rate in excess of 25%. Ten years later, in 1985, it stood at $447 billion. Thus, large "deposits" had begun to "float" through the markets—rapidly moving money in a constant search for the best available rates. Relationships counted for very little in all of this; price considerations determined financial transactions.

COMMERCIAL PAPER

Another price-driven product that became increasingly important was commercial paper (CP). Issued in the United States as early as the beginning of the nineteenth century, this form of debt allowed the issuer to borrow directly from the investor—bypassing the traditional banker and saving both parties the expense of the middleman. Originally CP found a small market. The CP market did not assume major importance until the late 1960s, when the Federal Reserve began pursuing tight monetary policies. Its popularity continued to flourish in the new interest rate environment of the 1970s and 1980s (see Chart 3.3).

Because commercial paper is essentially an unsecured promissory note, only well-known, creditworthy companies at first had access to funding through this market. As in the market for public debt, a large part of corporate America remained shut out because it lacked the credentials of investment-grade ratings.[40] Over time, however, the financial system came to rely increasingly on prices, and more corporations gained access, provided they were willing to pay the right price.[41] This growth in the market produced serious problems. One of the most significant was the 1970 failure of Penn Central Transportation's commercial paper, which caused widespread instability in the CP market. In the wake of this crisis, many other CP issuers found themselves suddenly excluded from this funding source. With Penn Central in trouble, many investors became frightened about other issuers as well. Their logic seemed to be: if Penn Central can go bad, so can others. This insecurity led to a rapid and massive abandonment of the CP market by investors. The market virtually dried up.

With the sudden disappearance of the CP market, CP issuers needed a new source of short-term money. They had little choice but to return to traditional relationship channels, such as bank credit lines. This necessity created a sudden surge in the demand for bank credit, forcing banks to honor credit lines to many corporations at the same time. The sudden demand for bank loans led to a near-crisis, and the Federal Reserve was forced to infuse emergency liquidity into the system. It also led to a reaction in CD market. I have already outlined the overall pressures that set the stage for deregulation of (selected) CD rates. It was, however, the liquidity problems of the banking sector in the wake of the Penn Central crisis that rang up the curtain on the first new freedoms. Free rates on short-term, large CDs enhanced the funding

40. As they did with publicly issued debt, ratings agencies rated the quality of commercial paper. For the banking sector itself, the CP market provided access to funds, as bank holding companies issued such liabilities to fund their banking subsidiaries.

41. A new feature was developed whereby the issuer of CP obtained a letter of credit from a bank, thus in effect buying insurance from the bank for the investors in its paper.

CHART 3.3
Growth of the CP Market
1965–1981

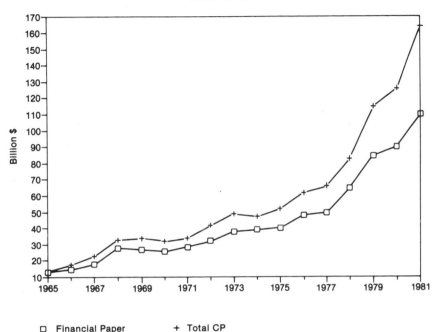

□ **Financial Paper**   + **Total CP**

Source: Federal Reserve Bulletin, various editions.

ability of banks and helped them survive such pressures as the CP crisis.[42] The speed with which the CP market collapsed, and its sudden and threatening impact on the banking sector, provided an early example of the risk associated with reliance on price-driven financial instruments rather than on stable, long-term relationships.

Eventually, the CP market recovered, and many investors and issuers returned to it, finding it an effective way of raising and placing funds outside of the traditional relationship system, and at slightly more favorable prices. Such savings were especially important in the new era of generally higher interest rates in the 1970s. Thus a CP market developed for lesser-known companies; they used lines of credit to back up their funding needs and bank guarantees to sell their paper in the market. By 1987, the CP market stood at $357 billion, of which 22.7% had been issued by nonfinancial corporations.[43]

42. See note 31.
43. See Board of Governors of the Federal Reserve System, *Federal Reserve Bulletin,* various issues (Washington, DC: Federal Reserve Board).

CORPORATE BONDS

A marked shift toward price banking was also evident in the market for public corporate debt. Bonds, like commercial paper, originally could be issued only by well-known companies—those with a rating of BBB or higher.[44] Bonds that traded with ratings of less than BBB were sometimes referred to as "Fallen Angels," because they had typically started life as investment grade and had been downgraded because of changes in the credit quality of the company that issued them. In the traditional system, no company with less than a BBB rating could access the public market, regardless of its willingness to pay higher rates of interest to investors. But in a system that was increasingly reliant on the price mechanism, this had to change, as the development of the public debt market for low-grade debt now makes clear.[45] In this high-yield bond market, almost anyone willing to pay the price could issue securities. So the "junk" bond market grew from an issue volume of less than $1 billion in 1977 to $1.2 billion in 1981 and then shot up to $30.9 billion in 1986.[46] This rapid growth hid difficult problems; not until the late 1980s did some of the most serious risks—the reason for the high yield—come to light.

The development of a single new SEC rule illustrates this same shift toward price reliance from another angle. As of late December 1980, SEC regulations permitted so-called shelf-registration (Rule 415), which allowed a company to go through the time-consuming process of preparing a *possible* issue well in advance of the *actual* issue, and to put SEC clearance on a "shelf." Once a favorable window of opportunity in the market opened (low interest rates), an issue could proceed.[47] Again, short-term price volatility and its impact on the profitability of the firm were increasingly important.

44. For several reasons, only debt rated BBB or higher had been acceptable for large classes of institutional investors.

45. Many have argued that a *relationship* with Drexel Burnham Lambert was a prerequisite for access to the developing high-yield market. Still, it should be clear that the high-yield market was designed to function as a price-driven market.

46. The rapid growth of issue volume in the high-yield market and the tendency of the bonds to become troubled later in their life (if at all) in effect reduced overall default rates, when bond defaults were considered as a percentage of total outstanding issue volume. See E. Altman, "Measuring Corporate Bond Mortality and Performance," *Journal of Finance* 44 (1989):909–922; and P. Asquith, D. Mullins, and E. Wolff, "Original Issue High Yield Bonds: Aging Analyses of Defaults, Exchanges and Calls," *Journal of Finance* 44 (1989):923–941.

47. For an extensive analysis of the changes in the registration procedures and an evaluation of the new environment, see J. Auerbach and S. Hayes, *Investment Banking and Diligence: What Price Deregulation?* (Boston: Harvard Business School Press, 1986).

MONEY MARKET FUNDS

Another key element in the rise of price banking was the inception and growth of money market funds. Although mutual funds were invented in 1924, the money market mutual funds were not developed until half a century later. They played a major role in breaking the relationship system.

We have seen that in the early 1970s regulators reluctantly freed some of the interest rate ceilings in response to pressures from the Euromarkets. Still, regulators wished to retain as much power as possible. They kept the restrictions on smaller-sized deposits, because, in contrast to the large corporate depositors, small individual investors could not easily escape the regulated system. The retail investor could not, like the representatives of large banks and corporations, fly to London to do transactions. But financial entrepreneurs recognized a new opportunity: Why not pool money from retail investors and invest in the deregulated wholesale money market? The answer signalled the birth of the money market fund, which provided a practical escape route for the retail investor. By the early 1980s, more than 450 funds offered this service, up from zero in 1974. By 1987, total savings invested in these funds stood at $316 billion. A large portion of it came directly out of the regulated, low-interest deposits that U.S. bankers so cherished as a cheap source of funds. Once they became competitive with deposit accounts and life insurance investments, money market funds proved effective in removing domestic regulations. Banks and insurance companies, forced to compete with these price-driven products, argued for further removal of price (interest rate) restrictions on their own products. The regulators' willingness to loosen interest rate restrictions on deposit accounts must be understood in this context, as price-performance-oriented products infected market after market.

These vignettes illustrate the breakdown of the old relationship system.[48] A pervasive shift toward price-driven instruments had taken place throughout the financial industry, and it was sanctified by the principle of deregulation. As I will suggest below, further deregulation of many financial instruments during the 1980s underscored the authorities'

---

48. On U.S. financial deregulation in the early 1980s, see A. Gart, *The Insider's Guide to the Financial Services Revolution* (New York: McGraw-Hill, 1984); G. Bentson, ed., *Financial Services: The Changing Institutions and Government Policy* (Englewood Cliffs, NJ: Prentice-Hall, 1983): C. Williams, "The Transformation of Banking," *Reprint Collection No. 15051* (Boston: *Harvard Business Review*, 1984); A. Carron, *Reforming the Bank Regulatory Structure* (Washington, DC: The Brookings Institution, 1984); and *Economic Report of the President* (Washington, DC: U.S. Government Printing Office, 1984):145–174.

ideological shift toward a philosophy of greater reliance on markets. But this shift had much deeper roots. In Chapter 2 I noted that widespread disappointment with Keynesian demand management in the 1970s led to supply side economics and the inflationary environment of the same period. With less pressure to adjust policies for the external balance constraint, inflation rose and interest rate variability increased. In response to these factors, prices assumed a more and more dominant role in financial transactions, and relationships lost value.

Thus, it is too simple to say merely that deregulation, internationalization, securitization, and so forth occurred in the 1970s and 1980s. They occurred because of fundamental forces in macro- and international economic conditions. Whether the price-driven system will prove compatible with stability remains to be seen. Some proponents of price banking argue that the stability of the traditional system was excessive, and that a degree of instability in the present system may be beneficial, helping to promote the most efficient allocation of funds. Still, recent events have brought this proposition into question and have reminded the financial community that greater instability means greater risk. The following section examines some of the risks that have emerged. One demonstration of the results of this instability may be found in the pages of banks' balance sheets: they clearly show far more risks, as higher funding risks have come to be matched by higher asset risks.

ASSET COMPOSITION OF BANKS

In the years immediately after World War II, the role of the commercial banks was, to a large extent, simply to take in funds through deposits and invest them in assets that had very stable returns. By 1950, almost 50% of the total assets of banks were invested in the most stable securities—government and tax-exempt obligations. By 1970, this ratio had dropped to less than 30%, while business loans had grown from less than 20% in 1950 to almost 30%; and mortgage loans from 9% to 14% over the same period. Given these figures, it is hardly surprising that bank portfolios began to show more risk during these years. Commercial loan demand was high, and the need to fund government expenses had fallen. (See Table 3.4.)

The riskiness of the banks' asset portfolio was not only a function of the shift in funds-needs away from the government and toward corporations, however. The costs of funds also helped banks decide what type of loans to make. Attracting enough funds to satisfy a large demand for loans can become expensive, especially when funding is based on price factors rather than on relationships. A bank that decides to grow its

TABLE 3.4
Selected Assets and Liabilities of Commercial Banks
(as a percentage of total financial assets)

Selected Assets	1946	1950	1960	1970	1980	1988
U.S. govt. securities						
Treasury securities	56.3	41.7	26.8	12.1	7.8	6.6
Agency securities	0.8	1.2	1.0	2.7	4.1	5.9
Total	57.0	42.9	27.8	14.8	11.9	12.5
Tax-exempt securities	3.3	5.5	7.7	13.6	10.1	5.2
Corporate & foreign bonds	1.9	1.7	0.6	0.6	0.5	2.8
Loans						
Mortgages	5.4	9.1	12.5	14.2	17.7	22.8
Consumer credit	1.9	4.9	8.9	12.7	12.2	12.6
Bank loans n.e.c.	13.2	18.7	27.4	29.3	30.8	25.8
Open-market paper	0.3	0.5	0.9	1.6	1.1	0.4
Security credit	2.4	2.0	2.6	2.5	1 4	1.2
Total	23.2	35.1	52.3	60.2	63.3	62.8
Vault cash	1.5	1.4	1.5	1.4	1.3	0.9
Reserves at Federal Reserve	12.0	11.8	7.4	4.7	1.9	1.1
Selected liabilities						
Checkable deposits	65.5	63.8	54.3	36.7	23.1	19.0
Small time & savings deposits*	25.5	24.6	31.5	34.8	32.0	36.4
Large time deposits**	0.0	0.0	0.5	10.4	18.4	14.2
Fed funds and security RPs	0.0	0.0	0.0	0.9	7.7	8
Net interbank claims	NA	NA	NA	3.6	− 1.9	− 0.7
Corporate bonds	0.0	0.0	0.0	0.6	1.6	3.7
Open-market paper	0.0	0.0	0.0	1.8	4.6	3.6
Miscellaneous liabilities	1.9	3.2	4.2	7.0	13.6	12.4
Total liabilities***	93.6	93.0	92.1	96.1	99.1	96.6
Financial assets ($ billion)	134	150	230	518	1,482	2,938

NA = Not available

*Includes larger ($100,000 +) deposits before 1970.

**Only includes large negotiable CDs before 1970.

***Includes liabilities not listed above.

Note: Some categories do not add up to subtotals because of rounding. In addition, since some types of financial assets are omitted, the selected assets will not add up to 100% of all financial assets.

Source: Board of Governors of the Federal Reserve System, *Flow of Funds Accounts,* various editions.

balance sheet in a price-oriented environment may find itself driven toward making higher-yielding loans (which may require that the quality of some of the loans be compromised), simply to offset higher funding costs. The relationship among funding methods, reliance on price-driven instruments such as CDs, and the composition of banks' assets, was succinctly explained by two executives of Citicorp, in their excellent presentation of Citibank's history:

> [The CD] would solve the funding problem, thereby opening the way to faster growth. Instead of matching loan commitments to the supply of bonds that could be sold, banks would now be able to book loans they thought profitable, knowing the funds would be available in the market at price. Moreover, market funding would solve another traditional banking problem: liquidity. If banks could find funds whenever needed in large, efficient CD and Eurodollar markets, they would be able to shift their assets portfolios away from low-yielding but highly liquid U.S. government securities toward higher-yielding but less liquid assets such as loans and municipal securities.[49]

In sum, two major changes took place. Lending shifted from the government to the private sector, and funding became less relationship- and more price-oriented (see Chart 3.4). Faced with new challenges but handicapped by old rules originally designed for another era, regulators began a general move toward deregulation rather than reregulation.

FINANCIAL DEREGULATION

Over some two hundred years the U.S. financial system has undergone a gradual and difficult process of change. Recent years have seen growing pressure for financial reform, although such reform has not been easy to implement. Commissions to study the need for regulatory reform have become an almost permanent feature of the financial industry, and reform acts were repeatedly submitted, debated, and shelved.[50] Because the financial industry affects virtually every individual and corporation it is difficult to satisfy, or at least not offend, major interest groups; hence, the U.S. Senate and House of Representatives find it hard to agree on legislation.

49. H. Cleveland and T. Huertas, *Citibank 1812–1970* (Cambridge, MA: Harvard University Press, 1985):256.

50. See, for example, S. Jones, *The Development of Economic Policy: Financial Institution Reform* (Ann Arbor: University of Michigan Research Division, 1979):83–99, 141–210.

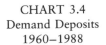

CHART 3.4
Demand Deposits
1960–1988

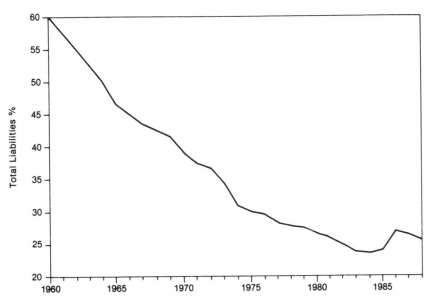

Source: *Federal Reserve Bulletin*, various editions.

As I mentioned earlier, several financial instruments were developed that allowed the largest borrowers and issuers to avoid tight regulation. But it took somewhat longer for the benefits of new financial instruments to reach small depositors. When market interest rates began to exceed the legal limits of Regulation Q, regulators initially tried to reduce the number of market-based options available to small depositors. Until 1966, for example, savings and loan associations had not been subject to limitations on deposit interest rates. The Interest Rate Adjustment Act of 1966, however, empowered the Federal Home Loan Bank Board to set maximum deposit interest rates for its members.

These barriers began to crumble almost as soon as they were erected. In 1972, for example, Massachusetts courts approved a savings account that customers could access with "negotiable orders of withdrawal" (NOW), which were very similar to checks. New Hampshire savings banks were eager to follow, and in 1973, Congress authorized all banks and thrifts in New Hampshire and Massachusetts to offer NOW accounts. By 1979, all banks and thrifts in New York and New England could offer NOW accounts. These innovations, along with the money market funds already mentioned, helped to advance the deregulation of interest rates for small-denominated deposits.

Because interest group lobbies and other factors make timely legislation hard to achieve, changes in regulation have more often been reactive than proactive. The Depository Institutions Deregulation and Monetary Control Act (DIDMCA) of 1980, which allowed commercial banks to pay interest on checking accounts (provided the deposit holder fulfilled some basic requirements), is an example: more than two years were required for its passage. Furthermore, DIDMCA created a committee to supervise the phaseout over a six-year period of controls on most deposit interest rates. It also authorized the Federal Reserve to set reserve requirements for all depository institutions, so that banks would no longer be tempted to leave the Federal Reserve System to take advantage of looser state reserve requirements. The dismantling of controls on deposit interest rates accelerated when Congress passed the Garn-St. Germain Depository Institutions Act of 1982. The act created two new savings vehicles (money market deposit accounts and super-NOW accounts), which had even fewer limitations than did traditional NOW accounts.

Restrictions on bank holding companies acquiring brokerage institutions were also loosened: the acquisition of Schwab by BankAmerica Corporation tested the willingness of regulators to stretch the interpretation of banking acts such as Glass-Steagall. Similarly, as the ubiquitous automated teller machine (ATM) rendered branching restrictions less effective and sometimes obsolete (and because some states wanted their banks to be more competitive with large money-center banks), legislation related to regional conglomeration was enacted. Nationwide banking proposals advocated by various banks, and even by Federal Reserve Chairman Volcker, also surfaced.[51]

Mortgage-backed securities enabled originating financial institutions to sell securities backed by packages of government-guaranteed mortgages, thereby decoupling the traditional relationship that had been characteristic of mortgages. This fast-growing market was yet another response to the price-oriented environment. It met little regulatory challenge and was facilitated by institutional change, when mortgages insured by federal agencies became widely available. Similarly, the use of

51. See "Fed Backs Interstate Banking," *New York Times,* April 25, 1985: D1, D13. See also E. Corrigan, *Financial Market Structure: A Longer View* (New York: Federal Reserve Bank of New York, 1987).

variable rate mortgages was sanctioned by federal regulators in the late 1970s.[52]

PRICE BANKING AND STABILITY

With change no longer proceeding at the speed of a slide show, but more like a fast-moving film, it becomes impossible to catalogue all the elements of U.S. financial deregulation. What matters for the purpose of this book is the underlying trend represented by this stream of changes—the breaking of traditional relationships and their replacement by price-driven transactions.

Though it is readily apparent that the United States has moved toward price banking and that regulators have lost some control, the specific effects of these changes—especially on the long-term stability of the American financial system—remain difficult to identify. The greater freedom with which financial institutions are now able to operate could well create an increasingly stable environment, as growing diversity in the sources and uses of funds reduces any likelihood of a liquidity crisis. The ability to buy money in the CD market might alleviate the liquidity fears (except where solvency is an issue) that have sparked bank runs in the past. Similarly, some of the problems that have traditionally plagued thrifts might be mitigated if new instruments in the mortgage-lending market allow them to resell their mortgages through mortgage-backed securities and to write variable rate mortgages. (Recent problems in this industry highlight new risks, which are discussed later.)

Despite these potentially favorable effects, however, there is evidence to suggest that banking has entered a period of increased instability as a result of new risks associated with the system.[53] Whether such instability will be temporary or permanently embedded in the newly developing system remains to be seen. As banks increasingly fund themselves with purchased, price-sensitive money, the potential for major withdrawals and for sharp increases in the cost of funding grows apace. In this case, new safeguards may be needed. FDIC deposit insurance, for example, is already of dubious effectiveness in forestalling liquidity problems be-

---

52. State chartered S&Ls have used variable rate mortgages much longer—in California, since 1928. In 1979, the federal S&Ls were allowed to use them. See F. Ornstein, *Savings Banking: An Industry in Change* (Reston, VA: Reston Publishing Company, 1985).

53. See, for example, E. Corrigan, *Financial Market Structure: A Longer View*. In this brochure, Corrigan presents a provocative view of the overhaul of the financial system and its regulatory structure.

cause investors in the large CD market are not included; they are likely to withdraw funds from banks with deteriorating credit. Similarly, funding through CP issues of a holding company means that much less stable money is available.

Many examples of instability within financial markets in recent years come to mind. Earlier, I referred to the problems in the CP market precipitated by the collapse of the Penn Central Transportation Corporation. The unprecedented speed with which the market responded to that problem is characteristic of the system of price banking; there are no relationships to inhibit reactions by the participants.

Consider too the 1982 failure of Drysdale Government Securities, a new, relatively unimportant government securities dealer, which had been active in the repurchase (repo) market. The repo market grew impressively during the late 1970s, as higher and more volatile interest rates made repos increasingly useful instruments to take advantage of short-term price fluctuation. But price volatility also helped undo Drysdale. With the shift to price banking, securities holders could borrow against their assets, rather than holding onto them for a long period. Assets could thus be acquired and financed immediately through repos. Drysdale, it now seems clear, engaged in questionable practices to build large positions in repos. What is more important, though, is that Chase Manhattan, an acknowledged expert in government securities, became deeply involved with Drysdale, and was forced to take a large write-off against current earnings amid rumors of significant losses when Drysdale ran into difficulty. Chase was drawn ever more closely into dealing with Drysdale by the reduced importance of stable relationship money, as well as by the momentum of an incessant quest for purchased funds. Transactions between these two institutions can be seen as purely price-driven events.

A third example of the new instability occurred in the summer of 1984. Continental Illinois Bank of Chicago had entered into extensive dealings with a dubious partner, Penn Square Bank. Continental had pursued an aggressive growth strategy, relying on purchased money (CDs and Eurodollars) to fund both originated and purchased loans. At the time this strategy commanded respect, at least in some quarters: *Dunn's Review* for 1980 ranked Continental among the five best-run companies in the United States. But when substantial problems emerged at Penn Square Bank, the associated questionable loans on the books of Continental (in excess of $1 billion) undermined confidence in the viability of the Chicago bank. By the summer of 1984, rumors about the overall quality of Continental's loan portfolio caused a major withdrawal of funds. At this time, however, in contrast to the experience of the early 1930s, small depositors did not cut and run; they were insured by the FDIC. Instead, it was the large CD and foreign depositors who made for the exits. These depositors had no continuing relationship with Continental, but had merely parked their money there because of price factors. They had no incentive to stay with the bank. They simply redeposited their holdings in other parts of the money market. When these large withdrawals brought Continental to the brink of failure, the FDIC felt compelled to insure *all* depositors, regardless of size. It did extract an equity position in the bank and holding company, to provide at least partial compensation for its risk. (I return to this incident in greater detail in Chapter 7.)

The recent problems of the S&L industry in the United States provide the most convincing evidence of the new instability and conform well to the interpretation advanced so far in this chapter. First, in response to competitive funding pressures, as other depository institutions and money market funds drove retail deposit rates up, the thrift industry asked for, and got, interest rate freedom. But then, with rising funding rates, profit pressures occurred because the asset portfolio—typically consisting of long-term mortgages—was made at historically lower rates. Not surprisingly, the S&Ls next requested new freedom for the asset side of their balance sheets as well. And regulatory reaction did indeed empower the S&Ls to broaden their investment portfolios with higher-yielding (and often more risky) assets, without adjusting the federal insurance premiums for the deposits.

Under these conditions, S&Ls could grow at will and fund themselves in a price-driven market (while remaining essentially subsidized through a nonmarket-related insurance premium).[54] With regional economic shocks, many assets began to show that their high yields were linked with low quality. Add to this a dose of fraud, a captured legislative branch of the government, and the unwillingness of regulators (for political and financial reasons) to take early action. These ingredients formed a volatile mixture that exploded into public visibility in 1989.

54. Several economic rationales for the behavior of the S&Ls can be provided. Because of government insurance, depositors of CDs had no incentive to monitor the asset quality of the S&Ls. S&L managers maximized the insurance subsidy from the government by increasing the risks of the asset portfolio; consequently they held a limited downside (the equity value of the shareholders) but a high upside potential, because they attained subsidized market funding due to FDIC insurance. In ordinary financial markets, the control that prevents such gambles comes through the bond/debt holders. With highly risky assets they will ask for high returns. In the S&L case, government insurance (at rates insensitive to the particular asset composition of the bank) took this control mechanism away, while Congress granted the S&Ls greater investment freedom that facilitated their policies.

CUSTOMER RELATIONSHIPS UNDER PRICE BANKING

Theoretically, in a purely price-driven world, various institutions offer similar products at similar prices. These prices, reflecting all available information about the product quality, result in an optimal allocation of all available funds. Even in a purely price-driven world, however, there may still exist some role for a relationship betweeen a financial intermediary and the borrower or lender. Such a relationship would give an intermediary the right to make a bid for a financial transaction at a competitive price. This relationship might be developed in several ways: for example, the ability to offer various financial products from diverse product areas (each of which would have to be priced competitively) could allow an intermediary to bid for various aspects of a customer's business. Similarly, in investment banking, a well-established relationship might allow a bank access to a client and thus provide the opportunity to offer products and services at competitive prices. In an emerging financial world, where customers are predisposed to look for the best possible prices, it is hardly surprising that a number of commercial banks have created relationship managers—executives who work to assure that their bank captures the right to sell financial products at prices as attractive as those of its competitors.

The new type of relationship is fundamentally different, however, from the type that prevailed before price banking. To a large extent, traditional relationships *substituted* for price competition; the new relationships *complement* it. In the old system, price and product restrictions limited growth opportunities and assured profitability for many financial institutions. Thus, relationship banking produced the slow and careful growth of both assets and liabilities. In the new environment, aggressive pricing policies and innovative behavior can effectively circumvent the traditional boundaries within which financial institutions once operated. Today, relationships are just another tool, like aggressive pricing and product development, for attaining market share in a price-driven world. Later chapters will look at what this situation implies for the current environment, and at the strategies being employed by financial services firms. Before pursuing the implications of this situation, however, I turn to events in two other major capital markets, Japan and the United Kingdom. Both form an integral part of the story.

4

THE JAPANESE FINANCIAL SYSTEM

The transformation of war-exhausted Japan, with its dearth of natural resources, into a very large creditor nation has been nothing less than spectacular. When a single nation builds such large claims against the rest of the world, other countries must be acting as borrowers. In this sense, the United States has obliged Japan. It is as if a confluence of national interests conspired to allow policymakers in *both* countries to procrastinate over adjustment policies: for Japan, policies that would increase consumption relative to production; for the United States, policies that would increase production relative to consumption. Neither adjustment appeared in time to prevent a severe imbalance. In the process of accumulating international assets, Japan's financial markets were propelled to global importance.

As a parallel to my discussion in Chapter 3, I intend to consider the Japanese financial market changes in the 1980s as the outcome of long-term developments. In particular, the past decade's changes in Japan's international asset position and in its national financial system can only be understood in the context of its extraordinary economic growth over nearly five decades. Many describe this performance as the Japanese miracle. Yet the use of the term *miracle* only obscures many causes that lay behind Japan's success. In analyzing this success, observers have focused on various aspects of Japanese society, and several have explored the capital markets. The latter sort of analyses have often rested on the assumption that Japan's export success was built at least partly on a lower cost of capital. It has been an especially popular explanation among U.S. business executives who had lost world market share.

But to suggest that the cost of capital was crucial to Japanese success is to oversimplify. Although I ascribe an important role to financial considerations, it is the entire Japanese financial *system*, which allocated funds in a particular way, that becomes the focus of my discussion, rather than the simple cost of capital calculations. I show how Japan's carefully crafted financial system allowed some firms to have preferential access to funds. It was a financial system that rationed capital, that created insiders and outsiders, and that allowed for a "guided" allocation-of-capital mechanism in which price and product freedoms were curtailed; rather than prices, relationships were central. The Japanese relationship system functioned for almost three decades after World War II. But just as in the United States, the 1970s and 1980s greatly altered the relationship environment. Underlying macro- and international economic forces (similar to those at work in the United States) broke the traditional Japanese system. To evaluate the impact of these forces, this chapter looks at the evolution of the Japanese financial system over time and ends by considering changes that are transforming the system at this moment.

In the postwar years, Japan's successful industrial reconstruction was accurately reflected in consistently high GNP growth rates. It was only in the 1980s, however, that remarkable international current account surpluses catapulted Japan's capital markets to international prominence. Furthermore, in the 1980s, just as in the United States, the Japanese capital markets gained new freedoms to develop and price financial products. As a result, many foreign players are now actively seeking to enter Japan's capital markets, and Japanese financial institutions are becoming increasingly important players in key foreign capital markets. In fact, Japanese financial firms, always eager to diversify their product base, have actually begun to dominate some pockets of the international markets. Later chapters will show how this development has affected the basic strategies of financial services firms.

The new domestic freedoms and large current account surpluses that enabled Japanese financial services firms to become important players in the international arena will undoubtedly force major adaptations in the nonfinancial sector of the Japanese economy as well. Although different industries typically hold very different types of assets, it is always through the liabilities side of the balance sheet that the pervasive influence of the financial sector is felt. The national financial system plays a fundamental role in every nation's economy; and in virtually all countries, over time, authorities exert a deep and far-reaching influence over financial transactions. The particulars of a national system typically reflect the preferences, cultural norms, and vital concerns of the nation. Japan is no exception: its financial system was specifically designed to facilitate rapid industrialization, a high savings rate, and cooperation among players. In the jargon of modern financial theory, the system seems to have dealt very efficiently with the many information asymmetries and agency problems that exist among borrowers, lenders, managers, and (stock) owners.[1]

A national consensus emphasizing economic growth, investments, and restricted consumption was reflected in the granting of great power to both the Ministry of Finance (MOF) and the Bank of Japan (BOJ). Centralization was also evident in the broad authority given to a few city banks and long-term credit banks, which provided loans to help finance much of Japan's industrialization effort. A national savings system was established, operating through the nation's widely branched post office network. Tax incentives stimulated and channeled retail savings, while poorly developed pension systems and generous bonus schemes contributed to individual savings.[2] Also, the proverbial Japanese work ethic and a lack of leisure time hampered consumption.

Two controls were especially important to the Japanese financial system: strict regulation of prices (interest rates); and careful segmentation of product markets. Together they produced a lack of alternatives in financial transactions and a great reliance on special relationships rather than the price mechanism for financial arrangements. In this, as my chapters on the United States and the United Kingdom show, Japan was not alone. What was unique to Japan was the method by which the relationships were fostered. That method reflected Japan's distinct history, culture, and goals. These factors shaped the role of the central authorities and created power balances and dependencies.

THE ORIGINS OF JAPAN'S FINANCIAL SYSTEM

The roots of Japan's financial system can be traced to the period after the Meiji Restoration of 1868.[3] This era brought an end to more than two and a half centuries of national isolation and fundamentally

1. For a more complete exposition, see D. Meerschwam, "The Japanese Financial System and the Cost of Capital," in P. Krugman, ed., *The United States and Japan: Trade and Investment* (Chicago: University of Chicago Press, forthcoming.)

2. Although it is not immediately obvious from standard economics that the lack of a contributory pension scheme will enhance personal savings, or that year-end bonuses (especially with rational, intertemporally optimizing agents) will enhance savings, these institutional designs *in combination with* cultural and historical norms, seem to have provided Japan with a comparatively high savings rate, especially in relation to that of the United States.

3. For accounts of the prewar Japanese financial system, see R. Goldsmith, *The Financial Development of Japan, 1869–1977* (New Haven: Yale University Press, 1983):16–106; and G. Allen, *A Short Economic History of Modern Japan*, 4th ed. (New York: St. Martin's, 1981):49–62.

changed the shape of most Japanese institutions.[4] The financial system that developed can be directly linked to the desires of the new rulers to transform Japan into a modern industrial economy. A policy of "Enrichment and Industrialization" called for changes in the roles of entire classes of society.[5] In this transformation, the role of the Samurai became particularly important to the development of the financial system. Deprived of its traditional powers, privileges, and obligations, this warrior class became involved with the practices of the banking business.

The leaders of the Meiji Restoration appropriated the taxing power that had traditionally rested with the feudal lords. In lieu of pensions and other distributions, the new central government offered to the Samurai class, first in 1873 and again in 1877, pension bonds that capitalized the pension obligations.[6] Economic problems, however, reduced the value of these bonds. The government attempted to resolve these and other problems through the National Bank Act of 1872, but it was not successful until 1876, when a revision of the National Bank Act led to conversion of the bonds into national bank ownership.[7]

The numerous national banks—by 1879 there were 153 of them —were responsible for currency issue. They did not function satisfactorily in a society undergoing rapid change and plagued by hostilities (e.g., the Satsuma Rebellion in 1877). Often poorly managed, their excessive issuance of notes in an unconvertible currency led to rapid inflation. Finally, in 1881, Minister of Finance Matsukata recommended the

---

4. Ieyasu Tokugawa's rise to dominance in 1603 ended a period of feudal, local strife in Japan. To consolidate his power, Tokugawa effectively closed the country off to foreign influence. Not until 1868 did a coup of disaffected nobles break the power of the Shogunate.

5. A policy intended to develop a "Rich Country, Strong Army" was instituted. See, for example, E. Reischauer, *The United States and Japan*, 3rd ed. (New York: Viking, 1964):10–11. Also, see Bank of Japan, *Money and Banking in Japan*, L. Pressnell, ed. (London: Macmillan, 1973):3–5.

6. See Allen, *A Short Economic History of Modern Japan*:43–48.

7. See ibid.:46. Quotes S. Okuma: "Now this [Samurai] class, beyond the functions which had appertained to it under the regime which had passed away, was ignorant of the ordinary means of gaining a livelihood, and now being suddenly released from these functions, was greatly in danger of falling into a state of indigence and perhaps into pauperism, unless some calling could be found for its members. The Government, consequently, with the objective of finding a means by which the military class could turn their public debt bonds to account in obtaining a livelihood, and moved also by the want of circulating capital in the country and the general tightness of money, adopted a plan to confer a double benefit, the principle of which was the establishment of national banks by the military class on the security of the public bonds held by them."

establishment of a central bank to redeem unconvertible notes.[8] The result was the Bank of Japan, founded in 1882. Based on the model of the central banks in Europe, it was given broad powers. Shortly after its founding, the Bank of Japan began to monopolize note issuance, and, as the powers of the bank expanded, the outlines of Japan's modern financial system emerged.[9]

The system that developed was centralized: the Bank of Japan's broad powers (albeit shared and surpassed by the Ministry of Finance) were felt widely. The authorities were given an active role in fostering and shaping specialized financial institutions. For example, the Yokohama Specie Bank (currently the Bank of Tokyo) was founded in 1880 as a private initiative to finance international transactions. It was strongly supported by the authorities and, in 1887, other banks were formally prohibited from encroaching into its specialized field.[10] Other specialized financial institutions also developed, among them insurance and trust companies, credit cooperatives, and mutual banks. A postal savings network, founded in 1877, gave authorities direct access to funds for financing preferred industrial undertakings.[11]

Specialized banks became characteristic of Japanese finance and remained unchanged even after the Occupation.[12] They were especially helpful in targeting finance according to maturity (short-term or long-term) or purpose (international trade, agriculture) during periods in which the demand for credit remained high because of industrialization. Of course, such specialized banks were not unique to Japan. In fact, the Industrial Bank of Japan (1900), a credit bank that provided long-term loans to industry, and the Hypothec and other Japanese agricultural banks, originally designed for long-term finance related to real estate, were reminiscent of the French system.

With the help of various government-sponsored financial institutions, authorities could influence the prices (interest rates) of financial prod-

---

8. Wholesale prices were estimated to have increased by 12% between 1868 and 1876. Between 1878 and 1881 they increased by 52%. Derived from H. Rosovsky, "Japan's Transition to Modern Economic Growth," in H. Rosovsky, ed., *Industrialization in Two Systems: Essays in Honor of Alexander Gerschenkron* (New York: Wiley, 1966):91–139.

9. For a concise statement, see Federation of Bankers Associations, *Banking System in Japan*, 9th ed. (Tokyo: Federation of Bankers Association, 1984):1–5.

10. See Bank of Japan, *Money and Banking in Japan*:15–16.

11. The postal savings system started to redeposit its funds with the Deposit Bureau (later the Trust Fund Bureau) of the Ministry of Finance.

12. On the development of special banks and other financial organizations, see Bank of Japan, *Money and Banking in Japan*:13–22, 29–35.

ucts. This situation did not, however, deter the growth of private financial organizations. By 1901, the number of commercial banks exceeded 1,800. Liquidations and government-supported amalgamation reduced this number drastically, particularly after 1920. In 1928, a new Banking Law established minimum capital levels for banks, reducing their numbers by half. By 1931, 683 banks operated in Japan (down from more than 1,400 in 1926), and concentration in banking continued. By 1936, there were 418 banks; by 1945, a mere 61. The number of savings banks was similarly reduced.[13]

Within the commercial banking sector, the reduction in the number of active participants did not represent the only important development; segmentation of the financial product market also continued. Segmentation before World War II was partly a response to the needs of the munitions industry, especially as authorities increasingly exercised control over the utilization of funds.[14] Later, banks in major Japanese cities dealt with the challenges of industrializing Japan, while the smaller local banks concentrated on the needs of rural areas.[15] City banks often had strong ties to industrial groups (zaibatsu) and provided the funds that they required. Local and rural banks were concerned mostly with gathering funds. Thus, a natural flow of funds developed, from the smaller local and rural banks to the larger, city banks.[16] In sum, three essential features of the Japanese financial system developed in less than half a century: specialization, price regulation, and centralization. These characteristics would remain at the core of Japan's new financial system.

World War II left Japan's financial system badly shaken, but reconstruction began quickly. New fiscal policies and new directives for banks reflected attempts by the Occupation forces not only to break the power of the zaibatsu, but to abolish the special relationships that had existed between the zaibatsu and their core banks.[17] In effect, the traditional

13. Ibid.:25–27; and Federation of Bankers Associations of Japan, *Banking System in Japan*:2.

14. The Temporary Funds Adjustment Law (1937) and Bank Fund Utilization Order (1940) had given the authorities formal power to channel investments and control the flow of funds in Japan.

15. T. Adams and I. Hoshii, *A Financial History of the New Japan* (Palo Alto: Kodansha International, 1972):104–108.

16. The call money market played the major role as the conduit of funds.

17. Fiscal conservatism had originated with the "Dodge Line." In 1949, a commission led by Joseph Dodge, financial advisor to the Occupation forces, recommended a policy of balanced budgets. For accounts of financial stabilization policies during the Occupation, see Adams and Hoshii, *A Financial History of the New Japan*:53–56; and G. Allen, *Japan's Economic Recovery* (New York: Oxford University Press, 1958). Also, see J. Cohen, *Japan's Postwar Economy* (Bloomington: Indiana University Press, 1958):87–91.

system of specialized banks became inoperative. The Yokohama Specie Bank, for example, was reconstituted as an ordinary commercial bank and renamed the Bank of Tokyo. The Hypothec Bank was similarly reorganized, and the Industrial Bank of Japan elected to function as a bond-issuing institution.

Save for altering appearances, these measures proved unsuccessful. The financial institutions reformed in apparent accordance with the new directives, but old relationships still prevailed among the various players. The traditional system was never destroyed, it simply went into hibernation.[18] Many traditional relationships resurfaced after the Occupation, as did the overall system of specialized financial institutions, in which each financial intermediary operated in its own well-defined product market. Designed in the aftermath of the Meiji Restoration to promote targeted and guided credit allocation—for the dual national purposes of industrial progress and a strong military—the old system could now be used to drive a single-minded policy of reconstruction. With the national consensus that economic growth was the country's most important goal, a financial relationship system could flourish.

THE JAPANESE RELATIONSHIP SYSTEM

This financial system saw Japan through the period of remarkable growth that continued during the 1950s, 1960s, and early 1970s.[19] As in the United States, however, pressures on the traditional system began to force change in the mid-1970s. For both countries, the most notable change was the shift away from relationships and toward market-determined prices in financial transactions. This similarity between Japan and the United States is surprising, given the very different antecedents of each national financial system: one highly decentralized, the other

---

18. A similar development was seen in Germany. Attempts by the Occupation forces to reshape the German economy could not destroy its long-standing relationships. For example, W. Manchester, *The Arms of Krupp 1587–1968* (New York: Bantam, 1970):736–770, relates how Alfried Krupp von Bohlen, convicted at the Nuremberg trials, organized his business interests from prison.

19. For accounts of the postwar, traditional-phase Japanese financial system, see Adams and Hoshii, *A Financial History of the New Japan*; Bank of Japan, *Money and Banking in Japan*; H. Patrick, *Monetary Policy and Central Banking in Japan* (Bombay: University of Bombay, 1962); H. Wallich and M. Wallich, "Banking and Finance," in H. Patrick and H. Rosovsky, eds., *Asia's New Giant: How the Japanese Economy Works* (Washington, DC: The Brookings Institution, 1976):249–315; G. Ackley and H. Ishi, "Fiscal, Monetary and Related Policies," ibid.:153–247; and W. Monroe, *Japan: Financial Markets and the World Economy* (New York: Praeger, 1973).

centralized; one highly legalistic, the other dependent on informal power relationships; one the outcome of more than two centuries of experimentation, the other assembled in less than two decades. But, on the other hand, the similarities must be understood as the outcome of the same fundamental forces already described in earlier chapters. These forces affected both systems. To see how this happened, I first concentrate on the nature of relationships in Japan and then describe their erosion during the 1970s. I explain how the breakdown in local relationships in domestic finance was hastened during the 1980s by the increasing irrelevance of national boundaries, a change already described in connection with U.S. developments in Chapters 2 and 3. For Japan, the international capital flows created the need to place large accumulations of funds abroad. It was increasingly drawn to international markets, and as a result it began to lose its individual distinctiveness. Still, it will be seen that these international pressures were second in importance to the domestic pressures that arose in Japan in the mid-1970s.

To understand the changes in traditional relationships in Japan over the past decade and a half, one must first briefly review the system as it operated during the first two decades after World War II—Japan's high-growth phase. As the system of specialized financial institutions resurfaced in the wake of the Occupation, separation by maturity and purpose of finance were reestablished.[20] Also, powerful industrial groups—not always identical to the old zaibatsu but highly reminiscent of them—reappeared. In this uniquely Japanese arrangement, one particular bank (of the 13 city banks[21]) might maintain close relationships with a group of industrial firms that often held significant cross-equity ownership among themselves.[22] Before exploring the methods by which the dependencies and power balances that led to relationships among these institutions were enforced, I will briefly describe some of the major players in the Japanese financial markets during the postwar years.[23] (See Table 4.1.) Readers already familiar with the financial institutions in Japan may prefer to turn immediately to page 123.

---

20. For a review of the principal fields in which different types of Japanese financial institutions operated until the mid-1970s, see Wallich and Wallich, "Banking and Finance," in Patrick and Rosovsky, *Asia's New Giant*:278–284; and Bank of Japan, *Money and Banking in Japan*:142–145, 148–318. On the flow of funds during the postwar traditional phase, see ibid.:104–115.

21. Including the Bank of Tokyo.

22. Until 1977, banks could have up to 10% (1953 Anti-Monopoly Act) equity ownership. Since then this share has been reduced to 5%, effective as of 1987.

23. For an excellent treatment, see Y. Suzuki, ed., *The Japanese Financial System* (Oxford: Oxford University Press, 1987).

TABLE 4.1
Selected Japanese Financial Institutions

The Bank of Japan

Banks
  City banks
  Regional banks
  Trust banks
  Long-term credit banks

Foreign Banks

Financial Institutions for Small Business
  Mutal banks
  Credit cooperative associations
  Credit associations
  Labor credit associations

Financial Institutions for Agriculture, Forestry, and Fishery
  Credit federations of agricultural cooperatives
  Agricultural cooperatives
  Mutual Insurance Federation of Agricultural Cooperatives
  Credit Federations of Fishery Cooperatives
  Fishery cooperatives

Securities Finance Institutions
  Securities finance companies
  Securities companies

Insurance Companies
  Life insurance companies
  Nonlife insurance companies

Government Financial Institutions
  People's Finance Corporation
  Housing Loan Corporation
  Export Import Bank
  Japan Development Bank
  Agriculture, Forestry and Fishery Finance Corporation
  Small Business Finance Corporation
  Finance Corporation of Local Public Enterprise
  Small Business Credit Insurance Corporation
  Environmental Sanitation Business Finance Corporation
  Okinawa Development Finance Corporation
  Hokkaido Development Finance Corporation

Government
  Trust Fund Bureau
  Postal Savings System
  Postal Life Insurance System

Source: Bank of Japan, *The Japanese Financial System* (Tokyo: Bank of Japan, 1978), p. 7.

THE CITY BANKS

Commanding a central place in Japanese finance were the 13 city banks. They kept the loyalty of powerful industrial groups by a unique understanding of their clients and by their ability to provide funds to members of the group on terms that did not necessarily reflect each company's constant performance.[24] City banks' relationships with client companies were often reinforced through equity holdings in the companies, although a legal limit to such investments existed. Apart from being financiers, these banks were often close counselors of their clients, and they orchestrated rescue efforts if any of "their" companies got into difficulty. Moreover, retired bank officials frequently moved to the companies, thus cementing relationships between city banks and their clients. An intricate network of permanent channels existed to foster understanding and a free flow of information.

Four of the 13 city banks (Sumitomo, Mitsui, Mitsubishi, and Fuji) carried forward zaibatsu, the earliest dating from the sixteenth century.[25] Six other city banks represented the outcome of later amalgamations; these banks created new groups, with participants that were typically less well known than those in the more traditional groups. Excluding the Bank of Tokyo, the remaining two city banks were forced to adopt an ordinary bank charter by the Occupation; they did not return to their original specialized status.[26]

---

24. In general, the value of long-term relationships in banking as a means of reducing information cost is well understood. However, the Japanese system seems to have taken this notion much further. Students of the system have claimed that members of the industrial groups were awarded profitable business opportunities within the groups. See the discussion of the transfer pricing issue in the context of industrial organization literature in R. Caves and M. Uekusa, "Industrial Organization," in Patrick and Rosovsky, eds., *Asia's New Giant: How the Japanese Economy Works*:459–523. For a recent econometric study of a similar effect, see T. Hoshi, A. Kashyap, and D. Scharfstein, "Corporate Structure, Liquidity and Investment: Evidence from Japanese Panel Data," Working Paper No. 2071-88 (Cambridge, MA: MIT, 1988). These authors test a model whereby the relationship structure (captured in an imperfect information setting) allows members of the groups with bank access to invest more favorably as the system reduces information asymmetries.

25. The number of city banks has remained at thirteen since 1973, though the total fluctuated somewhat in the earlier postwar years. See Bank of Japan, *Economic Statistics Annual, 1983* (Tokyo: Bank of Japan, 1984):55. In 1978, the number of city bank offices was about 2,700, with an average of 210 offices per bank. See Federation of Bankers Associations of Japan, *Banking System in Japan*:30.

26. See S. Bronte, *Japanese Finance: Markets and Institutions* (London: Euromoney Publications, 1982):13–14.

TABLE 4.2
Selected City Bank Liabilities
(¥ trillion and as a percentage of total assets)

Year	Deposits		CDs		Bank Debentures		Call Money		BOJ Loans	
1950	619	55.5%	—		—		2	0.2%	95	8.5%
1955	2,407	75.3%	—		0	0.0%	75	2.3%	29	0.9%
1960	5,580	73.0%	—		0	0.0%	238	3.1%	435	5.7%
1965	12,499	66.3%	—		45	0.2%	926	4.9%	1,136	6.0%
1970	24,298	65.9%	—		126	0.3%	2,044	5.5%	2,124	5.8%
1975	52,875	65.4%	—		738	0.9%	2,366	2.9%	1,468	1.8%
1980	85,418	69.5%	106	0.1%	1,395	1.1%	4,549	3.7%	1,796	1.5%
1985	114,814	59.2%	489	0.3%	2,599	1.3%	6,835	3.5%	3,121	1.6%
1986	137,542	62.4%	610	0.3%	3,192	1.4%	11,012	5.0%	5,181	2.4%
1987	158,699	63.2%	637	0.3%	3,536	1.4%	12,384	4.9%	5,156	2.1%
1988	172,816	61.3%	951	0.3%	4,147	1.5%	12,415	4.4%	5,456	1.9%

Source: Bank of Japan, *Economic Statistics Annual* (1989), pp. 50–51.

Because legislation prohibited funding through long (three-year) debentures, the city banks obtained most of their funds through deposits and the call money market. Especially during the period of rapid economic growth in the years before the oil shock of 1973, loans from the Bank of Japan were used in funding the loans made by the city banks. (See Table 4.2.) I return later to this system, which became known as "overlending." Here it is useful to note that overlending represented another example of the careful balances and dependencies already mentioned.

In Japan, city banks played a powerful role. Their offices in large population centers allowed them to enter retail markets, and as I have noted, former bank officials frequently held key management positions with clients. With these advantages, neither loan rates nor deposit rates represented competitive weapons for the city banks (as shown below). Instead, long-lasting relationships provided the real advantage. Table 4.3 shows an extreme example of the strong identification of banks and corporations with each other. In order to gather deposits in an environment that lacked competitive pricing, banks fostered relationships through ease of access, service, and gifts (not unlike the free toasters given out by U.S. banks).[27] They all became standard tools in city bank business—but under terms defined by strict cooperative agreement among the banks themselves.

27. See, for example, Suzuki, *Money and Banking in Contemporary Japan*:56.

TABLE 4.3
Financial Services Firms of "Reconstituted" Zaibatsu

Mitsubishi Group

Banking	Mitsubishi Bank	#4 city bank
	Mitsubishi Trust	#1 trust bank
	Nippon Trust	#7 trust bank
	Hachijuni Bank	leading regional bank
	Shinwa Bank	small regional bank
Insurance	Tokyo Marine & Fire	#1 non-life co.
	Meiji Mutual Life	#4 life insurer
	Nisshin Fire & Marine	middling non-life co.
Leasing	Diamond Lease	middling leasing co.
Consumer Finance	Diamond Credit	middling consumer credit co.
Securities	Nikko Securities	#3 securities co.
	Ryoko Securities	middling securities co.
Property	Mitsubishi Estate	#2 property developer

Mitsui Group

Banking	Mitsui Bank	#7 city bank
	Mitsui Trust	#3 trust bank
Insurance	Taisho Marine & Fire	#3 non-life co.
	Mitsui Mutual Life	leading life insurer
Leasing	Mitsui Leasing & Development	small leasing co.
Property	Mitsui Real Estate Development	#1 property developer

Sumitomo Group

Banking	Sumitomo Bank	#2 city bank
	Sumitomo Trust	#2 trust bank
	Kansai Bank	middling ex-mutual bank
	Mie Bank	small regional bank
Insurance	Sumitomo Marine & Fire	#4 non-life co.
	Sumitomo Life	#3 life insurer
Leasing	Sumisho Lease	small leasing co.
	SB General Leasing	middling leasing co.
Securities	Daiwa Securities	#2 securities co.
	Meiko Securities	middling securities co.
Property	Sumitomo Realty & Development	#3 property developer

Fuyo Group

Banking	Fuji Bank	#3 city bank
	Yasuda Trust	#4 trust bank
	Chiba Kogyo Bank	middling regional bank
	Ogaki Kyontsu Bank	middling regional bank
	Shikoku Bank	leading regional bank
	Higo Bank	medium-sized regional bank
	Higo Family Bank	middling ex-mutual bank
Insurance	Yasuda Fire & Marine	#2 non-life co.
	Yasuda Mutual Life	leading life insurer
	Nichido Fire & Marine	middling non-life co.
Leasing	Fuyo General Lease	small leasing co.
	Fuyo General Development	middling leasing co.
Securities	Yamaichi Securities	#4 securities co.
	Daito Securities	middling securities co.
Property	Tokyo Tatemono	leading property developer

Source: The Economist, March 25, 1989, p. 92.

Thus, relationships played a central role in the intermediated funds market. In the market for directly placed funds (debt and equity), however, the role of the city banks was restricted; like the commercial banks in the United States, city (and other) Japanese banks could not enter into securities distribution or underwriting.

THE POSTAL SAVINGS SYSTEM

In modern Japan, the network of city banks branches is dwarfed by 22,000 postal offices, which also gather retail funds. Instituted as early as 1874, the postal system grew remarkably; a century after its inception, it held more than ¥19 trillion in personal savings accounts.[28] By 1988, the total stood at over ¥120 trillion, compared to ¥173 trillion of deposit accounts at city banks, and ¥121 trillion at regional banks. Funds gathered by means of this system were placed through the Trust Fund Bureau of the Ministry of Finance (which had to put funds in local or central government investments), through government-affiliated organizations, and through a few other specially designated borrowers. Other intermediaries, such as the Post Office Life Insurance and the Postal Annuity Special Account, absorbed additional savings.

THE LONG-TERM CREDIT BANKS

Funded through one-year discount debentures and five-year ordinary debentures, the long-term credit banks (Industrial Bank of Japan, Long-Term Credit Bank, and the Nippon Credit Bank) specialized in longer-term finance. Since 1952, these banks operated under the Long-Term Credit Bank Law. Although in theory it is possible for a financial institution to fund long and finance short (or vice versa), such business policies carry interest rate risks (as the U.S. S&L industry discovered in the early 1980s). Simplifying somewhat, it is fair to state that in Japan long-term suppliers of funds were allowed to issue debentures; while suppliers of short-term financing, unable to issue long-term debt instruments, were forced to rely on deposits as their primary funding source. (Compare Tables 4.2 and 4.4.)

28. In 1974, this compared to ¥46 trillion in deposit accounts at city banks and ¥29 trillion at regional banks. See Bank of Japan, *Economic Statistics Annual, 1988* (Tokyo: Bank of Japan, 1989):49–56, 99. The postal savings system was popular because the tax structure often made the returns on these deposits somewhat more attractive than on comparable bank deposits, and because deposits could be, in effect, made anonymously. There were limits on the amount that an individual investor could place in the postal system, but the system was nevertheless extensively used.

TABLE 4.4

Selected Long-Term Credit Bank Liabilities

(¥ billion and as a percentage of total assets)

Year	Deposits		CDs		Bank Debentures		Call Money		BOJ Loans	
1950	95	44.8%	—		49	23.1%	0	0.0%	15	7.1%
1955	47	12.3%	—		285	74.6%	1	0.3%	0	0.0%
1960	87	7.6%	—		880	76.5%	8	0.7%	8	0.7%
1965	242	8.1%	—		2,262	75.6%	1	0.0%	27	0.9%
1970	809	12.4%	—		4,640	70.9%	—	0.0%	49	0.7%
1975	2,745	16.3%	—		11,033	65.6%	40	0.2%	53	0.3%
1980	3,434	12.8%	196	0.7%	18,213	67.8%	150	0.6%	1	0.0%
1985	5,646	12.6%	578	1.3%	28,855	64.4%	1,866	4.2%	281	0.6%
1986	5,337	10.9%	741	1.5%	32,779	67.1%	2,009	4.1%	352	0.7%
1987	6,644	11.8%	1,529	2.7%	34,637	61.7%	1,403	2.5%	449	0.8%
1988	6,782	11.4%	2,607	4.4%	37,303	62.9%	1,660	2.8%	534	0.9%

Source: Bank of Japan, *Economic Statistics Annual* (1989), pp. 60–61.

Though designed to define a distinction in maturity of liabilities *and* assets, the Long-Term Credit Bank Law referred only to a funding differential between the long-term and ordinary banks. During a period of a stable, upward-sloping yield curve, city banks could have engaged in long-term lending as well, either by rolling over their short-term loans or by stretching their maturities. Given an upward-sloping yield curve, such maturity transformation would not only have been profitable, but would have fallen in line with banking policies in many other countries, especially during the 1950s and 1960s.

In Japan, however, during the postwar reconstruction years, with great demand for funding from the corporate sector, it was expected that the differences in funding strategies between the long-term credit banks and city banks would lead to a "natural" distribution in lending. With city banks facing more loan applications than they could fund, the longer end of the maturity spectrum was left to the long-term credit banks. These banks were restricted in terms of the types of projects to which they could apply funds; they were kept from encroaching on the turf of the city banks.[29] Securities transactions were restricted for the

29. Typical lending opportunities for the long-term credit banks in the postwar years were electric power, steel, chemicals, and so forth. "The main function of the long-term credit banks is to provide long-term funds to industry. Until the 1970s, the three long-term credit banks channeled loans into industries whose development the government considered essential for the Japanese economy." See Bronte, *Japanese Finance: Markets and Institutions*:31.

long-term credit banks as well, in order to preserve the domain of the securities houses.

TRUST BANKS

Originally formed under the Trust Law and the Trust Business Law in 1922, trust banks also provided long-term financing.[30] Today's trust banks are the outcome of various alterations in the trust banking system, which took place during the period of inflation following World War II and the separation of the banking and the securities business in 1948.

Boundaries between trust banks and ordinary banks were blurred under the 1945 Concurrent Operations Law, but in the mid-1950s, authorities reverted to a policy of stricter segmentation. City banks that had entered the trust business were called upon to divest their trust departments, while trust banks had to choose between a principal focus of ordinary or trust banking. Typical of the Japanese system, the renewed segmentation was achieved through "administrative guidance"; it did not have official force as law, and Daiwa Bank successfully resisted such administrative pressure.[31]

The trust banks that operated after the exit of the city banks were allowed to enter into both trust and ordinary banking business, provided they strictly separated their banking and trust business accounts, which had to operate from separate offices. Furthermore, it was expected that trust activities would constitute the main business focus of these banks. For these trust activities, the banks were accorded the status of long-term credit institutions, and they relied primarily on negotiable trust loan certificates for raising funds, and on deposit accounts for their banking activities.

REGIONAL BANKS

Local banks and mutual savings and loans banks operated similarly to city banks. They gathered deposit funds and provided business loans, and they were not allowed to issue bank debentures. One major distinc-

30. Earlier trust business derived from the Mortgage Debentures Trust Law, 1905.

31. The successful opposition by Daiwa shows how difficult it is to generalize about the Japanese financial system. Although the hierarchical structure of the system is generally accepted, exceptions can be found. Carefully balanced relationships of power existed, though often not formally determined, and the stability of the system in the postwar years reflected both the hierarchical nature of the system and the willingness of the players to participate.

tion between local and city banks could be found in the size of their borrowers: local banks typically provided financing to medium- and small-sized companies, rather than to the largest industrial corporations.[32] Their funding usually reflected a higher proportion of retail deposits, and local banks often supplied additional funding to city banks, which, especially during the period of rapid industrialization and growth, were net borrowers in the call market.

Japan's mutual savings and loan banks derived from the Mutual Loans and Savings Banks Law of 1951. Like the local banks, these banks specialized in lending to small- and medium-sized institutions, typically long term. They relied on deposit accounts from individuals for funding. The mutual installment loan, unique to these institutions, allowed for long-term loans to be repaid in installments.

Other specialized financial institutions that targeted specific product areas include rural banking organizations (that concentrate on agriculture, fishing, or forestry) and credit associations and cooperatives. Founded under the Law for Small Business of 1949, credit associations and cooperatives typically deal with the small-loans business, relying on various types of deposit funding.[33] The rural financial organizations, mostly cooperatives, are particularly important in supplying seasonal funding for the agricultural sector. In addition to private institutions that supply financing for rural business, several specialized government institutions operate (e.g., the Agriculture, Forestry and Fishery Finance Corporation).

FOREIGN EXCHANGE BANKS

The Yokohama Specie Bank, transformed by the Occupation into an ordinary bank and renamed the Bank of Tokyo, was redesignated a special foreign exchange bank in 1954, after the passage of the Foreign Exchange Bank Law.[34] Although other banks obtained licenses for foreign exchange dealings, and although the Bank of Tokyo was also con-

32. As Bronte points out in *Japanese Finance: Markets and Institutions*:51–66, some of the largest local banks, particularly those closest to Tokyo, are as big as the smaller city banks, blurring the distinction between the two types of institutions.

33. Many officially sponsored institutions exist for aiding Japanese small business. See Bank of Japan, *Money and Banking in Japan*:239–279.

34. A host of regulations limited international currencies transactions, and it was not until 1952 that banks licensed to deal in foreign exchange were allowed to hold open positions. Even later, frequent direct control was exercised by the Bank of Japan, and market intervention was standard. See, for example, an account of the events of August 1971 in Monroe, *Japan: Financial Markets and the World Economy*:18–34.

sidered a city bank, it nevertheless remained distinct. Its specialization in international financial transactions kept it from establishing a domestic branch network but allowed it to build an international network instead. Lacking local domestic branches from which to gather deposits, the Bank of Tokyo was—in contrast to other city banks—allowed to issue long-term debentures.

SECURITIES HOUSES

In Japan, as in the United States, the securities and the banking businesses have been separated. Article 65 of the Securities and Exchange Law (1948) originally effected this separation under the Occupation, and it remained in force when the Occupation came to an end.[35] Note how the decision to retain the segmentation of the system under Article 65 complements the *return* to segmentation and specialization in those sectors where the Occupation tried to change the system in the opposite direction.

After the Occupation and a period of stock market gains (1955–1960), the importance of securities firms increased. Sluggish market performance in the ensuing years and a veritable crisis in 1964 brought about industry restructuring—a consolidation movement not unlike the consolidation in the banking industry before World War II. Mergers were the preferred way of dealing with the crisis, but some of the larger houses obtained large loans (e.g., Yamaichi borrowed from the Bank of Japan).[36]

Although more than two hundred companies are now licensed to engage in the securities business, the industry is dominated by four firms—Nomura, Nikko, Daiwa, and Yamaichi. These powerful securities firms played a very visible role during the late 1980s because of the burgeoning public securities markets. This contrasts with the influence they had in earlier times, when they were mostly active as brokers for a few publicly listed bonds and a small number of shares traded in the stock market.[37]

35. Contemporary Japanese securities firms, which still derive most of their revenue from underwriting and brokerage activities, play a role different from that played by U.S. firms, which, since the mid-1970s, have derived a larger part of their revenues from advisory fees. Even when underwriting and brokerage were the main activities of U.S. firms, the strong wholesale characteristic of the U.S. institutions did not develop in Japan, where retail distribution remains important.

36. See, for example, Japan Securities Research Institute, *Securities Markets in Japan, 1986* (Tokyo: Japan Securities Research Institute, 1986):1–8.

37. Japanese stock exchanges had been authorized since 1874 and actually opened in Tokyo and Osaka in 1878.

THE MINISTRY OF FINANCE AND THE BANK OF JAPAN

Of all the financial institutions that operate in Japan, the Ministry of Finance and the Bank of Japan stand out as unquestionably the most important.[38] Positioned at the top of the hierarchical system, they exercise both formal and informal control over a wide array of financial decisions. In terms of authority, the MOF ranks formally above the bank.[39] The Bank of Japan Law (1942) provides the MOF with legal powers to steer the bank (which has the usual powers of a central bank), but in reality, the relationship between the two institutions is one of consultation and coordination.[40]

The Bank of Japan is banker to the government, lender of last resort to the commercial banking sector, and Japan's monetary policy authority. A Policy Committee, founded in 1949 at the urging of the Occupation powers, was retained after the Occupation and remains the supreme policymaking body within the bank.[41]

As noted earlier, the BOJ engages in both formal and informal oversight of the banking sector. Interest rate policies are effected through discount rate policies and, only recently, through open market operations.[42] Bank influence extends beyond the use of these powers, as in the exercise of guidance in the lending decisions of the commercial

38. On the bank's overall organization, see Bank of Japan, *The Bank of Japan: Its Organization and Monetary Policies* (Tokyo: Bank of Japan, 1973).
39. Although the Bank of Japan jealously guards its independence, the Ministry of Finance can give it administrative orders. But balances exist as well. For example, the MOF determines the maximum note issuance, while the bank determines how much to actually issue within the established limits. Similarly, the MOF appoints a supervisory comptroller of the Bank of Japan.
40. Though similar in function to the other central banks, the Bank of Japan is not wholly owned by the government; 45% of BOJ shares are held by the public at a fixed dividend of 5%. See Suzuki, *The Japanese Financial System*:313.
41. Its membership includes: the governor, representatives of the MOF and the Economic Planning Agency, and four specialists from the fields of finance, industry, commerce, and agriculture.
42. For a more detailed discussion of Japanese monetary policy and tools, see Suzuki, *Money and Banking in Contemporary Japan*:149–224. Patrick, *Monetary Policy and Central Banking in Contemporary Japan*:90–107, notes that open market operations were not used in Japan. Given the lack of major debt issues and the avoidance of a free market structure for interest rates, this was not surprising. In 1962, the BOJ introduced a "New Scheme for Monetary Control," in which it attempted to introduce instruments that would allow for open market operations, but its efforts were frustrated by the Ministry of Finance. It was to be more than a decade before a bill discount was finally established. See Bronte, *Japanese Finance: Markets and Institutions*:144, 205–218.

banks—a tool used frequently to exploit the dependencies in the system, as I explain below.[43]

The MOF exerts perhaps even more influence over financial affairs than does the Bank of Japan. It is the most prestigious of all Japanese bureaucracies, and it attracts the most highly regarded candidates for its job openings (typically students from the law department of the University of Tokyo). The MOF is divided into various bureaus, run by career bureaucrats acknowledged to be experts in their field, who stand in close formal and informal contact with the major players in the Japanese economy. All top bureaucrats report to a politically appointed minister. The various bureaus of MOF (Budget, Tax, Banking, Finance, Securities, International Finance, and Customs and Tariffs) rarely rely on their ample formal powers, preferring instead to issue informal directives and guidance. These statements carry enormous weight.

Thus, the Japanese financial system is heavily influenced by the desires and intentions of two top bureaucracies, not always in perfect agreement but working in close consultation with one another.

SPECIALIZATION AND MARKET SEGMENTATION

From the preceding, it should be clear that the Japanese system has been characterized by product market segmentation.[44] This segmentation is no accident, nor is it the result of long-term historical evolution. The skeleton of the system was assembled in less than two decades, in accordance with the Meiji reformers' clear objectives: economic growth and modernization. The system used guided fund allocation to facilitate industrialization. But after half a century of operation, it was seemingly

---

43. "Moral suasion" is the term used to describe the effects on bank behavior of signals given by the money authority to indicate displeasure with the current behavior of the financial institutions. The signals used in moral suasion do not rely on actual policy actions, but instead on the persuasive abilities of the authorities. *Madoguchi kisei* (window guidance) is the practice whereby the Bank of Japan seeks to ration credit through the amounts individual banks may lend to customers. On the subject of window guidance and moral suasion, see Bank of Japan, *Money and Banking in Japan*:158–159; Suzuki, *Money and Banking in Contemporary Japan*:166–181; Patrick, *Monetary Policy and Central Banking in Contemporary Japan*:161–166; and Bronte, *Japanese Finance: Markets and Institutions*:145–146.

44. Several observers have argued that within the segmented product areas, there was lively competition among the various institutions. See, for example, E. Sakakibara, R. Feldman, and Y. Harada, *The Japanese Financial System in Comparative Perspective* (Washington, DC: U.S. Government Printing Office, 1982):24–38; and Suzuki, *Money and Banking in Contemporary Japan*:56.

destroyed by the Occupation.[45] As soon as the Occupation powers departed, however, the system reappeared with many of its old features intact; some specialized market franchises were actually enhanced by selective retention of Occupation reforms such as Article 65.

Specialization of financial institutions was never unique to Japan. What was unusual about Japan was the hierarchical and centralized nature of the entire system; in particular, the great power of the Ministry of Finance and the Bank of Japan. Equally important was the way in which formal dependencies were generously reinforced through informal structures, such as the system that parachuted executives from higher ranks into positions of power at lower levels.[46] Thus, bureaucrats from the MOF or the BOJ often found more profitable employment with private financial institutions in later stages of their careers. The banks themselves, in turn, often parachuted executives to subsidiary corporations or to companies that relied on banks for their financing.

Similarly, frequent informal meetings between bureaucrats and bankers were standard. Quarterly "discussions" (if not reviews) of lending decisions not only assured input from the authorities but must also have, in effect, carried implicit guarantees on these lending decisions.[47] Most important, the interdependencies and balances in the segmented system were reinforced by careful control of the prices of the various financial products. Specialized financial institutions, operating in well-defined product markets and often bound to their clients by relationships of long standing, limited financing alternatives for the various corporations. In addition, a lack of price differentiation among products reduced the incentive for participants to break these relationships.

The importance of long-term relationships in Japanese financial transactions has plenty of parallels. In every country, financial affairs tend, by their very nature, to be sensitive and confidential. As I noted already in Chapter 3, they are based on intangible factors such as confidence, character, and the willingness of borrowers to share sensitive information with the suppliers of their funds. For lenders that know just how fragile the claim to repayment is, special relationships are equally valuable. Japan used a highly centralized system to foster repeated transactions between specialized financial institutions and their customers. For such a system to operate, it was necessary to minimize the incentives

---

45. See Allen, *A Short Economic History of Modern Japan*:189, 204.

46. The Japanese term *amakudari*, which describes this system, is sometimes translated as "Descent from Heaven." It indicates the esteem in which the bureaucracies are held.

47. The frequent informal meetings are not unique to banks and their customers. In Japan, meetings between competitors under an industry umbrella are not unusual.

for lenders or borrowers to break out of the relationship system. By allowing powerful borrowers access to funds through city and long-term credit banks, and by assuring the funding base of these banks, the institutional prerequisites for the system were put in place. Strict price regulation completed the job.

PRICE REGULATION

In Japan even today, price regulation of financial instruments remains extremely strict. It is perhaps ironic that a "Temporary Interest Rate Adjustment Law" instituted in 1947 still stands at the center of the price structure for funds.[48] The discussion that follows concentrates on price regulation during the years before the mid-1970s, when the system began to undergo significant change. During that period, the freedom to conduct financial transactions was restricted by the specialized nature of financial intermediaries, each of which operated in its own domain. The freedom to conclude financial transactions at negotiated prices was virtually nonexistent.[49]

Price regulation in the Japanese financial system was broad and deep. Formally, almost all interest rates moved tightly together along linkages established by the Temporary Interest Rate Adjustment Law.[50] Furthermore, the authorities had controlling influence over several financial intermediaries (e.g., the postal savings system) and could exercise informal influence over most others.[51] Examples abound: price regulation

48. Explanations of the 1947 law, also translated as the Temporary Money Rates Adjustment Law, may be found in Adams and Hoshii, *A Financial History of the New Japan*:131–145; and Bank of Japan, *Money and Banking in Japan*:116–131. Although the official discount rate and bank interest rates were first linked directly in May 1957, the discount rate and the various bank rates were "coordinated" during the previous decade. See Adams and Hoshii, *A Financial History of the New Japan*:131–132.

49. As in many other countries, bankers in Japan required borrowers to hold compensating balances. Although such balances can allow for an effective interest rate in excess of the posted rate, there is no evidence that they were used as a price-competitive weapon.

50. On the control and structure of Japanese interest rates, see, for example, Adams and Hoshii, *A Financial History of the New Japan*:131–146; and Suzuki, *Money and Banking in Contemporary Japan*:37–61. Bronte notes: "For many years the short-term prime rate was determined by a cartel of the city banks. Since 1969, that rate was always pegged at 1/4 percent over the Bank of Japan's official discount rate." In *Japanese Finance: Markets and Institutions*:16.

51. Interest rates on postal savings system deposits are set by the Cabinet on the recommendation of the Postal Committee. Occasionally, difficulties have occurred in assuring compatibility between the postal rates and other deposit rates reflected in the decisions of the MOF and BOJ. Such issues have typically been resolved through negotiation.

controlled the rates city banks could pay for their deposits, and they were also restricted from offering deposit accounts of longer maturity. For the long-term credit banks, rates were determined by the Ministry of Finance, the Bank of Japan, and the banks, acting in close consultation. The rates that trust banks could offer on savings instruments were regulated, as were the rates that local and mutual savings banks could set in their funds-gathering.

A similar lack of rate freedom prevailed in lending. Both city and long-term credit banks consulted over lending rates; in effect, the banks cartelized them. Between 1955 and 1975, the Federation of Bankers Associations of Japan was instrumental in setting the cartelized structure. (During the early 1970s, it was set at 25 basis points over the BOJ's discount rate.) When in 1975 concerns about the Anti-Monopoly Law forced a discontinuation of this practice, the cartel lived on under a new mechanism whereby a single bank—typically the one that chaired the association—signalled the new rates.[52] The rate charged by the long-term banks not only reflected the official discount rate; in combination with the banks' funding costs it also assured the profitability of the banks through spread banking. Overall, prices of financial instruments were not the result of competitive market forces, but rather of set relationships with centrally determined rates.

Foreign observers and admirers of Japan's rapid economic growth have often argued that the financial system allowed for regulated, low interest rates, which gave Japan a capital cost advantage that led, in turn, to economic growth and export success.[53] There can be little doubt that the authorities controlled *many*, and severely influenced *all*, interest rates, and that these rates did not necessarily reflect market conditions. Yet it is wrong to imply that rates were regulated to low levels that gave special stimulus to *overall* investment activity in the private sector.

No authority can regulate rates downward and affect the overall level of investments without other measures to support that policy. In the Japanese example, if the rates set by the authorities and those the city banks charged their industrial customers had been too low (i.e., below

---

52. See Bronte, *Japanese Finance: Markets and Institutions*:16–17; and Federation of Bankers Associations, *Banking System in Japan, 1984*:90–91.

53. Assuming that an interest rate policy was used to stimulate targeted investments, a simple Keynesian multiplier model can be used to explain (at least partially) the spectacular Japanese growth performance in the postwar period. On the argument that the low interest rate policy was designed to encourage investment, see Suzuki, *Money and Banking in Contemporary Japan*:37–61; Goldsmith, *The Financial Development of Japan*:155; and C. Pigott, "Financial Reform in Japan," *The Federal Reserve Bank of San Francisco's Economic Review* (1983):25–44, esp. 26.

free market rates), other borrowers of equal quality would, by definition, have wanted to borrow as well. Capital rationing at the regulated interest rates was thus a necessity, especially since Japan had strict controls on international financial transactions, which closed escape routes for those not awarded favorable treatment at home. As a result, interest rates were low for favored industries, but not for those industries excluded from the preferential prices.

The role of Japan's financial structure in supporting its spectacular national development was therefore not simply to create low interest rates. As I noted, the system of centralized powers, specialized financial institutions, and regulated prices reduced freedoms in financial transactions and gave rise to a network of heavy dependencies. The regulated price mechanism, which did not always reflect market conditions, allowed those at the higher end of the hierarchy to influence capital allocation decisions. Further support came from other specially designed features of the Japanese economy, as well as from cultural and historical norms. For example, regulated low deposit rates did not deter the nation's high savings rate. (See Chapter 2, Table 2.4.) In addition, several observers have noted that a variety of tax incentives provided subsidies for savings, so that a large national savings pool accumulated to fund the investments required for growth.[54]

While these characteristics encouraged funds-gathering in the economy, institutional arrangements contributed further to the growth environment. Lending to industry at regulated rates reflected implicit government guarantees, which were based on frequent reviews of the banks' balance sheets and on the special guidance exercised by the authorities. Similarly, a Japanese antirecession cartel law had the effect of smoothing cash flow expectations for corporations in several cyclical industries. Such a system, under even the most standard notions of corporate finance, lowers the business risk of the enterprise, reduces the cost of capital, and allows for growth financed through debt (as I explain below). Even in the debenture market, institutional design favored well-established corporations. Since corporations could only issue fully secured obligations, outsiders were put at a significant disadvantage, and well-established corporations had better access to capital.

---

54. Note that the two ideas that have been used to help explain the high savings rate—favorable tax treatment and the unimportance of low deposit rates—are somewhat contradictory. One relies on a low price-elasticity of savings, the other on a high one. Despite the somewhat unsatisfactory nature of the proposition, cultural norms may have played the important role. Especially given Japan's natural-resource poverty, saving attained a very favorable connotation.

I have already mentioned another factor that was central to the success of the system—strict regulation on international capital movements, which closed escape routes for institutions that wanted to transact outside that system. The importance of these limitations during the Bretton Woods era was enormous. For the Japanese authorities to have devised a system of limited alternatives under strict controls would have been a futile exercise if free international capital flows had allowed corporations to seek funds in foreign capital markets.

Of course, the institutional arrangements that governed Japanese finance cannot be understood apart from the overall system. Just as in other areas of the economy, relationships, informal understandings, and dependencies played a major role.

INTERDEPENDENCIES IN THE SYSTEM

This section outlines only a few of the interdependencies endemic to the Japanese system, beginning with the relationships among the city banks, the Bank of Japan, and industrial corporations. As I have noted, the main function of the city banks was to supply short- and medium-term finance to industrial corporations. With an inactive equity market and a poorly developed public debt market, loans from "their" bankers were of essential importance to these corporations. During the rapid growth phase of the economy, the appetite for such loans was large; for any high-growth corporation, capital requirements typically exceed the level of retained earnings.[55]

With long-term credit banks dedicated to long-term funding, and mutual savings and local banks in effect proscribed from the territory of the city banks, it was up to the latter to satisfy much of the high demand for loans. Because interest rate regulations created an imbalance in the supply and demand for capital, city banks had ample opportunity to make larger loan commitments than could be fully supported by their funds-gathering activity, a situation that became known as the

---

55. As long as the retained earnings are insufficient to fully finance the investments, additional borrowings or equity issues must be made. Thus, even at the firm's sustainable growth rate—the rate at which the sales growth is equal to the growth rate of equity due to retained earnings—additional debt financing is required. See Meerschwam, "The Japanese Financial System and the Cost of Capital," in Krugman, ed., *The United States and Japan: Trade and Investment,* for a discussion of the internal and external funding needs of industrial corporations. The heavy reliance on bank loans is clearly seen in that data.

"overloan" problem.[56] This problem was solved in two ways: (1) through rationing (only those with well-established credentials and relationships had access to the preferential funds); and (2) by obtaining additional (though often only marginal) funds from the Bank of Japan (see Table 4.3). These latter funds had nothing to do with the traditional role of the central bank as lender of last resort, but reflected the willingness of the BOJ to supply additional funds. At the same time, these (marginal) funds must have enhanced the informal power of the officials in their guidance of the city banks.[57]

This system was both a result of the price regulation and product market segmentation and a reinforcement of these practices. It was a system that held rewards for all established participants: the major corporations obtained funds at the regulated rates, the banks got their profits, and bureaucrats at the top of the hierarchical system solidified their influence and control. Thus, established participants had few incentives to break the system. For those who stood outside it, the relationship system offered no advantage. For them, funds, if available at all, were expensive, since access could only be obtained through nontraditional channels.[58] But precisely because they were not powerful corporations, and because the overall system performed well, these outsiders did not pose a serious threat.

Yet another similarity can be seen between developments in Japan and the United States. The two systems were very different, but in both of them the relatively high economic growth in the 1950s and 1960s reduced incentives for financial innovators to break the system. The

56. See Wallich and Wallich, "Banking and Finance," in Patrick and Rosovsky, eds., *Asia's New Giant*:284–290; Suzuki, *Money and Banking in Contemporary Japan*:3–70; A. Koizumi, "The 'Overloan' Problem: Characteristic Feature of the Banking System in Japan," *Hitotsubashi Journal of Commerce and Management* 2(1962):53–65.

57. City banks have at times exceeded the level of loans suggested by the Bank of Japan through *fukumi kashidashi* (off-balance-sheet loans). However, it is likely that the quantity of such loans has been small. See Suzuki, *Money and Banking in Contemporary Japan*:178.

58. There are examples of successful financial innovators, sometimes placed in industries far away from finance. One example is related in M. Crum and D. Meerschwam, "From Relationship to Price Banking: The Loss of Regulatory Control," in T. McCraw, ed., *America versus Japan* (Boston: Harvard Business School Press, 1986):261–297. They show how some did try to attack the system, among them a new supermarket entrepreneur who, lacking well-established relationships, overcame obstacles to financing through repeated innovation. It was a long time before the efforts of such individuals showed real success, and only when overall change had made the system receptive to innovation did wide acceptance follow.

prosperous and stable global economy of that period helped both relationship systems to flourish. In Japan, the success of the system in generating growth became a condition for its own continuation. Loan demand remained high, corporations continued to grow, and the economy performed well in accordance with the objectives of the MOF and BOJ.

Another example of the careful balances created in the Japanese financial system during the high-growth phase can be found in government financing. With a policy of balanced budgets since the Occupation (the Dodge Line), the borrowing needs of the authorities remained low. Indeed, until 1965 no significant public debt issues took place.[59] When the authorities did make debt issues, they used a mechanism that allowed them to place the bonds without upsetting the carefully balanced system of regulated interest rates. The MOF guided the establishment of a system whereby *required* public debt absorption occurred through the financial sector. Bonds were placed at rates that were below those required by competitive private placement, yet consistent with the overall regulated interest rate structure.

One year after their absorption by banks and other financial institutions, bonds were typically resold to the Bank of Japan.[60] This method was used because the MOF was barred from placing bonds directly with the BOJ. Fears of immediate monetization and inflation were the rationale for this restriction.[61] Because of the small size of the issues and the rapid growth of the economy, this delayed monetization was not considered to be a problem. Indeed, given the growth rates of the late 1960s and early 1970s, the inflationary effects were minimal. Nor was this arrangement unfavorable for the banks. Selling the bonds back to the BOJ gave the banks the funds they needed to purchase the new issue allocated to them through the absorption mechanism. The resale process meant that few losses, and sometimes even small profits, were generated.[62]

---

59. The financial deficit of the public sector amounted to less than 2% of gross national product during the period 1956–1973. See Goldsmith, *The Financial Development of Japan, 1868–1977*:188.

60. This may be called "delayed monetization." Because the Bank of Japan buys the issues after one year and pays with new money, the money supply rises. The effects are similar to those that would have obtained had the bank bought the issues directly from the government upon the issue date. The difference is that the monetization is delayed by one year.

61. See R. Feldman, *Japanese Financial Markets: Deficits, Dilemmas and Deregulation* (Cambridge, MA: MIT Press, 1986):49–52.

62. In Chapter 5 on the U.K. system, a similar absorption mechanism is seen as the tender was covered.

Other examples of carefully balanced relationships can be found. The long-established links between the long-term credit banks and their clients meant that the banks had a thorough knowledge of their clientele. Furthermore, because the long-term credit banks had originally developed as official institutions, their relationships with the bureaucracies were strong. And because long-term finance (mostly related to long-term investments and the development of industrial power) was supplied by these banks, the role of the authorities in steering them remained great. Again, the system translated a consensus of national goals of growth and development into real actions.

It is, of course, impossible in so short a space to fully present or evaluate the complexity and richness of the Japanese financial system. Still, an overall picture clearly emerges of a highly stable system (there had been little or no exit or entry in the financial industry for a quarter of a century[63]), hierarchical in nature, with formal and informal controls exercised from above, and with long-term relationships between established partners. As with many other aspects of Japanese society, the chief impression the Japanese financial system gives—at least to outsiders—is one of balance, trade-offs, compartmentalization, and official guidance. Yet this is not to say that the system was totally bereft of freedoms, nor that it dictated the allocation of specified amounts of capital according to some all-encompassing economic plan. A more subtle set of dependencies, checks, and persuasions operated in Japan.

THE JAPANESE FINANCIAL SYSTEM AND THE COST OF CAPITAL

Did the Japanese financial system contribute to Japan's economic success? This question has been much debated, and it still generates considerable controversy. In its popular form, the debate is about the cost of capital in Japan, particularly in comparison with the United States.[64]

---

63. The restructuring of the securities industry should be noted, as should the actions taken to foster amalgamation and to allow the strongest players to survive.

64. The literature on the cost of capital controversy has grown rapidly. See, for example, A. Ando and A. Auerbach, "The Corporate Cost of Capital in Japan and the U.S.: A Comparison," Working Paper No. 1762 (Cambridge, MA: National Bureau of Economic Research, 1985); A. Ando and A. Auerbach, "The Cost of Capital in the U.S. and Japan: A Comparison," Working Paper No. 2286 (Cambridge, MA: National Bureau of Economic Research, 1987); C. Baldwin, "The Capital Factor: Competing for Capital in a Global Environment," in M. Porter, ed., *Competition in Global Industries* (Boston: Harvard Business School Press, 1986):185–223; G. Hatsopoulos, *High Cost of Capital: America's Industrial Handicap* (Waltham: Thermo-Electron Company, 1983); J. Hodder, "Capital Structure and the Cost of Capital in the U.S. and Japan" (Palo Alto: Stanford University,

Typically two types of arguments are presented: one rests on the assumption that Japanese interest rates were lower than those observed in the United States. The other, less concerned with the individual cost of debt or equity, looks at the weighted average cost of capital and notes that, since debt financing is usually cheaper than equity, traditionally higher leverage in Japan gave the firms a cost of capital advantage relative to foreign competitors.

For those who perceive a cost of capital advantage, the next step is typically to assume that "cheaper" capital allowed Japanese firms to pursue investment strategies different from those of their competitors. Given the widespread use of discounted cash flow models in making investment decisions, this argument sounds convincing. It should be clear from the description provided so far, however, that the cost of capital controversy is more complex.

As I noted already, it is not possible for authorities to regulate interest rates downward for *all* those that demand funds. If price regulation interferes with the free market mechanism, rationing has to take place. In Japan *some* firms did indeed obtain funds at the preferential rates, but others were denied that advantage. Thus, it is fallacious to suggest that the cost of capital was lower to "Japanese" firms, without being more specific about which ones. As far as the second hypothesis goes—the one that bases a cost of capital advantage on a different capital structure (less reliance on "expensive" equity)—the actual argument is more subtle.

First, institutional rigidities in effect forced high leverage. Accounts abound of the inefficiency of the equity markets as a new issues vehicle.[65] Furthermore, with a poorly developed bond market and a well-

---

Mimeo 1988); T. Luehrman and W. Kester, "Real Interest Rates and the Cost of Capital: A Comparison of the United States and Japan," *Japan and the World Economy* I (1989):279–301; I. Friend and I. Tokutsu, "The Cost of Capital to Corporations in Japan and the U.S.A.," *Journal of Banking and Finance* 11 (1987):313–327.

65. Although the equity market provided only a small share of the externally raised funds, the explanations for this phenomenon are not straightforward. Some argue that the Japanese preference for issues at par with subscription rights for existing shareholders deterred companies from going to the markets. See, for example, Wallich and Wallich, "Banking and Finance," in Patrick and Rosovsky, eds., *Asia's New Giant*:249–315. For an interpretation more related to the investor side, see Monroe, *Japan: Financial Markets and the World Economy*:124. However, finance theory has shown that such rights issues are not expensive to the firm and that they may constitute an efficient way to issue equity. A different approach suggests that Japanese executives considered dividend yield the appropriate cost of equity. With cheaper bank debt, a simple price decision was made.

established banking sector, leverage took the form of bank financing. In standard corporate finance, high leverage is equated with high risk. Not so in Japan. There, leverage was not supplied by arm's-length investors but by banks with intimate knowledge of their long-term customers. Furthermore, since bank loan portfolios were the subject of close scrutiny by financial authorities, bankers may well have viewed their lending as less risky, secured not only by their understanding (and by the assets) of their clients, but also by the authorities' implicit acceptance of their lending policies—if not for each individual loan, then surely for their overall portfolios.

Thus, during the 1960s, bank and bond financing provided approximately half the required funds. Within the externally raised funds, long- and short-term bank borrowing accounted for approximately 80% of the funding.[66] Over the same decade, leverage of Japanese manufacturing firms rose from 67% to 80%; comparable numbers for U.S. firms show an increase in leverage from 35% to 45%.[67]

The system devised further methods to support high leverage. The preferred groups with access to bank financing were not only supplied with funds at administered rates, they also knew that they could rely on assistance from the group bank and other group members in times of possible financial distress.[68] Thus, the risks of leverage were reduced by the system itself. The role of the financially supportive groups has more recently been studied in the context of investment decision making. Not surprisingly, it was found that firms with access to the preferential funding spent relatively more on investments.[69]

I have already mentioned Japan's antirecession cartel law. It was only one among many laws that sanctioned noncompetitive agreements for either targeted industries or corporations in times of trouble.[70] These exceptions to antimonopoly legislation once again facilitated high lever-

66. For a more careful breakdown of the data, see Meerschwam, "The Japanese Financial System and the Cost of Capital" in Krugman, ed., *The United States and Japan: Trade and Investment.*

67. Ibid. The definition of leverage employed here is: one minus the ratio of equity to equity plus total liabilities.

68. See, for example, S. Suzuki and R. Wright, "Financial Structure and Bankruptcy Risk in Japanese Companies," *Journal of International Business Studies* 16 (1985):75–110. Also see J. Abegglen and G. Stalk, *Kaisha, the Japanese Corporation* (New York: Basic Books, 1985):166–167.

69. See T. Hoshi, A. Kashyap, and D. Scharfstein, "Corporate Structure, Liquidity and Investment: Evidence from Japanese Panel Data" (Cambridge, MA: MIT Working Paper No. 2071-88, 1988).

70. See Caves and Uekusa, "Industrial Organization," in Patrick and Rosovsky, eds., *Asia's New Giant*:487, Table 7-4.

age among corporations. Cartel agreements reduced the fear of revenue volatility, making higher debt levels more supportable.

In short, those with access to funds were able to build leverage without having to pay the full price, since some of the risks associated with high leverage were absorbed by the system. Furthermore, the rationed capital system that awarded preferential access to those with well-established relationships may have been an effective method of dealing with the standard information and agency problems that plague most financial transactions.

Finally, the capital allocation system may have diverted investment decisions made by Japanese managers from the orthodox shareholder value-maximization paradigm. In contrast to U.S. banks, Japanese banks often own shares in the company to which they lend. Hence borrowing policies that benefit the bank to the detriment of the remaining shareholders may be seen.[71] This relates to the observation that Japanese managers, much more frequently than their U.S. counterparts, consider market share and market share growth to be the principal corporate objective. And although it seems contrary to the standard shareholder value-maximization model, Japan's institutional mechanism may have made the market share goal economically efficient: within the context of the rationed capital market, there are many examples in Japan of the license to produce future capacity being dependent on past growth. In a self-perpetuating cycle, growth became the access ticket to the preferential financing that sustained it.[72] In short, concentrating on the cost of capital in the sense of the prices of equity and debt finance is simplistic; it is more useful to concentrate on the contribution of Japan's system of rationed capital.

The financial system resurrected after the Occupation served Japan well. But its carefully designed balances and dependencies would make future shocks difficult to absorb, especially when they were generated outside the national economy. Such shocks became a dominant feature of the mid-1970s, as indicated in Chapters 1 and 2. As in the United States, they helped bring about the erosion of regulatory power and the transition away from the dominance of relationships. Again, just as in the United States, price-oriented financial transactions began to play a much more important role.

71. See M. Aoki, "Shareholders' Non-Unanimity on Investment Financing: Banks vs. Individual Investors," in M. Aoki, ed., *The Economic Analysis of the Japanese Firm* (New York: North Holland, 1984):193–226.

72. For an example from the steel industry, see T. McCraw and P. O'Brien, "Production and Distribution: Competition Policy and Industry Structure," in McCraw, ed., *America versus Japan*:77–116.

RUPTURING THE RELATIONSHIP SYSTEM

The Japanese financial system was fundamentally changed by macroeconomic forces during the 1970s and 1980s. Foremost among these was the oil shock of the mid-1970s, which effectively put an end to a period of very high growth. With it came a new need to fund large government budget deficits through public debt issues, as the authorities tried to fight the domestic recession that followed the oil shock. Again, there is a parallel with events in the United States. Macroeconomic policies in the mid-1970s were fully targeted to deal with the domestic economy, even as Japan's external sector worsened. But funding the current account deficits abroad increased interactions with foreign financial markets. Such markets—for example, the rapidly developing Euromarkets—afforded the kind of funding alternatives that Japan's old system had so carefully sought to limit; as Japan's current account swiftly (but temporarily) moved into deficit, the authorities reluctantly allowed firms to avail themselves of the new foreign freedoms. These new freedoms then increased pressures on Japan's regulated financial environment.[73] Admittedly, the freedoms were at first minor and given only to few corporations. But in the early 1980s they expanded. At this time the increasing success of the export sector not only reversed the current account deficit, but actually caused large capital account deficits to place the export earnings overseas. This further eroded the already weakened relationship system by introducing a large number of industrial corporations and financial intermediaries to the foreign markets, where they observed products, techniques, and prices very different from those characteristic of the traditional Japanese financial environment.

But, contrary to popular belief, increased *foreign* pressures in reaction to Japanese capital account deficits and current account surpluses in the 1980s were not responsible for the reform and liberalization of the domestic Japanese market. *Domestic* pressures caused by the oil shock shattered fundamental relationships and dependencies and put the system on a trajectory toward price banking. Foreign pressures were consistent with this transition; they did not cause it.

It should be clear from Chapter 2 that the rapid rise in oil prices in the mid–1970s had different effects in different parts of the world econ-

---

73. The Ministry of Finance has imposed significant restrictions on the ability of corporations to raise funds outside Japan. For example, it was not until 1975 that the first Japanese industrial firm had access to the convertible bond market in Europe. For an interesting description of the obstacles (and their remedies), see Nomura School of Advanced Management, "Ito-Yokado, LTD." (Abridged) #2-289-044. Boston: Harvard Business School, 1981.

CHART 4.1
Annual Growth Rates
1961–1980
Real GNP, Exports ($), and Imports ($)

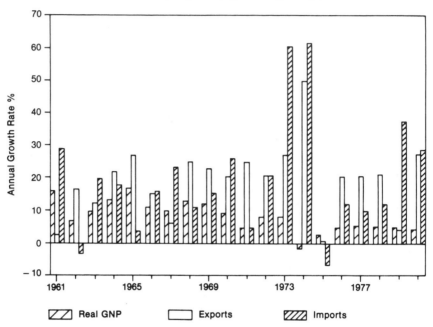

Source: Bank of Japan, *Economic Statistics Annual,* various editions.

omy. For example, several countries in Western Europe and the United States were able to balance their international accounts remarkably well, while a number of third world economies had to borrow extensively to finance energy imports.[74] Worldwide recession could not be avoided, however. In Japan, where growth had been strongly linked to export performance, expansion came to a dramatic halt, dropping from positive 9% for 1973 to negative 1% in 1974 (see Chart 4.1).

The impact of this dramatic reversal in growth rates on the Japanese financial system varied from player to player, but the change was profound for all. The city banks experienced a sudden halt in lending oppor-

74. This can most easily be seen in the international accounts of the major oil exporters. In 1973, their trade (oil) surplus stood at $18.6 billion. In 1974, it rose to $82.1 billion. It subsequently declined to $53.1 billion in 1975, rose slightly in 1976 to $65.2 billion, and then dropped again to $62.3 billion in 1978. The deficits on services and private transfers increased from $12.4 billion in 1974 to $35.0 billion in 1978. See *International Financial Statistics,* various editions.

CHART 4.2
Growth of City Banks' Loans
1970–1980

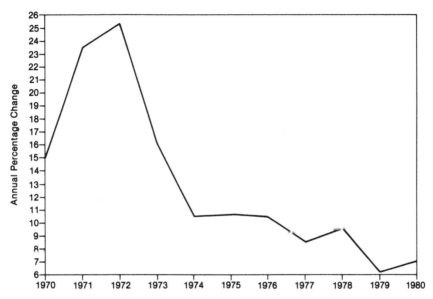

Source: Bank of Japan, *Economic Statistics Annual,* various editions.

tunities, and the growth rate of their loan portfolios was halved (see Chart 4.2). Slower growth meant less demand for bank loans, since a greater proportion of the funds that were now required came from the cash-rich corporations themselves.[75] The loss of lending opportunities had a no less dramatic effect on long-term credit banks. In a very short time, a system that had suffered from overlending came to be characterized by underlending.

As the need for private sector funds dried up, the need for public funds increased. I have noted how the authorities fought the recession with a standard expansionary spending policy.[76] Not surprisingly, the

75. Between 1960 and 1974, loans at city banks had grown at an annual compound growth rate of 19.3%. Between 1974 and 1981, growth stood at 10%. For long-term credit banks, growth rates also fell by half, dropping from 19.0% to 9.1%. See Bank of Japan, *Economic Statistics Annual* (Tokyo: Bank of Japan, 1983):55–56, 73–74.

76. I refrain from speculating about what made the authorities decide to issue debt rather than curtail expenditures or raise revenues. These issues lie in the realm of fiscal policy, with which I am not concerned here. On postwar Japanese fiscal policy, see G. Ackley and H. Ishi, "Fiscal, Monetary and Related Policies," in Patrick and Rosovsky, eds., *Asia's New Giant*:153–248; and J. Pechman and K.

CHART 4.3
Issue and Financing Need
1965–1988
(as a percentage of revenue)

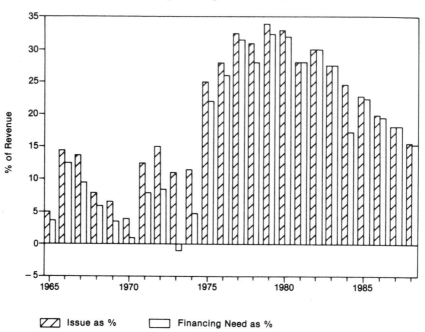

☐☐ Issue as %   ☐ Financing Need as %

Source: Bank of Japan, *Economic Statistics Annual*, various editions.

authorities' need for funds shot up (see Chart 4.3).[77] In 1965, when the first issues were made, the financing need of the government stood at 3.9% of total government revenue. Between 1965 and 1974, the need was on average 5.5% of revenue. In 1975, it jumped to 21.7% and remained above 22% well into the 1980s. Put differently, authorities issued (or borrowed) ¥197 *billion* in 1965; in 1974, they needed ¥5.2 *trillion*, double the 1972 issue. By 1977, the issue had again doubled.

The combined effect of the *economic slowdown* and *increased government financing* was to break one of the central balances in the Japa-

---

Kaizuka, "Taxation," ibid.:317–382; and Adams and Hoshii, *A Financial History of the New Japan*:285–302. For an account of more recent developments, see, for example, M. Rukstad, "Fiscal Policy and Business-Government Relations," in McCraw, ed., *America versus Japan*:299–336.

77. Financing need is defined here as the government debt issue minus the general account surplus. The latter reflects the excess of funding. Thus it is only the net required financing need I look at.

nese system. Although the government continued to place bonds through the forced absorption system at prices well below free market rates, this old proposition now became a losing one for the banks, and at a time when many of their traditionally profitable lending opportunities had disappeared. It was also a time, however, when the power relationship between the authorities and the banks was in transition. During the growth phase of the economy, overlent banks had sought financing from authorities whose own budget funding didn't rely much on placement of bonds through the banks. Now the banks, no longer overlent, had become an essential tool in satisfying the funding needs of the authorities. Yet the placement of bonds still relied on the nonprice-competitive issue procedure. Had bond prices reflected actual market conditions, the whole interest rate structure contrived by the Temporary Interest Rate Adjustment Law would have collapsed.

Unhappy with the status quo, the banks turned into advocates of change. They began seeking new customers, new pricing freedoms, and new products. Change also became attractive to Japanese corporations, now no longer in need of funds but with more money on their hands than they had opportunities for business investment. And later, when the renewed export success of the corporations increased their exposure to foreign financial markets, they developed a heightened awareness of new financing opportunities abroad. Foreign financial products became a fact of life for internationally operating corporations, which were exposed not only to the advantages of these products but also to their volatility.[78] Unable to insulate the domestic financial system from foreign influence, and in a weakened position because their own funding needs had increased, the authorities were forced to compete with foreign opportunities in terms of price and product freedoms.

In a sense, in the 1980s the Japanese financial system was defeated by its own success. Export success brought large current account imbalances to Japan. The associated international capital flows were incompatible with its tightly regulated financial system, which had started to show cracks, having already been compromised by the domestic effects of the oil shocks.

For many in Japan, the oil shocks had underscored the country's fundamental vulnerability and its dependence on foreign-owned natural resources. Ever since the Meiji Restoration, the country had been strug-

---

78. Two reasons apply. First, foreign direct investment in, for example, the United States could be seen as a foreign currency hedge. Second, the fear of trade restrictions in the wake of large U.S. current account deficits (which were seemingly unresponsive to exchange rate changes) would lead to foreign investments as a hedge against possible U.S. import restrictions.

gling to export enough to finance required imports of raw materials (without, at the same time, exhausting its foreign exchange reserves). Even as it industrialized, grew GNP with remarkable speed, and successfully rebuilt after the war, Japan recognized this basic vulnerability. So it is not surprising that in the 1980s the country focused anew on efforts to stimulate exports.[79] This time, however, the outcome would be very different, at least as far as the magnitudes involved were concerned. As I explained in Chapter 2, the prevailing view in the 1980s had become that large current account surpluses were perfectly feasible since they were to be offset by large capital account deficits without any formal forum for exchange rate or policy readjustment. I noted in Chapters 1 and 2 that new international institutional arrangements were expected to remove foreign reserves constraints, as well as to promote both macroeconomic policy independence and basically balanced international accounts. Governments acted on the former assumption, but real outcomes deviated significantly from the latter. Instead of becoming a balanced partner, Japan turned into the world's largest creditor nation, and its transformed capital market was propelled to international prominence.

In summary, what can be observed is less a national system transformed by revolution than a system, wounded by internal change, that increased the pace of its adaptation as it came into closer contact with foreign markets. Receptive to change, the Japanese capital market began to incorporate developments from other capital markets. It embarked on a steadily accelerating transition from the once-profitable relationships of the old regulatory order to a more flexible market orientation.

The changes that occurred in the Japanese financial system after the mid-1970s fall into two categories: product innovation, and price deregulation. Both reflect developments in other capital markets, particularly the United States.

Of course, financial institutions themselves were profoundly affected by these developments. As their customers' appetites for new products increased and their lending business deteriorated, the banks' incentives

79. See Crum and Meerschwam,"From Relationship to Price Banking," in Mc-Craw, ed., *America versus Japan*:290–291. With the exception of 1979 and 1980, the years of the second oil shock, Japan's current account was strongly positive. In 1986, the surplus in current account reached $86 billion. In 1974, Japan's merchandise exports were $54.4 billion, and its imports were $53.1 billion. By 1986, exports had risen almost fourfold, to $205.6 billion, while imports had only slightly more than doubled, reaching $112.9 billion. Thus, a growth rate of 11.7% for exports was offset by import growth of 6.5%. See *International Financial Statistics* (Washington, DC: International Monetary Fund, 1987).

to offer innovative products quickly increased. Furthermore, the traditional objectives of the banks—to honor and defend a system that offered them regulated profits, stability, and simplicity—no longer existed. Finally, with growing current account surpluses and capital account deficits, the financial institutions had become instruments for placing Japan's excess funds; they were exposed to foreign markets and learned new financial technologies.

THE MOVE TOWARD PRICE BANKING

The changes in the Japanese capital markets, in terms of new product offerings and regulatory reform, have been manifold. It is not possible to provide a complete listing, since many changes are still unfolding, but an impression of their depth and significance can be gained by looking at a number of instances of innovation and price deregulation that together show a clear pattern.[80] City banks successfully argued that they should be allowed to enter the over-the-counter market for government bonds, and competitive bidding for medium-term government securities was introduced. Securities firms succeeded in eliminating the requirement for full collateralization of corporate bonds, and, not surprisingly, credit rating agencies were also established. Bond and stock index futures were authorized, and call market rates were liberalized as the continuous setting of rates was allowed. Negotiable certificates of deposit were introduced, while traditional restrictions on the repurchase agreement (*gensaki*) market were loosened. A domestic commercial paper market was created, and money market certificates began to compete with deposit accounts. Later, Euroyen bonds issued by nonresidents appeared, and Euroyen CDs and bonds were placed with fewer and fewer guidelines. In short, a vast array of products and price decontrols served to change and complicate the system in Japan. (See Table 4.5.)

Both price deregulation and new financial products posed fundamental challenges for Japan's traditional financial structure. The impact of freer interest rates on the effectiveness of guidance by the Bank of Japan,

---

80. Some interest rates reflected market conditions even before the oil shock. Market pressures were reflected to a degree, for example, in the call money market (an interbank market) and the *gensaki* market (government bonds sold under repurchase agreement). Yet even these markets were influenced by the authorities, if only indirectly, since funds placed in them or obtained through them were used by intermediaries that were ultimately constrained by the overall posted rates. The authorities in Japan influenced the call market rates, and only in 1977 were more frequent interest rate adjustments seen there. In April 1979, when negotiable CDs were introduced, call rates were further liberalized.

TABLE 4.5

Selected Innovations in the Japanese Financial Markets

1977–1987

1977	City Banks allowed to see government bonds after one-year holding period in the secondary market Euroyen issues by nonresidents
1978	Competition in medium-term government bids Call rate liberalization
1979	Specifications for qualification standards for noncollateralized bonds Call and bill rate liberalization Negotiable CDs allowed Nonresidents allowed to enter the *gensaki* market
1980	Government bond funds introduced Tender procedure for four-year governments Additional freedoms for CDs Euroyen issues by residents Liberalization of foreign exchange regulations
1981	Further relaxation of government bond resales to the secondary market New freedoms for city banks to enter into repo transactions Relaxation of constraints on product offering in the deposit market
1982	New investment funds authorized
1983	Unsecured bond issues facilitated Secondary market sales of government bonds facilitated CDs liberalized Government bond time deposit accounts introduced Liberalization of Euroyen bank lending
1984	Bank dealing of government bonds Deposit market deregulation Overseas CDs and CPs allowed to be sold domestically Euroyen issue standards relaxed
1985	Rating agencies for corporate debt established BA market allowed, CD market further deregulated Call market deregulated
1986	Foreign membership on TSE CD market further liberalized Money market certificates and various deposit accounts liberalized
1987	Convertible bond issues relaxed for banks Stock index futures Domestic CPs allowed Deposit market deregulation Offshore financial futures allowed

Source: T. Cargill and S. Royama, *The Transition of Finance in Japan and the U.S.: A Comparative Perspective* (Stanford, CA: Hoover Institution Press, 1988).

for example, should be obvious. Similarly, the ability to issue bonds in foreign markets changed the relationships between corporations and the traditional suppliers of long-term funds. One of the central features of the Japanese financial system, the legal restriction against city banks raising long-term funds, was rendered almost meaningless by the development of the interest rate swap market, which in effect allowed for immediate maturity transformation of liabilities. The result was that long-term credit banks saw their traditional lending role eroded even further.[81] At the same time, the appearance of credit rating agencies signified the birth of a new method of judging corporate performance. And although some of these agencies are owned by banks, causing some observers to question their impartiality, they provide a new element of price-performance analysis for the bonds. Thus rating agencies may well begin to consider such issues as leverage very important in determining interest rates on bonds, especially since these securities are no longer fully collateralized.[82]

As Japan became a large international creditor nation and liberalized its domestic financial environment, its own financial institutions began to be interested in operating abroad, and foreign financial intermediaries likewise became interested in operating in Japan. Again, various forces interacted. Liberalization in Japan made profit opportunities for new players, such as foreign financial firms, seem more attractive, and the arrival of these new financial institutions subsequently moved Japan toward fuller innovation and product proliferation.[83]

Finally, one should note the pressures for financial liberalization from Japan's trading partners. I maintain that they did not cause the changes in Japan, but they were fully consistent with general demands that Japan liberalize its domestic economy in order to facilitate exports from its foreign partners. Not surprisingly, these demands increased in step with

81. In response, some long-term credit banks are using their in-depth knowledge of the corporate sector to develop consulting relationships with their clients.

82. Along with the financial environment, the tools of monetary policy have also changed. For example, moral suasion and guidance have become less effective, and room for open market operations has increased. The application of these relatively new tools of macroeconomic management will be important for financial markets inside and outside Japan, especially considering the strained trade relationship between Japan and the United States.

83. The growth of the number of foreign institutions active in Japan is not the only measure of their increased activity in the mid-1980s; the level of that activity is also significant. Morgan Stanley, for example, increased the number of employees in its Tokyo office from less than 20 to more than 500 in less than three years. See Chapter 7.

Japan's current account surpluses and foreign asset accumulation.[84] Anecdotal evidence of an uneven playing field is abundant—skis unsuited for "Japanese" snow, and bats inappropriate for Japanese baseball are among the most extreme cases. Indeed, there is a strong perception that Japan's economy is not as well organized to deal with imports as with exports. But as the discussion in earlier chapters showed, there is a fundamental economic relationship between Japan and the United States that provides a more satisfying explanation of the large imbalances: high net national savings in Japan and low net national savings in the United States. These will not be altered simply through liberalization of Japanese financial markets.

THE IMPLICATIONS OF PRICE BANKING

I have sketched Japan's transition from a system designed and built around price regulation and long-term relationships to one favoring

---

84. In 1984, in a joint report by Treasury Secretary Regan and Finance Minister Takeshita, the latter announced Japan's intention to:

- liberalize domestic capital markets spontaneously and positively in a step-by-step manner, which will result in a greater variety of attractive yen-denominated financial instruments with market-related interest rates and a more efficient allocation of capital;
- ensure that foreign financial institutions are accorded national treatment and the opportunity to participate fully in Japan's domestic financial system, including new and wider varieties of business areas; and
- provide for the development of Euroyen bond and banking markets which would make yen-denominated instruments more widely available to non-Japanese borrowers and investors.

Takeshita stated that the Ministry of Finance would ensure the prompt and thorough implementation of the measures announced in the report. Regan declared U.S. commitments to:

- continue its efforts to reduce the budget deficit, noting that recent congressional action has significantly enhanced the prospects that legislation will be passed this year that will have the effect of substantially reducing the U.S. budget deficit;
- welcome further issues of Japanese government-guaranteed bonds in U.S. capital markets;
- continue to ensure that its capital markets are open to foreign financial institutions and that they are accorded national treatment and the opportunity to participate fully in U.S. capital markets;
- continue to take into account fully the views of the Japanese government in its efforts to resolve the question of unitary taxation; and
- continue to cooperate with the Ministry of Finance in support of the international financial institutions.

more market-oriented transactions.[85] The result of this transition has been to give Japanese financial institutions new freedoms in the domestic markets, and to present their customers with a growing number of alternatives in financial decisions.

This implies that much more complex strategic decisions must now be made by financial intermediaries. Simplifying, one might argue that in the years in which the traditional system operated, senior executives in the financial services firms had to make few choices. They were allocated well-defined product markets, faced stringent price restrictions and a host of other regulations, and accepted many informal cooperative agreements.[86] The greater freedom inherent in the new environment, on the other hand, is attended by more choices and harder decisions. With foreign competitors eager to enter the growing market, Japanese firms must formulate strategic responses to actions taken by many who are unfamiliar with Japanese traditions. This applies equally to the foreign markets in which Japanese and non-Japanese firms compete. With the international capital imbalances between the United States and Japan increasing their dependence upon one another, and with the financial sector playing a crucial part in the economies of those two countries, the stage seems set for the financial industry to become a global (or at least a multinational) arena in which firms struggle for world leadership. This change obviously holds significant implications for the strategies of firms, a subject explored in later chapters. First, however, I turn to the third major international capital market, the United Kingdom, and consider how it fared during this time of transition.

85. For an insightful explanation of the changes in the Japanese financial system, see Feldman, *Japanese Financial Markets: Deficits, Dilemmas and Deregulation*:37–78.

86. Anecdotal evidence suggests that there were even directives to determine the quality of paper acceptable for greeting cards sent to bank customers.

5

THE U.K. FINANCIAL SYSTEM

When the London Stock Exchange abolished fixed commissions in October 1986, press reports described the deregulation of the City as the Big Bang. Many of these reports represented the story of the Big Bang in the United Kingdom as a dramatic and *sudden* change; however, it was not. As in the United States and Japan, events in the United Kingdom during the mid-1980s can only be understood as the culmination of *long-term* pressures, many of which were pervasive throughout the global economy. That the same forces led to financial deregulation in many different national markets during the early 1970s is less than surprising.

Like the changes in the American and Japanese financial systems, the alterations in the British financial system must be understood in terms of specific national historical developments, which combined with particular macro- and international economic pressures. Thus, London's Big Bang in 1986 should not be regarded as a watershed in British finance. It was one element of the gradual movement away from a system based on relationships and traditions toward a system in which prices played a far more important role. Again, the same two long-term trends encountered in earlier chapters reappear: first, the development of new international challenges and opportunities, and second, a shifting of the authorities' macroeconomic policymaking methods. Viewed in this larger perspective, the Big Bang becomes nothing more than a single significant incident.

To understand this movement from traditions to transactions, I begin by briefly reviewing some of the most important financial intermediaries, starting with the Bank of England. The unique position of "the Old Lady" in the system, along with the Bank's own perception of its role,

I am grateful to Ms. Nilgün Gökgür for providing extensive research assistance in writing this chapter.

provides insights into the U.K. financial system's traditional informal and unwritten rules of operation.

THE BANK OF ENGLAND

When London replaced Amsterdam as the leading international financial center in the eighteenth century, its banking institutions were scattered.[1] Merchants extended credit, the use of the Bill of Exchange became widespread, and discounting became standard practice.[2] The many and varied forms of financial services offered by intermediaries or principals were to become a permanent feature of the British financial center. Remnants of old customs would later be found side by side with more modern arrangements. For example, the role of the merchant engaging in finance stayed popular well into the nineteenth century, when one could still walk "into Twinings' bank and buy very good tea across the counter."[3]

As specialized financial institutions developed, the distinguishing characteristics of the British financial system became evident. In particular, a preference for *informal* relationships and understandings based on tradition can be seen in the institution that developed into Britain's central bank.

The Bank of England's special position as the final arbiter of good financial behavior emerged slowly over time. The Bank was originally granted no formal authority, but it managed to grow into a powerful, respected institution that could use moral suasion as a formidable tool for setting financial policy. Though formally the Bank did not differ from other banking institutions (for example, it had private owners and accepted deposits), its role as the goverment's banker and as banker to

1. Braudel notes, "It was only after 1730 that the Dutch commercial system began to break down in Europe, after fifty years of renewed activity from 1680 to 1730. And it was only in the second half of the century that Dutch merchants began to complain that they were being 'reduced to mere shipping agents or expediteurs who no longer intruded into the actual exchange transaction of goods.' There could be no better sign that the tide had turned. From now on, England was free from foreign interference and ready to take over the scepter of world trade." F. Braudel, *The Perspective of the World: Civilization and Capitalism, 15th–18th Century* (London: Collins, 1982):261.
2. For early developments in banking in Britain, see B. Anderson and P. Cottrell, *Money and Banking in England: The Development of the Banking System, 1694–1914* (Newton Abbot, Devon: David & Charles, 1974). Many original sources are presented there.
3. *Tales of the Bank of England with Anecdotes of London Bankers* (London: James Hogg, 1882):26.

other financial institutions gave it a unique position. Its power was further enhanced by its other role as the administrator (though not the architect) of monetary policy.[4] One observer of the British financial system noted:

> The Bank of England obviously works in a way that is different from that of other central banks, and this is largely a question of history. For centuries before the art of central banking was developed the Bank of England was only one bank among many in the City of London; all at a stone's throw of each other. Even today the Governor of the Bank of England regards himself primarily as a banker, and it is still true that all the important figures in the banking world meet frequently in the normal course of business and that they all work within a few hundred yards of each other. It is the fact that the British banking system consists partly of banks with extensive branching networks and partly of specialised banks within the City of London that enables the system to work without any written rules.[5]

The same author pointed out that the Bank operated in a system in which few "of the ground rules of the banking game were enshrined in statutes and regulations." Business was instead "done by convention and understanding."

The special role of the Bank of England did not, however, come about exclusively as a result of such understanding. In one way, it differed formally from other institutions: as early as 1694, the Bank had been made into a joint-stock bank. All other banks had to be private partnerships (with a maximum of six partners).[6] The partnership requirement prevented other banks from becoming large, nationwide institutions and thus potential challengers of the Bank of England. It also was thought that the small private banks would be more likely to operate prudently, since their well-known proprietors were personally liable. As in the United States, a preference for decentralization was observed. In the United Kingdom, however, the driving motivation does not seem to have been fear of centralization, which I suggested in Chapter 3 as the guiding force in the early development of the U.S. system. Another

---

4. Although the Bank of England's influence over the system is great, it *does not* determine monetary policy. In contrast to the roles of the Federal Reserve (which has considerable independence) and the Bank of Japan (which works in close consultation with the Ministry of Finance), the Bank of England is the agent of the Treasury. In comments to a House Select Committee in 1987, Chancellor of the Exchequer Lawson bluntly declared, "I make the decisions, the Bank carries them out."

5. J. Revell, *The British Financial System* (London: Macmillan, 1975):130.

6. A 1708 act reaffirmed the six-partner rule.

important difference between the two countries was that Americans saw reduced stability as a price that had to be paid to avoid the dangers of centralization. The British, on the other hand, were convinced that decentralization *enhanced* stability. In Britain the role of the individual liable partner, with his personal relationships and his sense of obligation to customers, was to guard the system from instability. As might be expected, the private banks subscribed to that view and opposed the establishment of new, joint-stock banks that could challenge them in their activities.[7] The consensus that small private banks ensured stability was shaken, however, by the financial panic of 1825. This led to the removal of some of the restrictions on the size of partnerships. In 1836, a committee investigating the banks declared:

> The Law [1826/1833] is not sufficiently stringent to insure to the Public that the names registered at the Stamp Office are the names of bona fide Proprietors. . . . The provisions of the Law are inadequate, or at least are disregarded, so far as they impose upon Banks the obligation of making their notes payable at the place of issue.

The report concluded:

> All these separate questions appear to Your Committee deserving of the most serious consideration, with a view to the future stability of the Banks throughout the United Kingdom, the maintenance of Commercial Credit and the preservation of the Currency in a sound State.[8]

As in the United States, it became apparent that there was a trade-off between decentralization and stability. But even so, it was not until 1857 that joint-stock banking became generally possible (some joint-stock banks had operated since 1826), and not until early 1858 that limited liability became feasible.[9]

7. R. Pringle, *A Guide to Banking in Britain* (London: Charles and Knight, 1973):21.
8. Quoted in Anderson and Cottrell, *Money and Banking in England*:299.
9. The existing private bankers opposed the development of the joint-stock banks, which they saw as a threat to their local monopolies. One such banker, R. Conway, wrote in 1825 in his *Treatise on a Loan Banking Company:*

> Of the view of a Loan Banking Company, notwithstanding the high estimation in which the private characters of the members may stand in public, the British Public . . . cannot be mistaken. No one, however dim his mental eye may be, save actual idiotism, but will clearly see . . . that the grand and primary object of an establishment of this nature is the attainment of an exorbitant rate of self-aggrandisement.

Quoted ibid.:267–268.

The Bank of England was Britain's main joint-stock bank for more than 120 years. During that time, its special position was consolidated, as traditions formed and informal understandings grew; no other formal arrangements for supervision were instituted. Yet the overall stability of the national financial sector—the Bank of England included—was less than perfect. In 1829, for example, the Bank came close to illiquidity after rumors started a run.[10] And though the Bank of England could not rely on a formal regulatory framework to support the features commonly associated with a central bank today, its preeminence remained unchallenged. Even as financial institutions grew and joint-stock banking caused conglomeration, no one questioned the special position of the Bank. In fact, the lack of formal regulation opened a window of opportunity for the Bank of England to establish informal control. Within this informal system, insiders could probe the boundaries of acceptable practice, and the Bank, in response, signalled its approval or disapproval, often using subtle messages. Outsiders who lacked the benefit of a long-standing relationship with the Bank could nevertheless attempt to enter the system; no official rules excluded them. But the price of admittance was acceptance of, or at least acquiescence to, the established rules of behavior.

That the Bank did not cease to be privately owned until 1946, when it was nationalized, is testimony to the ability of British bankers to operate in an informal system. The new Bank of England Act defined the Bank's place in the financial hierarchy as officially subordinate to the Treasury. As a consequence, with regard to monetary policy the role of the Bank was to execute, and not to formulate, policy.[11] But in terms of regulation, it was clear that the Bank was *the* authority. The act gave the Bank of England formal powers to regulate the banking community; it stated that the Bank could "request information from and make recommendations to the bankers," and that it could, "if so authorised by the Treasury, issue directions."[12] But though the Bank's newly bestowed status helped formalize its role as the central bank, its relations with other financial institutions continued to reflect its long-established traditions and informal understandings.[13]

10. Since the Bank of England was an ordinary bank, it took deposits from the public. Even after the general public was no longer able to hold accounts there, officers of the Bank continued to do so. See Revell, *The British Financial System*:134.

11. See note 4.

12. See J. Wadsworth, *The Banks and the Monetary System in the U.K., 1959–1971* (London: Methuen, 1973):105.

13. Wadsworth also notes that "statutory powers have apparently never been implemented. The position, as the Bank of England saw it in 1957, was expressed

Much of the power of the Bank of England derived from its extensive knowledge of financial markets and institutions. Frequent consultations with other institutions made it the repository of information. Even the geography of the London market helped. The governor of the Bank of England suggested that in just a matter of moments he could assemble the effective leadership of Britain's finance in his office.[14] Thus, even when formal powers began to be built into the system, the continual contacts among the various parties allowed for an additional level of supervision. Frequent consultation ensured that other banks did not deviate too far from the Bank's wishes, so that it was not necessary to issue directives. The Bank also had other ways of influencing the financial intermediaries. As lender of last resort to the discount houses (another group of financial intermediaries) the Bank achieved great influence over them, while its interventions in the short-term money market, gilt-edged market (through the government broker), and foreign exchange market further enhanced its power.

In short, the Bank effectively used moral suasion in a system of informal regulation and close consultation. In this sense, it was more like the Japanese system than that of the United States. An instance of the special character of the system can be found in evidence that the Bank's governor gave before the Radcliffe Committee in 1960. He declared:

> I have left the banks in no doubt during the recent phase of credit restriction, of my view that they should not allow their liquidity to fall significantly below 30 percent and I have made it clear that I reserved the right to make observations if there were any considerable divergence.[15]

In a complex system of dependencies and understandings, all the Bank needed was the ability to make "observations." Within this context, it is not surprising that the Bank's discount office, rather than a separate bureaucracy within the Bank, was responsible for supervision. Although

---

in a memorandum submitted to the Radcliffe Committee as follows: 'The Bank have had no formal control over other banks and no duty of inspection; the possibility that the Bank might refuse to continue to maintain an account for another bank has been historically an effective sanction. Since 1946, if the Bank think it necessary in the public interest, they may request information from bankers and make recommendations to them; and, if so authorised by the Treasury, may issue directions to ensure compliance with such a request or recommendation. This power has not been used.' " Ibid.:105.

14. See M. Moran, *The Politics of Banking—The Strange Case of Competition and Credit Controls* (New York: St. Martin's, 1984):15.

15. See Radcliffe Committee Report, Minutes of Evidence, quoted in Revell, *The British Financial System*:130.

overseeing the discount window and managing the money market were the office's primary tasks, it made extensive use of informal communications with financial institutions in order to understand the concerns of, and transmit its own desires to, the banking community. More formal, though perhaps not as legalistic as in the United States, was the Bank's influence over various lending and funding decisions of several other banks. Written quantitative and qualitative requests in relation to credit controls or specific lending priorities could be used in dealing with the financial community. But often, common understandings and general agreements in effect made the more formal request superfluous. When a "request" was made, the power of the Bank was sufficient to assure that no other bank could easily challenge its content. In executing monetary policy through these mechanisms, the Bank made extensive use of guidance and requirements on clearing banks' reserves. These clearing banks were the closest British equivalent to the American commercial banks, or the Japanese city banks, and they played a crucial role in financial affairs, if only because of their large size. (See Table 5.1.)

THE CLEARING BANKS

The segmentation of the financial product market in Britain resembled what was seen in both the United States and Japan, with one characteristically British exception: British institutions in each market segment formed "clubs" concerned with self-regulation and consultation among members. The clearing banks all held membership in the London Clearing House. Formally, mutual obligations (cheques) were cleared through this institution daily; but more importantly, it provided a forum to discuss a broad set of issues. For deposit gathering, the clearing banks used a vast retail branching network that covered most of the country. Like U.S. commercial banks, they made individual, commercial, and industrial loans. They also held a portfolio of government obligations. The wide geographical coverage enjoyed by the banks resulted from their taking advantage of the joint-stock banking provision after 1857, and from the movement to become nationwide institutions through amalgamation, which started in the late 1850s.[16] Not unlike public concerns about excessive banking power in the United States, public debate soon arose in Britain about the potential power of these banks. The growth of the banks raised concerns that (among other things) the Bank of England's ability to implement monetary policy might be

16. See J. Sykes, *The Amalgamation Movement in British Banking, 1825–1924* (London: P.S. King and Sons, 1926):4.

TABLE 5.1
The Shares of the U.K. Banking Sector and Other Financial Institutions in Deposit Liabilities
Percentages and £ Million

	1955	1960	1965	1970	1975	1980	1985
DEPOSIT BANKS							
London clearing banks	49.5%	43.4%	43.2%	28.7%	16.4%	14.5%	a
Scottish banks	5.8%	4.7%	4.4%	3.0%	1.7%	1.7%	a
Northern Ireland banks	1.0%	0.9%	0.9%	0.9%	0.5%	0.0%	a
Subtotal	56.3%	48.9%	48.6%	32.6%	18.7%	16.6%	15.9%
DISCOUNT MARKET	7.6%	6.6%	5.2%	5.8%	1.9%	1.8%	1.2%
ACCEPTING HOUSES, FOREIGN BANKS, AND OTHER BANKS							
Accepting houses	1.1%	2.4%	4.7%	8.1%	3.7%	3.9%	3.4%
Foreign banks*	6.0%	8.5%	19.4%	30.8%	55.2%	59.2%	67.6%
Other banks	—	—	1.5%	9.4%	13.2%	13.3%	9.6%
Subtotal	7.2%	10.9%	25.5%	48.4%	72.1%	76.5%	80.6%
TRUSTEE SAVINGS BANKS	5.0%	5.0%	6.4%	5.8%	3.5%	2.2%	b
NATIONAL SAVINGS BANKS	9.4%	9.7%	8.3%	1.5%	0.5%	0.4%	0.3%
FINANCE HOUSES	0.0%	1.9%	3.0%	1.9%	0.3%	0.2%	0.1%
BUILDING SOCIETIES SHARES & DEPOSITS	14.7%	17.0%	3.0%	4.0%	3.0%	2.4%	1.9%
TOTAL (£ million)	13,370	17,344	21,876	36,958	137,385	290,618	689,895

[a] Deposits of London clearing banks, Scottish banks, and Northern Ireland banks are not broken down but are included in the subtotal.
[b] Data on trustee savings banks can no longer be obtained from Financial Statistics after 1981.

* Foreign banks are American, Japanese, consortium, and other foreign banks and affiliates. British overseas and other foreign banks and affiliates. British overseas and Commonwealth banks are also included.

Source: Financial Statistics, *Bank of England Statistical Abstract*, no. 1 (1970), and *Bank of England Quarterly Bulletin*, September 1971, March 1976, March 1981, September 1986.

threatened. The consequences of amalgamation were questioned more generally when, between 1858 and 1868, 373 mergers between various banks occurred.[17] The Colwyn Committee was appointed by the Chancellor of the Exchequer in 1918 to evaluate the dangers of conglomeration in banking. Its instructions were to "consider and report to what extent, if at all, amalgamation between banks may affect prejudicially the interests of the industrial and mercantile community, and whether it is desirable that legislation should be introduced to prohibit such amalgamation or to provide safeguards under which they might continue to be permitted."[18]

Although the dangers inherent in concentrated banking power were recognized, the advantages of large, geographically diversified institutions were also appreciated. By having fewer but larger banks, it was supposedly easier for the depositors to ascertain their quality, while it allowed the banks to diversify their funding base; the large clearing banks were much less susceptible to rumors about insufficient liquidity and to associated bank runs. Furthermore, a systemic guarantee was widely credited: the authorities would not allow large banks to fail, since their failure would endanger the very health of the overall financial system. Here, all that was required was the perception of a guarantee. With depositors believing in its existence, the guarantee would never actually be tested; its existence would help prevent liquidity problems.[19]

The "Big Five" clearing banks (Midland Bank, Barclays, Lloyds, Westminster, and National Provincial) emerged from the amalgamation movement. By the outbreak of World War I, they were already established as the dominant nationwide retail banks.[20] The banks' funding

17. Ibid., Appendix I:193–195.

18. Quoted in D. Alhadeff, *Competition and Controls in Banking* (Berkeley: University of California Press, 1968):240. The Colwyn Committee's investigation came a decade after the investigations of the Pujo Committee in the United States, which had forced the breakup of money trusts such as the one that had developed around the interests of J. P. Morgan. See W. Shultz and M. Caine, *Financial Development of the U.S.* (New York: Prentice-Hall, 1973):462–463 and Chap. 3.

19. Of course, such a guarantee (or a deposit insurance scheme such as the FDIC in the United States) may create other problems. If depositors are unconcerned about the activities of the bank (since their deposits are guaranteed or insured), who stands watch against unwarranted risk taking by the banks? The monetary authorities, the providers of the insurance, and the guarantee itself are the natural candidates, but the American experience with S&Ls indicates that may not be adequate.

20. By 1913, the largest five banks accounted for 48% of all branches in Britain. By 1918 the percentage had risen to 83% and stabilized. In 1938, the combined liabilities of the five banks—of which Barclays accounted for 19%, Lloyds for 18%, Midland for 20%, Westminster for 15%, and National Provincial for 14%—represented 86% of the liabilities of all clearing banks in the United Kingdom at the time. See Alhadeff, *Competition and Controls in Banking*:246–247.

strategy relied on low-cost retail deposits; noninterest-bearing current accounts—the equivalent of U.S. demand deposits—represented almost 50% of total assets in 1970 (when the system began its transition from the traditional relationship era). In attracting the deposits, the London Clearing House functioned as the club for the big clearing banks. Apart from its official clearing function, it was used as a forum to set interest rates; thus, the clearing banks operated as a cartel. In contrast to the United States, where Regulation Q was for decades the formal avenue for rate setting, discussions in the Clearing House set prices for deposits through self-administration. The Bank of England's view remained important in these discussions; at least four times a year the governor of the Bank hosted the meetings, and between 1955 and 1971, the rate on time deposits was typically set 2% below Bank Rate.[21]

In lending strategy, informal regulation played a similar role, and interest rates were not used as a competitive weapon to gain market share. The asset side of the balance sheet also showed less than perfect competition for loans through the price mechanism. A Capital Issues Committee continued to operate in the years following World War II, but even after its abolition in 1957, credit controls and strong guidance from the Bank remained.[22] Furthermore, the clearers' ability to expand or contract their balance sheets was severely affected by the authorities' views on macroeconomic developments. The clearing banks were expected to observe an 8% cash ratio and a 28% (30% between 1957 and 1963) liquidity ratio. In addition, special deposit schemes were used repeatedly during the 1960s. For example, when macroeconomic conditions impelled the Bank to contract credit in the British economy in 1960, clearing banks were asked to place such special deposits with the Bank of England—at first 1% of their total deposits, and later 2%. Though these special deposits were only "requested," no bank could contemplate refusing.

The vignettes sketched above all point to the informal self-regulation and established relationships that were characteristic of the system. In this environment, moral suasion was a primary policy tool. The clearing banks did not object to their role as principal instruments of monetary management, since asset growth restrictions and the nonaggressive setting of interest rates led to a conservative asset portfolio and relatively stable profits. Given the developments reviewed in the chapters on the

---

21. Bank Rate was the rate of discount used by the Bank of England.
22. This committee had been set up in 1939 to oversee and coordinate investment decisions in Britain. See D. Sheppard, *The Growth and Role of U.K. Financial Institutions, 1880–1962* (London: Methuen, 1971):10.

United States and Japan, it should be no surprise that during the 1970s British banks began to object to their special status and the informal boundaries that had been laid down. The clearing banks would play an important role in the reorganization of the British financial system, but they were not alone in calling for reform. Some of the other players involved are briefly described below.

MERCHANT BANKS

A second group of important financial institutions, the merchant banks, concentrated on wholesale financial transactions. These banks engaged in wide-ranging activities, such as providing general financial advice, arranging mergers and acquisitions, factoring and leasing, foreign exchange dealing, financing shipping and foreign trade, and market-making in precious metals. Like traditional U.S. investment banks (before mergers and acquisitions advice and principal transaction started to dominate their activities), one of the most important functions of merchant banks was to raise funds for corporations through the underwriting of new securities. Therefore, membership in the Issuing Houses Committee—another typical British financial club engaged in the self-regulation of its members under the informal supervision of the Bank of England—was standard. The merchant banks' activities in corporate finance enabled them to establish close ties with industry and, to a certain extent, to serve as a conduit for the wishes of the Bank of England and the Treasury. Many merchant banks were involved in the acceptance business, which consisted of endorsing (accepting) bills that could then be rediscounted through the discount houses. It was another self-elected body, the Accepting House Committee, that monitored the activities of its members in this market segment. The committee was influenced, as usual, by the Bank of England. The Bank not only supervised the accepting houses, but also stood ready to assist them in times of distress.

DISCOUNT HOUSES

The discount houses, all members of the London Discount Market Association (LDMA), were unique to the British system. Their focus of operation was in the short-term (wholesale) money market, in which they provided liquidity for other financial institutions such as clearing banks, merchant banks, and local and state authorities. The traditional role of the discount houses was to discount (and thus finance) accepted paper that had passed through one of the accepting houses. The discount houses, in effect, engaged in fully secured lending, funding themselves primarily through loans from the other financial institutions. They operated as a conduit in the short-term money market, with the Bank of England functioning as their lender of last resort. The houses themselves could rediscount with the Bank of England and enter into the money market through Treasury bill purchases and sales, short-term (overnight) bank money, and sterling and Euro certificates of deposit. The Bank of England was closely involved with the discount houses. Not only did the Bank determine which assets it would be willing to rediscount, but it also carefully supervised whatever business activities the houses entered into and the quality of their balance sheets.[23]

In dealing with short-term state obligations (Treasury bills), the discount houses were required, until the 1970s, to cover the tender; they had to make syndicated bids for the full issue through the LDMA.[24] Note the similarity of this procedure to the forced absorption process of government issues in Japan, which was discussed in Chapter 4. As in Japan, the syndicated bid came into being after extensive consultation with the authorities—in this case, the Bank of England—rather than as a result of pure price consideration; and moral suasion was central in setting the price. Furthermore, an understanding that the clearing banks would not compete with the discount houses in the tender carried forward from the 1930s. Interactions between the discount houses and the Bank were thus manifold: rediscounting, supervision of balance sheets and product design, and the covered tender offer all assured frequent consultation. These common concerns meant that meetings between the governor (or deputy governor) of the Bank and the chairman of the LDMA were of great significance. With the typical British inclination for understatement, these meetings were known as the weekly "exchange of views." They provided the mechanism for what was, in effect, coordinated financial management, although the Bank and the LDMA both claimed that the Bank exerted "no undue influence" over the actual bid

23. See Revell, *The British Financial System:*215. In the 1970s, the Bank started to provide more formal guidelines, forcing the discount houses to invest at least 50% of borrowed funds in short-term gilts, local authority deposits, and assets that qualify as reserve assets to clearing banks. See J. Grady and M. Weale, *British Banking, 1960–1985* (London: Macmillan, 1986):55.

24. The syndicated tender was abandoned in 1971 with the introduction of CCC (see below). After 1971, the official obligation to enter the market with a syndicated tender was replaced by a system in which individual discount houses made bids at independent prices. All were forced to absorb the remaining nontendered part of the issue at a rate determined by the LDMA. See Revell, *The British Financial System:*223–227.

price for new issues of the gilts.[25] Still, it seems fair to suggest that the Bank Rate (the central interest rate that guided most other rates) was not really the outcome of a price-competitive tender driven by pure market forces. Consultation and coordination between the Bank and other financial institutions was guaranteed by the prevailing traditions.

OTHER FINANCIAL INSTITUTIONS

In the City, a host of other financial intermediaries also operated. For example, the building societies, like the clearing banks, provided savings instruments designed for retail depositors; they invested the funds in the housing market. Like many of the mutual savings banks in the United States, most building societies had started as friendly associations to save money, with which they intended to build housing for their members in a collective effort. Over time, however, the building societies increasingly began to function as true intermediaries. Their ability to pay slightly higher interest rates because of tax advantages allowed them to steadily increase their share of the retail deposit market. In 1953, 4% of British adults held accounts at building societies. By 1970, the percentage had risen fivefold, and by 1980 almost half of the British adult population were clients of the building societies.[26]

Like the other financial intermediaries, the societies had their own club. The Council of Building Societies Association (CBSA) was responsible for the regulation of its members until the Building Societies Act of 1962 put more formal supervision in place. A civil servant, the Chief Registrar of Friendly Societies, was appointed to oversee the behavior of the societies.[27] Still, the CBSA continued to "recommend" rates to its members and thus to prevent price competition, since members understood the importance of its recommendation. As might be expected, price fixing and adherence to the cartel's recommendations through the CBSA led to concentration. By 1983, the two largest societies, Halifax and Abbey-National, accounted for 30% of total funds in the industry.[28]

The retail deposit market was also targeted by the National Savings

---

25. See G. Fletcher, *The Discount Houses in London: Principles, Operations and Change* (London: Macmillan, 1976):122.

26. See M. Boleat, *The Building Society Industry* (London: Allen & Unwin, 1982):22–23.

27. Even though the societies are officially regulated through the Registrar's office, the Bank of England has itself occasionally exercised qualitative control. See, for example, Bank of England, *Annual Report 1966* (London: HMSO, 1966):11.

28. See P. Barnes, *Building Societies: The Myth of Mutuality* (London: Pluto, 1984):41, 62.

Bank. Like the postal savings system in Japan, the national savings bank used a well-developed post office network. Unlike its Japanese counterpart, however, the British system was not known for its efficiency and did not offer the tax advantages that Japan's savers enjoyed.[29] Funds that the national savings banks obtained were invested in state and local obligations.

Other financial intermediaries included trustee savings banks, which invested savings proceeds in government obligations; finance houses, which provided medium-term financing to private and corporate customers; and unit trusts and investment trusts, which offered convenient forms of professionally managed portfolios. Like the mutual fund industry in the United States, these trusts would gain a larger share of the financial flows over time; their ability to let small investors purchase a diversified portfolio—at a time when the price performance of the investment was becoming more important than dividends or interest payments alone—would make them stronger competitors for the established institutions.[30]

SELF-REGULATED STABILITY, 1950–1970

To understand the system in which all these institutions operated during the 1950s and 1960s, one must realize that additional informal relationships among the various intermediaries played a crucial role—quite apart from the forms of informal self-regulation described above. These relationships were often subtle and hard to define, but some of them can be identified. Most bankers were educated at the same schools; they held membership in the same social clubs. Informal understanding about the appropriate product boundaries was often reinforced through multiple contacts and cross-board membership. For example, merchant bankers served on the boards of clearing banks (see Chart 5.1). The impact of such arrangements seems to have been reflected in the strategies followed by the institutions involved. Take the retail deposit market: although this large source of funds was not legally off limits to underwriters of securities (the merchant banks) as in the United States and Japan, no merchant bank engaged in the practice of taking deposits;

29. See Bank of Japan, *Money and Banking in Japan*:360–367. Also F. Perry, *The Elements of Banking* (London: Methuen, 1975):122.
30. Insurance companies and pension funds also played important roles, and London was able to develop the leading insurance market in the world. Here again, informal self-regulation dominated, with the members of Lloyds setting the standards of behavior.

CHART 5.1
Directorships in Comon among 27 Financial Institutions

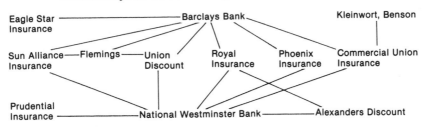

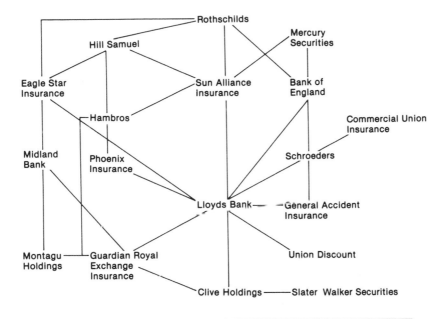

Source: Richard Whitley, "Commonalities and Connections among Directors of Large Financial Institutions," *The Sociological Review* (Routledge), November 1973, p. 623.

instead, it was well understood that the retail deposit market remained the preserve of clearers.

When border crossing did occur, it was usually indirectly, through subsidiaries. Clearing banks, for example, entered the merchant banking market through acquired subsidiaries after 1966.[31] The subsidiaries,

31. For example, Barclays Bank set up a merchant banking subsidiary and later formed Barclays-de-Zoete-Wedd. Also, mortgages were offered through the subsidiaries of various institutions and clearing banks, but the building societies could

naturally, then became members of the appropriate clubs. With membership came the inevitable obligation to play by the rules and to accept self-regulation: in the case of the merchant banks, the Accepting Houses Committee; in the case of the discount houses, the LDMA. The system leaves one with the distinct impression of informally regulated cartels, operating with little price competition and accountable to the Bank of England.

In this environment, the notion of fair play prevailed. That ethic dictated repeated transactions between well-known partners, which were possible only because all of them understood and accepted the rules of the game.[32] Asked, in the mid-1970s, to identify the reason for his banking success, Lord Poole of Lazard Brothers replied, "Quite simple, I only lent money to people who had been at Eton."[33] In short, the importance of relationships and unwritten rules was enormous, and both notions conformed to the stereotypical characterization of British society. And although the recurring theme of this and the two preceding chapters is that price competition was repressed in the national financial systems of the United States, Japan, and the United Kingdom, this convenient similarity in outcome must nevertheless be understood in the context of three systems that reflected distinct national characteristics but achieved a stable banking environment, each in its own way. In Britain a sense of fair play, adherence to traditions, and informal but very binding rules created a stable banking environment in the years after World War II.

This environment of unwritten rules, accepted by the local players, was perceived quite differently by foreign institutions. They viewed the absence of formal regulation as a license to develop their own rules for a different international game that just happened to be located in London. (As I explain below, this market remained largely distinct from the domestic British markets.) No British notions of fair play or complex

---

gather funds at an advantageous rate because of the tax advantages they bestowed on their investors. In Britain, the taxes on income derived from accounts at the societies were levied at the society level, at a rate effectively lower than the average rate. Similar advantageous funding for the housing market was also available in the United States, where interest regulation was more favorable for thrifts that invested in the housing market than for commercial banks.

32. See M. Lisle-Williams, "Beyond the Market: The Survival of Family Capitalism in the English Merchant Banks," *British Journal of Sociology* 35 (1984):241–271; and M. Lisle-Williams, "Merchant Banking Dynasties in the English Class Structure Ownership: Solidarity and Kinship in the City of London, 1850–1960," ibid.:333–362. Both cited in M. Clarke, *Regulating the City: Competition, Scandal and Reform* (London: Open University Press, 1986):50.

33. Quoted ibid.:14.

old-boy networks bound the foreign financial vendors to each other, to customers, or to the system. On them the subtle signals of the Bank of England would have no impact. Thus, overseas bankers brought products, techniques, and tools to London that they had developed in their own domestic markets. More importantly, they laid the foundations of an international market where price competition would reign supreme. This new market would lead to the evolution of new domestic markets (the parallel markets) in the foreign mold. The international market was unregulated and practically beyond the influence of the authorities. It was, at first, *separate* from the domestic market, but the new parallel markets—also much less controlled—would begin to provide a link to the major domestic markets. This link would be crucially important later, when fundamental forces for change (such as international asset flow changes in the global economy and the macroeconomic policy changes described in Chapters 1 and 2) reached Britain in the early 1970s. The parallel markets would then transmit these changes to the domestic markets and prompt the reorientation of the British financial system away from traditional relationships and toward more price-competitive transactions, just as had happened in both the United States and Japan.

THE INTERNATIONAL MARKET

Despite the decline of Britain as an international trade power after World War II, London's informal regulation, its time-honored financial institutions, and its English-speaking environment provided a natural haven for foreign financial institutions, particularly American banks. It was a place where they found themselves free of the rigid and legalistic regulations that prevailed in their own domestic banking sectors. Thus, London retained its position of prominence as an international financial center (see Table 5.2).[34]

Although British banks were instrumental in developing several of the Euromarket instruments, foreign financial institutions increasingly dominated the new markets.[35] The rapid growth of overseas banks is

34. On the development of the Eurodollar markets, see G. Bell, *The Eurodollar Market and the International Financial System* (New York: John Wiley, 1973); and H. Mayer, "Some Theoretical Problems Relating to the Euro Dollar Market," *Princeton Essays in International Finance*, No. 79 (Princeton: International Finance Section, 1970).

35. The merchant banking firm S. G. Warburg invented the Eurodollar bond in 1963 when it organized the financing of the Italian motor highway through a fixed-rate $15 million bond. See Clarke, *Regulating the City: Competition, Scandal and Reform:21.*

TABLE 5.2
U.K. Current Account
1950–1989
(£ Million)

	1950	1955	1960	1965	1970	1975	1980	1985	1989
VISIBLE TRADE									
Exports	2,261	3,073	3,737	4,913	8,150	19,330	47,422	77,989	92,537
Imports	2,312	3,386	4,138	5,173	8,184	22,663	46,061	81,120	115,530
NET EXPORTS	−51	−313	−401	−260	−34	−3,333	1,361	−3,131	−22,993
INVISIBLES									
All other than financial services	276	−13	−56	−59	−120	−623	−2,237	−313	1,968
Financial services*	82	171	229	240	709	2,374	3,976	6,606	4,186
NET INVISIBLES	358	158	173	181	589	1,751	1,739	6,293	6,154
CURRENT ACCOUNT BALANCE	307	−155	−228	−79	555	−1,582	3,100	3,162	−16,839

*Net service earnings of U.K. financial institutions, including insurance, banking (excluding interest earnings), commodity trading, and brokerage.

Source: Central Statistical Office, *Economic Trends*, January 1990, p. 50, and *Annual Supplement*, HMSO, 1986, pp. 128–129.

seen in Table 5.3.[36] Though mainly involved with wholesale, nonsterling business, some of these banks tried to gain access to the British home market.[37] Typically, these overseas banks stood in direct relation to one major foreign financial institution, sometimes as a branch and sometimes as the subsidiary of a holding company, depending on the home regulation of the parent.

Consortium banks, also formed by foreign banks, played a much less important role than did the traditional overseas banks, although one joint venture—Financiere Credit Suisse First Boston (CSFB)—became the leading player in the international securities market. Smaller European banks, in particular, saw the consortium structure as a means of competing with the larger American banks, but neither they nor the U.S. banks that joined consortiums (such as Orion Bank), were very successful. Nonetheless, the consortium banks that operated in London decided to form their own club, the Association of Consortium Banks.[38]

The remarkable growth of the nonsterling sector underscores the variety of competitive pressures that developed in Britain's financial industry. In the domestic (sterling) market, British vendors reigned supreme, although they faced changes that will be described below. In the rapidly expanding nonsterling market, however, these same large domestic British banks held no competitive advantage and played no special role; in fact, they never attained positions of leadership, as did CSFB, the American and German banks, and later the Japanese financial institutions.

Though British banks were not among the major players in the Euromarkets, Britain itself did benefit from the employment and profits generated by the international market, which furthered the economic objectives of the British government. Surpluses generated through the City were a valuable source of funds for Britain's balance of payments. These funds—although mostly produced by foreign players—apparently came at little cost; the domestic activities of the British clearing banks and other retail deposit-gathering institutions faced little competition from overseas banks.

36. These banks are different from the British overseas banks, which are British institutions set up to deal with foreign nations.

37. To enter the domestic side of the British financial market, foreign banks had to learn how to deal with its many traditions. As late as 1984, Citicorp unsuccessfully applied to the Committee of London Clearing Bankers. Instead it was suggested that the firm contact the Bankers' Clearing House. Unwilling to accept the decision, Citicorp was later rewarded with the institution of a committee that was to review the system.

38. See D. Channon, *British Banking Strategy and International Challenge* (London: Macmillan, 1977):178. The Bank of England approved the ACB in 1974.

For the merchant banks, competition was more direct. Their international opportunities were limited, since foreign institutions were typically better capitalized and enjoyed well-established relationships with many of the foreign issuers in the Euromarkets. Thus, British firms had no natural advantage in entering the international market, either on the issuer or distributor side. Still, most of these firms did not feel directly threatened by the expanding foreign institutions in the international market; within Britain itself, the relationships between the merchant banks and their clients were strong enough to assure continued profitability.[39]

THE PARALLEL MARKETS

The parallel markets are the second market, after the international market, that should be considered distinct from the traditional domestic markets. The parallel markets developed as early as the late 1950s but only grew to significant importance in the late 1960s. The sketch of the British domestic financial system presented so far depicts an environment in which the authorities' controls derived from subtle and complex understandings and relationships. For outsiders, this meant that opportunities sometime arose that were not easily tested by any set of formal regulations. The authorities, using their informal methods, were left to deal with such developments. Thus, in contrast to what has been shown for the United States and Japan, several market alternatives emerged within the British domestic market.

Until the late 1960s, these parallel or secondary markets did not threaten the main system.[40] They were not only condoned but actually looked upon favorably by the Bank of England. The antecedents of such markets could be found in local authority borrowing during the mid-1950s, but in the following decade other similarly unregulated markets developed outside the Bank's sphere of influence. Two of the most important were domestic clones of products introduced by foreign banks operating in the United Kingdom—a sterling interbank deposit market

---

39. In general, it was difficult for British institutions to engage in international transactions until foreign exchange controls were relaxed in 1979. Only then could British corporations raise foreign-currency-denominated funds through the Euromarkets and British institutions.

40. For a careful account of the parallel money markets, see P. Einzig, *Parallel Money Markets, Volume One: The New Markets in London* (London: Macmillan, 1971). Much of this section relies on Grady and Weale, *British Banking 1960–85:* esp. 121–123.

and a sterling CD market. Both were introduced two years after the arrival of their nonsterling counterparts.[41]

In the late 1960s, these newly developing markets grew to become a direct competitor for the traditional discount market. In that market, loans were secured, the Bank of England acted as lender of last resort, and the Bank also exercised authority to control interest rates. In the parallel markets, on the other hand, none of the above obtained; instead, it was a domestic wholesale money market, where price factors played a dominant role and where the Bank of England exercised little influence.

Why then were the parallel markets allowed to assume this role? Did they not threaten the traditional system? Several answers can be suggested. Some argue that the Bank hoped the parallel market would help, rather than hinder, the achievement of the Bank's objectives: in particular, the rates offered in the parallel markets could help attract foreign funds to Britain (in order to finance current account problems) without the need to raise Bank Rate.[42] Again, one can see the importance of the foreign reserve constraint already discussed in Chapter 2. Under the prevailing fixed exchange rate system, Britain had to defend sterling, and typically had to use higher interest rates to do so. However, these policies were deemed recessionary, and the authorities saw the parallel markets as a possible counterweight: if higher rates in those markets could be used to attract foreign capital to deal with external imbalances, and if those rates were not fully transmitted to the domestic markets (an arguable proposition), then the recessionary impact would be dampened. Inevitably, a comparison with events in the United States can be made: At about the same time (the late 1960s and early 1970s), the United States was also plagued with balance-of-payments problems that led the authorities, in very similar fashion, to segment the interest rate effects for the domestic and international sector. In Operation Twist, which I mentioned in Chapter 3, the authorities tried to use high short-term rates to support the dollar, while they attempted to keep long-term rates low. This U.S. policy proved unsuccessful; the British experience (as will be seen below) was also disappointing.

A second answer sometimes given to the question of why parallel markets were allowed to grow is that links between the traditional discount market (directly influenced by the Bank) and the parallel mar-

---

41. The sterling interbank deposit market meant that rather than solely relying on the discount market, banks could now use this new wholesale deposit market to fine-tune their deposit requirements.

42. See Revell, *The British Financial System:*287.

kets gave the authorities some influence over the new markets after all—if not over the *players* in these markets, than at least over some of the *prices* charged in them. The Bank set Bank Rate, which would influence the parallel markets by way of their links with the traditional market. Again, it is a somewhat questionable proposition, since ultimately demand and supply pressures in the parallel markets would be passed through to the primary market. But perhaps there was another, more important reason for the authorities to condone parallel markets. At their inception, these markets were relatively small, and they did not begin to play an important role until other events had helped propel them (and the banks most active in them) to prominence. For example, the sterling CD market started in 1968 with only £166 million of transaction volume. Yet by 1971, it had risen more than thirteenfold to £2,242 million. Over the next year, it more than doubled in size again. In other words, the authorities may at first have accepted the development of the parallel markets simply because these markets did not seem to threaten the primary market. But, by the late 1960s and early 1970s, as opportunities to do business in the nontraditional markets multiplied and as the number of players in them increased, the new risks these markets presented could be fully appreciated. When that happened, the authorities acted: unable to curb the new markets, they were forced to allow change throughout the whole financial system.

To say that the British financial services industry displayed stability from World War II until the early 1970s is not to imply that the relative market shares of the various institutions did not change. (See Table 5.3.) What remained stable was the basic industry structure and its methods of operation. It was only when new players entered the markets, often with new foreign techniques and ideas about finance, that the system's basic stability was compromised. The combination of the freedoms permitted in a self-regulated environment for those outside the traditional system and the new appetite of users and suppliers of capital for large, impersonal financial transactions caused a banking crisis unique in twentieth-century Britain. This crisis, which occurred in 1973–1974, signalled a transition away from the relationship system toward impersonal, price-driven transactions. It was Britain's turn to travel the road of change, a journey much like those of the United States and Japan.

BREAKING THE TRADITIONAL SYSTEM: CLEARING BANKS VERSUS FRINGE BANKS

The banking crisis tested the resilience of Britain's financial system. Sudden and severe pressures developed first in the so-called fringe bank-

TABLE 5.3
Relative Importance of Major Intermediaries' Gross Deposits
(£ Million)

	1950	1955	1960	1965	1970	1975	1980	1985
CLEARING BANKS								
Sterling	a	a	a	a	a	25,629	48,357	109,125
Nonsterling	a	a	a	a	a	4,408	13,039	41,475
Subtotal	7,132	7,521	8,465	10,623	12,058	30,037	61,396	150,600
% of Total	89	89	82	66	31	23	22	21
ACCEPTING HOUSES								
Sterling	a	a	a	686	1,370	2,263	5,296	11,358
Nonsterling	a	a	a	345	1,620	2,802	6,180	12,054
Subtotal	136	152	424	1,031	2,990	5,065	11,476	23,412
% of Total	2	2	4	6	8	4	4	3
OTHER BRITISH BANKS								
Sterling	—	—	—	219	1,850	8,867	16,663	32,353
Nonsterling	—	—	—	99	1,633	9,238	22,019	34,071
Subtotal	—	—	—	318	3,483	18,105	38,682	66,424
% of Total	—	—	—	2	9	14	14	9
FOREIGN BANKS								
Sterling	a	a	a	1,897	3,141	7,183	20,034	55,006
Nonsterling	a	a	a	2,338	17,334	68,707	152,109	411,077
Subtotal	712	808	1,467	4,235	20,475	75,890	172,143	466,083
% of Total	9	10	14	26	52	59	61	66
TOTAL	7,980	8,481	10,356	16,207	39,006	129,097	283,697	706,519
	100%	100%	100%	100%	100%	100%	100%	100%

[a] No breakdown for sterling and nonsterling available.

*Foreign banks are American, Japanese, and consortium banks, as well as other foreign banks and affiliates. British overseas and Commonwealth banks are also included.

Source: Bank of England Statistical Abstract, no. 1 (1970), and *Bank of England Quarterly Bulletin,* September 1971, March 1976, March 1981, September 1986.

ing sector and threatened to spread throughout the financial industry. To understand how the crisis of 1973 came about, and its impact on the system as a whole, it is first necessary to look at the interactions between monetary policymakers in Britain and the financial institutions.

Generally, monetary policy in Britain reflected changes in the development of macroeconomic thought. Macroeconomic management was handled differently, depending on the prevalence of either Keynesian or monetarist ideas; leading scholars sometimes deemed interest rates to be of the first importance, and at other times gave primacy to money growth rate targets. Policymakers adjusted their policies in tune to this theoretical debate. In the early postwar years, monetary policy had two objectives: interest rates were targeted to assure a favorable investment climate (in line with Keynesian ideas) and at the same time to guarantee the ability to attract funds from abroad if and when international transactions put the pound under pressure. (Recall the central role of the external balance constraint and its effect on monetary policy in Chapter 2.) Within this general context, especially in the aftermath of World War II, authorities at the Bank of England actively guided the investment decisions of the clearing banks, using many restrictions on capital allocation.

In setting overall monetary policy during the 1960s, British authorities employed alterations in Bank Rate, required liquidity ratios, and occasionally special deposits, together with qualitative controls. Open market operations, a primary tool of policy in the United States, played a role in setting liquidity and directing rates in the United Kingdom as well, although they did not stand at the center of policymaking. Authorities were assured that issues of public debt would be absorbed through the private sector, since the discount houses were obliged to tender for the full issue. In this scheme, a certain amount of interest rate volatility was implicit, but the tender price became, in effect, the outcome of consultation between authorities and discount houses. Still, the brunt of the monetary policy adjustments fell squarely on the clearing banks: when monetary policy was restrictive, banks were forced to constrain their credit; when policy was expansionary, they could increase the size of their loan portfolios.

In the 1960s, the loosening of many restrictions on lending created opportunities for intermediaries to compete for business, and the parallel markets began to grow. Authorities, hoping that these markets could be controlled through interest rate linkages with the primary markets and that the parallel markets would help provide liquidity, did not act to curb them. And indeed these relatively new markets provided ample liquidity. Among several groups of financial intermediaries, the fringe banks (which operated as secondary banks) availed themselves of the new opportunities, as they aggressively accelerated their lending activities (see "Other British banks" in Table 5.3).

In these new markets, banks could grow their liabilities without concern for their ability to attract deposits through traditional relationship channels. The fringe banks looked for money that could be bought. This is reminiscent of the development of the negotiable CD in the United States during the late 1960s, as well as the quotation in Chapter 3 (page 98) by the two Citicorp executives who chronicled the history of their bank. A strikingly similar quotation can be used to describe developments in the British market:

> These new markets brought with them the innovative banking technique of liability management, or endogenous deposit determination, first developed in the United States during the 1960s. A bank short of funds could simply go on out to these new wholesale money markets and bid for deposits. . . . They became potentially "advances driven" rather than "deposits driven."[43]

Because of this innovation, new players entered the market and began using untested instruments in unfamiliar territory. Lack of formal regulation had fostered the stable relationship climate but at the same time had left the door far enough ajar for new players to enter. With rising interest rates and increasing opportunities to make profits on the liabilities side of the balance sheet, outsiders started to push this door open, unhindered by many of the constraints that affected established players like the clearing banks. The latter, for example, had to observe the liquidity ratio, which reflected decades—if not centuries—of prior experience; in contrast, the fringe banks had little history to consult and few traditions by which to abide. Their managements consisted mostly of financial entrepreneurs rather than of the traditional financial aristocracy, and they were largely untested.

To operate as deposit-taking institutions, the fringe banks only had to obtain permission from the Department of Trade (which meant applying for a Section 123 certificate). Because these new financial intermediaries had no established relationship with the Bank of England, the usual system of moral suasion and informal but binding consultations did not apply. Add to this the lack of formal reporting requirements and the fact that liquidity constraints only applied to selected intermediaries (such as the clearing banks), and it becomes clear why supervision

---

43. P. Gardener, "Banking Crises and Risks," in P. Gardener, ed., *U.K. Banking Supervision, Evolution, Practice and Issues* (London: Allen & Unwin, 1986):5–6.

of the fringe banks was difficult. Nor did the Bank of England increase its supervisory staff in any way commensurate with the growth of the fringe banks: traditionally, informal and almost private relationships with the banking community had been maintained most effectively by a small group of well-known administrators. Even if it had wanted to monitor the fringe banks, the small staff of the discount office could not possibly have closely supervised such a rapidly expanding group of institutions.[44]

The various forms in which fringe banks developed have been described by Margaret Reid, in her study of the fringe banking crisis:

> In 1964, Hungarian-born Mr. Tom White, previously in the plastics industry, bought into the concern which he had built up, as Triumph Investment Trust, into a diversified group with some £200 million of banking, hire purchase, insurance, property and other interest. Mr. Herbert Despard, previously a Slater Walker man[45] moved in the late 1960s as a director and afterwards chairman of Cannon Street Investments (CSI), an investments concern which had once been a rubber company. In 1971 CSI purchased (from FNFC) a lending concern, Goulston Finance, which was later called Cannon Street Acceptances. Goulston had been part of Goulston Discount which had earlier been run by Mr. Sidney Davidson, a solicitor. In 1969 Mr. Davidson set up a private banking concern, Sterling Industrial Securities. . . . In 1968 three young financiers . . . bought sizable shareholdings in the J. H. Vavaseur commodity business. They afterwards developed it as a financial group with interests in foreign exchange brokering (through Harlow Meyer), banking (Vavaseur Trust), money management, property and films . . . (footnote added)[46]

For these financial corporations, the breathtaking speed of development and transformation was characteristic. Some institutions quickly grew into large companies. Slater Walker Securities (SWS), for example,

---

44. The reason for the growth of the fringe banks can be found in the general prosperity of the early and mid-1960s. It created a favorable environment for financial innovation; the demand for credit was high, the stock market showed gains (which meant that capital gains rather than dividends mattered), and an overall level of confidence in financial markets seemed to have returned in the wake of the strict controls of the 1950s. Real GNP growth between 1960 and 1965 stood at a compound growth rate of 3.13%. Although 1966 was a low-growth year, 1967 and 1968 showed growth rates of 3.5% and 4.0%, respectively. See *International Financial Statistics Yearbook, 1986* (International Monetary Fund, 1987). In this context, new, complex, and highly price-sensitive instruments began to supplant simple, noncompetitive, service- and relationship-based instruments.

45. Slater Walker was another major fringe bank.

46. M. Reid, *The Secondary Banking Crisis, 1973–1975, Its Causes and Course* (London: Macmillan, 1982):37.

would become, in only half a decade, a major financial institution, and by the early 1970s, its stock market capitalization made SWS one of the 50 largest corporations in Britain.[47] With the growth of fringe banks came respectability: major property companies and merchant banks began to do business with them. Now, the established players, bound by the traditional understandings, effectively gained exposure to a set of newcomer intermediaries, involved in novel activities that were based solely on price considerations.

The clearing banks needed to respond to the growth of the fringe banks. Competing on the basis of price was not—at least initially—an attractive option. Restrictive interest rates were a long and profitable tradition for clearing banks, and a linchpin of their business. Nor was it obvious that at first the clearers considered themselves constrained by liabilities. Early on, restrictions on loans and guidance from the Bank of England had effectively limited the need to be aggressive in funding, and no evidence exists that the cartelized interest rate setting was considered a hindrance in bank funding. Over time, however, the competition for funding from the fringe banks did look threatening. Still, some analysts have suggested that the clearing bankers believed their customers to be insensitive to interest rates. This may have been the case during the years of low rates, but it seems highly unlikely as interest rates began their long and sustained rise; between 1950 and 1979, interest rates rose from 2% to 17% as measured by Bank Rate.[48]

Thus, the lack of formal regulation allowed the newcomers (fringe banks) to grow rapidly, while the old players (the clearers) were restricted by informal regulation in testing their ability to gain presence in new markets. Between 1965 and 1970, clearers lost almost half of their market share, while other banks nearly doubled theirs (see Table 5.3). Furthermore, the lack of *formal* product market segmentation allowed the fringe banks to expand into several other areas, including share dealings, unit trusts, life insurance, property dealings, and loan services—all secured by real estate and largely financed through the parallel markets.

47. See C. Raw, *Slater Walker* (London: Andre Deutsch, 1977):191. Between 1966 and 1970, SWS bought 17 companies, and its market value increased from £4 million in 1964 to £135 million in 1969. Ibid.:191.

48. Alhadeff, *Competition and Controls in Banking*:329–331, gives one more reason for the apparent lack of price competition. He suggests that bankers believed that interest rate competition would have led to demand for time deposits as *substitutes* for interest-free checking accounts, thus driving up the costs for the banks without altering their fund availability. But in a world with general asset substitutability, it is less than obvious why, without interest rate responses from the clearers, funds would not be diverted to more aggressive competitors.

COMPETITION AND CREDIT CONTROL

The growth of fringe banks during the late 1960s presented a clear problem to the authorities. These new institutions operated mostly outside their influence and affected an important policy tool: the clearing banks. Remember that monetary policy tools in Britain were geared toward liquidity and reserve assets management (and requirements for noninterest-bearing special deposits) of the clearing banks together with Bank Rate policy.[49] Although the Radcliffe Committee had advised that these tools be extended to cover the nonclearing banks as well, fringe banks remained unaffected.

In this environment, three forces that would cause major change began to operate. First, the attractiveness of reserve asset and special deposit policies in monetary policymaking decreased in the face of increasing discussions about free market allocations. A 1967 report published by the National Board for Prices and Incomes was, for example, highly critical of the clearing bank cartel.[50] Second, a rethinking of monetary policy effectiveness hinted at the advantages of monetary management through interest rate changes rather than reserve asset management. Under this scenario, freed interest rates would allow for more competition in the financial industry *and* give the authorities freedom to use interest policy as a primary tool to devise monetary policy. Third, the ability of the clearing banks to obtain interest-free current account deposits was increasingly weakened by price-competitive alternatives in an environment of rising rates. Over time, deposits accounted for by the cheap current accounts fell.

The conservative government of Mr. Heath oversaw the change that the Bank of England presented in 1971 as Competition and Credit Control (CCC).[51] The most important provisions of CCC called for the clearing banks to dissolve their cartel and for the Bank of England to cease using them as its primary tool for policymaking. What was significant about this policy was its shift away from an environment very much reliant on the Bank's ability to exert moral suasion on a few well-disciplined institutions. Authorities wanted a system in which more

49. By varying the amount of special deposits, which often paid low interest, the Bank was able to contract or expand the money supply. See *Principal Memoranda of Evidence (Radcliffe Report)* VI (London: HMSO, 1960):41.

50. E. Nevin and E. Davis, *The London Clearing Banks* (London: Elek Books, 1970):195–196.

51. Competition and Credit Control was introduced in Bank of England, "Competition and Credit Control," *Bank of England Quarterly Bulletin* 11 (1971):189–193. Also see Moran, *The Politics of Banking: The Strange Case of Competition and Credit Control*:30–33.

impersonal policies, such as open market operations, would play a role. "Basically what we have in mind," the governor of the Bank said in 1971,

> is a system under which the allocation of credit is primarily achieved by its costs. . . . What we are therefore adopting is a new approach to credit control designed to permit the *price mechanism to function efficiently in the allocation of credit,* and to free the banks from rigidities and restraints which have so far too long inhibited them from fulfilling their intermediary role in the financial system. At the same time, it is hoped that these changes will favour innovation and competition, and in their way make some contribution to faster and sounder economic growth (emphasis added).[52]

In short, the switch to CCC increased reliance on price and reduced dependence on informal relationships. In this sense, implementation of CCC was a victory for the initiators of the fringe banking movement. These financial entrepreneurs had founded their growing firms on their ability to sharply price products, as well as to buy and sell financial instruments and money in various markets. At the same time, CCC could be a boon to clearing banks, allowing them to compete more directly with fringe banks. Competition was expected to be freer because the clearing banks were no longer the only institutions used to expand or contract the supply of credit; under CCC, a reserve requirement ratio was extended to *all* banks.

Another reason for the authorities' increased willingness to rely on the interest rate mechanism related to the external sector. Following serious balance-of-payments difficulties in the late 1960s, the devaluation of the pound sterling, and a standby agreement with the IMF in 1969, the balance of payments had once again begun to improve. After continuous deficits in the 1960s, the trade account had, by 1971, moved back into surplus. Now, without immediate external pressures, the focus on domestic effects of monetary policy seemed almost natural. The favorable international environment had freed policymakers from external concerns, at least temporarily. They were thus increasingly attracted by a financial environment in which markets would allocate credit to achieve optimal domestic investments. Unfortunately, the improvement in the international account was short-lived; and when external balance reappeared as a major concern, the combination of CCC, the parallel markets and the traditional market, *and* the fixed exchange rate system caused serious difficulty and brought the financial system to the brink of crisis.

52. See Bank of England, "Key Issues in Monetary and Credit Policy," *Bank of England Quarterly Bulletin* 11 (1971):196–198.

At first the new environment had appeared to function well. Even in 1972, when trouble eventually arrived, it was not initially to be found in the private sector. The onset of what was to become a major crisis appeared in the finances of the government sector. Rapid monetary growth and a lack of industrial investment opportunities fueled a boom in the financial and property sector.[53] General economic and political unrest (e.g., a coal miners' strike in early 1972 and a shortened work-week) precipitated a sterling crisis in mid-1972, which was exacerbated by worsening international accounts. Now, the international sector, which had looked so favorable in 1971, demanded full attention once again. Furthermore, because the Smithsonian agreement on (adjusted) fixed exchange rates was in effect, British policymakers found themselves in great difficulty.[54] Here, the basic issue raised in Chapter 2 is seen once again: the interaction between domestic macroeconomic management and the international accounts under fixed exchange rates. For the United Kingdom, a special dilemma arose as the authorities tried to stimulate domestic economic activity through low interest rates. Domestic demand increased (and hence, import demand remained strong), but pressures on the pound mounted and investment in the manufacturing industry remained low. With a worsening trade balance (and current account), and concomitant pressures on sterling, came the need to raise interest rates to defend the pound.

To extract itself from this predicament, the British government decided in July 1972 to float sterling rather than tighten interest rates. To keep interest rates low, they infused new liquidity, which was intended for industrial investment, but which actually allowed the fringe banks and other banks to continue to fuel the property boom. At the same time, domestic demand remained strong, the balance of payments deteriorated further, and the pound continued to weaken. To deal with these various problems, a restrictive budget for 1973 (which included a capital gains tax on property speculation) was presented. Also, interest rates rose in the summer of 1973 as the minimum lending rate (successor of the old Bank Rate) dramatically increased. In combination, these events

53. M3, a particular definition of the money supply, related to but broader than either M1 or M2, rose by approximately 30% in both 1971 and 1972.

54. Between 1967 and 1971, the trade balance of the United Kingdom had steadily improved and even turned positive. By 1972, however, this trend reversed. Trade balance figures for the years 1967 through 1974 were, according to the *International Financial Statistics* (Washington, DC: International Monetary Fund, 1982): −$1.6 billion (1967); $1.6 billion (1968); −$.4 billion (1969); $.1 billion (1970); $.5 billion (1971); −$1.9 billion (1972); −$6.4 billion (1973); −$12.5 billion (1974).

created a real estate bear market of historic proportions. Many of the fringe banks, whose loans were heavily collateralized with real estate, began to get into serious trouble as a result of higher interest rates and lower property values. (Bank Rate rose 8% between 1971 and 1973, using yearly averages.)[55] When two fringe banks (London and County Securities and Cedar Holdings) were brought to the brink of failure, fears arose that a systemic crisis was in the making. Suddenly, the new system was put to a major test. Not only were some of the newer institutions still outside the effective control of the Bank of England, but the traditional players under the Bank's influence were in danger of being contaminated by the many transactions linking various sectors of the financial system. The Bank of England had to assess just how many institutions would be involved in the crisis.

Through a series of meetings between the Bank of England and the clearing banks, it became evident that, owing to their many interbank loans and obligations, the potential for instability was enormous. Though the system had been designed precisely to avoid such situations, the commingling of unregulated price-focused institutions with informally regulated relationship banks seemed to have produced the worst of all possible worlds: price competition in funds-gathering, imprudent investments, and contamination of the overall system so that isolated closures of financial institutions became difficult. (Here, of course, a comparison can be made to the conditions that affect the S&L industry in the United States today.) To rescue the system from the spreading fringe banking crisis, the Bank of England organized an operation unparalleled in the history of the British financial system. Clearing banks and certain other financial institutions would be used to save the fringe banks by providing liquidity. Thus was born Operation Life-Boat.

There was a painful irony in this situation; the clearers who had trodden a more traditional path of prudence were asked to pay a penalty for the imprudent behavior of the upstart fringe banks. Furthermore, the crisis, which continued well into 1974, threatened on occasion to destabilize even the largest banks. At one point, even National-Westminster Bank was forced to deny a rumor that it had itself come under liquidity pressure.

The fringe banking crisis revealed the weaknesses that had developed in the British financial system during the late 1960s. The traditional system had not been set up to deal with new players, for whom price reigned supreme. The British concept of prudential regulation was based

---

55. See *International Financial Statistics* (Washington, DC: International Monetary Fund, 1980).

on informal rules; no formal regulatory powers existed. The authorities had tried to respond to the new price-oriented environment by forcing more competitive behavior from the traditional institutions while keeping formal regulation at a minimum; this set the stage for serious instability. When macroeconomic policy shifted from expansionary to contractionary, the fringe institutions were exposed, and they exhibited little ability to weather the storm. Lack of formal regulation and supervision had allowed these institutions to develop in an unacceptable way.

In the wake of these developments, it is hardly surprising that the Bank of England and the British government began to rethink some of the basic premises underlying the principle of informal regulation. An outcome of this process of reconsideration was seen in 1979, when a new Banking Act formalized many long-standing, unwritten rules. Only in 1979, for example, was the very concept of a bank clearly defined in legal terms.

Because they also influenced the methods of operation in British financial markets, the effects of international financial developments on the British financial system prior to this legislation need to be examined here. Although not as dramatic in their direct impact as the crisis of 1973, these international developments did exercise an important influence on the reshaping of the City.

INTERNATIONAL FINANCIAL PRESSURES

Despite Britain's economic decline after World War II, the eventual consolidation of the Euromarkets in London was natural. Yet the role of Britain's own institutions in this increasingly internationalized market rapidly diminished as foreign institutions aggressively entered London. Early on, in one pocket of the Euromarkets—the syndicated loan markets—British and American banks profited by their ability to recycle money from the cash-rich, oil-exporting nations to the cash-starved oil importers of the third world. London remained the dominant center for such syndication; by 1979, 65% of all such loans were organized from the City, and the lead manager share of the British banks rose.[56] (See Table 5.4.)

In international markets for securities and corporate finance advice, however, the British merchant banks were soon outdistanced by their

---

56. One of the major growth areas in which the clearing banks had participated was the recycling of petrodollars. This market started to slow down in the late 1970s, and it came to a natural halt as a result of the Mexican debt problem in 1982. It expanded again through the involuntary lending required in debt rescheduling.

TABLE 5.4
Percentage Share of U.K. Banks in Lead Managed
Syndications among Top Ten Banks

1977	4.0
1978	6.0
1979	6.0
1980	17.0
1981	20.0
1982	15.0

Source: R. McDonald, *International Syndicated Loans* (London: Euromoney Publications, 1982), p. 65.

American counterparts. The ability of the better-capitalized U.S. investment banks to handle the placement of issues through experienced sales forces, impressive distribution channels, and a large capability to hold inventory, was difficult for the British merchant banks to match; they were accustomed to smaller issues and a much more limited capital base.[57] Thus, although it was possible for a firm like S. G. Warburg to invent the Eurodebt markets, British firms never achieved positions of league-table leadership, except in the relatively small market for sterling issues. For example, by 1986, the sterling market had grown to issue volume of $10 billion. In contrast, the dollar market stood at $114 billion, the yen market at $18 billion, and the DM market at $17 billion.[58] London, and Britain generally, did profit from the internationalization of finance through the creation of employment opportunities (see Table 5.5) and a service account surplus, but it was only at the cost of allowing foreign institutions to build entrenchments in the City.

The growth of the overseas banking presence in London was remarkable (see Table 5.3): between 1970 and 1980, the number of foreign banks with offices in London more than doubled, from 165 to 353; by 1984, 470 foreign banks out of a total of 650 banks operated from the City.[59] U.S. banks were a particularly important presence in London. In 1978 more U.S. banks had offices in London than in New York, but

---

57. In the United States, the capital issue had also plagued several investment banks. Consolidations through mergers took place, and several investment banks aligned themselves with nonfinancial firms with deep pockets. Still others sought access to the public markets by transforming traditional partnerships into publicly traded corporations.

58. See Euromoney, *Annual Financial Report 1987.* Supplement to *Euromoney,* March 1987.

59. See J. Plender and P. Wallace, *The Square Mile: A Guide to the New City of London* (London: Century Publishing, 1985):26, 37.

TABLE 5.5
Employment Trends in the U.K. Financial Sector
(number of employees and percentage of total banking)

Staff Employed By	1975	1980	1984
London clearing banks	200,800	237,600	239,300
	65%	68%	63%
Scottish banks, Northern Ireland banks, merchant banks, and other banks	87,319	81,268	101,634
	28%	23%	27%
Foreign banks and foreign securities houses	20,881	31,132	42,066
	7%	9%	10%
TOTAL BANKING	309,000	350,000	383,000
	100%	100%	100%
Other financial institutions	106,000	120,000	130,000
TOTAL FINANCIAL SECTOR	415,000	470,000	513,000
Rate of unemployment in the U.K.	4.0%	6.8%	13.1%

Source: Committee of London Clearing Bankers, *Abstract of Banking Statistics*, vol. 2, May 1985; Parker, "Foreign Banks in London," *The Banker*, November 1981, p. 109; *Annual Abstract of Statistics*, HMSO, 1977, 1982, 1986–1987 editions.

their relative importance had declined.[60] After 1975 the Japanese banks gained a greater share—while the American banks garnered a smaller share—of international liabilities, reflecting the changing international asset positions of the two countries.

The success of the City's international financial transactions gave the authorities another reason to move away from strict reliance on informal relationships and traditions. I already noted the City's contributions to the balance of payments and to employment in the consistently weak British economy of the 1970s.[61] A less competitive manufacturing indus-

60. See C. Parker, "Foreign Banks in London: More Foreign Banks Open for Business," *The Banker*, November (1981):101–111.

61. One of the few positive developments in the U.K. economy during the late 1970s was the contribution of oil and gas exports from the North Sea. It was not until 1980, however, that the North Sea gas exports helped turn a chronic trade account deficit into a surplus. Moreover, the North Sea contributions were only temporary, and it was clear that the City would no longer be able to rely on a dominant international trading position to create a natural comparative advantage for its financial institutions.

try rendered the importance of the financial sector even greater. But though the financial sector's present contribution to Britain's international position was indisputable, no one could be certain about what comparative advantage the financial system might offer in the *future;* increasingly, other national markets offered new freedoms and opportunities, casting doubt on the future of London.

The City's past success in international finance had not occurred because British institutions could perform complex financial tasks at a cheap price (in fact, many of the innovative financial instruments introduced in the London market reflected developments in foreign markets);[62] but rather because London provided a haven for foreigners seeking to escape home regulation. So a seemingly paradoxical situation gradually emerged. The fringe banking crisis, together with increased price competition (CCC) on the domestic side of the financial markets, was leading the authorities to more formal regulation. At the same time New York, and later, Tokyo were becoming increasingly deregulated, thus eroding the chief advantage that London held for foreign players. In short, London's special international position was being threatened from both sides—by foreign as well as domestic pressures.

The economic importance of the international market meant that new British efforts at regulation would be primarily targeted to deal with the *domestic* side of the City. If the authorities were to extend formal supervision over the international sector, the market might relocate (although heavy investments in infrastructure would make such a move costly). At the same time, for the merchant banks, which had to compete with foreign players even for their domestic financing and advisory business, the need for competitive freedoms was pressing. For example, in brokering securities, would large institutional investors prefer to execute in New York rather than London, where many cumbersome traditions still prevailed? And in a domestic environment where the advantages of price competition were now being touted, were the traditional practices on the London Stock Exchange not unduly restrictive? In this light, the developments on the London Stock Exchange that led to the Big Bang can be seen as only a continuation of the much wider process of evolution sketched so far. Important as it seemed, that event merely offered further evidence of the ascendancy of price-driven transactions over traditional relationships.

---

62. In 1966, dollar-denominated CDs were introduced by American banks. Two years later, a sterling CD market opened. See Grady and Weale, *British Banking 1960–1985:*121–123. Of course, some instruments were developed by U.K. banks, the Eurobond being one example.

BREAKING TRADITIONS IN THE STOCK MARKET

The October 1986 changes in the U.K. stock market were widely publicized, and one American financial journal noted that London was "braving the new transactional era."[63] In essence, the Big Bang ended single capacity dealing, whereby jobbers made markets and held inventories of stocks while brokers placed orders and conducted transactions for their customers; it also enhanced the capital position of firms on the exchange by permitting new ownership structures that enabled old institutions to be sold to new, more diversified financial groups. Thus, the British stock exchange increasingly came to resemble other exchanges.

The Big Bang brought new price freedoms to the London securities industry, but it also brought new formal regulation during the mid-1980s, as various official bodies were instituted to regulate and oversee the industry. The latter seems to contrast with the developments of the New York market as it moved from regulation to deregulation (e.g., commissions were freed and shelf registration became possible through Rule 415). But though it is fairly accurate to describe the developments in the New York market in terms of pure deregulation, such a simple description does not apply to events in the London market. In fact, the British securities sector, like the remainder of the financial industry, had never really operated as an unregulated market; as with the banking sector, informal rules and relationships were pervasive.[64] London saw relatively little innovation because informal regulations gave the authorities the power to signal displeasure about early developments, long before they could be formally tested, and membership in the financial clubs effectively controlled entry, especially on the stock exchange.[65]

I noted that, for British merchant banks, competition with the much larger foreign firms had become more difficult in both the fixed-income market and in financial advisory services (e.g., mergers and acquisitions), where only the relatively small British market could be serviced with special advantage. And even in that last bastion of British influence, foreign firms began to show their power: more aggressive techniques, large distribution networks, and higher capitalization made them formi-

63. See *Institutional Investor* 20 (1986):255–278.
64. See Committee to Review the Functioning of Financial Institutions, *Wilson Report* (London: HMSO, 1980). The report argues that the difference between formal and informal regulation in Britain has been exaggerated, even though it does not question the basic description of London as a self-regulated market.
65. This contrasts sharply with the policies of many financial institutions in the United States. When BankAmerica acquired Charles Schwab, it meant that a commercial bank was entering the stockbroking business. The corporation tested the interpretation of the formal regulations and was able to purchase the broker.

TABLE 5.6
Equity Capital of Selected U.S. Investment Banks and Selected U.K. Merchant Banks

U.K. Merchant Banks	$ Million*	U.S. Investment Banks	$ Million
Kleinwort Benson	501	Merrill Lynch	1,888
S. G. Warburg	326	Salomon Brothers	1,181
Schroder Wagg	291	Dean Witter	961
Hill Samuel	286	Shearson Amex excluding	
Morgan Grenfell	270	Lehman Brothers	710
TOTAL	1,675	TOTAL	4,740

*Converted from pound sterling to U.S. dollar at 2.33 $/£.
Source: *Financial Times,* June 4, 1984, p. 14.

dable competitors for British firms.[66] (See Table 5.6.) Furthermore, the rules governing the London Stock Exchange not only made it difficult for outsiders to enter, but were actually a comparative disadvantage to the British firms that operated there. The changes that occurred on the London Stock Exchange in 1986 were essential if British institutions were to have any chance of regrouping and becoming competitive with the strong, rich, foreign institutions.

The reason that so much media attention was focused on the Big Bang may well have been that this episode of deregulation seemed to parallel events in the United States. There, in the mid-1980s, the press made much of financial deregulation and the spectacular incidents (such as Continental Illinois) that had occurred in connection with it. Events in the British stock market, too, provided good copy. But, like the other changes I discussed, the antecedents of the Big Bang go back a long time. The actual impetus for changes on the stock exchange originated a decade earlier, in 1976, when the Labour government's Secretary of State for Trade used the Restrictive Practices Act of 1956 to test the appropriateness of self-regulation, and specifically, minimum commissions, on the exchange.[67] Although not designed to provide a framework for investigating the stock market, the act did equip the Secretary with the tools to do so.

It is certainly reasonable to assume that the deregulation of the New

66. For example, when British Telecom was privatized, the difference in speed between the American distribution by Morgan Stanley and the distribution by the British merchant bankers was astounding. See Plender and Wallace, *The Square Mile:*49.

67. See N. Hewlett and J. Toporowski, *All Change in the City: A Report on Recent Changes and Future Prospects in London's Financial Markets* (London: Economist Publications, 1985):37–38.

York market, where fixed commissions were abolished in 1975, must have led British policymakers to consider similar measures. But the effects of abolishing minimum commission rates in the London market would be significantly different from those observed in New York. In London, without minimum rates, the very essence of the single capacity dealing system would be endangered. Traditionally, jobbers made markets in securities, while brokers engaged in the transactions with outsiders. Under a system of flexible commissions (which would probably be lower because of competition), the jobbers might want to deal with outsiders using brokers at a sharp discount as go-betweens. At the same time, brokers, with depressed profits from brokerage activity under negotiated commissions, might attempt to match their principals' transactions themselves, without putting those transactions through the jobbers. And all this would be happening when jobbers were also being affected by other changes in the system, such as increased block trading (which would be further enhanced by negotiated commissions) and rising interest rates. These large block trades, and concomitant inventory requirements with high carrying costs (interest rates), were already cutting into the profits of the jobbers and straining their capital. Finally, the other changes already mentioned that occurred in the British financial system at this time added to the atmosphere of volatility and change.

In 1979, the exchange was forced to hand over its rule book for external inspection by the Office of Fair Trading, whereupon it was reviewed by the Restrictive Practices Court. In their excellent study of the changes on the stock exchange, Plender and Wallace observed that

> seen from the Bank of England's perspective, the most worrying thing was not just that the Restrictive Practices Court Case against the Stock Exchange was preventing the change [that could have come from self-reregulation]. Either outcome of the case was potentially disastrous: if the Stock Exchange won, its constitution risked being set in concrete for another decade in which business would ebb away from the central market; if it lost, there was a powerful and more immediate threat from outside. Though in their speeches to foreign audiences Bank governors traditionally upheld the virtues of free trade and liberal investment policies, this liberalism had never extended to a desire to see domestic banking and securities markets opened up to the full force of foreign competition. The Bank had little doubt that the immediate removal of the ban on 100% corporate ownership of Stock Exchange firms would open the way to American domination of the more profitable end of the Stock Exchange's business, notwithstanding public protestations to the contrary by Sir Nicholas Goodison, the Stock Exchange chairman.[68]

68. See Plender and Wallace, *The Square Mile: A Guide to the New City of London*:93.

Another risk facing the exchange was that, even after allowing for outside ownership, the profitability of the jobbers and brokers might fall in a free rate environment. If this were to happen, one of the main purposes of the entire exercise—to make British securities firms globally competitive with the well-capitalized foreign firms—would be put in jeopardy.

Against this background, negotiations were conducted in 1983 between the Chairman of the Stock Exchange, Sir Nicholas, and Trade Secretary Parkinson. The agreement they reached was a compromise: negotiated rates would be instituted gradually, and as of October 1986 all transactions would be dealt with on the basis of flexible commissions. It was further agreed that the supervision of the exchange would be broadened to include outsiders, though no specific reference was made to full ownership by outside corporations.[69] Neither was the issue of single capacity dealt with clearly.

When it became apparent that a gradual transition toward negotiated rates was impractical, it was decided that all fixed commissions should be abolished simultaneously. This was the Big Bang. In this environment, single capacity dealing could not survive, and diversified institutions had to be able to buy both jobbers and brokers. Finally, majority outside ownership was accepted in March 1986. The stock exchange's journey from traditions to transactions had been completed. With the new environment came pressures to reorganize the industry. In the ensuing months, mergers and acquisitions went on at a feverish pace.[70] (See Table 5.7.)

One of the main reasons for the high number of takeovers and acquisitions was the view, shared by many British and U.S. financial firms, that a widely diversified financial organization providing broad services would have the best chance of survival in an increasingly internationalized system where price competition reigned supreme. (I return to this idea in Chapter 8.) In both London and the United States, financial supermarkets were envisioned and actually began to be built. Furthermore, looking forward to competition from foreign institutions such as Citicorp, Chase Manhattan Corporation, Nomura, First Boston Credit Suisse, Merrill Lynch, and American Express, many British bankers decided they needed to take over jobbers and brokers. Merchant banks

69. Outside (corporate) ownership of membership firms had been limited to 10% until 1982, when it was raised by the exchange members to 29.9%. See ibid.:96.

70. For a good description of the many takeovers and mergers, see ibid.: 110–116. Also see *New Markets After the Big Bang,* supplement to *Euromoney* and *Euromoney Corporate Finance,* 1986:28–29.

TABLE 5.7
Examples of Conglomerations in the London Securities Market

Ultimate Owner	Stockbrokers	Jobbers	Merchant Banks	Discount Houses
U.K. CLEARING BANKS				
Barclays	de Zoete & Bevan (March 1984)	Wedd Durlacher Mordaunt (March 1984)	Barclays Merchant Bank*	
Lloyds			Lloyds Merchant Bank*	
Midland	W. Greenwell (March 1984)		Samuel Montagu* (Midland's merchant bank subsidiary)	
NatWest	Fielding, Newson-Smith (July 1984)	Bisgood Bishop (February 1984)	County Bank*	
U.K. MERCHANT BANKS				
Barings	Henderson Crosthwaite (May 1984)	Wilson & Watford (December 1984)		
Hambros	Strauss Turnbull (March 1984)			
Hill Samuel	Wood Mackenzie (June 1984)			
Kleinwort Benson	Grieveson Grant (June 1984)	Charlesworth & Co. (June 1984)		
Morgan Grenfell	Pember & Boyle (October 1984)	Pinchin Denny (April 1984)		Target Group (May 1984)
N. M. Rothschild	Scott Goff Layton (December 1984)	Smith Bros. (December 1983)		
Schroders	Helbert, Wagg & Co., Anderson, Bryce, Villiers (August 1984)			
S. G. Warburg	Rowe & Pitman (August 1984)	Akroyd & Smithers (November 1983)		

Company	Acquisitions (with dates)
U.S. COMMERCIAL BANKS	
Citicorp	Vickers da Costa (November 1983); Scrimgeour Kemp-Gee (September 1984); Seccombe Marshall & Champion (February 1985)
Chase Manhattan	Simon & Coates (November 1984); Laurie Millbank (November 1984)
Security Pacific	Hoare Govett (June 1982); Charles Pulley (April 1984)
North Carolina National Bank	Panmure Gordon (December 1984)
OTHER U.S. FINANCIAL INSTITUTIONS	
Shearson Lehman-American Express	L. Messel (July 1984)
Merrill Lynch	A. B. Giles & Gresswell (June 1985)
Prudential-Bache	PB Securities, Down de Boer and Duckett (July 1984)
EUROPEAN BANKS	
Deutsche Bank	Morgan Grenfell (November 1984)
Union Bank of Switzerland	Phillips & Drew (November 1984)
Credit Suisse	Buckmaster & Moore (January 1985)
Credit Commerciale de France	Laurence Prust (June 1985)
Banque Bruxelles	Williams de Broe Hill Chaplin (July 1984); Henry Ansbacher (May 1984)

*Not purchased but developed internally.

Source: J. Plender and P. Wallace, *The Square Mile: A Guide to the New City of London* (London: Century Hutchinson Publishing, 1985), pp. 110–119; and *The Economist,* August 2, 1986, p. 61.

like S. G. Warburg (through its parent, Mercury Securities) and clearing banks like Barclays bought companies and diversified.[71] The stock exchange was no longer a club, with rules set only by its own members. The need for outside controls was recognized as new members were admitted. Central to all these changes was the realization that the British system's traditional organization had to be compromised if the stock exchange was to function better in the face of international competition.

FORMALIZATION OF THE BRITISH FINANCIAL INDUSTRY

Today's competitive institutions are able to offer a wider range of services to customers who, in turn, do business with a wider range of partners. Informal rules and dependencies play a lesser role than in the past. Deposit-gathering competition from the unit and investment trusts and from building societies has made clearing banks' reliance on no-interest checking accounts less feasible. Increased competition from foreign firms has put pressure on the well-established relationships between the merchant banks and their clients, and made it more important for them to offer the same services available from foreign competitors that operate in London.

Whether one calls the emerging British system regulated or deregulated depends on the benchmark taken. London has, for instance, much more freedom than Tokyo, even considering the deregulation that has taken place in the Japanese financial system over the past decade. Interest rate regulation is greater in Japan, and the market segments open to the various financial intermediaries are still heavily restricted by Article 65 and other rules and regulations. The comparison with the United States is harder to make. London still offers freedoms unknown in New York, although in some areas the U.S. market is actually less restrictive; overall the two markets now share many features. For example, a new scheme of deposit insurance introduced in the United Kingdom in 1982, which insures deposits of up to £10,000 for 75%, closely resembles the insurance offered through the FDIC and FSLIC in the United States.[72] In both countries, insurance premiums are independent of the quality of the assets—a provision that has drawn criticism from banks that consider their loan portfolios to be safer than average. More generally, the United Kingdom has followed the U.S. pattern of financial conglom-

71. For example, an American financial journal proclaimed the chairman of S. G. Warburg "Banker of the Year," because of his ability to broaden his institution. See *Institutional Investor* 20 (1986):124–126. Also see J. Maycock, *Financial Conglomerates: The New Phenomenon* (London: Gower, 1986).

72. See Clarke, *Regulating the City: Competition, Scandal and Reform*:41–42.

eration and product innovations that rely more on price and less on traditional relationships.

Though many elements of the transition described here actually provided new freedoms, the adoption of more formal rules implies that regulation actually occurred in the domestic U.K. market. The Banking Act of 1979 is perhaps the best example. Before its passage, the country had a banking system in which various financial institutions climbed a "ladder" of recognition and respectability; the higher they got, the wider the scope of banking activity permitted them. It was the Department of Trade that determined the position of each institution.[73] Once that department granted the certifications, the staff in the discount office at the Bank of England set supervision and reporting requirements, based mostly on nonstatutory agreements and understandings.[74]

The dangers of this procedure became apparent in the fringe banking crisis. The Banking Act rectified this problem by providing the first official definition of banks and of the activities in which they could engage. The act made explicit the criteria according to which the Bank of England could authorize a firm to act as a bank or to take deposits. At the same time, it established uniform minimum reserve requirements. Thus it extended the formal authority of the Bank of England, but retained flexibility in the use of tools for implementing policy.

One remnant of the old ladder of respectability that financial institutions used to climb remained in the new system: firms were divided into licensed deposit-taking institutions and recognized banks. Deposit-taking institutions were required to supply regular information to the Bank of England, while the recognized banks could only be *asked* to do so. The formal power to demand information from licensed deposit-taking institutions was intended as a safeguard against new players that were unfamiliar with the system. Graduation from deposit-taking status to that of a recognized bank could occur upon approval by the Bank of England. In short, some of the traditional nonstatutory (and self-) regulation was retained for the established banks, but now a formal framework existed to extend the authorities' control over many institutions that had previously been beyond supervision.[75]

---

73. It derived its power from the Companies Acts (1948 and 1967), rather than from a specific banking act.

74. See I. Morison, P. Tillett, and J. Welch, *Banking Act 1979* (London: Butterworth, 1979):12–15.

75. See P. Cooke, "Self-Regulation and Statute: The Evolution of Banking Supervision," in Gardener, ed., *U.K. Banking Supervision: Evolution, Practice, and Issues*:85–98, esp. 92–93.

TABLE 5.8
Regulatory Agencies and Their Responsibilities

Securities and Investment Board (SIB)
    Stock Exchange
    International Securities Regulatory Organization
    Association of Futures Brokers and Dealers
    Financial Intermediaries Managers and Brokers Regulatory Association
    Investment Management Regulatory Association
    Life Assurance Unit Trusts Regulatory Association*
Department of Trade and Industry
    Insurance companies
    General compliance with company law
    Unit Trusts Lloyds
Bank of England
    Banking (Clearing and all others as defined in the new Banking Act)
    Wholesale money and foreign exchange
    Gilts markets
    Bullion
City Panel
    Mergers and acquisitions

*Responsibility for the Unit Trusts is shared with the Department of Trade.
Source: The Economist, August 9, 1986, p. 66.

Other examples of the trend toward formalization can be identified: the founding and growth of the supervision department of the Bank of England, apart from the discount office, is one. The requirement that allowed outsiders on the Stock Exchange Council and that deprived the exchange of full self-regulation is another. In the past, the Prevention of Fraud Act (1958) provided for the licensing of firms dealing in securities. However, members of the London Stock Exchange or any of six other self-regulating institutions were exempt.[76] The Financial Services Bill of 1984 provided formalization here, since it defined the new structure, with a Securities and Investment Board (SIB) and six self-regulatory organizations (SRO) that derived their authority from the SIB. (See Table 5.8.) The SIB's board, appointed by the Secretary of State for Trade and Inventory and the governor of the Bank of England, therefore supervised the investment business in the United Kingdom in a new and

76. The six associations are: The London District Market Association; the Association of Stock and Share Dealers; the Law Society of Scotland; the U.K. Association of New York Stock Exchange Members; the Association of Canadian Investment Dealers and the Members of the Toronto and Montreal Stock Exchanges in Great Britain; and the U.K. Association of Tokyo Stock Exchange Members. See L. Gower, *Review of Investor Protection* (London: HMSO, 1982).

extensive way. Finally, the Insurance Companies Acts of 1974, 1980, and 1981 all increasingly formalized supervision of the insurance industry.

New forms of statutory and nonstatutory oversight emerged in the British financial environment in the 1970s and 1980s. As international and domestic pressures rendered the system of informal self-regulation less advantageous, the banking, investment, and insurance businesses saw greater statutory regulation, which defined more carefully the limits of acceptable behavior. In the new structure, more and more traditional rules have been formalized. Thus, events in the United Kingdom were different from those in the United States and Japan, where deregulation rather than formalization took place. This fact should not come as a surprise, since the traditional financial systems of all countries reflected the distinct traits of their cultures. But it should also be clear that important similarities have been revealed. In the next chapter, these similarities are reviewed as the three systems are compared.

6

THE THREE SYSTEMS COMPARED

In the preceding three chapters these common themes in the evolution of the major financial markets emerged: (1) a traditional phase, characterized by the reliance on relationships in financial transactions; (2) a move during the 1970s away from relationships and toward price-driven transactions; and (3) the growing importance of international financial integration. Given particular national preferences and concerns, distinct national characteristics, and the very different national foundations from which these systems developed, such similarities at first seemed surprising. But once the underlying layer of macro- and international economic cause and effect was uncovered, the similar evolutions became understandable. The underlying forces described in Chapters 1 and 2 *combined* with particular national characteristics and cultures to produce the similar results noticed in each country. Of course, this does not mean that the three systems ever were, or are becoming, identical. Indeed, important differences have been noted, for example in the development of national systems. The United States was marked by a fear of centralized financial power; Japan showed a preference for a clearly defined hierarchical structure; while the United Kingdom relied on informal clubs and traditions. Nevertheless, the outcomes of these differing developments mirrored each other; historically, all three financial systems fostered long-term relationships through market segmentation and a relative suppression of the price mechanism. In all three systems, financial transactions were heavily regulated, and multiple constraints on competition persisted as relationships flourished under the watchful eye of the authorities.

By comparing the traditional phase in each system, and contrasting each with the current environment, another similarity can be brought to light: the reduction in regulation has allowed many new freedoms and more flexible financial asset prices (interest rates) in all three systems. This development is consistent with the basic change outlined in Chapters 1 and 2, where it was shown how a traditional acceptance of capital controls (in stark contrast to attitudes favoring free trade in goods and services) was superseded in the 1970s by a new acceptance of international capital flows and flexible currency prices (exchange rates). Thus the old preference for freedoms in "real" transactions, which was coupled with suspicion of the price mechanism in financial transactions, gave way to the view that the price mechanism should govern financial transactions as well.

It is not just a similarity between changes on two levels (the international financial system and the three national financial systems), however, that shows up in the analysis presented: instead, the changes at one level affected the other, and often the two reinforced each other. For example, international capital flight from the United States forced deregulation in the early 1970s, first of large certificates of deposit and later of smaller-sized CDs. For Japan, an internationally induced recession in the wake of the first oil shock forced new domestic price freedoms. Later, during the second oil shock, current account financing needs encouraged regulators to look more favorably on companies availing themselves of opportunities in the Euromarkets. The United Kingdom underwent similar experiences in 1972, when international pressures first caused the pound to be floated; and later, as an interest rate shock threatened to destabilize the British financial system. As the three national systems changed, new instruments developed that facilitated the transfer of financial assets between countries. Investors became far more sensitive to the price performance of both domestic and international financial products than they had been in the past.

The outcome of all this has been a new set of uncertainties and potential rewards for policymakers, investors, issuers, and financial services firms. Relatively simple, stable, structured financial systems have given way to systems in which new freedoms allow for innovative financial strategies. This change represents a breakdown of boundaries in finance. Before exploring the broader implications of this breakdown of financial boundaries, I first review briefly the roles of central and commercial banks. Both were highly visible in all three national financial systems; they played important roles and are readily comparable.

THE CENTRAL BANKS

Though central banks operated in the United States, Japan, and the United Kingdom at the onset of World War I, their origins were different in each country. Repeated bouts of financial instability drove the U.S. government to set aside its mistrust of centralized power and finally to establish an institution that resembled a central bank. Though fragmented at its founding in 1914 (through the Federal Reserve Act of 1913), the United States' Federal Reserve System, like both the Bank of Japan and the Bank of England, grew into a powerful institution. In Japan, it was not financial instability in the sense of the U.S. bank panics, but the need to stabilize note issuance that led to the creation of the Bank of Japan and its high official position in 1882. In the United Kingdom, the power of the Bank of England had been building over a much longer time.

Eventually, in all three countries, the role of the central bank became to steer, regulate, and supervise. The central banks often used informal pressure to make their wishes known, more so perhaps in the United Kingdom and Japan than in the United States. All three central banks exercised great—though by no means exclusive—influence over their financial systems. They used this influence to make the banking sector a tool of monetary management. During the traditional phase of the system in the 1950s and 1960s, the policies of the central banks, the stability of the commercial banking sector, and the ascendancy of Keynesian beliefs, combined with (or resulted in) a generally prosperous, high-growth environment. During the 1970s, however, disenchantment with traditional Keynesian policies developed, particularly in the United States and the United Kingdom. Together with supply shocks such as the energy-price increases, this disenchantment led both the Federal Reserve and the Bank of England to formulate policies that facilitated inflation. Such policies were made easier by the elimination of the external foreign reserve constraint when the Bretton Woods system was dismantled. The outcome was more volatile and generally higher interest rates in both countries. In Japan, interest rates were also decontrolled; there, especially in the years after the oil shock, a standard Keynesian injection of government spending, without an offsetting increase in taxes, boosted demand, but also ultimately forced the Bank of Japan to alter the absorption mechanism of government debt and to allow for freer fluctuations in interest rates.

In all three environments, open market operations began to play a greater role in the central banks' management of monetary affairs—not surprising during a period characterized by new interest rate freedoms. Central banking authorities began to accept the validity of greater interest rate freedom and to change their thinking about monetary policy. They knew that their earlier tight control over domestic interest rates had to give way in the face of large international capital flows. Furthermore, loss of faith in the effectiveness of macroeconomic demand management developed while monetarist ideas (which carried interest rate volatility) resurfaced.

Briefly then, a new and untested environment appeared in the 1980s, with new policy ideas, new international opportunities to borrow or invest, and new interest rate freedoms for a host of financial products. Investors, issuers, and financial services firms faced an almost bewildering variety of choices. The commercial banks provide a good example of one group of financial institutions that had to respond to these new opportunities and risks. Again, they are easily comparable in the three national systems under consideration.

COMMERCIAL BANKS

The United States' money center commercial banking sector, Japan's city banks, and the United Kingdom's clearing banks exhibit marked similarities. Traditionally, these banks had played comparable roles as repositories of retail (and corporate) deposits, as lenders, and as intermediaries in a highly price-controlled market. And when national financial systems started to rely more heavily on price-driven transactions, similar changes could be expected to occur in the U.S. commercial, the Japanese city, and the U.K. clearing banks. The reliance of these banks on cheap relationship money would decrease as price-sensitive deposit alternatives became available, and some of their primary lending clients would discover direct funding methods as substitutes for traditional loans.

The banks were not identical in their responses to the new environment. Purchased money and rapid asset growth from loans to untraditional clients both appeared in the United States, in response to the emergence of new, price-sensitive products. In Japan, a slowdown in the demand for industrial loans led the major banks to attempt new product freedoms, just at the time of a newly emerging power relationship between them and the authorities, as the latter became large absorbers of funds. In the United Kingdom, the clearing banks started their transition to price-driven products after Competition and Credit Control had been adopted.

Yet despite such differences, important similarities can be found in the general attitude toward the traditional segmented and price-regulated product markets. In both Japan and the United States, banks began pushing to eliminate the remaining vestiges of the old legal separation between investment and commercial banking. In the United Kingdom, the Big Bang provided a variety of vendors with new opportunities for expansion, through subsidiaries, into the securities markets. A widening (and shifting) of activities was common to all countries as financial product prices increasingly reflected market conditions.

Also, just as the domestic product markets allowed new freedoms, international opportunities began to beckon. As clients turned to the international product market, many banks in the United States, Japan, and the United Kingdom attempted to gain a presence in the others' markets. With increased levels of international capital flows and a greater ability to move capital across national borders, a more integrated international capital market emerged that had fewer distinct national characteristics in the domestic financial markets.[1]

BREACHING PRODUCT BOUNDARIES

So far, only central and commercial banks have been mentioned. Yet in the financial systems of the three major countries discussed, a multitude of differentiated financial institutions have operated. Although the actual number of such institutions varied substantially from country to country, in each the authorities had chosen to support a variety of institutions that serviced particular segments of the financial product market. Such segmentation is not an inevitable form of financial organization, however. A country such as Germany, where universal banks operate, has created financial stability by adopting a very different structure. But in the three systems described here, all differentiated intermediaries performed the same basic function; by restricting the number of easily accessible, price-competitive alternatives, they reduced partner switches and enhanced relationships.

New developments breached the carefully established boundaries between these institutions. In the United States, for example, commercial banks purchased discount stockbrokers at home and abroad. Other examples of infringement of the Glass-Steagall Act abound; recently, for example, banks have been allowed to enter corporate bond underwriting. In Japan, the distinction between city banks and long-term banks was blurred by the application of new techniques such as swaps and funding in the Euromarkets. Boundaries in the United Kingdom collapsed as new entities combined interests of both merchant and clearing banks.

---

1. In such an environment, differences in capital and regulatory structure in the country of incorporation can provide a competitive advantage (or disadvantage) from the institutions' point of view and, thus, an incentive to escape the control of the authorities; financial services firms can shop around. Hence proposals for regulatory homogenization (e.g., internationally accepted capital adequacy rules) have naturally arisen, as financial institutions embarked on new activities. In general, business choices for the financial services firms have rapidly increased, a point I return to in later chapters.

And, it was not only the crossing of existing product boundaries that characterized this period. As I describe below, product innovation was spurred by the new emphasis on price performance and by a new ability to price particular product attributes. In combination, these two developments meant that the financial product market spectrum started to become a continuum.

In fact, it is now clear that for most remaining barriers, the question is *when*—and not *if*—they will be breached. All these recent changes have multiplied the choices available for financial services firms. Rather than being restricted by regulation, they have increasingly been able to define their business strategy themselves.

A popular strategic reaction to the breakdown of *local* boundaries inside the domestic product markets was (at one time) the financial supermarket. Similarly, the breakdown of *national* boundaries accompanying the growth of international capital transactions led to international diversification. (I shall return to this issue in Chapter 8.) In sum, the notion of segmentation within and between national financial markets is becoming obsolete. And if in the future the idea exists at all, it will be as the outcome of a strategic choice, rather than of regulated direction.

THE STABILITY OF THE EMERGING SYSTEM

One obvious concern arising from changes in the national financial systems concerns the stability of the emerging systems. In this respect, the problems of several U.S. banks have attracted considerable attention. The transition toward a price-driven environment seems to have left U.S. financial institutions more vulnerable than many of their foreign counterparts. One major incident—the failure of Continental Illinois—is explored in greater detail later. Here, a more general question arises: is instability inherent in the new form of organization? And, if so, may one expect to see examples of the same instability in Japan and Britain (especially remembering the fringe banking crisis)?

In answer, remember first that the movement toward price banking and the proliferation of product innovations has been most intense in the United States. Many of the newer Japanese and British instruments are mere copies of products first developed in the United States. Furthermore, Chapter 4 showed that in the Japanese financial system, oversight remains very significant. Also, the new freedoms offered in Japan emerged at a time when the country was experiencing rapid growth in its net foreign asset position, without major domestic economic dislocations. This may explain why the Japanese system has not, thus far, displayed the problems observed in the United States. For the United Kingdom, the stability of some institutions was endangered early in the transition phase, in particular during the fringe banking crisis, which held the potential of spreading to other banks as well. Formalization of the system through the passage of new legislation could be described as a partial response to the threat of instability.

The different speeds of innovation notwithstanding, there are reasons to be concerned about the stability worldwide: with increasing internationalization, instability in one market can easily spill into another. October 19, 1987, was a not-so-subtle reminder of the speed with which market malaise is transmitted. The question raised by the October 1987 stock market shock concerns the ability of the system to remain an effective carrier of *informed* price signals, even under unusual transaction pressure. But it is not just the growing volume of financial interactions between markets that is of concern. In fact, broader trade relationships are making the well-being of nations ever more dependent on developments within their partners' economies. In this light, the effects of large macroeconomic imbalances reflected in the international capital flows provide cause for concern. Adjustment is inevitable, and the institutional robustness of the system in dealing with large international asset price shocks has simply not been proven. Furthermore, with large, interest-sensitive international capital flows, the freedom of the authorities to deal with possible financial instability is highly reduced.

THE FORCES OF CHANGE

In earlier chapters I explored the fundamental forces that transformed the older world of stable relationships. Two types of forces worked to effect change in the financial systems: one, specific domestic events; the other, more generic issues. To see these forces of change in operation requires a brief review of the central issues of the previous chapters.

As early as the 1960s, the United States experienced important financial product innovations. But their impact did not truly emerge until they combined with higher and more volatile interest rates in the 1970s. First, during the late 1960s, fallout from macroeconomic management—when the costs of the Great Society combined with expenditures for increasing involvement in Southeast Asia—created balance-of-payments problems and credit crunches. As a result, the attraction of escaping domestic regulation increased for financial intermediaries and their clients, especially because exchange rate adjustment at the time seemed inevitable. When flexible rates emerged and eliminated the foreign reserve constraint, monetary policy—now fully targeted to deal with the domestic repercussions of the oil shocks—facilitated the onset of inflation. That brought higher and more volatile interest rates and created further incentives to be innovative in finance. A generally more favorable disposition toward free markets and deregulation in the late 1970s and early 1980s encouraged these trends and allowed them to flourish.

In Japan, one of the most significant reasons for change was the oil shock of 1974. It precipitated budget deficits and a shift in the national flow of funds, which triggered the move toward a new financial system, where prices played a more decisive role. In the 1980s, large current account surpluses put pressure on the country to accommodate more imports and to open up its economy; pressure to open capital markets was reflected in the accelerated entry of foreign financial intermediaries into Tokyo. The combination of export success and the country's increasing interaction with foreign capital markets and products opened the door to innovative, nontraditional financing techniques; the system became less relationship-driven and more price-oriented.

The changes in the U.K. financial system occurred as the fringe banking crisis (in part the outcome of a deliberate move toward increased financial competition) combined with new thinking about macroeconomic management and international economic pressures on the pound sterling. At the same time, the benefits of locating the Euromarkets in London were being weighed against possible incursions by foreign financial vendors into the domestic business of British financial institutions. In accordance with domestic pressures for increased competition, these international forces further emphasized price competition; in particular, the effects on the merchant banking industry and on the London Stock Exchange should be seen in this light.

These three brief paragraphs show some remarkable similarities in the underlying pressures that fostered diverse national events. One noticeable trend is that the 1950s and 1960s, the decades when traditional systems flourished, were characterized by economic stability; they saw relatively high growth and low nominal interest rates, and large international capital movements were not yet an issue. Belief in, and reliance on, Keynesian demand management gave authorities a preference for low interest rates, which were expected to stimulate investments. Though none of the three systems could regulate rates downward for the economy as a whole, they could at least apply some interest rate controls, offering the best access to funds at controlled prices to those firms that had the closest relationships with the regulated institutions.

Another general trend followed the many attempts to stabilize the financial systems—in all three countries, the authorities implemented market segmentation and price regulation, which reduced the power of individual institutions. One reason for this convergence was a common belief that the system left to its own devices would generate instability. Instances of such instability often prompted new regulation. But, as interest rates increased and new products rose to prominence, financial entrepreneurs and established players alike began to call for the removal of product market boundaries.

A third trend was the lack of prominence accorded to international financial transactions in the traditional systems. Under the system of fixed exchange rates, large sustained international capital flows between countries of comparable levels of economic development were not expected to be important; and short-term capital flows were deemed to be parasitic. As a result, controls on international financial transactions during the years of the Bretton Woods system closed most escape routes from the domestic relationship systems. If international flows occurred, they were viewed as the outcome of temporary trade imbalances. Such imbalances required monetary and/or fiscal policy adjustment; the foreign reserve constraint was thought to impose discipline.

Finally, I noted how the forces that would lead to the breakdown of Bretton Woods gathered strength during the late 1960s. Monetary authorities became increasingly concerned about the effect of their domestic actions on external accounts. Flexible exchange rates were expected to provide an answer, since they would free the policymakers from external constraints. I have already shown how wrong this thinking was; ultimately, large capital flows were generated. They assisted the changes in the domestic financial systems, speeding the move away from regulatory restraint toward greater price-driven innovation.

PRODUCT INNOVATION AND RELATIONSHIPS

Over the past two decades, price competitiveness of financial products has become much more important. At the same time, the products themselves have proliferated. The products all display a basic similarity—all allow for a transfer of purchasing power over time. In effect, the investor gives up *current* consumption power in return for greater *future* consumption power. As an example, consider a deposit account, a fixed-income security, and an equity security. What distinguishes these products are their specific *attributes*. For the deposit account, these are check-writing features (which used to be unique) and the safety afforded by the bank intermediary and government insurance. The fixed-income security is distinguished by pre-set annual interest payments. The equity security ties the fortunes of investors to the performance of a particular firm. Still, all three products fulfill the same basic function—they allow investors to postpone consumption now for consumption at a future date when the asset is sold. Only in their specific attributes do these financial products differ. Yet new freedoms in the financial markets allow financial innovators to price these various attributes independently; more than that, innovators can create new products by combining attributes and by targeting the combination to specific investors or issuers. For example, an issue of discount debt with attached but separable warrants creates, in effect, three securities: the discount bond, the warrant, and a "synthetic" convertible bond. The implications of such combinations are considered in a later chapter.

Generally, the traditional systems had provided relatively few opportunities to change product attributes or price these attributes competitively; thus, they offered little incentive to innovate. This situation contrasts sharply with the newer price-driven system. In the United States, the emergence of an options market offered the clearest example; here, one attribute of a security—the pure capital appreciation—was isolated and sold. Improved understanding of how to price such derivative products led to sharp pricing of other new products (such as packages of bonds and warrants or synthetic convertibles).

This type of financial engineering, whereby attributes are stripped from one product and appended to another, helped to develop the price-driven market; it became characteristic—to a greater or lesser extent—of all three national markets, where the number of possible products whose success depended only on the tastes and interests of the investors and issuers, was dramatically increased. Investors, in turn, displayed greater sensitivity to differential price performance during the transition to price banking. Proof of their changing attitude can be seen in the success of money market funds and in the relative decline of traditional instruments such as demand deposits (even after they began paying interest). This was a natural outcome of the higher interest rates of the 1970s.

During this transition, relationships declined in value but did not cease to play a role in financial transactions. For example, in the United States, several financial institutions created, or continued to maintain, relationship manager positions. But in contrast to the traditional relationships, which functioned as substitutes for price advantages, relationships became merely complements to price advantages; in an environment emphasizing price performance, relationship management ensures that intermediaries can make price-competitive bids.

In this context, a relationship enables the intermediary to offer a customer the best product at the most attractive price. Again, product innovation is involved, as increased attention to price performance forces the intermediary to design a product with the specific attributes the client desires and to price it competitively. Inevitably, many products will become more complex, which creates the risk that the complexity itself may become a deterrent to selling the product. Complicated combinations of borrowing strategies, in which one product is almost immediately transformed into other products by means of foreign exchange swaps, interest rate hedges and swaps, and other complex attributes, can sometimes lose their transparency and become difficult to evaluate.

One important contributor to the complexity of financial instruments, which I have not yet mentioned, is the rapid advance of information technology in the three financial systems. Improvements in computing and communications technology have played a major role in facilitating the transitions already described. It has been argued that information differences between issuers and borrowers are the raison d'être of intermediaries; indeed, financial disintermediation has taken place as technological developments have made information much more widely available. And though technological advances were not the driving force in the transition described above, the new opportunities for product complexity that they offer are thoroughly in the spirit of the price-driven environment.

Technological improvements, like product complexity, have also introduced new risks. Program trading and portfolio insurance—sophisticated strategies dependent on price-sensitive products—offer good examples. Although their value remains controversial, there can be no doubt that when their use was most called for, on October 19, 1987, institutional constraints limited their effectiveness. This did not happen because they were theoretically incorrect (although some debate exists), but rather because they were not designed to function in an environment of very large and rapid price changes, nor in the midst of order imbalances that cause prices to carry less and less information.

The abundance of choices in the price-driven environment contrasts sharply with the traditional phase of the national financial systems, when competitors offered a standard range of products, innovations in financial instruments were few and far between, and prices were generally undifferentiated. The present environment of choice can best be understood by contrasting it with the regulated simplicity that prevailed in the past.

THE DEMISE OF REGULATED SIMPLICITY

Whether or not regulation was optimal for its time, fundamental forces shifted to oppose it. Instead of reviewing the extensive literature on the causes and merits of regulation, the preceding chapters highlighted price and product restrictions as evolutionary steps in a long-term development that was spurred by periodic crisis. Inasmuch as the financial system is the conduit for capital to sectors of the economy, the authorities sought to influence it; explicitly, as in Japan and the United Kingdom, especially during the early postwar years, or implicitly, as for example through the special treatment of the home mortgage market in the United States.

Another effect of the traditional, regulated system was apparently to make it easier to chart macroeconomic policymaking. In the United States, open market operations were used to influence interest rates, which were expected to further domestic policy objectives. The authorities targeted central rates to effect expansionary aggregate demand policies or contractionary economic responses; they were confident they could predict the actions of the banking system, since members of the system had few choices. With well-established relationships, barriers to international capital movements, and pervasive interest rate controls, the effects of the macroeconomic policies seemed easier to predict.

Similarly, in the United Kingdom, several aspects of the traditional system benefited the macroeconomic policymaker. I noted the absorption of government issues through a negotiated tender, and many linkages between, and consultations about, interest rates. Direct lending ceilings and the special deposits of clearing banks were used in the traditional system to obtain contractionary or expansionary effects. In short, well-worn channels for policy execution existed.

The system in Japan was no less reliant on relationships in its monetary management. Again, the guaranteed absorption of government issues, a tightly regulated interest rate structure, and carefully balanced dependencies guaranteed great power to the authorities. This power was used both to keep overall interest rates low for those with access to the rationed system, and to enhance the influence of authorities and well-established players over the distribution of capital.

But nothing presented so far should be taken as a convincing argument in favor of regulation without some comparison with the alternative—monetary management under a free system. Furthermore, the effectiveness of national monetary policies during the 1950s and 1960s on real, rather than nominal, variables is increasingly being questioned. Earlier chapters make it clear that no *certain* causal connection has been demonstrated between the stable, high-growth years of the 1950s and 1960s and effective macroeconomic management. The high-growth environment may have resulted from more fundamental forces, and observers may have been misled in thinking that macroeconomic policies drove it. Thus, even when one grants that the traditional system facilitated the execution of certain types of macromanagement, it is not a logical conclusion that the system is *therefore* desirable, since the real effect of demand management remains questionable. This book is not, in any case, written as one more contribution to the economic policy-making debate, or to the literature of regulation. Instead, its focus is on the implications of change for the managers of financial services firms. The questions relevant to my topic are two: how the national systems developed up to the present; and what lessons can be learned about the likely course of their future development.

The importance of relationships and regulation (both formal and informal) in these three systems derived primarily from three factors: (1) the perception that the cost of financial instability (apparently associated with competition in financial services) to the economy as a whole would be high; (2) the desire of the authorities to exert some level of control over the allocation of funds; and (3) the system's gradual evolution during the postwar period of relatively stable growth and low interest rates, which reduced rewards for financial innovators. It took much trial and error for the systems to reach the smooth functioning of the 1950s and 1960s. In the United States, for example, a combination of segmentation and regulation flourished only after many unsuccessful attempts at different types of organization. And only with the creation of the Federal Reserve and later the acts of 1933 were the fundamentals of the traditional phase actually put in place. In Japan, the system began to develop after the Meiji Restoration, but its centralized nature did not become fully apparent until the period between the two World Wars. A more gradual development can be found in the United Kingdom, but even there the traditional system emerged only after the banking amalgamation movement and the slow usurpation of power by the Bank of England. In all three systems, regulated relationships functioned for less than three decades. It was as if a brief window of opportunity appeared, in a generally stable economic environment dedicated to economic growth or rehabilitation. The 1970s were a transition phase, and by the 1980s, the forces of deregulation had changed both the U.S. and Japanese systems, and reliance upon informal understandings between well-known partners had waned in the United Kingdom. Furthermore, increasingly powerful international financial transactions linked the three markets closely.

While national boundaries were broken, and macroeconomic policies that magnified national savings imbalances emerged, national financial systems served as conduits for the international flows of capital necessary to finance current account imbalances. Such capital flows may actually be seen by some as favorable; they allow for a better expression of the true savings and borrowing desires of the various countries. Still, they also allow for procrastination over unpopular policy adjustments since the financial system ceases to operate as a brake on capital movements. In the traditional system with multiple impediments to capital flows, it was more difficult to place significant amounts of domestic assets with foreign investors. Now, with new products and techniques (e.g., currency and interest rate swaps) and with investors and borrowers increasingly sensitive to the smallest basis point differential in yield, international financing of deficits has become much simpler. The ease with which the new instruments can be acquired may in itself be due to learning and familiarization; and it will also encourage the desire to invest in foreign assets. To put this more formally, using an international portfolio model, the desired shares of foreign assets as a percent of total wealth may well be functionally dependent on the ease with which the various markets can offer price-sensitive financial instruments.

Especially in light of the developments in the mid- and late 1980s, it now seems that the overall cost of large and sustained current account and capital account imbalances may lie in the adjustment costs of a long-postponed (hard) landing. Thus, all the changes, increased choices, and new uncertainties that are now an inherent part of the new environment follow from remarkably similar evolutions of three very different financial systems.

Before I consider the implications of these changes for financial services firms (the third level of financial change I identify in this book), it is useful to look at the individual actor who is ultimately affected: the issuer-investor. He or she operates in this new environment and provides the real challenge for the financial services firm. To simplify matters, I shall concentrate attention here and in the following chapters on U.S. institutions, issuers, and investors.

QUESTIONS FOR THE NEW ENVIRONMENT

Understanding the evolution of the three financial systems does not lead to infallible, straightforward predictions about the future shape of the financial services industry, or to a unique definition of optimal strategy. Precisely because the central characterization of the new environment is one of choices, as I shall argue later in more detail, firms will have to define their own distinct advantage.

What the evolution of the three systems does reveal is a series of pertinent *questions* for issuers and investors, and therefore for intermediaries, in the industry:

1. What is the relevant set of national markets?
2. What are the relevant products?
3. What are the probable macroeconomic policy scenarios and their price (interest rate) impact?
4. What are the predictable channels of transmission and how efficient are the markets?
5. What are the common mistakes and possible windows of opportunity?
6. What is the basis for superior advice and value creation?
7. What are abitrage opportunities?
8. What is the interest of the intermediary?

Although answers to these questions differ according to personal beliefs, consideration of the fundamental macroeconomic forces and changes in the national financial systems provides the essential precondition for every serious attempt to respond. Some of these issues may seem rudimentary, but experience shows that many issuers, investors, and intermediaries have not granted them sufficient attention.

THE RELEVANT SET OF NATIONAL MARKETS

I have shown already that the relevant market for investors and issuers is no longer limited to the domestic market. Many markets are open, and in them many similar products compete; the spectrum of instruments has widened enormously. Thus, before making investment or issuc choices, the set of relevant national markets to be considered must include even *seemingly* unrelated markets that may have an important indirect impact.

Take, for example, U.S. real estate investors. One would naturally assume that the U.S. real estate product is their central interest. Yet for them the actions of Japanese investors in the Japanese and foreign markets matter increasingly. To assess market opportunities in the United States, it is essential to determine, given high real estate values in Japan, how and if Japanese investors will decide to diversify internationally. Will they apply some of their capital gains in the U.S. real estate market? Similarly, will potential Japanese real estate investors—judging the Japanese market to be overvalued—decide to substitute, and thus to invest in comparatively cheap U.S. real estate? And if they do so, will this be a long-term or a short-term phenomenon? In other words, the Japanese market is relevant even for a U.S. real estate investor who is not planning to invest in Japanese products.

This, of course, is not a new issue. Take a closed domestic economy and assume that the only relevant investments are equities, bonds, and deposit accounts. For an investor considering the equity market, the bond market is also highly relevant, not only as an alternative, but because transactions in the bond market spill over into the equity market. Many classic contributions in the economics and finance literature have addressed this phenomenon. What I suggest is that, in the new environment, the multitude and complexity of relevant alternatives have vastly increased, as the breakdown of barriers between various product and national markets has created an unprecedented level of cross-market influences.

This means that it is hard for issuers and investors to determine which are the most relevant markets. The earlier analysis of fundamental forces can, however, help to explain how such a determination is made. For example, Chapters 1 and 2 showed that the international capital imbalances of the 1980s reflected fundamental savings imbalances, which must eventually revert, since no country can continue to borrow forever. Choices about the market in which the borrower or investor wants to operate are not just the result of a benign attitude to international capital freedoms by policymakers; the choices represent a long-term effect of basic forces. This means that multiple markets will continue to define the investors' and issuers' opportunity set. It implies that the attractiveness of a spectrum of increasingly complex products in the various markets has to be considered.

Given the linkages between the international markets, the relevance of any market will be affected by: (1) specific domestic conditions; and (2) the price that links the markets (the exchange rate). This price should be treated with caution, and its role should be minimized, unless an *explicit* decision has been made that the investor wishes to engage in a currency play. Of course, such a play is risky because the applicable rate cannot be forecast.[2] Although this observation may seem trivial or

2. In the previous chapters I showed that the adjustment in the external valuation of the dollar has not played the equilibrating role that had been widely predicted. Few analysts suggest that the current capital flows will revert through fundamental exchange rate adjustment; instead, most place emphasis on the savings mechanism. Here it becomes clear that forecasting exchange rate movements even for the medium term is extremely difficult. Instead, given the development of the swap market, extensive use of hedging can facilitate the accessing of different markets. Thus, specific national market opportunities have to be considered, which may be the result of supply and demand imbalances caused by factors such as local custom. Local market conditions and possible windows of opportunity have to be exploited and should be included in the relevant set of markets. Looking at the exchange rate, there is good reason to believe that, of all the asset markets, this is one of the most efficient. Thus, little can be expected from explicit forecasting, over and above what is already incorporated in the forward rate.

obvious, both investors and corporations have occasionally ignored it, sometimes at great cost. For example, many firms have failed to fully hedge the international currency flows that occur in the funding of their international operations. As a result, they have taken an *implicit* rather than *explicit* open currency position. While the latter is often disdainfully described as "speculation" and "not the business of this company," the former is often seen as merely a "normal consequence of international business." Yet unless currency speculation is explicitly desired, activities in foreign markets should be the outcome of the attractiveness of *local* conditions abroad, and the exchange rate effects should be isolated.

One implication of all this is that investors, issuers, and their advisors must evaluate local developments in various national markets. Of course, not every product market requires this scrutiny; few people, for example, would consider international markets in placing a deposit account. But for most financial decisions the potential payoffs increase as more markets are considered; at the same time, the risks grow and more uncertainties have to be faced. Ultimately, reliance on the market knowledge of international specialists becomes inevitable, and therefore the situation offers new opportunities for intermediaries with broad international intelligence about the relevant products.

THE RELEVANT PRODUCTS

A breakdown in product market segmentation has allowed many new products to emerge. These may be price-competitive clones of older products or genuinely new instruments. The market environment is such that more complex products are continually being created. Most product innovations take a place *between* two existing products, showing characteristics of both. For example, commercial paper occupies a place between a bank loan and a short bond, and becomes an alternative for both.

Product innovation requires both issuers and investors to have a carefully defined sense of their needs. And their needs are themselves increasingly complex, since the macroeconomic environment has become more uncertain than ever. The chief risk of complexity, however, is that it can obfuscate the true characteristics of a product. Take for example the development of the Perpetual Floating Rate Note (PERP) in the Euromarkets during the 1980s. It was the outcome of developments in the bond market whereby the product spectrum was filled up with products relevant to investors' needs. Bonds had traditionally carried coupons at a fixed interest rate (so that they were called "fixed-income instruments"), but the volatility of interest rates during the 1970s caused bond prices to fluctuate sharply. To respond to investor needs for higher certainty, a new bond was developed: the Floating Rate Note (FRN). The FRN provided for the frequent adjustment (annually or semi-annually) of interest rates to reflect changes in the market rates. Thus, every time the interest rate was adjusted, the security could be expected to trade close to par, and hence the investor was free from concerns about capital gains or losses as interest rates changed.

Investors realized, of course, that the interest rate was not the only factor that could affect the price of bonds. If the credit quality of the issuer changed over the life of the bond, its price would change as well. During the late 1970s and 1980s, however, volatility in interest rates proved far more important in causing bond prices to fluctuate than did changes in the credit quality of issuing institutions. By focusing on the interest rate risk, and ignoring the credit risk, FRNs were supposed to trade at par, since their coupons were regularly reset to reflect interest rate changes. But with the new product trading at par at the time of the coupon adjustments (say every year), it appeared that one could issue longer-term FRNs. A ten-year FRN (i.e., a FRN that pays coupons for ten years and principal in the tenth year) would trade at par at the end of each year, because of the floating rate coupon feature, and it would mature (at par) in the tenth year. However, an eleven-year FRN would, in effect, look identical for the first ten years of its life. In the tenth year, like the ten-year FRN, the eleven-year FRN would trade at par, albeit for different reasons.

In year ten, investors in the ten-year FRN would get the principal back (at par), but investors in the eleven-year FRN could resell the security in the market. There it would trade, because of the resetting of the coupon, at par as well; thus the investor would gain the same payoff stream as the investor in the ten-year note. But if an eleven-year FRN was, for the first ten years of its life, identical to a ten-year FRN, the same logic applied to a twelve-year FRN, and a thirteen-year FRN, etc. Finally, no leap of the imagination was required to see that a *Perpetual* Floating Rate Note (PERP) could be issued. It would never mature, but at the end of each year the investor could sell the bond at par.

For various reasons, these instruments sold well, and commercial banks became large issuers. However, since such instruments were fairly complex, many investors apparently had not accurately assessed their risks. When the credit quality of the banks came into question in the late 1980s, it was not the interest rate that caused price swings in the PERPs (they were semi-annually adjusted); it was underlying credit quality. As investors awoke to this problem, the market for PERPs came under severe pressure.[3] In short, the tailoring of new unseasoned products to the perceived needs of issuers and investors has sometimes resulted in risks that are only perceived over time. Here, the failed introduction of another complex new product provides a clear case in point. The Unbundled Stock Unit was designed to decompose a common stock into several separate attributes (i.e., dividend claim, a zero coupon bond, and a stock appreciation right). But despite developers' claims that the product offered unique benefits to issuers and investors, it failed to attract a market. Observers have suggested that it was simply too complex to make sense to many issuers and even more so to investors.

The definition of a relevant set of product alternatives has, therefore, to consider which product attributes are needed, which are offered by close substitutes, and whether the products are comprehensible. The development and competitive pricing of many complex new products could be seen in all three national systems as the inevitable outcome of long-term domestic and international forces. Since the international flows are long-term rather than temporary phenomena, and since the regulated simplicity of the traditional phases in the three systems was the outcome of a highly unusual confluence of factors, the only real limit on the development of products now lies with the needs and sophistication of issuers and investors. In order to succeed, intermediaries will have to become more sensitive to these needs; they will also have to become more ingenious at identifying specific opportunities, since the simplest needs are the most easily satisfied. The investor or issuer will therefore increasingly consider a relevant *set* of similar, but slightly different, products.

Investors and issuers can choose more easily from among the widening set of relevant products when the probable course of the macroconditions is understood. In the 1990s, however, the complexity of the new products is matched by the unpredictability of the overall macroeco-

3. In response to the problems of the PERPs, a new instrument was subsequently developed. Instead of adjusting the coupon only with respect to the underlying interest rate, now adjustments would also be made in response to changes in the credit quality of the corporation that issued the bond. If the credit quality deteriorated, the spread over the underlying interest rate would be adjusted upward, so that the bond would truly trade at par at the reset date. Of course, this is theoretically unsound. Suppose a company has serious cash flow problems, and its creditworthiness deteriorates. Now the coupon has to be adjusted upward. But if the cash flow problem is severe enough, it will only be exacerbated by this adjustment, since the higher coupon will itself worsen the creditworthiness of the corporation. The new feature of the bond is thus an umbrella that will be carried away in a downpour. Some of the provisions regarding a similar class of bonds, the so-called PIKs (Pay-In-Kind), suffer from similar problems.

nomic climate, which was discussed in Chapter 2. In combination, these two factors have made financial decisions more difficult to calibrate. Suppose an investor is interested in high-return, and therefore risky, investments. Suppose also that he or she has narrowed the set of appropriate investments to either equities or high-yield bonds of companies with different capital structures but in similar industries. Here, the investor must make forecasts about the sensitivity of the equity market and of the high-yield bond market to interest rate shocks; he or she can make the investment only after answering vexing questions about what the likely macropolicy scenarios might be.

THE MACROECONOMIC SCENARIOS

Thus, questions about macroeconomic developments have become more important than ever in recent years. Admittedly, new instruments like swaps seem to have mitigated somewhat the impact of macroeconomic fluctuations; both exchange rate volatility and interest rate uncertainty can be hedged. Still, even when hedges are available, overall macroconditions assert themselves through other channels.

Take the example of an investor's decision to buy high-yield U.S. corporate bonds. I have noted that a soft landing for the U.S. economy, viewed from an international accounts position, would have to involve an increase in the U.S national savings rate; a high employment–low consumption scenario is thus possible even without a major recession. In this case, there would be no need to significantly revise the growth forecasts of the cash flow projections that (seemingly) warranted issues of high-yield instruments.

I also suggested that the new international environment has allowed policymakers to procrastinate over unpopular policy choices. Here the potential for a hard landing has to be considered. Given the accumulation of international debt, and despite the fact that the current account deficit of the United States is indeed declining as a percentage of GNP, the forces outlined in earlier chapters suggest that the new uncertainties might cause rapid adjustments in interest rates and exchange rates. For example, at present a mild U.S. recession can hardly be fought with expansionary fiscal policy; budget problems preclude this. A recession could thus easily feed on itself (for example, reduced tax revenues and higher social security payments could exacerbate the budget deficit). In turn, foreign investments in the United States might slow down, causing an interest rate shock and putting severe pressure on the dollar. In such a case, investments in highly leveraged transactions could prove particularly risky.

Although this is only one of many possible scenarios, it does highlight the relatively high level of uncertainty associated with the current macroeconomic climate. The two largest market economies, the United States and Japan, have seen remarkably stable domestic macroenvironments during the 1980s, with relatively low inflation and high growth. As I indicated earlier, however, these conditions are unlikely to persist. My purpose here is not to present one particular forecast for the most important variables affected by the macroenvironment. Instead, I hope to make clear that now it is especially important for investors and issuers (and therefore for financial services firms) to question such scenarios. But only after acquiring an understanding of the driving forces of the current environment can any player generate a likely scenario.

Thus players must not only select the markets and products that fit their needs, they must also make a forecast about the macroenvironment. Although an understanding of fundamental forces remains the foundation for any informed forecast, the individual forecaster must depend on personal evaluation as well. For this, an appreciation of both market efficiency and channels of transmission is essential.

MARKET EFFICIENCY AND CHANNELS OF TRANSMISSION

As with other decisions in finance, choices about financial instruments matter less when the market is more efficient. Take, for example, a decision to avoid the currency swap market and, instead, to issue debt securities in a foreign currency. If markets are efficient, then current embedded interest and exchange rate forecasts reflect the market's expectations, and the individual investor or issuer has to have good reason to believe that he or she can supply *superior* forecasts.

The actions of most issuers and investors indicate that they, at least implicitly, often believe themselves to have made such superior forecasts. In order to prevent financial missteps, it is important to make such forecasts explicit. To do this, it is vital to understand the driving forces that caused the current environment and the major adjustments that are likely to occur. Again, an understanding of the past should lead to a better appreciation of the channels of transmission that have so far proved robust in macroeconomics and that are likely to remain predictable in the future. Not surprisingly, given the still rather limited understanding of the complex global macroeconomy, these channels rely mostly on common sense, rather than state-of-the-art economic modelling.

The most relevant channel of international transmission relates to the net saving behavior of countries. Net savings deficits and surpluses are inevitably transmitted through the capital markets as asset flows; they make strict national market regulation impossible. Of course, many national macroeconomic policies affect the net national savings. A U.S. policy of large budget deficits not offset by increases in private savings arose in the 1980s; inevitably, it forced net national borrowing, and the United States had to sell assets abroad. Thus, fiscal and monetary policies do have influence, even though the events of the 1980s have disillusioned many players and analysts who thought they understood these channels as they appeared during the 1960s and early 1970s.

Exchange rate changes provide a second important channel of transmission, but one that has become less transparent over time. The dollar's appreciation during the early 1980s seemingly conformed to the burgeoning U.S. current account deficits, but later these deficits remained robust despite a depreciation of the dollar. This is not to suggest that sophisticated economic models can no longer shed light on exchange rate movements; however, for practical decision making in finance, the prediction of long-term exchange rate movements does not represent a fruitful area effort. More reliance can be placed on belief in market efficiency and on using the current rate as a good predictor of the future.

A third set of channels of transmission centers on the effects of macroeconomic policy. Again, past history does not justify optimism for the future. I have already reviewed the changes in macroeconomic policy-making in the United States; at present, the impact of fiscal policy seems even less well understood than in past decades, and the political room to apply such policy even more restricted. Similarly, there is now less activism on the subject of monetary policy, and a stronger emphasis on its impact on inflation. If anything, then, it is riskier than ever to try to predict policy and its effects.

Just as before, my objective here is to show that one has to accept a new level of complexity and uncertainty. Although new opportunities exist, caution is required. It is most useful to explicitly consider channels that have proven valid during the historical periods already described; these are the channels that led to the current environment. In this sense, the outlook for the 1990s is pessimistic—complexity in products and uncertainty in economic outcomes. But it also holds the promise of new choices. The choices can be made as every investor and issuer considers a personal map of forecasts and needs, each of which will differ according to the individual. Furthermore, with many new product choices, market timing becomes more important, since the new products may open windows of opportunity at their inception.

OPPORTUNITIES IN MISTAKES

One source of windows of opportunity in the markets lies in new product introduction and in market imperfections related to less than perfect information about the product. New products can create imperfect information. The investor or the issuer has to assess the trade-off between the possible advantages associated with the new product and the riskiness that stems from its unproven nature. Here, the example of the PERP can be reintroduced: once the credit risks embedded in the instrument were recognized, market reaction to the PERP was swift and harsh—prices fell sharply. These prices became so low that a window of opportunity was opened for investors: heavily discounted PERPs turned (temporarily) into a very profitable investment, one that actually allowed for an arbitrage opportunity. By adding a stripped government security to the discounted PERP, a synthetic dated floating rate note emerged that was cheaper than the actual dated FRN.

A complex financial environment is a spawning ground for new opportunities. Investors and issuers must evaluate many different, complex products in search of extraordinary profit opportunities and for the sources of uncertainty or mispricing that create them. Thus, the task of having to identify relevant markets and relevant products is complicated by having to search for market failures that fit individual needs. In the face of this increasingly difficult task, the financial services industry must advise its clients. To do so, it must explain and interpret the fundamental forces that shape the financial environment, while demonstrating an ability to apply specific information about market opportunities. In short, the financial services vendor must be largely responsible for exploiting opportunities for product developments that are valuable to the clients.

ADVICE AND VALUE CREATION

For help in value creation, both issuers and investors rely on the intermediary. Thus, knowledge of local market conditions in various capital markets can be an important product for financial services firms allowing them to attract clients that reckon those markets to be relevant, but who have no reason to be familiar with the local conditions. Many such clients now exist, and the integration of markets assures that they will continue to seek advice about a broad array of market conditions.

As the environment increases in complexity, and confidence in the predictive ability of macroeconomic models declines, cross-national effects become even harder to calibrate. Interest rate forecasting, for example, now seems more difficult, because of new international capital flows and new views on macroeconomic management. One implication of this difficulty is that the advice of intermediaries will be valued less for interest rate and exchange rate forecasts than for information on market imbalances (favorable windows) and product applications to the specific needs of both issuers and investors. The high-yield bond market provides an example of a complex financial instrument that was useful to investors who had information about it at the right time.

When first introduced, these noninvestment grade bonds had no trading history. Thus, the "high-yield" reflected not only the relatively high credit risk of the issuing companies, but also what may be called product risk. No one really knew how the bonds would behave in the aftermarket. Risks aside, these bonds created value, at first, by giving issuers access to a new source of capital (cutting out the intermediary cost of traditional bank financing) and offering investors a new investment opportunity. Later, value was created by using the new instruments to finance innovative restructuring techniques (such as the LBO). Not surprisingly, as the market matured and came under increased scrutiny, the windows of opportunity closed. The price structure of the instrument has now been more closely examined, and studies show that the actual risk-return trade-off for investors may have been less favorable than originally estimated. In 1989, this translated into serious problems in the high-yield market and into a requirement for higher coupons on new bonds. An issue window had been closed.

Other methods for value creation arise from the ability of the intermediary to suggest complex financial strategies that benefit the client, mergers and acquisitions being an example. More mundane but potentially powerful sources of value creation lie in distribution capabilities or operation efficiencies that are offered by one intermediary relative to another. Here the value simply comes from doing a standard activity *better* (e.g., through tighter cost control), or from having such broad market information that temporary issue or investment opportunities are more easily identified for the client. The success that some of the largest intermediaries in the Euromarkets have had in obtaining favorably priced financing for their clients provides an example of the latter: their leadership position in the issue-league tables assured them of broad market information that profited both their clients and their own trading departments.

Another source of possible windows of opportunity, especially as the product market becomes more complex, is value creation through arbitrage. Better availability of information about market imbalances or the application of broad market information can allow the investor and issuer to generate real profits at low costs.

ARBITRAGE

As the complexity of the financial product market continues to increase, new arbitrage opportunities should appear.[4] *Arbitrage* identifies the creation of riskless financial strategies leading to returns in excess of the cost of capital committed to the activity.[5] Arbitrage activities can exist between national markets, between products, and over time. Of course, the effect of arbitrage is to eliminate the opportunities to engage in it—thus, it has been said that the function of arbitrage is to keep markets in line.

Still, temporary opportunities abound. For issuers and investors, it is essential to ask: What allows the arbitrage opportunity to exist? Although complex financial strategies are sometimes suggested to create arbitrage opportunities, these, in turn, must rely on some impediments to the flow of information and the contact between markets, and they should be made explicit. Similarly, many products offered to issuers and investors as value creating should be questioned against the background of the possibility of arbitrage. The recent infatuation of various firms with listings on foreign stock markets provides a good example. When it is suggested that a foreign listing will allow firms access to equity capital at a cheaper price (because of higher foreign multiples), there is no need for sophisticated financial models to refute that proposition; all that is needed is a simple arbitrage argument. Since the two listed prices will be arbitraged to parity, other factors have to be responsible for any possible value creation. These may be related to marketing factors, prestige, or similar causes, and they should be explicitly identified.

Skepticism should also apply to several complex arbitrage strategies employed in the late 1980s, which turned out not to be real arbitrage strategies at all. Already I have referred to the dramatic events of October 19, 1987: these undermined the arbitrage between a basket of listed

---

4. Of course, complex instruments may also eliminate some arbitrage opportunities. For example, the ability to take advantage of sluggish adjustments in particular stocks while the market as a whole moves is less likely if a broadly based market index is traded.

5. I purposely exclude the so-called risk-arbitrage activity engaged in by many investment banks. In this essentially speculative activity, very high risks are taken with the committed capital, most noticeably in the context of (expected) mergers and acquisitions transactions.

stocks and an index of similar stocks. The magnitude of the price fall in the equity markets, and the unexpected institutional constraints affected program-directed trading and rendered even "riskless" strategies highly risky. Similar institutional trading impediments can also occur in international markets or even in the domestic markets for products other than equities.

THE INTEREST OF THE INTERMEDIARIES

The traditional role of intermediaries as sellers of advice or as agents in transactions once seemed clearly understood. The intermediary served the client and the client's best interests. The lack of choice during the era of relationship-based finance almost assured the commonality of interest between client and intermediary. But that congruence of interest is less clear today. Potential conflicts of interest already have arisen between client and intermediary (some reflected in actual violations of securities laws), and the new financial environment provides great opportunities for more of these conflicts to occur. Take, for example, the increased activity of investment banks in the area of principal transactions (or merchant banking). What are the implications for a client that is advised by his investment banker on a certain transaction in which the banker may himself have a substantial position? Similarly, what of the policies of commercial banks that sell large parts of loans they originate in highly leveraged transactions? Typically, the originating bank will keep sizable commitment and origination fees (and in some deals may collect commitment fees for transactions even if they fail to materialize). What do such actions imply about the *true* interest of the advisor? Is the advisor creating value for the client or simply generating transaction fees?

Of course, the financial services vendor should be rewarded for its activity, be it advice, product development, or the execution of transactions. But investors and issuers must know where the intermediary's interests lie in order to understand their own. Take, for example, an offer to an issuer for a more aggressively priced issue. Here, the intermediary may argue that superior distribution competence leads to value creation. Similarly, a new product may truly offer advantages to the investor because it is an early entrant, benefiting from favorable supply and demand imbalances. But unless the intermediary can convincingly demonstrate where the client's value is derived from, it is possible that the only true value transfer is from the client to the intermediary. In contrast to the simple, stable relationship environment, today value creation for the intermediary no longer arises from an activity defined and priced by regulation. Financial vendors have to create strategies that lead to much more explicit value creation, and it is now the client—rather than the regulator—that must monitor how and where the intermediary creates value.

All this should *not* suggest that most, or even many, financial services firms operate in conflict with the interests of their clients. Value creation for the firm can and should take place in accordance—not in competition—with the interest of the client. The demise of a relatively noncomplex environment has led to new roles for intermediaries, and successful financial services firms must be concerned with their ability to create and demonstrate value as a result of strategic choices they make. Without that concern, they cannot survive. Such firms operate in an environment where the needs of clients have greatly changed and where opportunities and risks have multiplied at an equal rate. Financial services firms can assist their clients in this uncertain era by incorporating into their services an enlarged understanding of the driving forces of the new environment, such as I have outlined in the chapters so far.

MACROECONOMIC FORCES AND BUSINESS STRATEGY

The dynamic financial environment I have sketched was the outcome of the impact of macroeconomic forces on the domestic economies and of the growing importance of international financial transactions: together they changed national financial market structure in all three major financial centers. Individual financial firms have felt the changes as well. Again, the new products have provided new opportunities on the one hand, and have caused some traditional products and profit opportunities to disappear on the other. And from this process have emerged new strategic choices. The first of these has to do with the basic business purpose of the financial services vendor. Greater price competition and an increasing sophistication of issuers and investors have together called the value of pure intermediation into question; a manifestation of this is the trend toward disintermediation. Banks have been among the big losers in this trend, and for them a choice must often be made between reducing growth or turning to potentially riskier investments. The recent experience of a number of savings and loans institutions is a sad case in point; a group of these institutions decided to expand their asset bases away from the traditional outlet and into new, possibly higher-yielding assets. Using price-sensitive money, these institutions committed funds to assets that turned out to be of questionable value. In another shift in business focus, many financial institutions were attracted to advisory and fee generating activities because they require few assets.

Somewhat surprisingly, this has led several institutions to extend their advisory activities into principal transactions, returning once more to an asset-driven strategy, though now in the belief that capital gains on the assets—rather than spread lending—would provide profitability.

A second major area of choice relates to the international strategies of institutions; once again these affect all three key international markets. Observing the increase in international capital flows and the growth of opportunities afforded by improved communications and information technology in various national markets, many financial institutions have begun to build their own international networks. Whether or not such strategies will be successful remains to be seen; what is already clear is that the forces that draw issuers and borrowers from the capital markets of one country to those of another exert great attraction on financial institutions as well.

In short, as alternatives for clients increased, strategic choices for financial services firms became more important. New opportunities arose, and traditional activities were superseded by product market innovations. The last chapter discusses the implications of these developments for the strategies of individual firms. First, however, I present four vignettes that highlight some of the generic issues involved.

PART III

PRODUCT INNOVATION, MARKET ORGANIZATION, AND BUSINESS STRATEGY

7

BREAKING RELATIONSHIPS:
THE INTERMEDIARIES' RESPONSE

In the previous chapters I investigated interactions among various mac-roforces and changing regulations in three national financial systems. I showed how they precipitated a transition away from relationship and toward price banking over almost two decades, and I briefly examined some implications for issuers and investors. The focus now shifts to financial intermediaries and to the strategies that they have developed to meet new challenges. These strategies have varied both in their na-tures and their outcomes. As samples of that variety, consider the fol-lowing vignettes:

- In the summer of 1984, FDIC regulators were faced with an unusual problem: a commercial bank was about to fail, and the FDIC had to decide how to respond. That a bank was in need of assistance was not in itself so extraordinary—in the previous two years more than forty banks had closed, well in excess of the average yearly number of closings from World War II until that time. What was new was the impressive size of the institution in difficulty. With assets of $41 billion in 1983, Continental Illinois Bank was the eighth-largest bank in the United States, and the forty-ninth-largest in the world. Yet by the summer of 1984, the bank was close to failure. Between 1981 and 1984, $1.6 billion in shareholder value was destroyed, and assistance had to be sought from the authorities.
- Citicorp, the largest U.S. commercial bank, concluded the acquisi-tion of a British securities firm, Vickers Da Costa, in early 1984. In 1986, Vickers Da Costa was one of six foreign institutions allowed to purchase a seat on the Tokyo Stock Exchange and to engage in securities transactions. Thus, a U.S. commercial banking corpora-tion gained access through a British firm to the Japanese securities industry, which was formally (through Article 65) closed to entry by any commercial banking organization. This was a step toward

internationalization and blurring of the traditional boundaries between commercial and investment banking.

- Morgan Stanley, one of the largest and most powerful U.S. investment banks, was also allowed to purchase a seat on the Tokyo Stock Exchange in 1986. For Morgan Stanley, this was only another step in a strategy to rapidly build its international presence. In 1980, its Tokyo office, which had been in operation since 1970, employed fourteen people. By 1987, it employed approximately 500, as many as had comprised the whole firm in the early 1970s. Here was an example of the impact of internationalization and its large demands on firms in terms of choices and capital commitments.
- In 1988, First Boston, the prominent U.S. investment bank, and Credit Suisse First Boston, a joint venture between the U.S. firm and Credit Suisse, the powerful Swiss commercial bank, announced plans to merge. Through complex cross-ownership, senior managers in the two firms, the Swiss bank, and later a Japanese investor, would eventually hold ownership of the merged entity. Thus, a Swiss commercial bank became the largest equity holder in a major U.S. investment banking firm. This fundamental restructuring of First Boston and CSFB resulted from internal management problems, based, in turn, on rapidly changing opportunities in the international markets and associated changes in banking strategy.

These four vignettes illustrate remarkable developments in the business strategies of financial intermediaries. These developments represent a decade of change (1980–1990) and highlight issues already discussed in preceding chapters: the impact of price-sensitive funding opportunities (Continental), the new ability to broaden business activities (Citicorp), the breakdown of national boundaries (Morgan Stanley), and the difficulty in managing these transitions (CSFB and First Boston). More significantly, perhaps, all four vignettes demonstrate the growing importance of strategic choices for financial services firms. New freedoms have forced firms to choose among many new alternatives, while increased price competition and product innovation have fundamentally compromised many of their traditional sources of profitability. The new freedoms have brought opportunities and additional risks. The four vignettes point to generic, underlying trends that are essential to understanding the overall environment.

CONTINENTAL ILLINOIS CORPORATION AND THE FDIC

In the late spring of 1984, Continental Illinois became the largest U.S. bank to face possible failure since the widespread financial dislocations of the 1920s and 1930s. Media attention focused on problems at the bank, and hectic activity ensued as regulators, bank officials, and prospective investors tried to find ways to resolve the crisis. Potential instability was not limited to the failure of the bank itself (or even to the bankruptcy of its holding company); many feared that repercussions from Continental's problems would be felt throughout the U.S. banking sector. The main problems of the bank were easy to identify. It had a questionable loan portfolio, and it was in the midst of funding difficulties because of the reaction of the price-sensitive markets, on which it had relied heavily for financing.

The basic solution to Continental's problems was also not hard to discover—deposit insurance promises had to be fulfilled, capital infused (possibly with help from the FDIC), and the equity position of bank shareholders would be adjusted. The real issue, however, was the challenge of understanding how the problems had occurred, what might be done to prevent repetition at other banks, and what signals would be sent to other banks as part of any solution approved by the regulators. In this respect, many perplexing questions emerged: What, for example, should happen to holders of the holding corporation's commercial paper, especially in relation to FDIC-insured depositors? Should these commercial paper holders, to whom the FDIC held no obligation and who had been rewarded with rates that should have reflected the riskiness of the bank, benefit from a rescue plan? What action should be taken with respect to Continental's management and board, under whose governance the problem had developed? What lessons could be learned about the appropriateness of uniform premiums for FDIC insurance, given the vastly different asset-growth strategies of member banks?

In theory, at least, the FDIC's responsibility in this matter was clear. According to the Banking Act of 1933, the FDIC was the agency

> whose duty it shall be to purchase, hold, and liquidate . . . the assets of national banks which have been closed by action of the Comptroller of the Currency, or by the vote of their directors, and the assets of State member banks, which have been closed by actions of the appropriate State authorities, or by vote of their directors; and to insure . . . the deposits of all banks which are entitled to the benefits of insurance under this section.[1]

In practice, however, stricter judgment was needed. Would it be best (and cheapest) to liquidate the bank? In this case, any shortfall between the recovery value of the bank's assets (minus certain senior claims) and the liabilities to insured depositors would have to be paid from the FDIC

---

1. Banking Act, 1933, Section 8, and Federal Reserve Act, 1916, Section 12a.

insurance fund. In this case, too, the potential for a widening problem had to be calibrated, because Continental's problems could easily contaminate other banks. Alternatively, were other solutions possible, and, if so, what kind of help and what conditions for assistance should be contemplated?

Remember that FDIC insurance was originally designed to safeguard against liquidity problems. Since liquidity problems can occur because of a loss of depositor confidence in the bank rather than from insolvency, it was thought that the insurance scheme would not only help retail depositors of banks that faced runs, it would also help prevent these very troubles from the start. Insured depositors would have no incentive to start a run on the bank.[2] But events in the summer of 1984 made it clear that FDIC insurance was less effective than anticipated in keeping depositors' money in Continental Bank. To understand why, and to see how the nationwide move from relationship to price banking helped create the situation, it is useful to look briefly at the history of Continental Illinois Bank.

Continental's crisis in 1984 was not the first time that officials had been forced to engineer its rescue. It had come close to failure during the Depression, and not until 1939 was the bank able to buy back preferred stock that had been held by the Reconstruction Finance Corporation (RFC), an agency established in 1932 to deal with various credit problems. The RFC had begun to function as a bail-out facility for troubled banks, through its authorization to purchase preferred stock, notes, or debt. Though neither large nor powerful enough to restore full confidence in financial markets, the RFC was, in some important respects, a forerunner of the FDIC. Continental was one of the larger banks it helped, through a purchase of $50 million of preferred stock.

After the 1930s, Continental's comeback began, first under its chairman, Cummings, and later, between 1959 and 1969, under the leadership of former Secretary of the Treasury Kennedy. The bank grew, functioning mostly as a wholesale bank to large industrial Midwestern corporations. The wholesale nature of the bank was no accident; state banking laws in Illinois were among the most restrictive in the nation, allowing no within-state branching, so that a large retail operation was

---

2. A liquidity crisis may actually *cause* a solvency problem. A liquidity problem refers only to an inability to quickly liquidate assets in order to satisfy liability holders. The need to resolve this problem, however, may force the institution into a fire sale of its assets. If in such a fire sale, assets are sold at low prices, illiquidity can turn into insolvency.

not feasible. Continental Illinois and its main competitor, First Chicago, serviced the corporate sector instead.

First Chicago was often described as the dominant wholesale bank in Illinois, but by 1975 both it and Continental held about $20 billion in assets. In that year, Continental's return on total assets (ROTA) was 0.59%; its return on equity (ROE), 14.4%; and the ratio of total assets to equity (TA/E), 24.5. Between 1975 and 1981, Continental's assets grew at an annual compound growth rate of 15.1%, and its earnings at 14.0%. As a result, in 1981, the bank's ROTA stood at 0.56%, its ROE was at 15.4%, and its asset-equity ratio had increased to 27.5. During the same period, First Chicago's asset base grew more slowly, at the rate of 9.0%. In 1981, its ROTA was a meager 0.36%, its ROE, 9.4%, and its TA/E, 26.4 times.

Continental's performance was in many respects remarkable. From 1975 to 1981, real GNP grew in the United States at an annual compound growth rate of 3.4% (even though annual inflation of 9.13% propelled nominal growth to double digits). Continental, situated in one of the economically hardest hit parts of the country, showed *real* asset growth almost twice as high as the economy's growth rate. Achieving such growth in the middle of the Rust Belt, while at the same time maintaining a high ROE, earned accolades for Continental's management. In 1980, *Dunn's Review* ranked Continental one of the five best-run companies in the United States.

One can see in Continental's strategy a clear example of the application of the new choices available under price banking. In 1971, relationship money—domestic demand and time deposits—funded 57.1% of Continental's total assets. By 1981, this figure had fallen to 31.9%. For (noninterest-bearing) demand deposits, the percentages stood at 31.7% in 1971 and 19.3% in 1981. Price-sensitive money showed, however, a very different picture: In 1971, foreign deposits (identifiable as purchased money) funded 28.7%, and other purchased funds 10.3% of assets. By 1981, these percentages had increased to 31.2% and 23.4% of assets, respectively.

Continental had thus funded a rapid asset growth strategy with purchased, rather than relationship, money.[3] This strategy of using purchased funds to finance an asset buildup requires that the assets yield sufficient revenues to cover the costs of the purchased funds. Thus,

---

3. Recall from Chapter 3 (page 98) that many observers viewed the CD as a solution to the banks' funding problems. Chapter 5, similarly noted that U.K. banks became "advances-driven" rather than "deposit-driven," as new funding instruments developed there.

Continental's aggressively funded growth strategy required the bank to fund assets that would cover the cost of the (expensively) purchased funds. The economic slowdown in the Midwest and a generally sagging economy limited demand for loans from large corporations—the bank's traditional business—so Continental found new lending opportunities in the oil industry, which was booming in the wake of the oil shock.

Continental had gained some energy sector experience in the early 1970s and had upgraded its energy group; but now the situation required Continental to compete much more aggressively for energy lending with well-established banks located in oil producing states. Thus, Continental was driven to purchase loans from the secondary players that flourished in the new price banking environment, where funds and assets could be bought and sold. Note that the same unfortunate interaction between the funding and lending risks would be observed in the savings and loan industry a decade later, and had been observed a decade earlier in the United Kingdom in the development of the fringe banking crisis described in Chapter 5. With more expensive funding in the price-driven markets, assets had to yield higher returns, not only to cover the higher funding costs, but also to compensate the bank's equity investors for higher risks. Thus, the bank was inexorably driven toward a riskier balance sheet. And though at first the results seemed positive, problems began to appear by the early 1980s. Continental's link to an unimportant Oklahoma bank was the herald of misfortune.

The Penn Square Bank was a small one-unit bank situated in an Oklahoma City shopping mall. Its fortunes grew with the oil boom of the 1970s, yet the growth of its asset base, from $59 million to $288 million between 1976 and 1979, represented nothing more than the tip of the iceberg. The figure much understated actual loan generation at the bank; many loans that were made did not remain on Penn Square's balance sheet, but were sold to banks like Continental that could not generate all the loans they wanted for themselves, because their traditional clients had begun to use new products. To become large players and make large loans, banks like Penn Square fully availed themselves of the price-driven financial environment. They made loans and then sold the paper realizing that they did not have to keep the loans on their books. With many asset-hungry money center banks just asking to take loans off their hands, Penn Square was able to sell $2 billion of assets between 1976 and 1980! Continental was rumored to be the holder of more than $1 billion of them.[4] Though investigations after the 1982

---

4. "Penn Square: Ever Again?" *The Economist*, August 21, 1982, 284:62–63.

closure of the Oklahoma bank revealed shoddy management practices, the events at Penn Square proved important for another reason.

Penn Square's failure was, in retrospect, merely an incident. Its real significance lies in the fact that several of the largest and most prominent U.S. banks had established close but undiscerning business relations with Penn Square, a bank with lending practices that were appalling to any knowledgeable observer. So when, in 1982, that bank had to be closed by regulators, the focus shifted to the question of how banks like Continental had gotten involved. This question proved especially troubling because it became clear that Penn Square was not an isolated incident. During the same summer, troubles at another "upstart" financial firm—Drysdale Securities—again dragged some highly regarded institutions into the public spotlight, in this case Chase Manhattan. Furthermore, concerns about the banks' possibly imprudent asset management were not helped by the deepening third world debt crisis. What became clear was that in their quest for growth, some of the largest and most experienced banks had placed prudence in the backseat. Thus in 1982, the Continental strategy began to look doubtful if not dangerous. Still, the impressive size of this major bank helped postpone the final crisis for another two years.

During this period, Continental's management seemed more aware of the manifestations of its problems than of their causes. In the bank's 1983 annual report, for example, chairman-designate Taylor noted that:

> As we move towards a brighter future, we are dealing directly and firmly with the realities of today . . . . The problems that the organization has been grappling with since July 1983 are substantial. They arise from a group of credits in our loan portfolio primarily related to the loan participation purchased from Penn Square Bank and a few other large energy-related credits. The balance of our loan portfolio has some problems, but I do not feel that these are out of line with other major banks. . . . While aware of the difficulties, we are proceeding confidently. We have sound strategies and programs to position Continental for the future and for the vigorous pursuit of profitable opportunities.[5]

Taylor's statement raises several interesting issues. Although he ascribed the problems of the bank directly to the energy-related loans, one should consider them a mere symptom of the larger issue. The real cause is to be found in the funding of a rapid-growth strategy with purchased money requiring high-yielding and, therefore, risky assets.

A second point deserving attention is Taylor's suggestion that the

5. Continental Illinois Corp., *Annual Report,* 1983.

problems at Continental were not "out of line with [those at] other major banks." Though there is an element of truth in this statement, especially in light of the rapid buildup of third world loans by various other large U.S. banks, two caveats apply: One is that those other banks that followed more diversified funding strategies were less likely to encounter immediate problems. The other is that other banks' mistakes can hardly justify Continental's strategy; indeed, many of these other banks had been viewed unfavorably by the stock market, where banks' P/E ratios have significantly underperformed those of the market. Between 1961 and 1969, money center bank P/E ratios stood on average at 85% of the S&P Index. Between 1970 and 1983, they averaged 65%, and from 1982 to 1986, the years in which the debt crisis had been given high press coverage, 51%.[6]

A third issue raised by Taylor lies in his promise to continue the "vigorous pursuit of profitable opportunities." Taken at face value, his statement seems unobjectionable; yet it fails to mention the risks of these profitable opportunities, especially in combination with the funding strategy employed.

When the crisis finally struck Continental in May 1984, observers should really have been surprised that the markets took two years to fully catch up with the problem—and not that a near-failure occurred. Rumors of Japanese (and other foreign) investors withholding funds from Continental began to circulate at the same time that questions arose concerning the accuracy of the bank's estimate of its nonperforming assets. What is significant here is that once these rumors started, the wholesale funding sources on which Continental relied quickly dried up—in the world of price banking, money moves fast. Though FDIC insurance indeed kept most small depositors from moving, their relative importance in Continental's funding had diminished. For the large corporate depositors and money market investors that had bought Continental's paper, there were no incentives to stay with the bank.

When the large, price-sensitive suppliers of funds decided to place their money elsewhere, Continental, plagued with solvency concerns related to the quality of its assets and liquidity concerns arising from its inability to fund itself in the purchased funds market, could not survive. The only remaining question was how the FDIC would fulfill its obligation "to purchase, hold and liquidate . . . the assets of national banks which have been closed by action of the Comptroller of the Currency."

Events at Continental Illinois were one of the worst possible results of the larger trend toward price-driven financial transactions. Of course,

6. Salomon Brothers, Inc., *A Review of Bank Performance*, 1988:118–119.

it can be argued that Continental's experience is not an indictment of price banking but an example of its success. In a free capital market, investors should be offered an opportunity to invest along a scale of risk-return combinations. In this view, Continental's rapid-growth strategy would only be seen as offering equity investors a more complete set of investment opportunities. Buyers of Continental equity bought a participation in a high-risk strategy with potentially high rewards. (Had oil prices risen again after 1982, Continental's oil investments would have paid off handsomely.) In such a view, where financial markets are considered much like all other markets, it is seen as a mistake for the FDIC to provide deposit insurance unrelated to the quality of a bank's underlying assets and at uniform insurance premiums, since this keeps the market from functioning freely and removes the monitoring function of investors. In this view such insurance is part of the problem, not part of the solution. Though some theoretical elegance can be found in this reasoning, it now seems clear that such a perfectly free, unregulated capital market is not likely to occur. Not only does much academic work point to possible market imperfections, but regulators and legislators oppose a totally unregulated financial industry. Therefore, the possibility of an environment free of regulation will not be explored here.

The effects of changing regulation on bank strategy are impossible to ignore in the Continental case. Mistakes made there resemble the errors that plagued regulators, legislators, and managers of the S&L industry half a decade later. Dramatic failures in the S&L industry clearly called into question, if not the entire concept of deregulation, then at least its implementation. Indeed, suggestions for reregulation have been put forward to deal with what seems, again in retrospect, a simple problem. When S&Ls were allowed to become more price competitive in funding, as money market certificates were introduced in 1978, they faced asset growth problems similar to those of Continental when it started to fund itself with more expensive purchased money.[7] For S&Ls, the required high-yielding outlets for the purchased funds became feasible as the Depository Institutions Deregulation Act (1980) and Depository Institution Act (1982) increasingly widened the number of approved investment vehicles. With greater reliance on federally insured, high-paying deposits, the stage was set for an estimated $300–$400 billion problem, as the high-yielding assets revealed their true risks. Not all S&Ls got into trouble, but serious dangers to these institutions were inherent in

---

7. The next chapter returns to this issue and briefly discusses how a risky lending strategy may actually be optimal from the bank's perspective since it maximizes the value of the subsidized insurance premiums.

a world of price banking, deregulation of investment alternatives, and continued insurance. In short, the lessons taught by Continental seem to have been ignored.

And though concern about the S&L industry has commanded much media attention recently, it should be clear that the same type of problems could emerge for the commercial banking sector as well. In the price-driven financial environment, with FDIC insurance at uniform premiums, the asset quality of banks can be expected to deteriorate. Thus, it cannot come as a surprise that now the size of the FDIC insurance fund, in relation to possible future claims from the commercial banking sector, is emerging as an issue of public debate.

Furthermore, the problems that plagued Continental may now be spreading to regional and smaller banks, in a reversal of the loan sales from smaller to larger banks (Penn Square to Continental). With many large money center banks aggressively engaged in highly leveraged financial transactions in the late 1980s, large banks kept the origination fee and sold the assets down to smaller banks. Little imagination is required to envision a scenario in which a higher interest rate climate causes problems in those loans. This is more likely because the process of loan sales decouples relationships between originators, lenders, and borrowers. And, as origination fees become substantial, the role of credit analysis itself may be jeopardized. In the future, smaller banks may perhaps be dragged down by the aggressive lending of the largest ones.

Though it has magnified risks for financial intermediaries, the move toward price banking has also brought many potentially favorable opportunities: New products can be offered, and foreign markets are within reach. New and different business strategies are possible, as Citicorp's acquisition of a British securities firm illustrates.

CITICORP AND VICKERS DA COSTA

With 63,700 employees, 1,630 offices in 94 countries, $860 million in net income, $5.8 billion in equity, and assets of $135 billion (exceeding those of any other bank), Citicorp was, in 1983, the largest banking organization in the world. It was also one of the most internationalized, with the United States accounting for only 38% of its net income. Citicorp's international focus was not a recent phenomenon. The bank had begun early to build an international network; it had become involved with domestic and international securities transactions before the financial dislocations of the 1930s, and before Glass-Steagall excluded commercial banks from the securities business. (Earlier, in the 1920s, National City was the largest distributor of securities in the world and the fourth-largest originator of securities in the United States.)[8] In those pre-Glass-Steagall days, both U.S. securities and foreign issues were originated, underwritten, and distributed through the bank's substantial retail distribution network. Once excluded from the securities industry, the bank refocused on commercial banking. Then, during the 1950s and 1960s, Citibank became a dominant international bank, active in a variety of financial product markets, but with acknowledged expertise in making large loans to major corporations. The bank was also successful in product innovation (e.g., development of the negotiable CD in 1961), and it followed different strategies in different national product markets, in accordance with local and U.S. regulations.

As Citibank outgrew its competitors, its size and its groups' geographic and product spread gave rise to frequent internal reorganizations, which often reflected new emphases on particular market segments. During the 1960s and 1970s, Citibank had been considered an international wholesale bank and important sovereign lender, but by 1983 Citicorp was broadly organized into three banks—the Institutional Bank, the Individual Bank, and the Investment Bank. The "Three I's," as many called them, were not equally important in terms of earnings generation. Not surprisingly, given the limited growth potential of the large institutional loan market during the 1970s and 1980s, the Institutional Bank grew less rapidly than the other two. Between 1970 and 1980, net interest income after loan loss expenses grew at 15.5%; fees, commissions, and other income grew at 18.9%.[9]

At this time, the corporate lending business' decline seemed irreversible. Even Citicorp's own inventiveness (such as the CD) ultimately helped other price-driven instruments to gain popularity and fostered disintermediation: large customers bypassed the loan department for the CP market, while large corporate deposits left the bank, often to be placed in the CP market as well. Other traditional clients availed themselves of direct financing opportunities offshore as domestic competition for funds became more costly.

Citicorp responded to these developments in several ways. Like Continental, it shifted its target borrower group. There was a group of cash-

---

8. See H. Cleveland and T. Huertas, *Citibank 1812–1970* (Cambridge, MA: Harvard University Press, 1985):139, 152.

9. In light of the large write-offs in 1987, the interest income could be considered overstated if more conservative reserving had been charged against it.

hungry borrowers that Citicorp knew well through past experience: third world borrowers.[10] The bank increased lending to third world countries as a means of generating the asset growth that could no longer be found in either the United States or Europe. One senior executive at Citicorp was quoted as saying:

> We all kept waiting for spreads to turn around and they never did. In a sense, we ended up allocating loans according to price. We held back in Europe, where spreads fell first each time. We loaned instead to borrowers that remained above our threshold. As a result, Latin America doubled its book while Europe and Asia grew slowly. Neither Brazil nor Mexico was pushing for the narrowest spreads then.[11]

In terms of asset quality this lending strategy yielded effects similar to those experienced by Continental Illinois in the 1980s, but Citicorp applied a much broader funding and product market strategy. In particular, its Individual Bank started to play a more important and more profitable role. Profits generated here and elsewhere in the bank (e.g., in a highly successful currency trading operation) bought Citicorp the time it needed to build up its loan loss reserve, so that the dubious portfolio of third world debt did not threaten the existence of the organization during this period.[12] In particular, Citicorp actively developed both its consumer and its other fee-based activities. This emphasis on a fee-based, rather than asset-growth, strategy is easy to explain once the financial goals of Citicorp have been examined. With an ROE growth target of about 18%, earnings growth targets of 15%, and dividend payout ratios that had often been at 30%, the corporation was financially constrained.[13] In such a situation, it is clear that both asset sales (to control leverage) and nonasset-intensive fee-based income become highly attractive; both increase ROA and ROE. In addition, in financial markets fees from advisory services—primarily generated in mergers and acquisitions transactions and in highly leveraged financial transac-

10. Before the 1930s, Citibank had been the second-largest underwriter for Latin American debt securities.

11. Quoted in P. Wellons, "Cross-Border Learning by Citicorp in the 1980s," #381-146. Boston: Harvard Business School, 1981.

12. Citicorp dramatically increased its loan-loss reserves in May 1987; it announced an increase of $3 billion, thereby setting a new industry standard, which was subsequently raised by its competitors.

13. See Citicorp *Annual Report,* 1988:2. Using a simple sustainable growth-rate calculation, the targets imply significant equity issues, given that fuller leverage would be costly in rating terms and could conflict with regulatory capital requirements.

tions—exploded during the 1980s. Consequently, the attractiveness of those areas of investment banking where Glass-Steagall was no barrier became compelling. In fact, initiatives in the investment banking field became a standard response for many of the large commercial banks.

For Citicorp, the attractiveness of investment banking obviously carried memories from the pre-Glass-Steagall days, when the bank had been both a significant underwriter and a major retail distributor. But Glass-Steagall excluded Citicorp from the important trading and underwriting segments of the U.S. investment banking business.[14] Nevertheless, Citicorp could profit from a trend occurring within the investment banking field. There, financial advisory services had begun to command extraordinary rewards, especially in the financial restructuring arena. The general trend toward price-driven financing and the proliferation of financial products compelled corporations to seek more help and to consider financial restructurings that had been impossible in the traditional environment. (For example, the high-yield bond brought hitherto impossible transactions into the realm of financial feasibility.) Neither advisory services nor new lending activities related to financial restructuring were outside the legal limits of Citicorp. Thus, with its traditional lending business in decline, the high rewards in those areas of investment banking open to Citicorp now beckoned.[15]

Though the Investment Bank was one of the firm's "Three I's," it did not look like a conventional investment bank. In 1983, Citicorp's Investment Bank contributed $128 million to profits, of which 60% ($77 million) derived from activities described as "investment banking," 20% ($26 million) from "investment management" services, and another 20% from "international private banking." (Some investment-banking-related income, such as Citicorp's highly profitable foreign exchange trading efforts, was reported through the Institutional Bank.)

Of the $77 million attributed to investment banking, approximately 50% was produced in the United States; 30% in Europe, the Middle East, and Africa; and the remaining 20% in the non-U.S. Western Hemisphere. In the latter two areas, this income derived from a scattered set of products and services that were dependent on local business custom and regulation. In the United States, where $38 million of investment banking income was generated, Citicorp was a player in the origination

14. Citicorp and other banking corporations were permitted to enter a variety of government, state, and local securities activities. And indeed, Citicorp was a major U.S. government securities trader.

15. Although I concentrate on its investment banking activities, Citicorp's most important and successful initiative actually occurred in the retail market.

markets for certain municipal securities, several Euroissues, and its own commercial paper. Yet its distribution activities were weak. In trading and positioning, Citicorp held an important but declining position in U.S. government securities. Citicorp had some presence in the advisory business, but mostly in smaller transactions. In the mergers and acquisitions market, for example, Citicorp typically represented smaller corporations. Not surprisingly, many of the larger transactions were executed by the top-tier U.S. investment banks, which boasted of their experience. On Wall Street, mergers and acquisitions deals were likened to brain surgery, for which one would go to the most experienced surgeon without regard to price.

Thus, even for a player of Citicorp's financial power, high reputation, and overall caliber, formidable barriers existed. In corporate securities underwriting and distribution, legal barriers prevailed; in advisory services, other players were already well established. Still, the potential rewards of investment banking activities compelled Citicorp to design a strategy that would allow it, if not to circumvent existing legal obstacles, then at least to prepare itself for the day when the legal barriers between investment banking and commercial banking might come down. Such expectation of deregulation was fully justified by the financial climate of the early 1980s, and many observers of the financial industry considered a breakdown of remaining product boundaries to be only a matter of time. Also, many suggested that this breakdown would lead to the emergence of a few large international institutions capable of spanning the entire financial product line. Advocates of this proposition almost always counted Citicorp among the surviving institutions.

In pursuit of its investment banking strategy, Citicorp would have to use all of its inherent advantages to wrest territory away from experienced players. The growing importance of international transactions could provide it with an extra advantage. Many U.S. investment banking firms were attempting to expand their international networks, while also experiencing rapid domestic growth. At the same time, foreign securities firms sought entry to the U.S. market, both to learn U.S. financial techniques and to gain a foothold there. Citicorp's advantage lay in its worldwide presence (and the broad information it could therefore gather), its ability to readily access many foreign markets, and its experience in managing a global financial network. Furthermore, Citicorp's experience and strengths in specialized product lines, such as foreign exchange, could provide leverage in other transactions. In short, an internationally focused strategy, set in accordance with U.S. regulatory constraints, seemed to make good sense for Citicorp.

To mount a broad investment banking strategy seems to require a basic securities trading and distribution function—if not for the sake of the profits it generates, then at least to support other investment banking services through the information gathered in trading. Thus, in anticipation of future regulatory freedoms to enter the U.S. securities market, an international equity business was a natural step for Citicorp. Given these considerations, its purchase of foreign equity capabilities makes sense. Prevented by local regulation from entering the Tokyo and New York equity markets, Citicorp turned to London. There, like many other players in anticipation of the Big Bang, Citicorp entered the securities business with its purchase of Scrimgeours, a British broker.

Citicorp's other British brokerage acquisition, Vickers Da Costa, should be viewed within the context of this same strategy—to build an international equity presence. This small U.K. broker, already in possession of a securities license in Japan, dealt mostly in Far East securities. Seeing the acquisition as a possible means of gaining a toehold in the Japanese equity market, Citicorp tested the letter and spirit of Article 65. Thus, Citicorp embarked on an international equities strategy, leveraging its international experience and its ability to manage large, geographically diversified institutions.[16]

Citicorp's purchase of Vickers Da Costa subsequently gained it a seat on the Tokyo Stock Exchange, where Vickers was among the first foreign firms to be awarded access. In this sense, Citicorp did indeed succeed in establishing an international equity presence.

Of course, the long-term effectiveness of Citicorp's international investment banking strategy has not yet been demonstrated, and some retrenchment is already in evidence. Citicorp's exit from much of the London gilt and equity market in 1989 provides another story, not

---

16. The acquisition of Vickers was reportedly the outcome of pressures within the bank to expand the international equities strategy. International Private Banking (IPB) is said to have pressured for the acquisition of a foreign broker. Highly profitable during the mid-1970s, IPB became important in placing the funds of high net worth individuals, especially those from the Middle East. It is not surprising that these investors turned to Citicorp; uneducated in the workings of the U.S. capital markets but familiar with the largest banking institutions, they were naturally attracted by a bank with Citicorp's reputation. Citicorp first gained through spread banking as it took deposits and made loans, and later through placing the funds in safe government securities.

But the IPB's customers eventually became more sophisticated, and the shift to price banking promoted the notion of performance investing. This forced the IPB to provide more sophisticated investment strategies. One such strategy involved international equity investments, for which an international equity presence would be highly desirable. The opportunity to gain such a presence came with the Big Bang and the rapid restructuring of the U.K. securities industry.

taken up here. But this outcome illustrates the riskiness of invading tempting new markets. The next vignette provides an example of how one prominent U.S. bank carried out another such enterprise.

MORGAN STANLEY'S TOKYO BRANCH

Morgan Stanley, Inc., long one of the premier U.S. investment banking firms, had a large international network in place in the late 1980s. In 1986, the company employed approximately 5,300 people. Of this number, its more than 700 London and 500 Tokyo employees together represented more than twice the *total* number of Morgan Stanley employees in the early 1970s.

Of course, such rapid international and domestic growth was not exclusive to Morgan Stanley: firms like Goldman Sachs, Salomon Brothers, and First Boston, along with many British and Japanese firms, displayed similar appetites for expansion. Their international strategies, recently adopted except for earlier forays into the Euromarkets, represented a new trend in investment banking. All sought the profit opportunities that existed (or were expected) abroad and the boost that international standing would bring to their domestic banking activities.

For this expansion, different rationales have been offered. Some argue that many investment banks were largely following "me-too" strategies—one bank copying the potentially successful international strategy of another in order not to be left out. Others suggest that the entry of foreign banks into the United States demanded a reciprocal response. Another, more positive rationale was that the increase in international capital mobility and price-driven banking transactions in the domestic markets around the world fostered the development of financial technologies and techniques that could be applied across geographic markets.

The use of the term "globalization" to capture this latter line of thought suggested that, in effect, a single, globally homogeneous market was being created, and that financial intermediaries should aim to exploit economies of scale and scope. Yet, hard evidence for globalization is less abundant than its popularity among the press and various market participants would suggest; instead, few products seem really to be traded globally, except foreign currencies and selected government securities. Still, many professed a belief in the inexorable move toward financial integration of the markets. Morgan Stanley, for example, in its first annual report as a publicly traded company (1986), noted that:

> We are now witnessing the emergence of a global securities market. This market has few national boundaries, and is open to virtually all investors,

issuers, borrowers, or savers. Price is established by supply and demand from around the world, rather than a single domestic market and transactions often take place on a twenty-four hour basis. Morgan Stanley operates in these global markets on an integrated worldwide basis.

Morgan Stanley has had an active presence in Europe for nearly 20 years, and opened its office in London in 1976. Today we have a London staff of over 700 people. Morgan Stanley continues to be a leader in the management and distribution of public offerings of debt and equity securities in the Euromarket, the business that drew the firm to London originally. . . .

Based on our trading volume in equity and convertible securities we are now the leading non-Japanese broker on the Tokyo Exchange. . . . In our Tokyo fixed-income activities, we have expanded trading beyond Eurodollar, U.S. Treasury and U.S. federal agency securities to include yen bonds, floating rate notes and U.S. corporate bonds. The Tokyo office increased its activity in arranging complex interest rate transactions for Japanese investors and almost doubled its volume of foreign exchange transactions. We have also remained a leader in mergers and acquisitions for Japanese companies, particularly those investing in the United States. We continue to be a major dealer in foreign equities for Japanese investors through our Tokyo office. For Japanese investors interested in purchasing Japanese stock, we have put in place in Tokyo a sizeable Japanese equity research staff.[17]

Morgan Stanley's professed international strategy appeared to engage all aspects of Japanese investment banking.[18] The firm aimed at broad participation in equity, fixed-income, and foreign exchange markets, as well as advisory services and international asset management. This broad product market strategy contrasted with the strategies being pursued by a number of competitors, who had decided to concentrate on niches.

For a U.S. firm to follow a broad investment banking strategy in Tokyo seems daunting. There, firms engaged in foreign exchange trading face regulatory constraints not present in the United States. Few opportunities exist in equity underwriting, not only because the four large Japanese securities houses are formidable competitors in this market, but also because custom makes it difficult for foreign securities firms to enter. In fixed-income underwriting, foreign investment banks have had little success historically, and only recently have they been allowed to enter segments of the government securities markets. Though firms like Morgan Stanley have been able to show some success in equity trading, they have not attained anything approaching the market share

17. See Morgan Stanley, *Annual Report,* 1986.
18. Morgan Stanley was one of the few firms praised for its strategy management in "A Survey of Wall Street: Where to From Here?" *The Economist,* July 11, 1987:22.

of the large Japanese institutions. Still, even a small share in this market (Morgan Stanley's share was reportedly .5% to 1% by 1986) can generate significant profits, especially given the fixed-commission structure still employed in Japan and the large volume of transactions.

Advisory services also proved to be a difficult market, and one very different from any of those that Morgan Stanley had taken part in so successfully in the United States. Although cross-national mergers and acquisitions have shown some growth, the domestic Japanese corporate restructuring market has been small.[19] Similarly, many of the more advanced products and advisory services employed in complex financial transactions in the United States are not yet standard fare in Tokyo. One could argue that the current modest level of such activities does not deny their future potential. Still, even if these opportunities grow, the question remains: to what extent will the large Japanese securities houses, familiar with local markets, customs, and clients, continue to present a formidable, if not insurmountable, barrier to foreign firms?

In this respect, note how very different the Japanese and U.S. investment banking industries are. Table 7.1 outlines the activities and income generation of some prominent U.S. and Japanese investment banking firms and presents some relevant statistics. Several U.S. firms generate 70% to 75% of their revenues from advisory services and principal transactions, the remaining 25% to 30% of revenue being derived from underwriting and distribution. In Japan, the inverse is true—trading and underwriting are the predominant activities. Since much of the trading is done for a retail distribution network, the vast difference in compensation per employee is not surprising. To put it simply, highly paid talent provides complex advice in the United States, while in Japan lower-paid salespersons engage in distribution.

Thus, a firm with a strategy for becoming an international investment bank is necessarily attracted to the rapidly developing Tokyo market, but its entrance there cannot be justified by present opportunities. The success of foreign firms in Tokyo depends heavily on future developments, and particularly on the anticipation of further liberalization in the Japanese markets. This expectation raises another question: whether, and how soon, the forces that led to a greater emphasis on more complex financial products and services in the domestic United States market will be able to create an equivalent environment in Japan.

---

19. For an account of the Japanese mergers and acquisitions market, see W. Carl Kester, *Japanese Takeovers: The Global Contest for Corporate Control* (Boston: Harvard Business School Press, 1991).

Again, the future importance of international capital flows—which almost forced foreign players to enter foreign capital markets during the 1980s—will have to be evaluated. One can conceive of a world in which some degree of balance is restored to international capital accounts, but in which the *openness* of the various capital markets does not change. If this occurs, the success of Morgan Stanley's international strategy is possible. If it does not, any commitment of resources could be futile. Indeed, several investment banks have recently tried to decrease their international commitments, apparently questioning the continued internationalization of markets, or at least their ability to profit from the trend or their ability to finance the costs of a prolonged startup phase. Still, Morgan Stanley's broadly based international strategy has won many accolades from industry observers. And though internal allocations make it difficult to get reliable estimates of costs and revenues, one can try to estimate some of the commitments.

That they are large is beyond doubt. Take, for example, Morgan Stanley's Tokyo employment of 500 people, and assume that approximately 20% are U.S. citizens. Using the average direct compensation figure ($140,000) from the table, U.S. personnel cost can be estimated.[20] Because lower-level personnel in the Tokyo office are typically not of U.S. nationality, the average U.S. personnel compensation should be increased, say to $200,000–$250,000. Given that the total employment cost for a U.S. citizen in Japan is, according to industry analyses, approximately two to four times U.S. compensation, total U.S. personnel costs could easily run to $50–$100 million. Add to this the costs of the Japanese employees (who arc presumably paid at a higher rate than the Japanese industry average of $60,000, in order to attract them to non-Japanese firms), and total personnel costs could jump to between $70 and $120 million. Other expenses (rent, office costs, and so forth) can also be assumed to be well in excess of what they would be in the United States; the table suggests that an additional $100 million would be needed for a 500-person office. Total direct costs may easily exceed $200 million.

Here, the question is obviously one of investments versus expected future payoff. Firms like Morgan Stanley are betting that the future payoff from pursuing the currently limited business opportunities in Tokyo will be at least as great as the costs of entry. Furthermore, while

---

20. Note that all cost projections in this paragraph are based on the author's calculations and do *not* utilize any information provided by Morgan Stanley. Consequently, they should only be considered estimates.

TABLE 7.1
Selected Data on Securities Firms
1986

	Morgan Stanley	First Boston	Salomon Brothers (Inv. Bank)	Merrill Lynch	Nomura	Yaimaichi	Daiwa	Nikko
Employees	5,300	4,493	5,957	47,900	9,455	7,512	8,540	8,398
Revenue[a,*]	$1,428	$1,310	$2,066	$6,909	$4,963	$2,405	$3,202	$2,815
Rev./Employee	$269,434	$291,565	$346,819	$144,238	$524,907	$320,154	$374,941	$335,199
Tot. Expenses[a,*]	$1,106	$1,065	$1,279	$6,134	$1,941	$1,120	$1,353	$1,348
Exp./Employee	$208,679	$237,035	$214,705	$128,058	$205,288	$149,095	$158,431	$160,514
Compensation & Benefits[a]	$695	$706	$838	$3,473	$704	$470	$500	$466
C&B/employee	$131,132	$157,133	$140,675	$72,505	$74,458	$62,567	$58,548	$55,489
Net Income Before Taxes[a]	$323	$245	$787	$773	$3,023	$1,263	$1,802	$1,420
Net Income[a]	$201	$181	NA	$454	$1,347	$515	$728	$541

Total Assets[a]	$29,190	$48,618	$78,164	$53,013	$17,844	$13,246	$20,253	$12,750
Cash[a]	$385	$115	$1,224	$1,871	$4,285	$1,819	$3,881	$2,159
Sec. Owned[a]	$9,511	$18,337	$41,324	$15,515	$6,932	$4,261	$4,780	$2,853
Sec. Repo[a]	$14,189	$20,017	$18,797	$21,405	$5,530[d]	$2,790[d]	$11,057[d]	$7,247[d]
Other[a]	$5,105	$10,149	$16,819	$14,222	$1,097	$4,376	$535	$491
Equity[a]	$798	$958	$3,454	$2,876	$5,094	$2,217	$2,958	$2,750
Revenue -Int. Exp.[a]	$1,428	$1,310	$2,066	$6,909	$4,963	$2,405	$3,202	$2,815
% Investment Banking	46[b]	51	20	14	13	23	18	17
% Principal	33	30	57[f]	15	17	5	14	11
% Brokerage Commissions	15	9	[e]	31	62	61	56	53
% Other	6	9	23	39[c]	8	12	12	12

*Excludes interest expense.
[a]$ Million
[b]Approximately 70% of which comes from mergers and acquisitions. Thus 32% of total revenues is generated through M&A.
[c]Real estate, insurance, and asset management contributed 65% of this.
[d]Refers to secured loans.
[e]Not separately reported, but included in "Other."
[f]Includes underwriting.

Source: Annual Reports (1986).

Tokyo represents an opportunity for future expansion, the cost of creating and maintaining a presence there can be subsidized by current successful domestic operations. If the Japanese market should blossom into a highly profitable environment, as did the United States in the 1980s, then the cost of early entry will be recouped. If those opportunities do not materialize, however, expansion will not only have proven costly, but it could create a lot of internal disorganization. Large international ventures provide benefits, but they also present management challenges, especially when environmental change does not allow for a continuation of previously profitable strategies. This observation brings the fourth vignette to mind: Credit Suisse First Boston's challenge of managing an organization in a changing international financial environment.

CREDIT SUISSE FIRST BOSTON

The merger between CSFB and First Boston, announced in September 1988, seemed somewhat surprising. CSFB had been a highly successful joint venture, entered into by a Swiss commercial bank, Credit Suisse, and a U.S. investment bank, First Boston, in 1978. Ten years later, the merger of the parent and the joint venture was not a move made out of strength; serious management problems had made the existing setup unworkable. And although First Boston, a publicly traded company, had problems with damaging personnel losses in its highly profitable mergers and acquisitions department, there was no reason to believe that the merger was intended to solve that problem. The real reasons for the move were changes in the international capital markets, the increasing erosion of local boundaries in international finance, and the resulting difficulties in managing complex organizations. Each of these forces has been described earlier. Interestingly, these same forces were, to a large extent, responsible for the creation of CSFB as a joint venture in 1978. They were also responsible for the extraordinary success of CSFB during the ten years in which it operated as a joint venture between two financial intermediaries from different countries.

CSFB's 1986 net income of SFr 225 million represented a 26.8% return on equity and an annual compound growth of 41.5% since 1979. The firm dominated the new-issue league tables in the Euromarkets, was widely respected for its professionalism, and was known to have a highly effective trading capability. Few of its competitors could match its record. It seemed that careful strategic planning of Credit Suisse and First Boston had paid off, and that the unusual entity created by their joint venture was not only viable, but enormously successful.

To comprehend the reasons for CSFB's success and to grasp the inevitability of the organizational changes that occurred, one must look briefly at the origins of the firms. Rather than attributing CSFB's remarkable performance solely to brilliant strategic planning, it is better to acknowledge that CSFB was to some extent created by accident. Credit Suisse had been involved in a joint venture in the Eurobond markets with the New York investment banking firm White Weld; this occurred at the time that U.S. regulation and current account problems drove domestic borrowers abroad, adding to the importance of the Euromarkets (as outlined in Chapters 2 and 3). The first issue in the Euromarkets had taken place on behalf of an Italian firm, but increasingly during the 1970s, U.S. corporations entered the market. In the Eurobond markets, as elsewhere, the success of investment banks (often registered by their market share of new issues underwriting) was determined by two factors: access to issuers, and access to investors. For a number of reasons, large Swiss banks displayed great placement power, while U.S. investment banks had traditional access to U.S. corporate issuers.

Building on an earlier relationship, Credit Suisse and White Weld had formed a joint venture that performed quite successfully, climbing to second position on the league issue tables between 1973 and 1977. When White Weld was acquired by Merrill Lynch in 1978, Credit Suisse decided against continuing the joint venture with a firm as large as Merrill Lynch. Wanting nevertheless to keep the operation alive, the Swiss bank considered a number of other U.S. partners. After being rebuffed by several that wanted to explore the Euromarkets on their own, Credit Suisse's search for a partner with good access to important issuers brought it to First Boston.

First Boston had recently experienced financial difficulties and was eager to form a joint venture that would bring new capital into the firm. The alliance with Credit Suisse accomplished this by placing a large block of First Boston shares with the new entity, which became CSFB. CSFB's shares, in turn, were held by Credit Suisse and First Boston. William E. Mayer, chairman of the executive committee at First Boston, observed that the cash infusion and stock deal "saved our business and made it takeover-proof."[21]

The joint venture's mandate seemed well defined. First Boston was to continue its investment banking activities in the United States and Credit Suisse its banking activities out of Switzerland; CSFB would concentrate on issuing and trading securities in the Eurobond markets. CSFB suc-

---

21. See "The Healthy Hybrid," *The Wall Street Journal* (European ed.), April 22, 1987:1, 8.

cessfully pursued its assignment. It attained a leadership position in its first full year of operation, and the firm profited from the rapid growth of the Euromarkets. Between 1978 and 1986, issue volume grew at an annual compound rate of 40%, from $12 billion to $176 billion in the fixed-income market, and CSFB prospered along with the markets. One reason for the firm's success, other than the high quality of its employees, was that no other firm was organized in the same way. Most U.S. investment banking firms had decided to pursue their own Euromarket strategy, and the consortium banks that tried to emulate CSFB's success were frequently hindered by their parents' own attempts to enter the markets independently. CSFB's success seemed to derive from its perfect fit with the new and rapidly growing environment. By 1986, it was the dominant player in the $176 billion fixed-income Euroissues market.

But CSFB's success went beyond its ability to derive profits from underwriting and distributing issues; trading the seasoned issues became, in fact, its main source of income. Of course, links existed between CSFB's leadership position in the issue market and its ability to generate trading profits. With lead management status and the ability to "run the book" of an issue, much information generated inside the firm could be valuable in trading decisions. By 1986, trading revenues stood at SFr 190 million, surpassing underwriting fees of SFr 151 million. Advisory services—in contrast to U.S. investment banks—accounted for very little of CSFB's revenue.

As the 1980s progressed, however, the sources of profitability began to change. With more competition in underwriting, spreads started to fall. As Hans Joerge Rudloff, vice chairman of CSFB, noted in early 1987:

> The bear market in profitability began in 1986 and the markets will be even less profitable this year. With dozens of new mice nibbling at a cake which is getting smaller, you have to be a pretty crafty rat to get a good slice.[22]

The reduction in spreads referred to by Rudloff had actually occurred even earlier. Spreads had fallen as the straight, fixed-rate bond market matured and new players entered; but newer markets, such as the one for floating rate notes and bond cum equity warrants developed, in which initially spreads were once again higher.

CSFB had skillfully made the required transition, following its success in the fixed-bond market with success in these newly developing mar-

22. "A Survey of the Euromarkets: Now for the Lean Years," *The Economist*, May 16, 1987:4.

kets. But by the late 1980s, continued adjustment and adaptation had become far more difficult. At that time, the most promising new bond market—Japanese yen issues—was managed by Japanese investment banking houses. (Between 1985 and 1986, the yen share of all issues almost doubled, from 5% of total issues volume to approximately 10%.) The international yen-denominated issues reflected the new freedoms granted by the Japanese authorities, whose domestic markets also relied increasingly on the price mechanism. Now, Japanese firms dominated the yen market through aggressive pricing complemented by close customer relationships.

But reductions in spreads and underwriting commissions were not the only manifestations of change; as in the U.S. domestic market, issuers and investors were becoming more sophisticated about prices and more interested in complex products. CSFB's annual report for 1986 recognized this trend:

> In the past new issue activity was substantially dependent on the net financing needs of the borrowers. Today, swap-induced active management of assets and liabilities triggers capital markets' new issue volume which is independent of borrowers' net financing needs. . . .
>
> As a consequence of product innovation, financial intermediaries (particularly the traditional investment and merchant banks) have seen their historical roles altered. In the past they served as direct intermediaries between borrowers and investors and were rewarded with commissions; in general, they did not take principal risk. . . .
>
> While many obstacles to free capital flows still exist, it nevertheless can be stated that the liberalization of the past three years has radically altered the forum in which issuers, investors and financial institutions conduct their respective businesses. For the most part, investors now can satisfy their desires to achieve the highest risk-adjusted return. And borrowers are unrestrained in their freedom to seek the lowest risk-adjusted cost of money.[23]

In this annual report, the issues raised are clearly consistent with the forces of change identified earlier. They are also consistent with the observed behavior of U.S. investment banks, in which income generation through underwriting and distribution shifted toward principal transactions and advisory services. If similar changes were to occur in the Euromarkets and the local European markets, problems could arise for CSFB because of its particular structure and relationships with its parents. First Boston, for example, which had become highly successful in the U.S. advisory business, had to compete with other U.S. investment banks, such as Goldman Sachs and Morgan Stanley, which were actively

23. Credit Suisse First Boston, *Annual Report*, 1986.

trying to make their advisory services international. It was not only the expected profitability of these international transactions that mattered; the ability to perform international transactions at all became part of a sales pitch to land U.S. business. Now, the stage was set for competition between the various parts of what had until now been a harmonious and tightly efficient firm. CSFB wanted to take advantage of new international product opportunities, and First Boston was determined to do likewise, if only to remain on par with its U.S. competitors.

Against this background, it is not surprising that problems arose in the complex interactions between CSFB and First Boston. In international advisory services, for example, who should be calling on clients, CSFB or First Boston? Similarly, for designing complex products, who should take leadership, First Boston or CSFB? The structure of CSFB, given the nature of its cross-ownership, would not allow for any easy determination of the allocation of profits and revenues. Reportedly, the implementation of joint strategies proved to be far more difficult than had been anticipated. A *Wall Street Journal* article in early April 1987 referred to the problems that First Boston and CSFB had in sharing the international equity business. "We are like wolves; we think territory," said vice chairman Rudloff of CSFB, admitting that an attempt to resolve these conflicts had given rise to a "terrific shouting match."[24]

With the September 1988 announcement of the merger between the two firms, it was evident the partners had concluded that the joint-venture structure, once so useful to them both, was no longer viable. Though CSFB had operated remarkably well for a time as an "independent" unit, market conditions had changed, becoming inconsistent with the old organizational structure. Business strategy had to adjust. In some respects, this outcome confirmed the prediction of the chairman of the old Credit Suisse White Weld, who was rumored to have preferred a combination between Dillon Read and Credit Suisse. Worried that a structure such as CSFB would not be able to survive bad times with pressures from two strong parents, he had believed that a smaller U.S. partner would be more attractive.

In the proxy statement to the merger agreement, management expressed the issue in this way:

> The difficulties that have arisen include conflicts between First Boston and [CSFB] regarding business strategy in certain capital markets, conflicts regarding responsibility and compensation with respect to products, services, and customers, which involve the geographic area of both organizations and reluctance of professionals to transfer from one organization to the other.

24. See "The Healthy Hybrid."

In many cases, neither organization has been able to take advantage of attractive business opportunities pending the resolution of these difficulties. As a result, the personnel of both organizations have devoted significant amounts of time to managing these issues thereby *reducing employee productivity* [emphasis added].[25]

Note how the changing international product market opportunities and ensuing competitive pressure led to what was essentially a management problem. Although strategy seems to have been clearly set (and in the past, to have been highly successful), with new pressures the actual management tasks at CSFB became so formidable that it started to affect the productivity of the employees—a cardinal sin in investment banking, where professionals pride themselves on being "producers" rather than "managers."

The difficulties experienced by CSFB and First Boston in managing a complex organization in rapidly changing markets also reflect on other investment banks. How can firms like Morgan Stanley or Goldman Sachs manage the compensation, location, and other organizational problems that multiply with internationalization? Remember that Citicorp's enormous experience in managing large, internationally operating firms was identified as a possible source of advantage. Admittedly, one may note that this experience relates to managing an employee force very different from the one that is required for a successful investment banking operation. Still, one could also observe that as financial product market boundaries have been broken and the product market spectrum has filled up, the skills required of commercial bankers and investment bankers have come to resemble each other more and more closely.[26] In this sense, changes in the financial environment have not only made the world more complex for the CFOs who face more choices in the financing alternatives for their firms; the new strategies open to financial services firms increasingly require strong management capabilities, which have not traditionally been a recognized strength at the often loosely managed investment banking partnerships. (This issue is considered in Chapter 8.)

The events described above are illustrative of the interaction between

25. See "Proxy Statement to the Proposed Merger," 16.
26. Consider, for example, the skills necessary for a calling officer. Unless these include broad familiarity with a range of investment banking products and corporate finance strategy, the calling officer will be unable to land business for the bank. Similarly, the banking officer engaged in loan sales for the bank (and the officer responsible for making the loans, and the credit officer) has more in common with a salesperson at an investment bank than with the traditional loan officer of a commercial bank. (See also Chapter 8.)

the changing environment, business strategy, and industry structure. First, new opportunities created the environment in which CSFB flourished. Then, new product developments and new players, along with the dissemination of financial techniques such as those employed in mergers and acquisitions transactions, forced the reevaluation of old strategies and the reconsideration of old alliances. Before looking to the more general lessons for financial services firms, I briefly list a few other major strategic responses of U.S. financial intermediaries to their new environment.

OTHER STRATEGIC RESPONSES

In hindsight, the costly failures associated with the asset growth strategies of Continental Bank, the S&Ls, and the holders of third world debt all form one class of strategic responses and can easily be traced to the new opportunities of the price-driven financial environment. In contrast to their outcomes, at the time they were developed these strategies were admired and embraced by many.

One response to the price-driven era, which sometimes appeared in combination with an asset growth strategy, involved broadening the funding base. New products such as CDs and Automated Teller Machines eroded intra- and interstate branching restrictions. Furthermore, individual states or groups of states began to allow regional banks. The attraction of interstate banking is supposedly that it widens the funding base and economies of scale in operations, while it generates a more diversified loan portfolio on the asset side. Some large regional banks were created, and several money center banks expanded well beyond their traditional home base. Banks bought smaller out-of-state institutions, sometimes because they seemed cheap (especially if they operated in parts of the country with depressed economies), sometimes simply to gain access to new geographical areas. Chemical Corporation's acquisitions of Texas Bancshares—the largest commercial bank in Texas—and New Jersey's Horizon Bank show how some have bet on diversified regional strategies. It is too early to grade their success, other than to point to the expected operating economies, which have so far proved elusive.

Another strategic direction taken by commercial banks has been to expand their product base into the securities industries, avoiding Glass-Steagall restrictions by limiting their services to those offered, for example, by a discount broker. (Bank of America acquired Charles Schwab, although several problems later led it to sell that unit again.) Chase Manhattan's offering of CDs with rates linked to a stock index (which blended loan and securities products) provides another example, while its acquisition of two British brokers signals more direct expansion into the securities business.

In the United States, the clearest shift in investment banking has been the growing reliance on advisory services and principal transactions for revenue generation. This shift away from such traditional sources of revenue as trading, brokerage, underwriting, and distribution has not been unexpected. The abolition of fixed minimum commissions in trading transactions and the increase of competition in underwriting through changes such as Rule 415 precipitated an inevitable migration to advisory services and principal transactions. This shift holds implications for the capital positions of firms that have focused on these activities. And indeed several firms decided to go public in the 1980s or to link up with deep-pocket companies. Another reason for this same phenomenon, may, of course, have been that the price at which many of these transactions took place were highly attractive to the owners (partners).

The importance of the firm's capital base was recently underscored when one of the star performers of the 1980s, Drexel Burnham Lambert, filed for Chapter 11 protection. The story of Drexel's rise and fall is well known and fits easily into my earlier interpretation of fundamental forces for change. First, the firm took brilliant advantage of the opportunity to create new products for a price-sensitive market, and it exploited windows of opportunity in the capital market. But as bond prices deteriorated and the market window closed, Drexel's special position of market leadership was undermined, legal difficulties arose, and the value of its inventory of noninvestment grade bonds was questioned by outside suppliers of capital; Drexel could no longer fund itself in the price-competitive market. Like the events that forced Penn Central Railroad and Continental into reorganization, it was the CP market and Drexel's inability to purchase funds that heralded trouble.

The role of capital is equally crucial in a relatively new financing technique offered by investment banks called bridge financing. It is another response driven by the strategy of aggressively searching for transaction volume and fees. In this arrangement, the investment bank itself provides the client with the financing needed for a financial restructuring. Not until after the deal is completed is money actually raised in the market; it can then be used to repay the bridge loan. Apart from the capital need generated by such a transaction, interesting questions are raised regarding the Glass-Steagall Act. One of the rationales for Glass-Steagall was to prevent conflicts of interest between lenders and underwriters. Bridge loans can recreate these conflicts. The incentives for the investment banker to sell the securities that are supposed to replace its bridge loan are significantly reinforced—failure of the securities issue means that the investment bank cannot free up its own investment in the transaction and may possibly face serious losses if the credit quality of the borrower declines. Furthermore, since the size of the bridge loan can be very substantial relative to the firm's capital position, the riskiness of this strategy could become evident if the macroeconomic forces cause some of the highly leveraged transactions to fail.

Though so far no attention has been paid to changes in the insurance industry, it too had to find strategic initiatives as its operating environment was affected by the trends I have discussed. For example, insurance companies moved to hold riskier assets. Their traditional reliance on high-quality private placements and other highly rated investments was partially supplanted by purchases of high-yield and high-risk bonds (with or without equity conversion features). Competition for funds from sources such as high-yielding money market funds increased the insurance firms' costs and required higher returns.

Another example of the increased price competition that has affected insurance companies even in their least performance-driven product—term life—was their decision during the late 1970s and early 1980s (when very high interest rates prevailed) to use their annual investment income to set premiums low in order to attract funds in a price-competitive market.[27] When rates fell, and premiums could not be adjusted, serious losses occurred. An equally well-known mistake was made with the introduction of the Guaranteed Investment Contracts (or Guaranteed Rate of Return Contracts). Betting that short-term interest rates would remain high, the insurers offered guaranteed long-term returns, well above the reigning long-term rates. These long-term rates were below the current short-term rates (i.e., the yield curve was inverted). When the yield curve became upward sloping again, the innovative, price-driven GICs became expensive liabilities for the issuers.

As they became more performance-oriented, insurance companies did not just expand their product base—some even entered the investment industry more directly through acquisitions. For example, The Prudential acquired Bache Securities, and Aetna purchased large stakes in the British merchant bank Samuel Montagu, and in Federated Investors, Inc., a money manager. Travellers bought Dillon Read, and Sun-Life entered the U.S. mutual fund industry by buying the oldest fund man-

27. In the industry this became known as "cash flow underwriting." When short-term rates fell, the insurers were faced with real problems since without the high-interest yield the premiums were not sufficient to cover claims.

ager in the United States: Massachusetts Financial Services. Conversely, several investment banks, such as Merrill Lynch, tried to expand into products traditionally perceived to be the domain of the insurance industry.

In the mid-1980s, many argued that the breakdown of product market boundaries and conglomeration across product lines would drive firms to strategies that would inevitably lead to financial supermarkets. Institutions such as Sears and American Express attempted to implement such strategies. The move toward price banking, the erosion of traditional relationships, and the reduced regulatory interference with market transactions all seem to have provided an appealing rationale. A broad product line would afford an intermediary a new type of relationship, allowing it to make the first bid, at *competitive* prices, for a transaction; as noted before, the relationship here is a complement to price competitiveness, not a substitute. If economies of scope exist among the various products—and this so far has been difficult to show—such a strategy could be successful. I return to this issue in the next chapter.

At the same time that some institutions were trying to become financial supermarkets, others were pursuing a strategy at the opposite extreme. The 1980s also saw financial investment bank boutiques begin to flourish, and some of the most profitable commercial banks were smaller regionals.[28] Firms developed niche strategies, often aimed at the most lucrative end of the financial product line.

Thus, the filling up of the product market spectrum has not been the only development of recent years. Increasingly, a wide array of financial services firms actively compete in many different market segments. What again becomes evident is a world of enormous choice, diversity, and complexity. Inherently, this world includes great risks and the need for a very careful definition of objectives, strategic strength, and value creation.

---

28. Boutiques specializing in mergers, acquisitions, and general corporate finance emerged. James D. Wolfensohn, Inc., is one example of the new class of small investment banks. The Blackstone Group provides another. Here the focus is on the high-quality advice segment of the product market, although some firms sometimes supply funds to take principal positions in transactions suggested to their clients.

Principal transactions have also constituted a segment of the market for specialized boutiques. The remarkable success of the firm started by Messrs. Kohlberg, Kravis, and Roberts in structuring leveraged buyout transactions is the clearest case in point. The popularity of the financial technique employed here, the leveraged buyout, is a direct consequence of the change in the new financial environment and of new instruments such as the high-yield bond, even though the technique itself had been developed earlier. And though some firms, such as Forstmann Little & Co., eschewed the use of the high-yield bond, many availed themselves of the new opportunities.

8

SETTING STRATEGY IN A CHANGING
ENVIRONMENT

For financial services firms, the most important implication of the myriad changes in finance on the local, national, and global levels is greater freedom of choice. Strategy now assumes a much more important role, and the potential risks and rewards for the financial intermediaries (and thus for their owners, employees, and clients) have become great—so great, in fact, that some firms have been unable to remain independent entities while others have generated extraordinary riches. Strategy has mattered enormously, and the multiple tie that often characterized the industry in the past has been replaced by a race with clear winners and losers.

This chapter analyzes the impact of the changing environment on financial services firms. It shows that financial services firms have become in many respects firms like any other, and that they have to focus increasingly on explicit methods of *value creation*. This focus has been mandated by competition. The old regulated simplicity of the operating environment for financial services firms no longer exists; instead, strategic choice has claimed a dominant role everywhere.

To create value in the current environment, firms must pursue *distinct advantage*. The exploitation of such advantage creates value both for the client and for the firm; without it, the firm's very existence may not be justified. Thus an essential role of strategy is to explicitly formulate distinct advantages and the means to make use of them.

Although value creation and distinct advantage may seem simple and even trivial notions, the financial industry has had a hard time recognizing them. Firms have often pursued "me-too" strategies rather than those that exploit distinct advantage. This is perhaps not surprising, given a history of markets, prices, and products defined by regulation. The importance of strategy arose at a time when it was most difficult to formulate and implement—namely, during a period of change.

Looking toward the future, there seems little doubt that the cycle of change has not ended. Further deregulation appears likely in several product areas (e.g., the underwriting powers of commercial banks), and reregulation is to be expected in others (e.g., the eligible investment portfolios of savings and loans associations); there is no evidence to suggest a long-term maintenance of the status quo. This means that the process of strategic choice will continue and that the concepts of value creation and distinct advantage will remain the focal point in the search for strategy formulation.

THE FINANCIAL PRODUCTS

Before looking at the strategies of the financial services firms, it is useful to separate their activities. They operate in three basic areas:

1. Products (and services) that relate to a financial instrument's capacity to transfer wealth over time.
2. Advisory services.
3. Pure intermediation (such as brokerage services).

With the instruments in the first category, the buyer gives up current consumption while the issuer gains the funds to consume now. At the same time, the buyer and the issuer contract to reverse these positions at some future date. This wealth transfer over time can be considered the core of the financial instrument; the provisions of the contract (i.e., the way in which the product is designed) should be seen as product specific attributes, as I proposed in Chapter 6. There, I used the example of two seemingly very different products—a deposit account and an equity investment—both of which had the same core function. Despite their differences, both provide the investor with a means to save; the equity can be sold at some future date, and the deposit can be redeemed. Yet they differ in *specific attributes:* one has a predetermined rate of return, the other provides (uncertain) dividends and capital gains.

In many ways, the traditional U.S. financial environment proved highly restrictive in designing and pricing the specific attributes of products. Financial services firms had few incentives or opportunities to be innovative or price competitive; given the regulatory-defined product, there was little room to rearrange or competitively price specific attributes. This, in turn, affected the second basic activity of these firms: advisory services. With few products and limited alternatives, the role for advice was limited as well. In fact, corporate finance was often little more than bank lending in a world where, for many, the capital market seemed almost synonymous with the bank.

The changes outlined in previous chapters all widened the set of specific attributes that could be offered through new financial instruments. Some "products" were actually nothing more than these specific attributes, now fully decoupled from the core product—interest rate swaps and stock options are simple examples. Some of the new attributes reflected new pricing freedoms, other technological innovations, and still others new attitudes to financial transactions. For example, negotiable CDs gave banks access to funds at decontrolled rates, at the same time giving investors a deposit instrument with the resale attributes associated with negotiable securities. Commercial paper combined specific attributes from the standard bond market (direct, disintermediated funding) with attributes from the short-term loan market. Later, the employment of letters of credit on commercial paper incorporated aspects of the insurance market to enhance the credit quality of the instrument.

The high-yield bond is yet another example of the changes in the attributes of financial instruments. Traditionally, only investment grade bonds could be issued, but proponents of high-yield bonds argued that by combining the characteristics of the publicly traded bond with a high-risk/high-yield, privately placed term loan, a new product could be created to the advantage of both issuers and investors.

As financial products increased in complexity, and as it became possible to price and trade specific attributes of products (e.g., the rights to capital appreciation of a common equity in a stock option), financial advice became more sophisticated and therefore more valuable. Financial services firms could advise clients in the creation of value through innovative management of the liabilities side of the balance sheet. But such advice naturally interacted with other activities of the financial services vendor. For example, can advice about appropriate capital structures or a particular financing alternative be given to a client by a financial services firm that lacks trading capability in the equities market where price and distribution information is generated? And if so, can such a presence be sustained without also maintaining a presence in other national equity markets (as discussed in Chapter 6)? Here, advisory competence may be related to fundamental strategic choices about capital commitments to build international networks. In short, while the complexity of the financial product market enhances the value of advisory services, the vendor's ability to provide these services is related to its strategic choices in other activities as well.

For the third activity mentioned, pure intermediation, similar issues apply. Again, the complexity of the decisions required of the financial firms reflects the growing complexity of the markets. For example, in contrast to the regulated environment, where commission structures were fixed, price competition has now driven these commissions down. In the new environment, value can be created through efficient service and superior execution. Though perhaps difficult to achieve, this seems conceptually straightforward. It is not, however. Depending on its over-all strategy, a firm may view brokerage services as the required comple-ment for other, more rewarding financial services. Brokerage services may be seen as the loss leader that is more than compensated for by profitable underwriting and advisory activities for the same client. In this case, a firm that follows an efficient and cost-effective strategy in brokerage may still be undercut through cross-subsidization of a com-petitor. And though such cross-subsidization is surely not a new issue in corporate strategy, it has attained a new importance for the financial services industry because of the expanding product markets that firms can enter. Thus, overall strategy and the contribution of all activities to value creation must be considered together. Furthermore, strategists must never forget that the underlying forces that drive the industry are also subject to significant change (as discussed in Chapters 1 and 2).

THE MECHANICS OF CHANGE: CORPORATE RESTRUCTURING AND LBOs

An illustration of the complex interaction among macroeconomic pres-sures, market changes, and product innovation can be found in the development of the leveraged buyout (LBO), partially financed with publicly traded noninvestment-grade securities.[1] What made this phe-nomenon possible? First, the development of a new financial instrument, the high-yield bond. As noted, the bond simply combined existing attri-butes within a new instrument. But what accounted for its popularity? Issuers were found so easily partly because the new bonds increased funding alternatives at what seemed like attractive prices. And more importantly, the bonds made new financial structures feasible, since in many cases the credit officers at banks would have been unwilling to grant equivalent loans.

Of course, investors had to be found to invest in securities with virtu-ally no trading history. Here, marketing provided the bridge between issuers and investors. It combined with new needs of particular invest-

---

1. The actual LBO phenomenon predates the high-yield bond. Private place-ments and bank finance were tools used earlier to effect these transactions. Later, however, it was the success of the high-yield bond that elevated the technique to new prominence.

ors, such as aggressive insurance companies, S&Ls, and high net worth individuals. As I noted earlier, these investors were driven by the competition of the mutual fund and money market instrument sectors. The roots of this competition can be traced to the macro- and international economic events of the 1970s, which forced investors to seek higher-yielding assets in order to achieve competitive returns. In this environment, the more daring investors were willing to buy high-yield bonds. Thus, a market for noninvestment-grade securities developed.

But more is required to explain the sensational growth (and initial high rewards) of the debt-financed buyouts and to account for their reduced returns as time passed. Why were the early ones so successful? Here one can see again the interaction of financial product market changes and underlying macroeconomic conditions. Shortly after the LBO phenomenon started in the late 1970s and early 1980s, the stock market embarked on a sustained rise. LBOs were often predicated on the idea of selling off components of the company and returning the remainder to public investors at a later date, so many early LBOs were profitable simply because of rising equity markets. Companies were bought low and sold high. Also, the early LBOs became feasible and profitable in a generally prosperous climate of low nominal interest rates, as inflation receded in the 1980s. Thus the macroenvironment played a fundamental role in the success of LBOs.

There may be other reasons why the LBOs were successful. Many argue that inherent in the publicly traded stock corporation is a conflict of interest between managerial objectives and shareholder interest, and that this conflict is caused by corporate boards' inability (or unwillingness) to monitor management. And although issues of management's fiduciary responsibility can be raised, several examples do show that, after replacing equity with bonds, the cash flow requirements necessary to service the debt forced companies to improve efficiency or change strategic direction.[2] Of course, a more mundane reason for the success of early LBOs may have been that the bonds issued were simply mispriced—the high yield was perhaps high in relation to prime rate or other standard benchmarks, but not relative to the true risks. In this case, the promise of high yield is a self-fulfilling prophecy: if the bonds are mispriced (i.e., the rates are too low), then the transaction is less

2. One other reason for the possible value-enhancing effect of the LBO for debt and equity holders is the potential reduction in tax obligation often associated with the recapitalization of the firm. However, it can be argued that the actual amounts of debt in the capital structure of several of the releveraged firms exceed the optimal level, even taking the potential tax benefits into account.

likely to fail, since the cash flow requirements become smaller. However, if after some time suspicion of the risk-return trade-off begins to be registered in the markets, then the self-fulfilling prophecy of high yield is undone. As higher rates are required by the investors, the higher interest payments of the releveraged corporations may actually make cash flows insufficient to cover them.

Finally, I suggest another reason for the high rewards to early investors in the LBOs. When these transactions were new, when few understood how to carry them out, and when their success was not yet proven, there was little competition for the deals. This prevented high prices for the acquisition of the equity that was to be replaced by the debt. But success drew others to the market, driving acquisition prices up. This inevitably heightened the risks of the later transactions (since the higher acquisition price meant that more debt was required to finance them), while driving the possible returns down.

In all of this, the financial services firms found new demands for their advisory services. At the same time, another potentially rewarding role for these firms emerged: principal transactor in deals. By having better information about—and more experience with—these types of transactions, agents could become principals, and invest their own capital in deals. Indeed, many did so.

Financial services firms thus have to decide how to allocate their capital and their human resources among an increasingly abundant number of alternatives. In this sense, their strategy dilemma looks more and more similar to that of nonfinancial firms. But how far can this convergence be taken? And what are the unique aspects of financial services firms? These questions are important because, if there are enough similarities with nonfinancial corporations, the standard strategy frameworks that other industries have found useful may be applied here as well.

ARE FINANCIAL SERVICES FIRMS REALLY DIFFERENT?

A basic proposition here is that the real differences between financial and nonfinancial firms are linked to the relative importance of particular features, rather than to absolutes. One example can be found in the interactions among the many products provided by the financial services firms, all of which require different inputs. Although such interactions are not unique to the financial services firm, they do seem more abundant. Take the simple bank loan: it requires skills very different from those utilized in corporate advice service, yet such advice comes into play when a financial transaction suggested by the firm requires substantial bank lending. In this sense, a financial firm is neither like a producer of a particular product (e.g., a car manufacturer) nor like a pure advisor (e.g., a legal counselor). Instead, it covers both areas.

Another characteristic that distinguishes the financial services firm is that in many products and services offered by these firms, the *future* plays a more important role than for most nonfinancial firms. Again, take the bank loan as an example; its core function has been defined as the transfer of consumption power over time. The client's ability to fulfill a future obligation is of central importance to the bank; thus, the bank retains a direct interest in the client even after the loan is made. This contrasts with, for example, the attitude of a car manufacturer, which has less and less interest in the client as the sale recedes. In this sense, future developments are more important for the financial services firm than for many other firms, and its business is characterized by an element of uncertainty.

Another difference relates to the financial intermediary's required capital commitment for future strategy implementation. Typically, investments in plant and equipment are relatively low, thus allowing financial services firms some flexibility to adjust their balance sheet over time.[3] This connects directly to another difference between financial firms and most other corporations: the capital structure of the firms themselves. Regulatory requirements for minimum capital mean that the financial services vendors have fewer freedoms than industrial corporations. Thus one of the areas of strategic importance for many nonfinancial firms, the leverage structure of the balance sheet, is different but at least as complex for the financial services firm.

Financial capital is, of course, only a part of the capital equation. Human capital is the other essential factor. For example, in advisory activities, an obvious comparison can be made to consulting, law, or accounting firms. But as I noted, there are also differences. For financial firms, advice depends partly on the optimal utilization of information produced in other activities (trading and distribution of securities). Therefore, while most pure advisory firms (e.g., a law firm) have little, if any, need for capital, financial advisors may deem capital indirectly necessary to gain market information. In recent years some financial firms have tried to avoid this capital issue and thus to become more similar to pure advisory firms—the investment banking boutique is a

---

3. Of course, the balance sheets of many financial services firms are relatively large in relation to their capital. The basic business activity of most of them calls for large holdings of securities. However, in contrast to the balance sheets of nonfinancial firms, most of the assets are *financial* assets.

clear case in point. As I noted earlier, not only has the product market spectrum filled up, but the spectrum of financial firms has expanded as well. As a result, investment banking boutiques may combine with other firms that have broad market intelligence. In effect, they "purchase" their market expertise by including the other firm in the deal. Again, in the new environment particular attributes are bought and sold as free-standing components—in this case, market intelligence.

The list of differences between financial and nonfinancial firms could be continued. But none of these differences are so fundamental that the standard frameworks of strategy formulation cannot be applied. What matters is to adjust these frameworks properly, so that they capture the unique aspects of financial firms.

By using a popular competitive strategy model, the traditional strategies employed by financial services firms in the 1950s and 1960s can easily be analyzed, as can those strategies emerging today.

Take these three propositions: (1) the financial services firm is similar to other firms engaged in production of particular products and services using mixes of human and financial capital; (2) as with other firms, the success of operations can be measured in various ways, but a conveniently measurable one exists: owner wealth maximization; (3) the firms' strategies to maximize owner wealth will determine not only their own performance but also the industry structure. To analyze the implications of these three propositions, it is useful to group the various forces that shape the industry structure and the firm's strategy. The framework used here is simple but sufficient to deal with the traditional environment. It will also put the larger forces of change into perspective.

REGULATORY-DEFINED STRATEGY

Michael Porter has identified five forces—distinct but interrelated influences—that drive industry competition.[4] These are: (1) the threat of entry, (2) effects of the availability of substitute products, (3) the power of suppliers to the firm, (4) the power of clients of the firm, and (5) the pressures from existing competitors.

These five forces, according to Porter's framework, "jointly determine the intensity of industry competition and profitability." He adds that "the strongest forces are governing and become crucial from the point of view of strategy formulation."[5] Porter also notes that the "strength

---

4. See Michael E. Porter, *Competitive Strategy: Techniques for Analyzing Industries and Competitors* (New York: Free Press, 1980).
5. See ibid.:6.

of the competitive forces in an industry determines the degree to which [the] inflow of investments occurs and drives the return to the free market level, and thus the ability of the firms to sustain above-average returns."[6]

The emphasis here on *sustainable* above-average returns to investors may be somewhat misleading, since it is possible for current owners to capitalize on expected future returns so that the new investors, despite favorable competitive forces, only attain average returns. Thus, an investment banking partnership that has created a distinct competence in mergers and acquisitions advice may decide to capitalize on future returns by selling the partnership (at a high price) to the public. Now, to the new investors, despite the distinct competence of the bank, and even assuming that the talented employees do not leave, the returns will not be abnormal, given the high acquisition price. The partners have already capitalized on the five favorable forces in the act of selling the partnership.

But while, in Porter's framework, five forces determine competitive strategy, these forces are themselves the outcomes of other forces. For example, government enters Porter's framework primarily through its influence on the *threat of entry*. But, if one adjusts the framework to allow for a more active role of government, it can easily be applied to the financial services industry in its traditional phase. During that phase it was seen that government was *the* dominant force. It entered the financial industry through pervasive regulation and its powers over monetary and fiscal policy. For example, economies of scale (or scope), whether or not they existed in the financial industry, could hardly be explored because of product and geographic market segmentation.

Similarly, I argued in Chapter 3 that regulatory restrictions on the ability to price products competitively increased the likelihood of repeated transactions between the same players. This allowed financial institutions to become more familiar with the clients to whom loans were made. Because of the typically highly confidential nature of financial information, long-standing relationships were deemed desirable. For those in need of funds, long-standing relationships appeared to make future access to funds more likely. As I noted in Chapter 3, severe price restrictions represented the government's successful intervention to increase switching costs and thus to limit financial alternatives.

In the area of the *substitute products,* regulation was no less a determinant. It was suggested earlier that most financial products can be

6. Ibid.:5–6.

characterized by a transfer of purchasing power, with product differentiation achieved by separating and repackaging specific product attributes. Before the advent of the price-driven system, product development was limited by regulation and a lack of price competition among products. Only later, when new products that relied heavily on price performance were developed, were traditional players forced to come up with competing products.

Meanwhile, the *power of suppliers and buyers* also seemed relatively unimportant in the financial services industry. Few buyers or sellers accounted individually for a large share of the revenues of intermediaries. Again, regulation was the limiting factor, prohibiting, for example, a bank from making loans to an individual client in excess of a certain percentage of bank capital.

Finally, consider the intensity of *competition among rivals*. During the strictly regulated phase of the industry, lack of aggressive price competition, along with authorities' concerns about concentration, muted the intensity of rivalry. This phase has been compared to a marathon race that ended in a tie, with the strongest runners being held back while the weakest were helped to the finish line. Certainly, some differences in performance emerged, and some runners were stronger than others. But the very low failure rate suggests that rivalry was not a fundamental determinant in most segments of the industry. Furthermore, the overall prosperity of the economy during the traditional phase allowed many firms to achieve goals without impinging on the territories of their competitors, even if regulation had permitted them to do so.

This is not to suggest that the authorities fully determined the industry structure and the strategies of all financial intermediaries. The issues pointed to here are of varying importance in different product segments of the industry. In fact, firms followed a number of different strategies. Some intermediaries were more successful than others, for example, in creating barriers to entry, and this discrepancy was reflected in their performance. Yet the role of the federal and state governments in the traditional phase of the financial industry remained pervasive.

THE NEW QUEST FOR VALUE CREATION

A highly regulatory-dependent system functioned well during the 1950s and 1960s. But as Chapters 1, 2, and 3 demonstrated, inflationary pressures of the 1960s, supply side shocks of the 1970s, and policies that followed in the wake of the breakdown of the Bretton Woods system all conspired to change the world of finance.

In the United States, those pressures for change eventually affected the entire industry. Some innovations took place early on, but they were of only minor importance at the time of their inception, and they did not yet threaten the regulatory-defined environment. The initial inception of the CD, the early removal of Regulation Q for specific deposits, and the move toward negotiated commissions in the mid-1970s were all early milestones in the long road toward deregulation. It was not until the 1980s, however, that deregulation found its fullest expression.

The changes wrought by deregulation fundamentally affected various facets of the Porter framework. Development of the CD market spurred *price competition and rivalry* among established industry players, not only in funding, but also in lending; players had to make higher-yielding investments in order to service the cost of purchased funds. Development of the CP and other securities dependent on disintermediation was nothing but *forward and backward integration of various buyers and suppliers,* providing, at best, a shift from clients in one segment of the financial industry (the banks) to clients in another (the underwriters in the investment banking industry).[7] As the product market widened and new instruments appeared that relied on appending competitively priced attributes of one type of product to other products, *pressure from substitute products* dramatically increased. Improvements in the ability to price risks facilitated the creation of substitute products and also reduced the information costs that had helped create barriers to entry. Rather than having to rely on a long-term relationship with a bank, a competitively priced letter of credit appended to a commercial paper program allowed firms access to new markets. Rapid advances in information technology also facilitated product development. More sophisticated technology allowed for further improvement in pricing ability. It gave buyers and suppliers more power and put pressure on industry participants to supply more sophisticated advice. With the indexed futures and option-pricing techniques, for example, issuers could design more complex instruments, taking advantage of opportunities in one segment of the capital market and applying the new techniques to transform the attributes of the funds raised.

In short, all of the factors that affect the five forces of the Porter framework moved away from regulated simplicity and toward deregulated complexity. Furthermore, the large international capital imbalances described in Chapters 1 and 2 heightened domestic pressures for

---

7. Concerned about this shift toward investment banking, Bankers Trust explored the boundaries of the Glass-Steagall Act through its decision to underwrite CPs. The bank claimed that the CP did not so much represent a corporate debt security as it did a simple, unsecured, short liability.

breaking local boundaries and limited the ability of authorities to respond to innovations.

All this meant new freedoms for financial intermediaries. It also meant that a fundamental reassessment of the value creation process had to take place. The legitimacy of the firm no longer derived from its well-defined (and regulatory-allocated) product market; new opportunities for value creation had to be sought. As the fundamental macro- and international economic forces outlined in Chapters 1 and 2 made markets increasingly contestable, strategy no longer played a minor role. In order to achieve profitability, firms would now have to demonstrate explicit value creation. This mandate explains changes such as the shift in the primary activity of many investment banks. As the traditional activities of underwriting and brokerage became less profitable, the firms moved into areas where the five forces of Porter's framework would allow higher profits: advisory services for mergers and acquisitions and principal activities are two examples.

Mergers and acquisitions activities are especially useful as a tool for evaluating the new environment. There are high barriers to entry in that field because of the complexity of the activity and the need for a good reputation. Competition is primarily seen among existing players (with a few exceptions, such as firms comprising former employees of the established firms). Since mergers and acquisitions put the very existence of a corporate entity at stake, advisors are typically selected not on the basis of price but on the basis of reputation and experience—scarce resources for any new entrant. Buyer power, or forward integration, is virtually nil, because of the complex nature of the product and the relative infrequency with which most clients have reason to use it. Simply, it does not pay for most corporations to employ their own in-house mergers and acquisitions advisor, and besides, regulatory and legal forces encourage firms to obtain outside counsel. Pressure from substitute products is virtually absent—there is no alternative to advice. The intensity of the rivalry among firms within the product market can perhaps be counted an unfriendly force, but even here there are mitigating circumstances, especially when one considers the overall richness of the product and the small set of players. First, note that high fee structures may actually serve as a quality signal, and thus it may be fully rational not to compete on price. Also, because of the typically very large transaction costs of the overall deal (e.g., a multibillion dollar transaction with tens of millions of dollars in legal fees), one can expect to see relatively little price bargaining from the buyer side over the investment banker's fee. Thus, rivalry seems to be expressed as competition for market share based on perceived competence rather than as competitive pricing of products. Given the fairly small set of players, a cartelized, rather than competitive, price structure exists.

However, at least one of the five forces could prove distinctly unfriendly: supplier power. Here, an untraditional view of supplier power should be taken. In most industries supplier power rests with outside vendors, but for this particular financial services product, supplier power rests with human capital—the firm's own employees. The impact of human capital on the effectiveness of the investment bank in the advisory field relates to two factors: the quality of the advice, and the reputation of the firm. The first will be much dependent on individual employees (even though some support may be derived from the use of information technology). The second depends on the outcome of the transactions and the visibility of the firm, which may or may not relate directly to the individual employee. This latter issue proves essential in considering strategy.

Suppose a publicly owned investment bank is highly successful in generating advisory fees. Does this mean that its shareholders benefit? Not necessarily. Depending on the compensation structure, all the profits may be expropriated by the talented individual producers who generated the rewards. Thus to create value for the *institution*, avenues have to be found for reminding the individual producer that his or her value-creating activity is dependent on the firm; if not, that individual has every incentive to leave, unless he or she is awarded the full contribution. In other words, there are the risks in setting up mergers and acquisitions departments in which individual "stars" develop. Such an environment should be contrasted with one in which individuals are not allowed to attain high profile, so that they remain reliant on the deal flow as generated by the firm's reputation. For producers in these latter firms, revenue generation has to be shared with the institution.

Similar issues pertain to other aspects of the investment banking industry as well. Take highly successful traders. If traders are successful because of their individual abilities, in effect little of their value can be expropriated by the firm (other than that commensurate with the provision of the infrastructure of the trading facility); again, compensation issues reflect supplier pressure. If, on the other hand, the successful trader derives much of the profits from the effective use of information flows generated within the firm, compensation pressures can be resisted; either the revenues are shared with the institution or the trader may be asked to leave and to try to generate the profits at another firm—one that may not provide the trader with information flows of equal utility. In short, value creation for the firm is optimized when the environment created is *complementary* to the skills of the employees.

In the quest for value creation, when competition for market share takes place among vendors unwilling to compete on price (as in mergers and acquisitions advice), other benefits have to be offered in order to land business for the firm. The phenomenon of bridge loan financing is nothing more than one such method to help complete the deal, retain the client, and enhance the value of the institution over that of the individual player. This situation again calls for complex strategy determination, since it has implications for capital requirements and for the institution's funding strategy.

The creation of several successful regional banks constitutes another example of an approach to value creation. A regulatory climate increasingly permissive toward interstate banking has led several nonmoney-center banks to rapidly expand beyond their traditional state borders, claiming value creation through economies of scale. Several of these super-regional banks, which continue to be oriented toward the middle-market and smaller companies, claim to have achieved significant operating savings through the mergers that created them. Here, value creation derives from the basic intermediation function (most applicable to the small and mid-sized markets), together with effective amortization of costs, such as computer networks and advertising expenses. In this case, the value creation relates perhaps more to efficient production organization than to the functions traditionally associated with banking. Although it is premature at this stage to judge their ultimate success, interstate conglomeration does seem to create value; some of the regional banks have shown good performances and market payoffs.

Asset management—increasingly popular with all kinds of financial institutions—is another useful avenue of value creation for financial firms. In this method, value creation relies on information gathering and processing capability, and on the ability of investment specialists to provide superior returns. And though it is in theory difficult to explain why the performance of asset managers should dominate that of specialized or diversified market portfolios over sustained periods, these services may be valuable inasmuch as they afford small investors convenient access to diversified portfolios at lower transaction costs.[8]

Though technological change has led to speculation about a cashless society, the financial intermediaries' traditional role in the facilitation of the payments mechanism still constitutes an important source of value creation to society. This is true despite the diminishing returns in

8. Although some funds in the mutual fund industry have outperformed the comparable market indexes (for example, the Magellan Fund offered by Fidelity), the overall industry performance is exactly as might be expected: slightly below the market index.

these activities caused by changes in Porter's five underlying forces. Deregulation of deposit account interest rates, for example, has increased the funding costs to banks and reduced the appeal of spread banking. But though fewer abnormal returns may be available, respectable profits should nevertheless be generated for those offering high efficiency in the facilitation of the payments system.

One final example of value creation is the function of channeling investments to particular sectors of the economy. Before the 1980s it was a regulated source of value creation, and it provided particular financial institutions with their raison d'être. The savings and loan industry comes to mind: by allowing them to raise deposits with government guarantees and by forcing them to invest in the mortgage industry, the authorities enabled the S&Ls to create value. A mechanism was provided to channel the funds to a sector of the economy the authorities deemed desirable. In this context, the demise of segments of the S&L industry is not surprising. With new instruments available to fund mortgages more directly, with new government-supported mortgage guarantees and with the broadening of the S&Ls' own investment opportunities including high-yield securities, the traditional method of value creation simply disappeared. As a result, the S&Ls took an incentive structure set up to channel funds to one industry and, in a dramatic shift, applied it to the gathering of funds for different investment outlets. The mismatch between the old incentives and the new activity has led to value *destruction* and to the problems that presently plague the S&L industry.

The examples given above are only a few from a long list. They illustrate the importance of determining where and how value can be created. It should be clear from the presentation so far that precisely because of the large set of choices now available, it is not possible to present a single program for success. But given the fundamental trends described in Parts I and II of this book, it is useful to look more closely at the basic products that can now be offered by almost all financial services firms. From these products and services, the firms will have to derive value and justify their existence.

VALUE CREATION AND PRODUCTS

Although individual firms must decide for themselves how to build, defend, and expand distinct advantages, it is possible to identify the basic opportunities inherent in the activities of most financial services firms. I have noted that many of these activities are closely interrelated. Indeed, the ability to design specific new products often facilitates the advisory function in complicated transactions that are driven by the application of these products. Similarly, information advantages provided by the advisory product may facilitate principal transactions. For example, advisors have sometimes taken principal positions in transactions in lieu of part of their advisory fee.

The interconnectedness of the products raises one of the major issues that firms must consider: how much of an integrated, one-stop financial services firm should they be? To put it differently, if economies of scope offer an advantage, can the natural barriers to exploiting them be overcome? In particular, transfer pricing, bonus allocation, cost control, and contributions of employees are notoriously complex to evaluate and manage, since the products and services feed on one another and multiply. (The occurrence of this problem at CSFB was discussed in the previous chapter.) Thus, while synergies may exist and may offer some integrated firms new opportunities for value creation, the firm's success in making use of such opportunities will still depend on its own ability to deal with the barriers to execution.

Having determined in which product markets to compete, firms have to design financial products and strategies for their targeted issuers or investors. What matters here is the quality of the financial engineers and their ability to cooperate with other employees close to the investor or issuer. Communication between product designers and those with contacts to clients should not be one-directional; a firm's incentive structure should allow employees directly involved with clients to profit from the placement of newly developed products, and if necessary these same employees should be required to identify additional needs, which the financial engineer can then work on. The failure of the Unbundled Stock Unit provides a classic example of the difficulty in organizing such communication. On the other hand, the introduction of a mutual fund that solely invested in senior bank loans made in highly leveraged transactions shows how marketing skills and financial engineering can be successfully combined.

The potential of new products relies on: (1) attaining a large market share through perceived product specialization and attendant trading capabilities, and/or (2) taking advantage of opportunistic profits generated while the market for the product is not well developed. An example of the latter can be found in Salomon Brothers' one-time ability to sell stripped U.S. Treasury-backed securities in Europe, taking advantage of interest rate differentials. A strategy of market dominance may be found in Shearson Lehman's ability to create a strong position in the short-term floating rate preferred stock market (money market preferreds).

Market dominance of new products such as money market preferred stock or high-yield bonds can be highly profitable; yet only a few product markets in which one firm maintains dominance, at least for a period of time, have developed during the last decade and a half. On the other hand, the life spans of most new products are continually being shortened by rapid imitation. Thus, abundant opportunities exist, not for long-term market dominance, but for taking advantage of temporary anomalies in markets. Again, the caliber of employees involved in product development is crucial, since some of the attributes included as components of the new products are not easily priced when initially packaged together. Of course, the ability of the financial firm to spot windows of opportunity in the capital markets matters here as well; so does marketing ability.

For existing products, more standard sources of value creation apply. Excellence of execution, efficiency in distribution, and effective use of information technology and other delivery vehicles all play a role. As with any ordinary production organization, efficiency and rigorous cost control can and should be pursued, in accordance with the distinct advantages of the firm. An example is Chemical Bank's decision to hire an outside transportation service to deliver checks, rather than owning a fleet of vehicles. Complex financial engineering is one way to create value; carefully managed operations are another.

Finally, two of the most popular and profitable methods of value creation used in recent years have to be mentioned again: advisory services and principal transactions. For the latter, most financial services firms suggest that employee quality is the primary determinant of success. And indeed, as I noted earlier, the individual ability of the advisor matters, since it can influence the value contribution of (and subsequently the reward to) the financial firm itself. But the firm has to define its own contribution over and above that of the employee. For example, reputation, deserved or not, may be a major factor in generating business opportunities. A client's reliance on reputation may be fully justified if the investment bank is being hired by a management concerned about its board's reaction. In such a case, the driving motivation may simply be the management's desire to reassure the board that it has obtained "the best advice money can buy." The skills of the individual employee are then only complements to the firm, and the rewards can consequently be shared.

In some extreme cases, financial services firms may actually experience a trade-off between the quality of the individual employee and the reputation of the firm. The risks of allowing stars to develop were mentioned already. To put it differently, the ownership of the deal-flow in advisory services may be a result of individual employee reputation or of firm reputation. Clearly, in generating returns to the firm, as much of this deal-flow ownership as possible should be tied to the firm.

Principal transactions have become another avenue for financial services vendors to reap rewards. These can be profitable for two very different reasons. One relies on a firm's superior ability to judge the risk-return trade-off offered by particular securities, relative to the market. Here, the firm uses the same information available to others in the market, but more cleverly. A second source of profitability accrues to firms that enjoy superior information flows.

An example of the latter is the possible profitability of the trading operations of several leading underwriters. In the previous chapter this was seen at CSFB, where issue dominance helped trading profits. If trading profitability derives from better market intelligence regarding bond placement, the firm, rather than the individual bond trader, should reap the benefits. In this case, one would expect highly successful traders who switch firms to lose some of their superior returns. Here, value creation for the firm results from (legal) internal information sharing between underwriting and trading groups. A major difficulty in translating this profit potential to actual performance may lie in finding compensation structures that allow for the most efficient information flows, while at the same time preserving legal safeguards against misuse of information.

Value creation in the financial services firm is thus attributable to four main factors: (1) exploitation of temporary anomalies in new product markets; (2) efficiency in production technology and organization of standard financial products; (3) superior ability to combine employee competence with resources "owned" by the firm; and (4) better information in principal transactions as a result of client relationships or of market dominance. A broad product line may constitute another factor, not in the sense that clients of one product line will automatically be receptive to products of another (though this may occur), but rather because information generated in each product line can be applied in others.

The foregoing discussion suggests that several traditional functions of financial intermediaries have come under pressure in the new environment. Indeed, some classes of institutions or products may reasonably be termed "dinosaurs." Pure intermediation in the mortgage industry has been largely supplanted by the mortgage-backed security. Many short-term bank loans to large corporations have been replaced by commercial paper. Underwriting and brokerage activities have become competitively priced and no longer offer the same rich profit opportunities. The list is long, and it touches almost all financial intermediaries.

In general, two distinct types of value creation are taking place: One relies on the traditional intermediation function, and it is typically geared to the less sophisticated investor or issuer. The other relies on highly complex financial products and strategies, and it is targeted to larger, more sophisticated players. Traditionally, this distinction has been less sharp. A money center commercial bank often profitably provided the largest U.S. corporations with entirely standard products. Some of the most important investment banks generated their returns through brokerage and underwriting at fixed commissions. Such simple strategies are now becoming less viable, since value creation no longer occurs as as result of the exploitation of regulated product markets.

In the new environment, financial firms must consider not only where value creation is possible but also what particular application of distinct advantages will make it happen. Evaluation of a firm's own distinct advantage and subsequent strategy determination and implementation can be very difficult in a changing environment where competitors employ new strategies. The herd behavior that has often resulted may not even be completely irrational from the point of view of individual companies. In fact, such behavior might derive from an evaluation of the competitive environment that goes something like this: "getting it wrong while others are getting it wrong" or "getting it right while others are getting it right" is less *profitable* than being the sole successful firm, but much less *costly* than being the sole unsuccessful firm. Already the rapid international expansion of U.S. firms in London and the subsequent large layoffs in many of these same institutions has provided an instructive example of herd behavior, which can also be ascribed to the many large money center banks that earlier decided to make substantial loans to LDC borrowers.

In sum, financial services firms must, and increasingly will, determine their existing distinct strengths in relation to the four activities that can create value; this will shape the future financial environment.

THE FUTURE SHAPE OF THE FINANCIAL MARKETPLACE

Internationalization

Speculating about the future shape of the financial marketplace is as risky as it is difficult, yet certain trends can be discerned. One trend is the development of linked, but distinct, national markets in coexistence with truly global markets. In the national markets, the distinct characteristics and preferences of issuers and investors will be serviced through strategies responsive to them. It is, for example, hard to imagine that the

United States will experience broad cross-ownership of equity securities between corporations, as is the case in Japan. Similarly, it is unlikely that Japanese securities will be traded with the same intensity (during business hours) in New York as in Tokyo. Even with 24-hour trading, Japanese institutional investors will probably deal during their office hours and execute during Japanese trading times for their Japanese stocks, since little comparative advantage could be expected from trading in Japanese securities during New York time. And even with an increase in the holdings of foreign securities by the managers of global portfolios, there is little reason to believe that those securities will not be traded primarily in their local markets.

Similarly, it is unlikely that U.S. depositors would be better served by deposit accounts located in Tokyo, even if they offered some important rate advantages; convenience of access obviously dominates in this case, even though Japanese banks may buy into the U.S. market and offer the product locally. The same applies to insurance products; it is not probable that Japanese corporations will be able to offer superior products from a Tokyo base. Yet these various markets will be linked. With products such as government securities being traded worldwide, and with a deep and globally operating foreign exchange market, capital transfers from one market to another will continue to take place, and international portfolio diversification will continue to play a role. The latter will occur because the technology is available and the diversified product adds value for certain clients; the former because it allows the international trading system to continue functioning with less than perfectly balanced accounts. But even in the absence of imbalanced accounts, the increased speed and ease of information dissemination across national borders make insulation of national capital markets highly unlikely.

Thus, continued internationalization will take place in the form of transborder capital flows, and the markets will resemble one another in many respects, including the adoption of similar products. But even for products that resemble each other, local characteristics of issuers and investors will persist, based on informational differences. Only for some of the least information-dependent products, such as currencies and U.S. government bonds, may the market indeed be globalized, the nationality of issuers and investors being largely immaterial.

The implications for the international strategies of firms are: (1) that entry into foreign product markets needs to be considered from the perspective of individual product lines for which particular firms might have distinct advantages, possibly through operating efficiencies; and (2) that market intelligence will have to be gathered in many different markets as well as in the local market. This is not to suggest that large international networks will be optimal for all commercial or investment banks or for all product lines. There is no reason to believe, for example, that U.S. investment banks will ever play an important role in retail distribution in Japan. Similarly, capture of a large share of overall trading on the Tokyo Stock Exchange is unlikely, since few U.S. firms can bring comparative advantages to this activity. It is equally unrealistic for commercial banks to assume that their lending business to the middle and smaller business market will ever be truly internationalized.

But linked international markets, which create the broadest set of financial instruments available, remain a factor in international strategies. To offer a client floating rate Euroyen financing, to be swapped to floating rate dollars, and subsequently to fixed-rate dollars, requires broad market intelligence and even access to international distribution channels. Similarly, a commercial bank that engages in secondary loan sales may need an overseas presence in order to gather distribution information. The real question for the institutions is to what extent required market intelligence relies on active participation in various markets through local branches, and how many true local opportunities exist abroad.

Overall, there is little evidence to suggest that large, internationally operating firms will realize significant advantages over firms that decide to follow more locally focused strategies. U.S. banks that have reduced the size of their operating presence in London (and some also in Tokyo) provide one potent example. Similarly, a large presence in the Euromarkets may be advantageous to firms that rely heavily on Euroissues for their corporate finance activities, but there is little reason to expect that the market will be profitable for newcomers with slight experience and a client base not much focused on these international opportunities.

After a phase of "me-too" internationalization, some firms will probably find their overseas strategies simply too costly relative to profit opportunities, and they will return to a more locally focused strategy. However, a few large, internationally oriented firms with activities in the international market that relate to particular strengths, such as technological advantage or strong client demand for international transactions, will continue to operate and prosper internationally.

The U.S. Market

Given the forces now in place, financial services firms will increasingly offer more products with similar characteristics. I called this the filling up of the product spectrum. This phenomenon is not always immediately obvious, since the products are seemingly very different. Once they are properly analyzed, however, they reveal their similarities. An example is the recent phenomenon of mutual funds that invest in high-yielding senior loans. Although unique in one sense, this product can be compared to another new debt security issued by a specially created "bad bank" that bought low-quality loans at deep discount (thus making them into high-yield assets), in the recapitalization of the Mellon Bank. Both products offer retail investors participation in high-yielding bank loans.[9]

As the product spectrum becomes glutted, differentiation will be achieved only through greater product complexity; and this will create a major challenge for marketers, whose task it will be to explain and sell the features and benefits of the increasingly complex products to clients.

With product proliferation inevitably comes some further segmentation of the labor force employed in the financial services industry. But the segmentation will be different from the one that characterized the traditional phase of the system. Rather than strict segmentation *by* firm, segmentation *within* firms will occur. Employees on the client side of products and advice will have to rely on a common pool of skills. Thus, the traditional difference between an investment banker and a calling officer will become less pronounced, even though some specialization will persist. Likewise, information technology specialists and back-office personnel will become more similar from firm to firm. As I noted before, financial services firms will increasingly be allowed to enter similar fields of operation, and products will resemble each other. As product specialization becomes the outcome of choice rather than of regulated direction, employees will be more easily comparable among firms that *choose* to engage in similar activities.

Another determinant of the shape of the future U.S. financial industry will be the momentum with which the advisory market develops. As long as advisory transactions continue to pay high fees, and price competition reduces the appeal of intermediated products, the attraction of the advisory market will persist. Independently of mergers and acquisitions activity, the increasing availability of complex products should

---

9. Of course, there are differences between the two products. In the case of bonds in the bad bank, the investor attains the high yield on the underlying loans because of the discount at which Mellon Bank sold them to the bad bank. Here the loans are of poor quality but have been priced down to take account of this, so that a high yield appears. In the mutual fund example, the high-yield loans are not ordinary loans that have been priced down because of poor credit quality, but rather face-value loans that are made at a high yield to reflect the initially risky financing structure of the highly leveraged financing of the corporation.

continue to reward those who are able to provide advisory services that match these products to individual clients' needs.

Further refinements in information technology and its application in the financial firm constitute another major determinant of the U.S. financial industry's future. One can imagine a world in which the dissemination of information has developed to such an extent as to render intermediation unnecessary. In this circumstance, only the engineering of peripheral attributes would justify the existence of the financial services firm. If complete information were available to all investors and issuers about all other issuers' and investors' needs, the riskiness of various investment opportunities, and the pricing of risks, the role of the financial intermediary would effectively be ended—except in advisory services. A mild form of this scenario can be seen in the development of the CP, CD, and high-yield markets. No one, however, foresees the kind of information flows necessary to make *all* intermediation obsolete. It is only necessary for the financial firm to realize that for the simple intermediation function without traditional regulation, a *factory* function is supplied. In other words, for this activity production efficiency has to reign supreme, economies of scale are likely, and conglomeration is to be expected.

Future Regulation

Although everything I have discussed so far has shown how regulatory control was overwhelmed by fundamental underlying forces, regulators will continue to affect the future shape of the financial industry. Given a number of failures (such as the S&L industry, and the alleged impact of index arbitrage on the October 1987 stock market collapse), debate about deregulation and reregulation has attained a high currency. Still, the present state of the financial services industry has made a return to the earlier, regulated, simple environment impossible. For example, regional banking has become a fait accompli over the last five years, breaking down traditional geographic segmentation in the United States; this change can be considered irreversible. The demise of fixed commissions is another example, as is the obsolescence of strict deposit rate regulation.

A further breakdown in the increasingly permeated wall between the securities industry and the commercial banking industry can also be expected. A resurrection of the barriers is not feasible, the most important reason being that the old boundaries have been blurred. Too many products combine specific attributes from both sides—e.g., bridge loan financing through investment banks, underwriting of commercial paper by commercial banks, the origination of senior bank debt by commercial banks in some highly leveraged recapitalizations, after which the loans are sold down. Here, banks function effectively as underwriters, rather than as lenders. Future segmentation between investment and commercial banking will be the outcome of strategic choices made by institutions themselves—not the result of regulation. As the product market spectrum has filled up, the natural barrier between the two traditionally different industries has been lacerated.

As a result of the new business opportunities that have emerged for financial services firms, one aspect of the traditional, regulated system that remained during the years of transition will have to be rethought: Several of the government-supported insurance schemes seem increasingly one-sided. They provide downside protection for the financial services firms' investors, but do little to affect the asset structure of the intermediaries. It is no longer only S&L deposit insurance that is questioned; several commercial banks, faced with potentially large write-offs on their LDC and real-estate lending portfolios, have reignited the debate about FDIC insurance. Even government-sanctioned institutions such as the Government National Mortgage Association (GNMA), that are backed by the full faith and credit of the U.S. government and that play a central role in the securitization of mortgage pools, may see their roles questioned. In all these examples, the same basic issue is highlighted—how much nonmarket-priced government insurance is warranted in an increasingly market-price-oriented system. One may confidently predict that rethinking of the current structure will occur.

A final consideration with regard to the future shape of the financial services industry has to do with the present high visibility of the financial market and the public scrutiny that attends it. High visibility, large individual rewards, and incidents of widely publicized abuses all invite political scrutiny and provide an opportunity to create political capital. Hence, in setting strategy and evaluating risks and opportunities, financial intermediaries need to be even more concerned with the possible reactions of regulators and policymakers than other corporations have to be.

STRATEGY, COMPLEXITY, AND MANAGEMENT: FINANCE IN THE 1990s

There can be no doubt that new skills will be required of successful managers everywhere in the financial industry. Managers in nonfinancial industries had to learn about complex new financial instruments and techniques during the 1980s; now, managers in the financial services industry have to learn about strategy management. The learning process for many managers in nonfinancial firms was difficult. They complained that in a world in which the liabilities side of the balance sheet took up more and more of their attention, they were unable to concentrate fully on the asset side of their operations. This was especially true during periods of possible takeover, when senior management was forced to concentrate exclusively on unfamiliar financial engineering techniques, often for long periods of time. And indeed, in a remarkably detailed account of the largest LBO in corporate history, senior management at RJR-Nabisco has been portrayed as being completely preoccupied with financial matters.[10] Similarly, some have argued that as the result of new financial techniques, increasingly important management decisions are in effect dictated by the liabilities side of the balance sheet; R&D policies, marketing decisions, and plant and equipment purchases are good examples.[11]

The parallel for the financial services firm should be obvious. The other side of the same coin that provided new financial strategies for industrial corporations is that corporate strategy plays a more important role for the managers in the financial services firm.

Such corporate strategy determination requires skills that financial services firms do not always possess. Traditionally, investment banking partnerships prided themselves on the lack of managerial assets, arguing that producers were all that was required. But rapid domestic and international growth has forced many of these organizations—now largely corporations—to pay more attention to how they are managed. Large money center banks, often in possession of international networks, have experienced the same awareness.

In the simplest terms, management's task will be to define and implement strategy. This book does not deal with the issue of management implementation in the financial services industry. This is a major topic that deserves a treatment of its own.[12] Still, this book hints at issues of

10. See B. Burrough and J. Helyar, *Barbarians at the Gate* (New York: Harper & Row, 1989).

11. Of course, others have argued that these financial constraints represent nothing but the most effective way to compel good management. In this view, financial constraints do not detract from the manager's ability to employ the assets of the firm, but simply assure their most efficient use. For a prominent proponent of this view, see M. Jensen, "Agency Costs of Free Cash Flow, Corporate Finance and Takeovers," *American Economic Review* 76 (1986):323–329. For an earlier view on these issues, see G. Donaldson, *Managing Corporate Wealth* (New York: Praeger, 1984).

12. For a study concentrating on the investment banking industry, see R. Eccles and D. Crane, *Doing Deals: Investment Banks at Work* (Boston: Harvard Business School Press, 1988).

relevance, three of which are listed here. The first is the need to assure that the employee is integrated into the organization, so that the firm can capture the value that is created. The second is the ability to effectively deal with compensation issues that arise from both cross-product information effects and business development (e.g., how to compensate the calling officer who works with a client for several months on a loan product that is sharply priced but that carries with it a swap highly desirable for the swap group). The third issue concerns the dilemmas inherent in managing highly paid, entrepreneurial producers on the one hand and an elaborate organizational infrastructure on the other. The ability to manage both will be crucial, especially at a time when efficiency and cost control will play an increasingly important role.

Another requirement for effective management will be the ability to assure that the often tenuous boundary between legal and illegal activity is not crossed. This is especially important in the financial services industry, not because of some ethical weakness in those that populate the industry, but simply because of the nature of its products and the methods of value creation. An important reason for the existence of many firms is the exploitation of informational advantages, which provide an important source of value creation. But it can easily lead to legal (and/or ethical) problems. Especially as products become more complex, and as the size of many financial firms grows, management faces a major task in confronting this issue.

I have merely hinted at some important strategy implementation issues. For strategy formulation, this book may be more useful, not in providing a set of winning strategies but in describing the context in which particular strategies must be set. Greater choice, increased complexity, and the uncertainties of dealing internationally form this context.

The new strategic choices of the financial services firms themselves add another level of complexity. The strategies of competitors, whether successful or mistaken, can have serious impact on the firm's own operating environment, and at the same time complicate the required macroeconomic policymaking evaluation. Two examples can be used to highlight this observation—one from the recent past, and another dating from the onset of the turbulent 1970s.

As I noted in Chapter 3, when Penn Central railroad failed, its commercial paper problems caused widespread dislocation in the CP market. That impacted the banks (as many corporations called backup credit lines) and forced the Federal Reserve to infuse liquidity. Institutional failure directly affected monetary aggregates and, therefore, the financial firms' operating environment; thus firms that had nothing to do with Penn Central were severely influenced in their strategies. More recently, the Chapter 11 filing of Drexel Burnham Lambert caused widespread problems for Drexel's competitors in the high-yield market, and even spilled over into the investment-grade bond market, thus affecting a large set of institutions; strategic errors at Drexel defined the environment of others.

In this sense, the trend toward reduction of regulatory control comes at a highly inopportune moment; it is a time when the fundamental macroforces seem particularly difficult to predict. Furthermore, institutional uncertainty may exacerbate this difficulty. For example, several commercial banks in the United States are faced with questionable real estate portfolios (and perhaps increases in their funding costs as well), and the difficulties at these banks could reduce their lending in other areas. Such a bank-induced monetary squeeze (not unlike the institutional problems in the context of the Great Depression[13]) would at present be much more difficult to fight with expansionary fiscal or monetary policy, considering the overall large deficits on the U.S. current account. Here, the argument presented so far in this chapter—that from a corporate strategy perspective the financial sector is quite similar to the nonfinancial sector—requires some adjustment. Because of its role as supplier of credit, the financial services industry is more directly affected by, but also more directly of importance to, the overall macroeconomic environment.

Of course, one of the rationales for the traditional regulation of the financial industry relied precisely on this argument. But as was seen in the preceding chapters, the fundamental forces of change have made the highly regulatory nature of the system untenable. Thus, as new strategic choices for financial services firms arise, the costs of poor strategy may go well beyond the effects on the individual firm. More strongly put, a perfectly optimal individual strategy may carry serious social costs, in light of the current state of regulation. The example of S&Ls that maximized the insurance value of the FDIC by investing in highly risky assets comes readily to mind. I noted earlier that for these S&Ls the high-risk strategy may have been perfectly optimal, since a large part of the costs was carried by the insurance authorities.

It is likely that in the 1990s the business strategies of financial services

---

13. See Ben Bernanke, "Non-Monetary Effects of the Financial Crisis in the Propagation of the Great Depression," *American Economic Review* 73 (1983): 257–276. Also, note the visit that Chairman of the Federal Reserve Board Greenspan paid to local banks in the summer of 1990 in order to discuss the lending policies of banks in the Northeast United States.

firms will be scrutinized more closely by policymakers because of problems in several sectors of the financial industry and concerns over some of the financing techniques popular in the 1980s, as well as because these strategies interact with an economy that is tilting toward recession. Given the constraints on U.S. fiscal and monetary policymakers (which are especially binding in the 1990s), this scrutiny will come at a time when the impact of *any* macroshock on the financial system is extremely difficult to calibrate.[14]

To complicate matters further, there is as yet little experience with the transmission effects of some of the newer products to other financial markets. For example, what effect will a possible weakening of the senior bank loan market for highly leveraged transactions have on holders of these loans that bought them in the secondary market? Will traditional models of rescheduling such loans be adjusted because many of the loans are no longer held by the originating banks? And what will be the impact on those that bought the loans? Similarly, how will possibly large changes in either exchange rates or interest rates affect the (supposedly) matched books of the swap suppliers? One can construct a scenario whereby a macroeconomic shock to the highly leveraged financing structure of many industrial corporations causes defaults on swap obligations to occur—thus further exposing the intermediary.

In short, the overall level of uncertainty has greatly increased. One may of course argue that a large set of different strategies, made possible in the new environment of choice, will diversify the risk to the entire financial system. Using this interpretation, the S&L problem in the United States may be considered a case of undiversified risk, one caused by government incentives for too many firms to pursue the same strategy. There is reason, however, for more basic concerns; financial firms in other sectors marched lockstep along the same paths to difficulty—for example, LDC and real estate lending, and rapid international expansion.

All this means that the breakdown in financial boundaries on the three levels I identified earlier has *not* been one-directional. Just as the environment affected the firms, so the firms' new strategies helped to shape the environment. The replacement of simplicity and stability with

---

14. In 1989, the interest cost represented 88% of the deficit. (This reflects the *on-budget* interest expense and deficit. If the *off-budget* items are included, net interest expense for 1989 rises to 111% of the deficit, because the off-budget balance shows a surplus of $53 billion.) Although in the past the interest component accounted for large parts of the total deficit (for example, in 1981 the comparable numbers were 96% and 88%, respectively), it is the overall magnitude of this item, and the authorities' lack of control over it that further reduces policy freedoms.

choice and complexity is yet to be tested. Such choices and complexities have been seen at the firm level, the financial system level, and the macroeconomic level, and have brought with them another important change: response time has dramatically shortened as the speed of change has increased. For example, on the macrolevel the metamorphosis of the United States from the largest international creditor to the largest debtor nation occurred within a mere ten years. Similarly, Japan surged to international asset prominence in a very short time. On the level of the national financial systems, key changes came in rapid succession over a period of less than ten years. Things have been no different on the level of the financial firm; the rapid decline of Continental Illinois and the meteoric rise and fall of Drexel Burnham Lambert provide ample evidence.

So while one message of this book speaks to the enormity of change, another declares that these changes occur rapidly. Not only does this make strategy formulation more difficult, it also introduces a note of irony: now that the importance of strategy has been recognized, increased uncertainty and shortened response time have made it far more difficult to formulate. Thus, financial services firms face a difficult trade-off between opportunistic value creation (which tries to adjust its behavior in synchronization with the unfolding environment) and strategies focused on longer-term distinct advantage. Only rarely do they occur concurrently.

Although both avenues have their attractions, each carries heavy costs. Opportunistic behavior may be nothing but the "me-too" strategy that leads a firm to frequent and expensive entry and exit from product markets (indeed, this conclusion has been justified by several aborted internationalization efforts) and it can create organizational upheaval. Pursuit of long-term advantage may at times represent an unsuitable goal for financial product markets that change rapidly.

Regardless of the direction that management decides to take, an adequate understanding of the forces that shape the environment remains the prerequisite for successful strategy. In contrast to their outcomes, these forces have been remarkably stable. Like the current of a river, they are constant and knowable, even as the ripples on the surface continually change. I have traced the underlying forces across time and from country to country. These durable forces can be a compass for firms that need to establish strategic direction. Naturally, the particulars of each firm's course will depend on its starting position and the specific definition of its target. In addition, every successful firm must be sufficiently flexible in its planning to circumvent the inevitable obstacles that appear over time.

CONCLUSION

This discussion of the factors that should determine strategy does not constitute a nice, neat road map to success. Few seasoned observers can have expected such a map. In an industry where increased competition, fundamental uncertainty, and rapid innovation are the visible characteristics, no easy road to success can be found. But this is no cause for pessimism. The same daunting terms could be used to describe other industries where highly successful firms did emerge. Strategic choice represents an essential challenge, through which firms must justify their continuing existence; but it also offers a new opportunity for success.

At the beginning of this book I noted that the only constant in the new financial environment was change. The foregoing chapters have discussed widespread changes that affected financial affairs in fundamental ways: international financial transactions changed; the national financial systems of the United States, Japan, and the United Kingdom all changed; and the behavior of financial services firms changed with them. The events of the early 1970s played a pivotal role. During those years, the groundwork was laid for significant alterations in the financial terrain that became visible only in the 1980s. It was in the 1980s that international capital imbalances and their attendant international capital flows reached unusual levels. And during the 1980s, the novel strategies on which financial services firms had earlier embarked began to show up in some spectacular failures (along with a smaller number of successes). The topology that became visible during the 1980s owed its shape to more fundamental underlying forces for change that developed in earlier decades.

In this sense, then, the 1970s were literally pivotal; they turned one financial world into quite another. For the three levels—international and macroeconomics, national financial systems, and financial services firms—the years before 1970 were characterized by regulated simplicity. This I attributed to a generally favorable economic growth environment, low nominal interest rates, well-learned lessons from earlier financial instability, and a willingness by authorities to control financial transactions, both internationally and domestically.

This last point is especially important, because the common mindset of policymakers was responsible for the stable regulatory climate and institutional arrangements. These arrangements, in turn, shaped the traditional relationship environment in which financial services firms operated. Although the authorities of most countries professed support for free international *goods* transactions—in accordance with the centuries-long development of standard international-trade literature in economics—they were not willing to leave international *financial* transactions free. I summed up this view as the "casino on top of the trading house" syndrome; and from it came the bias in favor of international capital controls and fixed exchange rates.

Authorities organized their domestic financial environments in the same spirit, imposing several limits on financial transactions. And within the three major financial centers, these impositions had quite different historical impulses: in the United States, it was a fear of centralized financial power; in Japan, a preference for centralization and hierarchy; and in the United Kingdom, reliance on informal traditions. Each distinct system reflected a particular set of national and cultural characteristics. Yet some commonality among all three nations existed in their reliance on relationships in financial transactions. In all three systems the authorities, after long experimentation, embraced systems that viewed free financial transactions as undesirable—systems that limited choices in finance and that repressed the price mechanism. These systems encouraged long-term relationships between well-known partners. In this heavily regulated financial environment, strategic choice was greatly reduced and rendered nearly impotent as a competitive weapon. This environment was favorable to many intermediaries since it allowed them adequate profits and provided access to capital for those clients that maintained relationships with intermediaries.

Because international capital transactions were subject to many international capital controls, which had been built into the system by engineers of Bretton Woods, escape routes were closed for those dissatisfied with (or excluded from) relationships in the regulated domestic system. Meanwhile, low nominal interest rates further reduced pressures for innovation and escape.

But forces for change were at work in the world that would break up the traditional system. These forces steadily gathered strength during the late 1960s and the 1970s. First, they breached the Bretton Woods system, and later they transformed regulated financial systems in the United States, Japan, and the United Kingdom. Such factors as flexible exchange rates, energy price shocks, new accommodative monetary policies, higher inflation, international account imbalances, the demise of Keynesian demand management, the ascendancy of supply side economics, and fundamental differences in saving behavior among major industrial nations all combined to fragment and then destroy the relationship system. In the financial world that has since evolved, transactions have begun to reflect both current market conditions and the particular needs of issuers and investors. Not everyone has benefited from this new regime. Financial services firms have seen their traditionally profitable niches erode; to survive, they have had to formulate new strategies and enter new product markets at home and abroad. In this altered environment, financial services firms—like other firms—have discovered the imperatives of value creation and the exploitation of distinct advantage. These require them to carefully evaluate their changed environment. Given the complex forces that have altered it, this is not an easy task. Many of the failures in the industry can be attributed to an inability to understand the complex nature of the changes that have taken place; recent financial history proves that such understanding is now crucial to success and even to survival.

Although this book chronicles the disappearance of a comfortable, low-risk tradition of doing business and presents a sober view of the future, it is not intended to sound a note of defeat. Instead it points to a new direction: one of careful strategy formulation and implementation. It looks to an era in which sound managerial decisions will be more difficult, but also potentially highly rewarding. In presenting this analysis, my hope is that it will contribute to the larger understanding of the dynamics and interactions required at all three levels for such sound management. When managers understand the major macro- and international economic forces and the broad historical developments of the three major international financial markets, and when they have a general framework for analysis of their own industry, there should be fewer surprises in store for them.

This book suggests that though the basic rewards for financial services firms can remain high, they will also be increasingly difficult to achieve. Firms must make skillful use of their new freedom to enter many different product markets and to price products competitively within them. Those that can manage the strategy process dexterously, and that prove their ability to incorporate the fundamental forces of change in their thinking, should continue to create valuable opportunities—for their clients *and* themselves.

BIBLIOGRAPHY

Abegglen, J., and Stalk, G. *Kaisha, the Japanese Corporation*. New York: Basic Books, 1985.

Ackley, G., and Ishi, H. "Fiscal, Monetary and Related Policies." In *Asia's New Giant: How the Japanese Economy Works*, edited by H. Patrick and H. Rosovsky, 153–247. Washington, DC: The Brookings Institution, 1976.

Adams, T., and Hoshii, I. *A Financial History of the New Japan*. Palo Alto: Kodansha International, 1972.

Adler, M., and Dumas, B. "International Portfolio Choice and Corporation Finance: A Synthesis." *The Journal of Finance* 38 (1983):925–984.

Alexander, S. "Effects of a Devaluation on a Trade Balance." *International Monetary Fund Staff Papers* 2 (1952):263–278.

———. "Effects of a Devaluation: A Simplified Synthesis of Elasticities and Absorption Approaches." *American Economic Review* 49 (1959): 22–42.

Alhadeff, D. *Competition and Controls in Banking*. Berkeley: University of California Press, 1968.

Allen, G. *Japan's Economic Recovery*. New York: Oxford University Press, 1958.

———. *A Short Economic History of Modern Japan*, 4th ed. New York: St. Martin's, 1981.

Altman, E. "Measuring Corporate Bond Mortality and Performance." *Journal of Finance* 44 (1989):909–922.

Anderson, B., and Cottrell, P. *Money and Banking in England: The Development of the Banking System, 1694–1914*. Newton Abbot, Devon: David & Charles, 1974.

Ando, A., and Auerbach, A. "The Corporate Cost of Capital in Japan and the U.S.: A Comparison." Working Paper No. 1762. Cambridge, MA: National Bureau of Economic Research, 1985.

———. "The Cost of Capital in the U.S. and Japan: A Comparison." Working Paper No. 2286. Cambridge, MA: National Bureau of Economic Research, 1987.

Aoki, M. "Shareholders' Non-Unanimity on Investment Financing: Banks vs. Individual Investors." In *The Economic Analysis of the Japanese Firm*, edited by M. Aoki, 193–226. New York: North Holland, 1984.

Armington, P. "A Theory of Demand for Products Distinguished by Place of Production." *International Monetary Fund Staff Papers* 16 (1969):159–178.

Artus, J., and Rhomberg, R. "A Multi-Lateral Exchange Rate Model." *International Monetary Fund Staff Papers* 20 (1973):591–611.

Asquith, P., Mullins, D., and Wolff, E. "Original Issue High Yield Bonds:

Aging Analyses of Defaults, Exchanges and Calls." *Journal of Finance* 44 (1989):923–941.

Auerbach, J., and Hayes, S. *Investment Banking and Diligence: What Price Deregulation?* Boston: Harvard Business School Press, 1986.

Baldwin, C. "The Capital Factor: Competing for Capital in a Global Environment." In *Competition in Global Industries*, edited by M. Porter, 185–223. Boston: Harvard Business School Press, 1986.

Bank of England. *Annual Report 1966*. London: HMSO, 1966.

———. *Bank of England Quarterly Bulletin* 11 (1971).

Bank of Japan. *The Japanese Financial System*. Tokyo: Bank of Japan, 1972.

———. *Money and Banking in Japan*. Edited by L. Pressnell. London: Macmillan, 1973.

———. *The Bank of Japan: Its Organization and Monetary Policies*. Tokyo: Bank of Japan, 1973.

———. *Economic Statistics Annual*. Tokyo: Bank of Japan, various issues.

Barnes, P. *Building Societies: The Myth of Mutuality*. London: Pluto Press, 1984.

Barro, R. "Unanticipated Money Growth and Unemployment in the United States." *American Economic Review* 67 (1977):101–115.

Bell, G. *The Eurodollar Market and the International Financial System*. New York: John Wiley, 1973.

Bentson, G., ed. *Financial Services: The Changing Institutions and Government Policy*. Englewood Cliffs, NJ: Prentice-Hall, 1983.

Bernanke, B. "Non-Monetary Effects of the Financial Crisis in the Propagation of the Great Depression." *American Economic Review* 73 (1983):257–276.

Bickerdike, C. "The Instability of Foreign Exchange." *Economic Journal* 30 (1920):118–122.

Bloomfield, A. *Monetary Policy Under the International Gold Standard, 1880–1914*. New York: Federal Reserve Bank of New York, 1959.

Board of Governors of the Federal Reserve System. *57th Annual Report*. Washington, DC: Federal Reserve Board, 1970.

———. *The Federal Reserve System: Purposes and Functions*. Washington, DC: Federal Reserve Board, 1974.

———. *Banking and Monetary Statistics, 1941–1970*. Washington, DC: Federal Reserve Board, 1976.

———. *Federal Reserve Bulletin*. Washington, DC: Federal Reserve Board, various issues.

Boleat, M. *The Building Society Industry*. London: Allen & Unwin, 1982.

Bolles, A. *The Financial History of the United States, 1774–1789, 1789–1860, 1861–1885*, vols. 1, 2, and 3. New York: Appleton, 1884–1886.

Brander, J., and Spencer, B. "Export Subsidies and International Market Share Rivalry." *Journal of International Economics* 18 (1985):83–100.

Braudel, F. *The Perspective of the World: Civilization and Capitalism, 15th–18th Century*. London: Collins, 1982.

Bronte, S. *Japanese Finance: Markets and Institutions*. London: Euromoney Publications, 1982.

Brown, W. *The Dual Banking System in the United States*. New York: American Bankers Association, 1968.

Burrough, B., and Helyar, J. *Barbarians at the Gate.* New York: Harper & Row, 1989.

Caroll, C., and Summers, L. "Why Is U.S. National Savings So Low?" *Brookings Papers on Economic Activities* 1 (1987):607–635.

Carron, A. *Reforming the Bank Regulatory Structure.* Washington, DC: The Brookings Institution, 1984.

Caves, R., and Uekusa, M. "Industrial Organization." In *Asia's New Giant: How the Japanese Economy Works,* edited by H. Patrick and H. Rosovsky, 459–523. Washington, DC: The Brookings Institution, 1976.

Chandler, A., Jr., and Tedlow, R. *The Coming of Managerial Capitalism: A Casebook on the History of American Economic Institutions.* Homewood, IL: Richard D. Irwin, 1985.

Chandler, L. *The Economics of Money and Banking,* 6th ed. New York: Harper & Row, 1973.

Channon, D. *British Banking Strategy and International Challenge.* London: Macmillan, 1977.

Citicorp. *Annual Report,* 1988.

Clarke, M. *Regulating the City: Competition, Scandal and Reform.* London: Open University Press, 1986.

Cleveland, H., and Huertas, T. *Citibank 1812–1970.* Cambridge, MA: Harvard University Press, 1985.

Cohen, B. "The European Monetary System; An Outsider's View." *Essays in International Finance No. 142.* Princeton: International Finance Section, 1981.

Cohen, J. *Japan's Postwar Economy.* Bloomington: Indiana University Press, 1958.

Continental Illinois Corp. *Annual Report,* 1983.

Cooke, P. "Self-Regulation and Statute: The Evolution of Banking Supervision." In *U.K. Banking Supervision: Evolution, Practice, and Issues,* edited by E. Gardener, 85–98. London: Allen & Unwin, 1986.

Cooper, R. *The Economics of Interdependence: Economic Policy in the Atlantic Community.* New York: McGraw-Hill, 1968.

———. "The Gold Standard: Historical Facts and Future Prospects." *Brookings Papers on Economic Activity* 1 (1982):1–56.

Corrigan, E. *Financial Market Structure: A Longer View.* New York: Federal Reserve Bank of New York, 1987.

Crockett, A. *International Money: Issues and Analysis.* Sunbury-on-Thames, England: Nelson, 1977.

Crum, M., and Meerschwam, D. "From Relationship to Price Banking: The Loss of Regulatory Control." In *America versus Japan,* edited by T. McCraw, 261–297. Boston: Harvard Business School Press, 1986.

Dam, K. *The Rules of the Game: Reform and Evolution in the International Monetary System.* Chicago: University of Chicago Press, 1982.

Davis, A. *The Origin of the National Banking System.* Washington, DC: U.S. Government Printing Office, 1911.

De Vries, M. *The International Monetary Fund, 1945–1965,* vol. 2. Washington, DC: International Monetary Fund, 1969.

———. *The International Monetary Fund, 1966–1971,* vol. 1. Washington, DC: International Monetary Fund, 1976.

――――. *The International Monetary Fund, 1972–1978*, vol. 1. Washington, DC: International Monetary Fund, 1985.

Dixit, A. "Trade Policy: An Agenda for Research." In *Strategic Trade Policy and the New International Economics*, edited by P. Krugman, 283–304. Cambridge, MA: MIT Press, 1988.

Dixit, A., and Stiglitz, J. "Monopolistic Competition and Optimum Product Diversity." *American Economic Review* 67 (1977):297–308.

Donaldson, G. *Managing Corporate Wealth*. New York: Praeger, 1984.

Dornbusch, R. "The Theory of Flexible Exchange Rate Regimes and Macro-Economic Policy." *Scandinavian Journal of Economics* 78 (1976):255–275.

Dornbusch, R., Fischer, S., and Samuelson, P. "Comparative Advantage, Trade and Payments in a Ricardian Model with a Continuum of Goods." *American Economic Review* 67 (1977):823–839.

Eccles, R., and Crane, D. *Doing Deals: Investment Banks at Work*. Boston: Harvard Business School Press, 1988.

Economic Report of the President. Washington, DC: U.S. Government Printing Office, various issues.

The Economist. "A Survey of the Euromarkets: Now for the Lean Years." May 16, 1987:4.

――――. "A Survey of Wall Street: Where to From Here?" July 11, 1987:22.

――――. "Penn Square: Ever Again?" August 21, 1982:62–63.

Einzig, P. *Parallel Money Markets, Volume One: The New Markets in London*. London: Macmillan, 1971.

Euromoney. *Annual Financing Report 1987*. Supplement to *Euromoney*, March 1987.

Federal Reserve Bank of Philadelphia. *Fifty Years of the Federal Reserve Act*. Philadelphia: Federal Reserve Bank of Philadelphia, 1964.

Federation of Bankers Associations. *Banking System in Japan*, 9th ed. Tokyo: Federation of Bankers Association, 1984.

Feldman, R. *Japanese Financial Markets: Deficits, Dilemmas and Deregulation*. Cambridge, MA: MIT Press, 1986.

Fleming, N. "Domestic Financial Policies under Fixed and Floating Exchange Rates." *International Monetary Fund Staff Papers* 9 (1962):369–380.

Fletcher, G. *The Discount Houses in London: Principles, Operations and Change*. London: Macmillan, 1976.

Francke, H., and Hudson, M. *Banking and Finance in West Germany*. New York: St. Martin's, 1984.

Frenkel, J. "A Monetary Approach to the Exchange Rate: Doctrinal Aspects and Empirical Evidence." *Scandinavian Journal of Economics* 78 (1976): 200–224.

――――. "Preface." In *The Economics of Exchange Rates*, edited by J. Frenkel and H. Johnson, vii–xii. Reading, MA: Addison-Wesley, 1978.

Frenkel, J., and Mussa, M. "Asset Markets, Exchange Rates and the Balance of Payments." In *Handbook of International Economics*, vol. II, edited by R. Jones and P. Kenen, 679–747. New York: North Holland, 1985.

Friedman, M. "The Case for Flexible Exchange Rates." In *Essays in Positive Economics*, edited by M. Friedman, 157–204. Chicago: University of Chicago Press, 1953.

Friedman, M., and Schwartz, A. *A Monetary History of the United States, 1867–1960.* Princeton: Princeton University Press, 1963.

Friend, I., and Tokutsu, I. "The Cost of Capital to Corporations in Japan and the U.S.A." *Journal of Banking and Finance* 11 (1987):313–327.

Funabashi, Y. *Managing the Dollar: From the Plaza to the Louvre.* Washington, DC: Institute for International Economics, 1988.

Gardener, P. "Banking Crises and Risks." In *U.K. Banking Supervision, Evolution, Practice and Issues,* edited by P. Gardener, 3–24. London: Allen & Unwin, 1986.

Gart, A. *The Insider's Guide to the Financial Services Revolution.* New York: McGraw-Hill, 1984.

Goldsmith, R. *The Financial Development of Japan, 1869–1977.* New Haven: Yale University Press, 1983.

Gower, L. *Review of Investor Protection.* London: HMSO, 1982.

Grady, J., and Weale, M. *British Banking, 1960–1985.* London: Macmillan, 1986.

Grossman, G. "Strategic Export Promotion: A Critique." In *Strategic Trade Policy and the New International Economics,* edited by P. Krugman, 47–68. Cambridge, MA: MIT Press, 1986.

Group of Ten. *Report of the Study Group on the Creation of Reserve Assets.* Washington, DC: G-10, 1965.

Haberler, G. "The International Monetary System Again Under Stress." In *The International Monetary System: A Time of Turbulence,* edited by J. Dreyer, G. Haberler, and T. Willett, 3–19. Washington: American Enterprise Institute, 1982.

Hammond, B. *Banks and Politics in America From the Revolution to the Civil War.* Princeton: Princeton University Press, 1957.

Harberger, A. "Currency Depreciation, Income and the Balance of Trade." *Journal of Political Economy* 58 (1950):47–60.

Hatsopoulos, G. *High Cost of Capital: America's Industrial Handicap.* Waltham: Thermo-Electron Company, 1983.

Hayes, R., and Abernathy, W. "Managing Our Way to Economic Decline." *Harvard Business Review* 58 (1980):67–77.

Haywood, C., *Regulation Q and Monetary Policy.* Chicago: Association of Reserve City Bankers, 1971.

Haywood, C. and Linke, C. *The Regulation of Deposit Interest Rates.* Chicago: Association of Reserve City Bankers, 1968.

Helpman, E., and Krugman, P. *Market Structure and Foreign Trade: Increasing Returns, Imperfect Competition and the International Economy.* Cambridge, MA: MIT Press, 1985.

Hewlett, N., and Toporowski, J. *All Change in the City: A Report on Recent Changes and Future Prospects in London's Financial Markets.* London: Economist Publications, 1985.

Hodder, J. "Capital Structure and the Cost of Capital in the U.S. and Japan." Palo Alto: Stanford University, Mimeo, 1988.

Horsefield, K. *The International Monetary Fund, 1945–1965,* vol. 1. Washington, DC: International Monetary Fund, 1969.

Hoshi, T., Kashyap, A., and Scharfstein, D. "Corporate Structure, Liquidity and Investment: Evidence from Japanese Panel Data." Working Paper No. 2071-88. Cambridge, MA: MIT, 1988.

IMF. *First Annual Report on Exchange Restrictions*. Washington, DC: International Monetary Fund, 1950.

———. *The Role of the Exchange Rate in the Adjustment of International Payments*. Washington, DC: International Monetary Fund, 1970.

———. *Articles of Agreement*. Washington, DC: International Monetary Fund, 1978.

———. *International Financial Statistics Yearbook*. Washington, DC: International Monetary Fund, various issues.

Institutional Investor. 20 (1986):124–126.

Japan Securities Research Institute. *Securities Markets in Japan, 1986*. Tokyo: Japan Securities Research Institute, 1986.

Jensen, M. "Agency Costs of Free Cash Flow, Corporate Finance and Takeovers." *American Economic Review* 76 (1986):323–329.

Johnson, H. "The Monetary Approach to Balance of Payments Theory." *Further Essays in Monetary Theory*. New York: George Allen, 1972:229–249.

Johnson, R. *Historical Beginnings: The Federal Reserve*. Boston: Federal Reserve Bank of Boston, 1977.

Jones, S. *The Development of Economic Policy: Financial Institution Reform*. Ann Arbor: University of Michigan Research Division, 1979.

Kane, D. *The Eurodollar Market and the Years of Crisis*. London: Croom Helm, 1983.

Kester, W. *Japanese Takeovers: The Global Contest for Corporate Control*. Boston: Harvard Business School Press, 1991.

Keynes, J. "The German Transfer Problem." *Economic Journal* 39 (1929):1–7.

———. *The General Theory of Employment, Interest and Money*. London: Macmillan, 1936.

Klebaner, B. *Commercial Banking in the United States: A History*. Hinsdale, IL: Dryden, 1974.

Koizumi, A. "The 'Overloan' Problem: Characteristic Feature of the Banking System in Japan." *Hitosubashi Journal of Commerce and Management* 2(1962):53–65.

Kouri, P. "The Exchange Rate and the Balance of Payments in the Short Run and in the Long Run: A Monetary Approach." *Scandinavian Journal of Economics* 78 (1976):280–304.

Krooss, H., ed., *Documentary History of Banking and Currency in the United States*. New York: Chelsea House, 1969.

Krooss, H., and Blyn, M. *A History of Financial Intermediaries*. New York: Random House, 1971.

Krugman, P. "Scale Economics, Product Differentiation and the Pattern of Trade." *American Economic Review* 70 (1980):950–959.

Kydland, F., and Prescott, E. "Rules Rather than Discretion: The Inconsistency of Optimal Plans." *Journal of Political Economy* 85 (1977):473–493.

Lancaster, K. "A Theory of Intra-Industry Trade under Perfect Monopolistic Competition." *Journal of International Economics* 10 (1980):151–175.

Lerner, A. *The Economics of Control: Principles of Welfare Economics*. New York: Macmillan, 1944.

Lisle-Williams, M. "Beyond the Market: The Survival of Family Capitalism in the English Merchant Banks." *British Journal of Sociology* 35 (1984): 241–271.

———. "Merchant Banking Dynasties in the English Class Structure: Ownership, Solidarity and Kinship in the City of London, 1850–1960." *British Journal of Sociology* 35 (1984):333–362.

Lucas, R. "Expectations and the Neutrality of Money." *Journal of Economic Theory* 4 (1972):102–124.

Luehrman, T., and Kester, W. "Real Interest Rates and the Cost of Capital: A Comparison of the United States and Japan." *Japan and the World Economy* I(1989):279–301.

Macedo, J. de. "Optimal Currency Diversification for a Class of Risk Averse International Investors." *Journal of Economic Dynamics and Control* 5 (1983):173–185.

Machlup, F. "The Terms of Trade Effect of Devaluation upon Real Income and the Balance of Trade." *Kyklos* 9 (1956):417–452.

Manchester, W. *The Arms of Krupp 1587–1968.* New York: Bantam, 1970.

Marshall, A. "The Pure Theory of Foreign Trade." *Scarce Tracts in Economics and Political Science,* no. 1. London: The London School of Economics and Political Science, 1879.

Maycock, J. *Financial Conglomerates: The New Phenomenon.* London: Gower, 1986.

Mayer, H. "Some Theoretical Problems Relating to the Euro Dollar Market." *Princeton Essays in International Finance,* no. 79. Princeton: International Finance Section, 1970.

McCraw, T., ed. *America versus Japan.* Boston: Harvard Business School Press, 1986.

McCraw, T., and O'Brien, P. "Production and Distribution: Competition Policy and Industry Structure." In *America versus Japan,* edited by T. McCraw, 77–116. Boston: Harvard Business School Press, 1986.

McKinnon, R. *An International Standard for Monetary Stabilization.* Washington, DC: Institute for International Economics, 1987.

Meerschwam, D. "J.P. Morgan's Mexican Bank Debt-Bond Swap," 289-013. Boston: Harvard Business School, 1988.

———. "The Japanese Financial System and the Cost of Capital." In *The United States and Japan: Trade and Investment,* edited by P. Krugman. Chicago: University of Chicago Press, forthcoming.

Merton, R. "Optimum Consumption and Portfolio Rules in a Continuous Time Model." *Journal of Economic Theory* 3 (1971):373–413.

Metzler, L. "The Theory of International Trade." In *A Survey of Contemporary Economics,* vol. 1, edited by H. Ellis, 210–254. Philadelphia: The Blakiston Company, 1948.

Monroe, W. *Japan: Financial Markets and the World Economy.* New York: Praeger, 1973.

Moran, M. *The Politics of Banking—The Strange Case of Competition and Credit Controls.* New York: St. Martin's, 1984.

Morgan Stanley. *Annual Report,* 1986.

Morison, I., Tillett, P., and Welch, J. *Banking Act 1979.* London: Butterworth, 1979.

Mundell, R. "The Appropriate Use of Monetary and Fiscal Policy for External and Internal Stability." *International Monetary Fund Staff Papers* 9 (1962):70–79.

———. *International Economics.* New York: Macmillan, 1968.

Muth, J. "Rational Expectations and the Theory of Price Movements." *Econometrica* 29 (1962):315–335.

Myers, M. *A Financial History of the United States.* New York: Columbia University Press, 1970.

Nevin, E., and Davis, E. *The London Clearing Banks.* London: Elek Books, 1970.

New York Times. "Excerpts from Connally News Conference." August 17, 1971:16.

———. "Fed Backs Interstate Banking." April 25, 1985:D1, D13.

Nomura School of Management. "Ito-Yokado," 289-044. Boston: Harvard Business School, 1981.

Ornstein, F. *Savings Banking: An Industry in Change.* Reston, VA: Reston Publishing Company, 1985.

Papell, D. "Monetary Policy in the United States under Flexible Exchange Rates." *American Economic Review* 79 (1989):1106–1116.

Parker, C. "Foreign Banks in London: More Foreign Banks Open for Business." *The Banker,* November (1981):101–111.

Patrick, H. *Monetary Policy and Central Banking in Contemporary Japan.* Bombay: University of Bombay, 1962.

Patrick, H., and Rosovsky, H., eds. *Asia's New Giant: How the Japanese Economy Works.* Washington, DC: The Brookings Institution, 1976.

Pechman, J., and Kaizuka, K. "Taxation." In *Asia's New Giant: How the Japanese Economy Works,* edited by H. Patrick and H. Rosovsky, 317–382. Washington, DC: The Brookings Institution, 1976.

Perry, F. *The Elements of Banking.* London: Methuen, 1975.

Peterson, P. *The United States in the Changing World Economy.* Washington, DC: U.S. Government Printing Office, 1971.

Phillips, A. "The Relation Between Unemployment and the Rate of Change of Money Wages in the United Kingdom, 1861–1957." *Economica* 25 (1958):283–299.

Pigott, C. "Financial Reform in Japan." *The Federal Reserve Bank of San Francisco, Economic Review* (1983):25–44.

Plender, J., and Wallace, P. *The Square Mile: A Guide to the New City of London.* London: Century Publishing, 1985.

Porter, M. *Competitive Strategy: Techniques for Analyzing Industries and Competitors.* New York: Free Press, 1980.

Pringle, R. *A Guide to Banking in Britain.* London: Charles and Knight, 1973.

Radcliffe Report. London: HMSO, 1960.

Raw, C. *Slater Walker.* London: Andre Deutsch, 1977.

Redlich, F. *The Molding of American Banking: Men and Ideas.* New York: Hafner, 1947–1951.

Reid, M. *The Secondary Banking Crisis, 1973–1975: Its Causes and Course.* London: Macmillan, 1982.

Reischauer, E. *The United States and Japan,* 3rd ed. New York: Viking, 1964.

Revell, J. *The British Financial System*. London: Macmillan, 1975.

Ricardo, D. *On the Principles of Political Economy and Taxation*. London: J. Murray, 1821.

Robinson, J. *Essays on the Theory of Employment*. New York: Macmillan, 1937.

Rosovsky, H. "Japan's Transition to Modern Economic Growth." In *Industrialization in Two Systems: Essays in Honor of Alexander Gerschenkron*, edited by H. Rosovsky, 91–139. New York: Wiley, 1966.

Rukstad, M. "Fiscal Policy and Business-Government Relations." In *America versus Japan*, edited by T. McCraw, 299–336. Boston: Harvard Business School Press, 1986.

Sachs, J. "The Current Account and Macro Economic Adjustment in the 1970s." *Brookings Papers on Economic Activity* 1 (1981):201–268.

Safire, W. *Before the Fall: An Inside View of the Pre-Watergate White House*. Garden City: Doubleday, 1975.

Sakakibara, E., Feldman, R., and Harada, Y. *The Japanese Financial System in Comparative Perspective*. Washington, DC: U.S. Government Printing Office, 1982.

Salomon Brothers, Inc. *A Review of Bank Performance*, 1988.

Scott, B. "National Strategy for Stronger U.S. Competitiveness." *Harvard Business Review* 62 (1984):77–91.

Sheppard, D. *The Growth and Role of U.K. Financial Institutions, 1880–1962*. London: Methuen, 1971.

Shultz, W., and Caine, M. *Financial Development of the United States*. New York: Prentice-Hall, 1937.

Smith, A. "Capital Theory and Trade Theory." In *Handbook of International Economics*, edited by P. Jones and P. Kenen, 289–324. New York: North Holland, 1985.

Solow, R. "What To Do (Macro-economically) When OPEC Comes." In *Rational Expectations and Economic Policy*, edited by S. Fischer, 249–267. Chicago: University of Chicago Press, 1980.

Stigum, M. *The Money Market*, rev. ed. Homewood, IL: Dow Jones-Irwin, 1983.

Stolper, W., and Samuelson, P. "Protection and Real Wages." *Review of Economic Studies* 9 (1941):58–73.

Suzuki, S., and Wright, R. "Financial Structure and Bankruptcy Risk in Japanese Companies." *Journal of International Business Studies* 16 (1985): 75–110.

Suzuki, Y. *Money and Banking in Contemporary Japan: The Theoretical Setting and Its Application*. New Haven: Yale University Press, 1980.

————, ed. *The Japanese Financial System*. Oxford: Oxford University Press, 1987.

Swanson, W. *The Establishment of the National Banking System*. Kingston, NY: Jackson Press, 1910.

Sykes, J. *The Amalgamation Movement in British Banking, 1825–1924*. London: P.S. King, 1926.

Tales of the Bank of England with Anecdotes of London Bankers. London: James Hogg, 1882.

Taussig, F. "International Trade under Depreciated Paper." *Quarterly Journal of Economics* 31 (1917):380–403.

Taylor, J. "Estimation and Control of a Macroeconomic Model with Rational Expectations." *Econometrica* 47 (1979):1267–1286.

Temin, P. *Did Monetary Forces Cause the Great Depression?* New York: W.W. Norton, 1976.

Tew, B. *The Evolution of the International Monetary System, 1945–1977.* London: Hutchinson, 1977.

Thompson, T. *Checks and Balances: A Study of the Dual Banking System in America.* Washington, DC: National Association of Supervisors of State Banks, 1962.

Torrens, R. *An Essay on the External Corn Trade.* London: Hatchard, 1815.

Triffin, R. *Gold and the Dollar Crisis: The Future of Convertibility.* New Haven: Yale University Press, 1960.

———. "The Evolution of the International Monetary System: Historical Reappraisal and Future Perspective." *Princeton Studies in International Finance, no. 12.* Princeton: International Finance Section, 1964.

Tsiang, S. "Fluctuating Exchange Rates in Countries with Relatively Stable Economies: Some European Experiences after World War I." *International Monetary Fund Staff Papers* 7 (1959):244–273.

———. "The Role of Money in Trade Balance Stability: Synthesis of the Elasticity and Absorption Approaches." *American Economic Review* 51 (1961):912–936.

U.S. Congress. House Committee on Banking and Currency. *Bretton Woods Agreements Acts: Hearings on H.R. 2211.* 79th Cong., 1st sess., 1945.

U.S. Department of the Treasury. *Report to the President: Geographic Restrictions on Commercial Banking in the U.S.* Washington, DC: Department of the Treasury, 1981.

Viner, J. *Studies in the Theory of International Trade.* New York: Harper and Brothers, 1937.

Wadsworth, J. *The Banks and the Monetary System in the U.K., 1959–1971.* London: Methuen, 1973.

Wallich, H., and Wallich, M. "Banking and Finance." In *Asia's New Giant: How the Japanese Economy Works*, edited by H. Patrick and H. Rosovsky, 249–315. Washington, DC: The Brookings Institution, 1976.

The Wall Street Journal (European edition). "Healthy Hybrid." April 22, 1987:1, 8.

Wellons, P. "Cross-Border Learning by Citicorp in the 1980s," 381-146. Boston: Harvard Business School, 1981.

Wheelwright, S. "Restoring the Competitive Edge in U.S. Manufacturing." *California Management Review* 27 (1985):26–42.

Williams, C. "The Transformation of Banking." *Reprint Collection No. 15051.* Boston: Harvard Business Review, 1984.

Williamson, J., and Miller, M. *Targets and Indicators.* Washington, DC: Institute for International Economics, 1987.

Wilson Report. London: HMSO, 1980.

Wolff, E. "Models of Production and Exchange in the Thought of Adam Smith and David Ricardo." Unpublished Ph.D. diss. Yale, 1974.

INDEX